MANHUNT

Seashore Saga of the Punnapra Vayalar Uprising

KV MOHANKUMAR
translated by Manjula Cherkil

Vitasta
LET KNOWLEDGE SPREAD
www.vitastapublishing.com

Published by
Renu Kaul Verma
Vitasta Publishing Pvt Ltd
2/15, Ansari Road, Daryaganj
New Delhi - 110 002
info@vitastapublishing.com

ISBN 978-93-86473-63-9

MRP ₹450
First Edition 2019

Artist: Soman Katalur
Cover by Somesh Kumar Mishra
Layout by Ram Kumar
Printed by Vikas Computer and Printers

For my Mother
Lakshmi Kutty
who poured out the story of the Punnapra-Vayalar
uprising into my scorched childhood
of insecurity and also,
for the martyrs who gave in homage
their own lives
to this legendary revolt

Contents

Acknowledgements

I wish to place on records my gratitude to Manjula Cherkil, a Research Associate for the Five College Women's Studies Research Center (FCWSRC), Mount Holyoke College, South Hadley US who translated the book into English.

MA Baby, a well-known personality in Indian politics and Member, Politbureau of the Communist Party of India (Marxist) who penned the foreword.

Publisher Renu Kaul Verma, the team of Vitasta Publishing, Kanagam King, and Papri Sen Sri Raman who added value to the book through her excellent editorial inputs.

Publisher's Note

Vitasta is proud to bring out the English translation of the award-winning Malayalam novel, *Ushnaraashi-Karappurathinte Ithihasam.* In India, one and all know about the Jallianwala Bagh massacre of April 1919 where the number of dead is put at anywhere between 380-1600. However, very few have heard of the Punnapra-Vayalar uprising, where the dead is said to be anywhere between 500-7000.

For long, there has been a debate on whether the Punnapra-Vayalar Uprising can be called a part of India's struggle for freedom from British rule. The revolt took place in a tiny princely State, against a British-appointed administration's draconic rule. That itself makes it a 'freedom struggle'. Today the debate has also taken the colours of the north-south discourse. Beyond all arguments, however, is the truth, that on the eve of Independence, in the knowledge of the Congress Party, its leaders like Mahatma Gandhi and many other stalwarts, a knighted administrator unleashed a willing and corrupt police force and a reluctant army on thousands of poor farmers, factory workers, fishermen and others and killed thousands. After reading this book, one might be tempted to ask, how long can one ignore history?

The English edition comes out on the eve of hundred years of the formation of the Communist Party of India. This book is not about communism, but yes, it certainly is about class struggle, a story of haves and have-nots, a story of poor people's struggles against authoritarian forces. With the English edition, we hope to bring non-Malayalam readers, an untold story of a People's Movement in India's not-so-distant past.

Translator's Note

The book, *Manhunt,* wades through the travails of the economically impoverished classes living in two sea shore villages, Punnapra and Vayalar in the kingdom of Travancore in what is now the State of Kerala, nestled in the southernmost tip of the Indian Peninsula. It talks about the atrocities of a feudal system perpetrated by a puppet King of the princely State, supported by colonial rule and the horrendous massacre of innocent men, women, children, the old and infirm by a fascist administrator who used the police and army recklessly in insensitive and illogical operations just a year before India attained freedom.

What happened in Punnapra and Vayalar was the explosion of suppressed feelings smouldering for a long time, bursting into violence and bloodshed on reaching the ignition point. It can also be considered as an instant reaction of the people against the administrative reforms introduced by Sir CP Ramaswamy Iyer, the administrator appointed by the British government who wanted to impose a method of governance based on an 'American Model' that people feared would make the situation of the common man in Kerala worse. The run up to such a reform resulted in events which led to killing of innocent people. The revolt or the struggle took the form of a civil war between the subjects of a native kingdom divided by the ruling class, landlords and officials and the ruled groups of workers, through whose efforts the economy of the kingdom thrived.

Author Mohankumar, himself hailing from the historical village, has taken care not to dwell on just the fictional representation of the uprising but also tells the simultaneous story of the historic truth in its real perspective. At the same time *Manhunt* is not just a historical novel. It is quite contemporary in the sense that the historical incidents are seen through the eyes of young Aparajitha, a research student from Delhi, who sets off to Punnapra-Vayalar to get an accurate account of the causes and effects of the uprising while searching for the roots of her own legacy.

The story traces the history of radical movements in Kerala, scanning a period of 90 years, vividly narrating the miserable state of men and women residing in poverty-stricken villages like Punnapra, Vayalar and Cherthala leading to the formation of the Communist Party regional branches in the 1930s to fight against the feudal misdemeanour of the ruling class and leads up to the present Maoist movement in India.

Through a three-year long literature survey involving relentless reading, research and by interviewing the old heroes of the struggle still alive, the writer has been successful in fleshing out many a hidden information lying dormant in the historic land of struggle. Sensitively depicting the warmth of relationships, between brothers and sisters, childhood friends, class mates, neighbours, joint family members, close-knit village communities and staunch followers of a particular political philosophy, creating events with detailed explanation of the background where they occur, environmental degradation, disappearing rivers and lush green forests and lost watersheds stolen by sand and other mafias, this is a narrative that reflects the creative and poetic story-telling capabilities of the author, and makes the reading of this book an unforgettable experience.

What's unique about the book is that rather than being overly reactive to perceived injustice in society, the work is prescriptive in influencing perceptual patterns and official policies. Instead of being a pristine chronicle of a particular time and place, it takes a unique position at the nexus of the past and future realities and hence the need to reach a vast global readership, which is the reason for an English translation of the award-winning Malayalam work, *Ushnaraashi*.

Foreword

The Punnapra-Vayalar Uprising was a landmark event in people's movement in India which was fought to achieve a situation where people could live as human beings. It marked the beginning of a transformation in their mindsets in terms of interpreting their social and political rights. It paved the way for a tremendous change not only in the State of Kerala (then still comprising several Princely states) but in the political consciousness of the whole of India, inspiring the peasant and the worker to embark on a struggle for freedom to wriggle out of the colonial British rule that fostered local exploitation. These uprisings broke out in October 1946 in two villages in Kerala, Punnapra and Vayalar, extending to their neighbouring places, bringing into prominence a tiny hamlet known as Karappuram in the erstwhile Travancore kingdom, a stellar occurrence in the history of modern Kerala.

> 'I thought that the sand here would be red, but it is black and white.' A friend from Neyyatinkara said this several years ago on his visit to Alappuzha. He had come to Alappuzha expecting deep red sand and his eyes wore a red tint as a result of the constant exposure to the red soil that marked his native place. I said, 'The spirit of this land is red, it cannot be seen outside'.

The quote above is from the introductory passage of *Flames of Resistance*, an essay on P Keshavadev, authored by the renowned critique Prof MK Sanu. 'Kerala's Paris Commune', this was how the beloved poet ONV described the Punnapra-Vayalar Uprising. *Ushnaraashi – Seashore Saga of the Punnapra-Vayalar Uprising*, the novel before us, tells the story of that iconic and legendary struggle in Alappuzha, which has too often turned wet, bathed by streams of warm blood.

I was one among those present at the release of the first edition of *'Ushnaraashi'*, at Alappuzha in August 2015. Within a few months, the second edition was out and thereafter a third one too. Now I am extremely happy that an English version is also being published. Why does this English work fill me with joy and excitement?

It is mainly because the novel emerges against the backdrop of all the historical happenings that had a great impact on the history of the world as a whole. What makes one happy is this political context where people get together to shake off the shackles of systemic slavery and this process assumes a great historical significance. Most certainly, this novel bridges the glaring gap existing in Kerala literature, of the absence of a literary work that comprehensively portrays the legendary uprising, accounting for its multiple experiences and complexities.

The author himself has made it clear. 'There are instances in history when silence is criminal. *Manhunt* is the story of the resurrection of my land which was passing through a cowardly silence. Being a writer born on that coast, if I do not write this story, history will convict me for my silence.' Over the past 70 years, Punnapra-Vayalar has become the premise of many creative works. P Bhaskaran's *Vayalar Roars* is the first one that comes to mind. Some of its verses continue to reverberate in the minds of Malayalis.

In 1948, a shadow drama of experiences of Punnapra-Vayalar that were still rife in the memories of Keralites was performed at the Purogamana Sahithya Sanghadana's meet held at Thrissur. It was directed by CJ Thomas and P Bhaskaran. That drama excited the meeting which was inaugurated by Mulk Raj Anand. The scene in which unarmed protesters tell the police aiming guns at them, 'No, comrades, don't! This protest is for you and for your land', emotionally disturbed the viewers. A few movies have also been made based on the Punnapra-Vayalar revolts.

There is no doubt that this revolt, which is a milestone in the history of Travancore, is complex enough to be comprehensively covered only through a meta narrative. There are at least two litterateurs of high standing from Alappuzha itself who were creatively proficient to write a novel based on the revolts, P Keshavadev and Thakazhi Shivashankara Pillai. Sadly, neither of them went in-depth into the subject in their works.

Keshavadev talks of the historical circumstances that led to the Punnapra-Vayalar Revolt and the workers' strike in Alappuzha in 1938 in his work, *Mirror*. Barring the nameless mention of a comrade who comes and goes like a wind, which can be safely attributed to the sporadic appearance and disappearance of Comrade P Krishnapillai, he did not make any attempt to give creative expression of the revolt itself in spite of the immense possibilities that it offered to bring forth a masterpiece.

Thakazhi talked of the period of Punnapra-Vayalar in *The Scavenger's Son* and *Randidangazhi*, but still did not refer to it adequately, despite even authoring a tome, *After Punnapra-Vayalar*.

Why did these great littérateurs shy away from this topic? P Keshavadev, despite working among the workers as a self-proclaimed communist, had differences of opinions with the Communist Party on various issues right from the beginning. This may be why, in spite of his abilities and positive circumstances, Keshavadev never attempted to write about the Punnapra-Vayalar Revolts. He might not have been interested in authoring a work with blind criticisms of the revolts. Researchers can enquire more into it.

Novel is an art form that helps to understand the complex relationships between human beings themselves as well as between human beings and nature. Then, what about drama? Have Shakespeare and Kalidasa left anything untouched in this universe in their works? Surely then, those who prefer poetry to other literary forms will argue that they made that transition because they were not a success at poetry. They will recall that when Roger Federer displays what a magician he is on the tennis court, is it not said that his strokes are as beautiful as poetry? Does that not reflect the glory of poetry as well?

Proponents of short stories, then, will raise the question, is there any complexity of life that has not been effectively dealt with by short stories? Clearly, those who have experienced romance as mesmerising as what has been portrayed in short stories will definitely not be able to ignore that question. Will literary criticism become creative at all, is a question that has been raised quite often. In several languages, a creative style of literary criticism has emerged which weighs the positives and negatives of creative works from different perspectives. *Manhunt: Seashore Saga of the Punnapra-Vayalar Uprising* while portraying historical events has intricately woven in the different perspectives through the experiences of the characters that play the key roles in those events.

A notable feature of this novel is the impressive presence of its female characters. The author's impeccable creativity comes to the fore in drawing up these characters without making any alteration to the primary historical perspective of the narrative, making it all the more engaging. The individual resistance of Neeli and Paru to the existing structures is as brave and courageous as any of the protesters in the forefront of the revolts. These feminine characters from disadvantaged sections bring into focus the intensity and depth of interpersonal relationships, fraternity and love. By presenting these characters on an equal footing to the protesters who fought against the cruelties of law and social systems, the author more than makes up for the absence of such feminine voices in the written histories of this struggle. Special mention also needs to be made about the subaltern representation in this struggle. Many of them were not only unable to make ends meet, but also had to deal with the systemic injustices meted out to them because of their social background. The novel weaves a beautiful tale of the legendary lives on the seashore depicting the travails of subaltern life and juxtaposing it with the resistance that rose from within it under the leadership of the Communist Party.

Beautifully transcending the boundaries of space and time, the novel also neatly fits in discussions on theories regarding the growth of Communism. While indicating that Communism should have a natural growth in the mindset of the people, it stresses on the need for the Communist Party to be built up at the political level. The following passage gives an indication:

> Che peeped at her from the cover page of the Bolivian Diary. He was sitting with the book kept open in his lap in a hideout formed by the branches of a tree in the dense Bolivian forest.
>
> 'Aleida', looking at her Che called.
>
> 'No, I am not Aleida', Aparajitha said. 'I am Aparajitha.

'OK Aparajitha, where are you now?'

'I am freezing out in this Delhi winter', she said. 'Can't you see this heavy thermal wear?'

Che detached the gun from his shoulders, polished it and started taking aim somewhere through the tress.

'Are you in a dream world?' Che enquired.

'Umm...', she said. 'I am watching the glorious arrival of the red sun... I am dreaming of the red flag hoisted on the top of the Red Fort.'

"If not today, tomorrow.' Che was confident. 'Time will make it inevitable.'

'You are right. If not today, tomorrow', she repeated. 'In India, a time will come when Communism triumphs; I keep dreaming of it. It is sure to happen in the near future.'

'What do you mean?' Che looked at her. 'Communism is not to be implemented, it has to sprout.'

The novel also draws a contrast between the public life of Communists and others. Here is an example of how the novelist accurately portrays how those who are not Communists waver in public life:

Everything turned topsy-turvy from the time of the Alappuzha meeting of the State Congress held at the Punnapra market ground... a gathering of the leaders who scrambled around. The dais was adorned by Pattom Thanu Pillai, TM Varghese, C Kesavan, Kumbalathu Sanku Pilla, Kannanthodathu Janardhanan Nair, R Sreekandan Nair, K Balakrishnan, Shankaranarayanan Thampi, Panambilli Govinda Menon, AP Udayabhanu, Janardana Kurup, all seated in a row. KS Joseph and VK Karunakaran, both hailing from Punnapra, were running around attending to every detail of the gathering. It was with great difficulty they had assembled the audience on the sea shore. Pattom Thanu Pillai

> concluded his presidential speech with a question as to what was wrong in implementing CP's American Model in Travancore on an experimental basis. This was opposed by Shankaranarayanan Thampi. That caused a furor among the gathering. Pattom warned that the Communists within the Congress Party will be expelled. The moment that was said, the audience let out cat calls and whistles. Pattom concluded the meeting and left the venue abruptly. Congress and Socialists parted ways.

The novel, despite being a work of fiction, is firmly rooted in its historical realities creating a trust climate between the author and reader. What makes it close to the heart of the reader is that the reader experiences the tense atmosphere surrounding the uprisings, pathetic lives of comrades who partook in the struggles, mental and physical agony suffered by the families of agricultural and industrial workers, cruelty of police actions, miseries of women and tales of children. It truly holds a mirror to the politics and society of those times, writ large in this novel. Rooted in fact, yet being a work of literature, the novel does justice to both history and literature. Not dealing in fairy tales, the novel bases its characters and events on concrete people and situations, which makes it a deeper experience in reading, doing justice to history. At the same time, having brilliantly captured the images of the uprisings, justice is done as a work of creativity as well. One cannot neglect the immense effort that the author has taken, which is profoundly reflected in the novel.

A serious observation of English literature reveals that in the meta narratives of Shakespeare and Tolstoy, their characters were real people who represented the dispossessed and the downtrodden, while post-modernism, which is the political philosophy of late capitalism, gave way to the creation of extreme fictional characters and stories.

In this age of post-modernity which seeks to substitute earth by extra- terrestrial elements, humans by robots, issues of seriousness by trivial impertinent topics and black and white realities by spectacular illusions, *Ushnaraashi*... stands apart. As the narrative spreads a canvas that depicts the true historical life of a society and touches the psyche of the reader, the aroma of human tenderness elevate the characters to unscaled heights of nobility.

The author has captured even the most complex historical moments and delicate nuances, portraying them as significant and gracious. The magic with which history is retold is mesmerising. It is worth noting that this happens at a time when mega narratives are sought to be replaced by capsule forms.

Thus, despite being a historical narrative, the novel has been able to do justice to creative expressions, gender voices, subaltern perspectives and political correctness. Its beauty lies in its attentiveness to detail and in its reflection of emotions. I congratulate the author on his creative genius in producing this impeccable work in English, which now makes the history of Punnapra-Vayalar revolts accessible to the entire world. Wish the readers an enlightening and enriching literary experience as well.

M A Baby
Member, Politbureau
Communist Party of India (Marxist)

Dishahara

'Apu, you should write. It's your father's wish that you become a well-known writer. ...a talented writer... like Bimal Mitra...Bibhutibhusan Bandopadhyay... our Madhavikutty...so deep and profound', her father had told her as they strolled under the cool shade of the neem trees hedging the Tolstoy lane.

Aparajitha tried to recollect the day of his final visit to her university campus in Delhi.

They were munching hot popcorn bought from the peddlers in front of Jantar Mantar. Father cut across the road and continued to walk towards the left.

'If you can write', he said, 'someday you should go there and write about the legendry uprising....'

'...I wanted to do that myself...but...well. It's yet another unfulfilled dream of your father.'

'Can't you try to do that even now? with that old pen of a journalist?', she clung to his fingers.

She could see those eyes glistening with tears of disillusionment.

'In the struggle to build up a People's Movement, I lost all my fire to write... a very long time ago.'

'Poor Comrade Sathyadas', she chided him. 'Even now he is good only at throwing his fists up and shouting slogans. But remember you may have to change your strategies; the new game is against corporates and mafias.'

A sad smile flashed on his lips and disappeared. 'If we get threatened by all that, can we survive? After all, you live only once.'

'Isn't that what I am also trying to say? There is only one life', she said. 'The ruling party will always be on their side. Even those who pretend to be the opposition also support them secretly.... Only a few, like my father, chooses to fight alone...!'

'Shouldn't there be someone to do that also? To protect this earth, to protect this society.... Do you know, where exactly the new liberal policies announced by the government on the pretext of economic development, have landed our country in? ...At the peak of inequality; the number of billionaires in our country has increased by four to five times. And what has become of the poor? What's the point in bragging about the reduction in poverty by manipulating the income-consumption data? On one side, the spiraling inflation; on the other side the gigantic growth in corruption as a byproduct of the new liberal policies! Can't you see these are facilities offered to multinationals to loot our natural resources...it has become inevitable that this trend is checked...it's time for a democratic socialist revolution in our country.' Despite the creeping cold of the city's evening mist, Father's veins started pulsating with emotion.

'Oh, I forgot to tell you. When are you planning your next visit to Kolkata? Your mother's album will be launched, on the tenth of next month. It has been titled *Dishahara*. Salil is going to be there. But will you be able to make it?'

'Mother called', she said. 'That composer seems to be unreasonably fascinated by her poems.'

'Poor Subodh', Father said. 'He was the one who gave music to all those poems. Your mother's poems impressed me only after he composed the music…they have become more meaningful now.'

Father translated those lines, and hummed.

My heart is losing its direction,
It doesn't look backward or forward
It has forgotten all its boundaries
To conquer the mountain peaks, breaking all the barriers…

Father turned to the road leading to Rajeev Chowk.

'Be careful', she laughed. 'By the time *Dishahara* is released, Snehalatha Chatterji will be a star. If that heart goes in the wrong direction… well there is no clue in which direction it may turn…'

Father burst out laughing at that. '*Dishahara… Dishahara….*'

As they reached the metro station in Rajiv Chowk, before disappearing into the crowd, he stopped, turned back and said, 'At some point in life, if you happen to dig for your roots, you will reach that historical land where you will find your father's roots too.'

Why did Father say that at their last meeting? Did he hear the footfalls of death approaching? Her eyes turned moist as the letters started appearing on the monitor.

If only Father was here to read these lines!
No. Father cannot be dead.
'*Illa, illa, marikhathilla...*' sound of final farewell calls from the comrades standing around her father's pyre, rang out in her ears.... 'No, no. Brave comrades never die...'
She had chanted that slogan at least a hundred times.
At the memorial of Comrade Pavan Das....
At the pyre of Comrade Joginder....
Beside the body of the beheaded Suman Bose wrapped in a red flag....
'No, Comrade Sathyadas is not dead.'

She thought, 'It may have been my father's cherished wish that has prompted me to visit this place. And Disha and Mrinalda just happened to be instrumental in making it possible. Anyway, I was bound to come here some day.'
'Comrade Sathyadas had his roots here and therefore mine too should be here. Those invisible roots have brought me here. Otherwise what made Disha invite me here when I was so uncertain about a place to settle down after the campus life in Delhi? And why did Mrinalda think it was okay for me to accept her invite? What made Mrinalda change his mind suddenly?'
She continued to reflect, sitting in front of the key board....
Her fingers ran over the keyboard ... *Vayalar*!

Sir CP's Manhunt

A congregation of dark clouds camouflaged the afternoon sun. *Neer Kozhi* (moorhens) burrowed in the water bubbles sprang to life in trepidation and ducked into the screw pine thickets growing densely on the banks of the backwaters. In the distance the sky and the sea merged.

The darkening sky spread its gloomy shadow on the surface of the placid backwater. Something about the ominous landscape filled people with a sense of foreboding that a major catastrophe was on its way.

'Was not the sun blazing all this time?' Comrade Sekharan thought, raising his head skyward. 'If only there had been a drizzle from the sky this burning sand would have cooled.'

It was already *Thulam* (October) tenth. Still there has been no sign of Thulam rain.

'No, this is not the sign of rain', Comrade Raman Kunju peered out of the camp kitchen hut. 'The rain clouds seem to be reluctant to pour down. As if they have foreseen something inauspicious.'

Dogs howled somewhere in the cashew thickets.

Comrade Sekharan's mind was suddenly on fire. He thought of Panikkarachan's earlier alerts, which had not been very pleasant. 'There were shootouts in Punnapra, Kattoor and Mararikulam. Many died. Taking that into account, they will surround our camp too. There will be a shootout here too. Quite a few among us are sure to die. Whoever values his life need not stay here. They may disperse quickly.'

As they heard him, the crowd had got emotional and agitated. They shouted in unison. 'Never, never, we will never leave.... If we live, we will live with dignity. Or else, if death is the only alternative, we will embrace it....'

It was almost two o'clock in the night when Panikkarachhan left the camp.

Last night, the sneaky army boats had approached the camp, through the backwaters. The comrades who stood watch without sleep had spotted the boats from a distance. Sharpened granite stones had pierced through the darkness, like highspeed missiles from the shore. The army had to flee for their dear lives.

'But the army can strike back anytime and if they come, there will be a deadly shoot-out', Comrade Krishnan warned, holding together a number of sharpened spears, measuring a length of exactly three and quarter feet with pointed tips, and examining them. 'The tips are deadly sharp...the moment the army closes in, target their stomachs....'

Comrade Sekharan looked around in trepidation. More and more people were arriving. Mothers, children, the infirm.... 'What will happen to them if the army barges in?'

'And the army has no eyes to see them', added Comrade Kunjan. 'They have only guns.'

Wading through the groups of comrades, a bunch of famished villagers entered the Vayalar Camp. Famished mothers pulling their tummy in, carrying infants on their hips, hungry toddlers tagged to their *mundu* (wraparound tied to their waists), followed by the elderly, with their backs bent.... All moved towards the camp kitchen....

'Menasserians...!' said Comrade Karunakaran. 'Didn't the army and the goons of the landlords burn down their huts and belongings? Their men, poor souls, mortally scared, fled for their dear lives....'

Comrade Raman Kunju had spotted them from a distance itself. 'All of you have a seat in the shed. *Kanji* (rice porridge) will be ready soon.'

A little girl holding a plate with broken edges came in last, her tiny legs wobbling. Her eyes were dry, cheeks sunken with their baby fat lost in hunger, thin lips turned black in the scorching sun...just a pack of bones wrapped in a torn dirty towel around her waist.

'Is this not the child of our Kelan Kumaran?' Sekharan recognised her.

She moved closer to the hearth eagerly looking into the pot boiling on it.

Poor thing, so famished, she looks as if she might jump into the boiling hot porridge on the fire, thought Raman Kunju. She must have been tramping all the way from her far away village!

'Don't you remember, Comrade', whispered Sekharan to Raman Kunju. 'Kumaran, who was tied to a coconut tree and beaten to death by the goons of Pattathil Kartha? This is that Kumaran's daughter.'

During those days, Raman Kunju used to live in Kumarakom. Listening to the conversation, the toddy-tapper Kittan looked at them. Kittan could never forget that scene.

Kumaran was the tenant of Kartha. He was in charge of one of Kartha's innumerable coconut farms. Kumaran was allowed to take the yield of two coconut trees for his services. When the two coconut trees allotted to him stopped yielding, Kumaran took the extreme step of felling a few coconuts from a nearby coconut tree. The punishment for that crime was severe and inhuman. Kumaran was tied to the same coconut tree from which he had plucked the coconuts and beaten to death by the goons of the farm owner.

At the time, Kittan was perched upon a coconut tree extracting toddy, a few feet away from the crime scene. He saw four or five goons walking towards Kumaran's hut. Kumaran's wife was busy dehusking a decayed coconut. Her toddler daughter was playing next to her, catching gold-headed worms using a thread made sticky with her saliva.

'Woman…!' Hearing the goons accosting the poor woman, Kittan's attention turned to the scene.... 'Where is your outcaste husband?'

'Masters!' the woman scrambled to her feet in panic. 'From yesterday he is bedridden and sleeping inside the hut without seeing the light of day.'

'After stealing coconuts from the Pattathil house, the scoundrel is hiding inside the hut?' the goons shouted.

They dragged delirious Kumaran outside the hut and kicked him brutally. Kumaran rolled on the ground and pleaded for his dear life with folded hands. They chased out his petrified wife and child who were screaming in terror. One of the goons tied Kumaran to the coconut tree. 'This is the very tree you stole the coconuts from...rot on that, you, worthless beggar', they bellowed. Others thrashed him with iron rods. Twirling their iron rods, they chased away the spectators who had gathered around, hearing the commotion.

Not knowing what to do, in shock, Kittan was still perched on top of the coconut tree. He climbed down only after the goons had left. By then Kumaran was dead. From that day, Kittan stopped extracting toddy from coconut trees. 'Even now my legs wobble when I climb the tree… the sound of Kumaran's wails still plays in my ears.'

'Kumaran's woman died of starvation just four or five days ago', Sekharan said. 'Now this poor girl is all alone! Who will take care of her?'

'Poor thing! She must be starving...her arms and legs are trembling.' Raman Kunju's heart went out to the little girl. 'Sit here my child. The porridge is almost ready', he said.

'Hurry up...hurry up…isn't everyone famished?' Comrades KC Velayudhan and Sreedharan entered the kitchen and registered their impatience. 'Start serving…. Aren't we starving from the morning?'

'Let the porridge cool down a bit. Anyway, all of us have waited so long. Have a little more patience.' Raman Kunju removed the pot from the fire with the help of Sekharan. Women comrades added grated coconut to the cooked green gram and stirred. The porridge was poured into bowls made of palm leaves stitched into shape.

'Now, all of you may please be seated in a row', Comrade Velayudhan announced.

Holding up her plate with broken edges, the child waded through the crowd....

Aparajitha stared at what she had written in disbelief. She wasn't aware of the characters emerging from unknown origins and flowing through her fingers tapping on the keyboard. Hidden in invisible spaces, they debated with her incessantly. Aparajitha went into a trance in front of her laptop. The open window in the room offered her a view of paddy fields.

Disha's mother had woken her early in the morning. While having breakfast with Disha and Niranjan, her mind was filled with the little girl's face...

Like the black and white Bengali movies of the olden days, those bygone scenes flashed in her mind.

...Travancore kingdom.... After the Second World War, the allied forces emerged victorious.

Though the Union Jack flew high, the firmly-laid foundations of the British Empire had become shaky.

Discharged from the British Indian army the young war heroes were back, without any jobs to hold on to.

The country was bogged down by scarcity, coupled with hoarding and black marketing of food grains resulting in famine and starvation. ...At the same time, fattened rodents feasted on the hoarded grains and multiplied in the granaries of the rich landlords.

Death slunk through the shacks of the poor which were in perpetual darkness for want of kerosene oil.

The little girl's face continued to haunt Aparajitha even as she returned to her keyboard.

In the islet of death, spiders spread diaphanous nets waiting for the prey. Shadows of fear settled in the dark pools of her eyes. The landlord's henchmen had killed her father in front of her eyes… her own screaming frightened face fleeing from the scene of violence….

Procession of ants drawn by the smell of death…. The lifeless body of her mother lying on the cow dung plastered floor….

… The child was sitting there in front of her, holding a plate with broken edges….

Aparajitha's fingers raced through the key board.

Comrade Raman Kunju served hot porridge to the famished child. Comrade Sekharan pinned a jack tree leaf into the shape of a small ladle and gave it to her to help her with the hot porridge. As she greedily scooped the food and brought it near her dry lips, Comrade Sreedharan called out from outside, 'Am I hearing that roaring sound again?'

Comrade sharpened his ears; just a while ago they had heard that roaring from the sky…Sir CP's yellow Dakota circled the area several times, scattering copies of his Press Communiqué and vanished. It was a message from the sky which ordered the resisting comrades to surrender.

'Army has taken over the administration of Ambalapuzha and Cherthala districts. A ban order is in force!' it said.

Agitated comrades gathered together, throwing their fists up to the sky chanting, 'End Diwan's rule…Chuck the American Model in the Arabian sea. *Inquilab Zindabad…Inquilab Zindabad*'.

'Is that Sir CP's aircraft coming back bellowing?'

'Look there...', somebody howled. 'The army is coming back through the backwaters....'

The comrades stopped eating the porridge. Gathering their weapons, sharpened spears, knives, axes, iron rods and deadly sharp granite stones, they rushed out.

From the western side, through the backwaters, the Diwan's army, consisting of hundreds of soldiers* armed from top to bottom with guns and other weapons, were approaching the Vayalar camp menacingly, accompanied by four or five boats filled with automatic guns and ammunitions.

They encircled the camp from three sides...south, north and west. Heavy boots thudded. The Comrades were also ready to face the imminent slaughter. They had to face the guns. No other option. They were ready with their strategies. Plans were already laid out.... As soon as the whistle goes, lie flat on the belly and crawl forward with body pressed to the ground, holding the sharp spears without lifting your head. As the enemy gets close, spring up and drive the spear into his belly.

The soldiers spread out in three rows, forming a barricade on the eastern side. The first row positioned itself face down on the ground. The second row stood on their knees. The third one took their place behind the second with their guns fixed with bayonets pointing at the comrades.

Masses of dark clouds in the sky froze, forming a canopy over the camp.

The moment Comrade Kumaran blew the whistle, comrades stretched out on the ground and started crawling forward, holding their spears towards the fencing.

---

* These were soldiers of the King of Travancore's army, commanded by the Diwan.

Gun fire erupted from behind the barricade. Fire balls from guns sped past.

The first one to get hit was Sreedharan – on his forehead.

'Don't get shaken comrades, move forward, move on.' The comrades recognised Sreedharan's voice. Blood gushed out of the wound on his forehead.

Sreedharan was not perturbed. Bullets hissed. Shrieking comrades dropped dead all around.

The moment a comrade crawling right in the front raised his head slightly, a bullet hit him, scattering his brains. Blood flowed. Comrade Sreedharan boldly stood up in front of the soldiers, stripped off his shirt, and beating and thrusting out his chest, pleaded: 'You are also our comrades. It's in your interest too. We are facing death for the sake of this country and countrymen. However, if you think you have to kill us for your survival then don't hesitate, go ahead.'

Unconsciously, the fingers of the King's soldiers loosened their grip on the triggers. They stood frozen, not knowing what to do. Sound of gun shots stopped for a while.

'Bloody fools' someone bellowed. 'F…ire….fi...r…e!!' It was DSP Vaidyanatha Iyer. He had removed his hat and was waving at them.

Again, the automatic guns blasted. Fire balls sped past. Comrades dropped dead. Limbs, flesh and bones scattered. Comrades continued their surge forward, carrying their spears.

'Amma…' from somewhere near the camp kitchen, a gut-wrenching cry…. Comrade Sekharan tried to glance in that direction, carefully tilting his head.

It was the little girl wriggling... red petals of a hibiscus flower scattered on her chest... she was still holding the spoon made of the jack tree leaf.

'You heartless ones... you hired murderers of Sir CP', Comrade Sekharan poised his spear, targeting the back of DSP Vaidyanatha Iyer who was walking towards the building. But he couldn't hit him, instead, a bullet hit his chest, spraying blood all round... his limbs grew weak.

Flinging his fist towards the sky, he screamed, 'Let the Diwan's rule go to hell. *Inquilab Zindabad.*' Comrade Sekharan's face hit the ground.

Che Guevera's Sweetheart

Her last few days in the campus in Delhi were like that. Aparajitha closed Che's *The Motor Cycle Diaries* after inserting a page marker.

She stood admiring the cover picture of the book, Ernesto Guevara lying flat on his back on the terrace of his house in Buenos Aires, gazing at the sky. She tried to recollect every word of the foreword written by Aleida which she read meticulously, as she picked up the book each time.

'Shall I tell you a truth?' Aleida Guevara, Che's daughter, would tell her. 'Each time I read this book, I fell more and more in love with the youth, whose persona, I felt, was transforming into the father of my childhood days.... I recollect my childhood moments of clinging to my father, sitting behind him on his motor bike after displacing Alberto Granado, and flying over mountains and lakes. Each time I read the book, I got to know the youth Ernesto more and more.'

She too had lost count of how many times she had read that book which her father had gifted her along with a red packet of *jalebi* and a big packet of Whisper on the day she attained puberty.

'How fast my Sarangi has grown up to become a big girl!' Handing over the book, Father drew her close to him and kissed her on her forehead. Holding her close and pressing his face on her forehead, Father had stood there for a long while. As the warmth of his tears seeped down through her hair, she raised her head.

Forcing a moist smile on his lips, Father said, 'I just thought of that sprightly little girl with black sweet tooth, babbling and running around in our courtyard…how fast my daughter….'

'See how fast time flows….' He caressed her tresses lovingly.

She also felt that time flew very fast on its wings.

How fast her father too walked away silently into oblivion without telling her anything…. She had so many doubts to clear with him. She wanted to know about what was going on in his mind. She knew her father had a lot of information to pass on to her. But then, who knew time would blow its final whistle so abruptly!

On nights when sleep eluded her, staring at the darkness through the windows she would ask, 'Where are you Dad? Do you know there are a lot of things I want to discuss with you? …without waiting to hear me out you….'

A firefly settled on the window bar, twinkling and spreading a tiny circle of light. She closed the window shutters, trapping the fly inside the room. It spread light in the room till she sank into deep sleep. On waking up, she found it inside Che's book in between the pages…having lost its luster.

Somebody knocked on the door. She opened it. It was Disha. She rushed into the room to escape from the scorching heat outside. She downed the entire water in the jug in one go and cooling herself, looked at Aparajitha

'What did you decide? I just had a discussion with Ranbir. He says, near Patiala, his family has a small farmhouse. You can stay there in comfort.'

'I don't think I want to go to Patiala. It's so far away…. And a strange place too…. Living there all alone….' Aparajitha said.

'But you won't be alone. He and his people will be around', argued Disha, settling on the cot.

She leafed through Che's book. 'Oh, how many times have you read this book, girl? Don't you ever get bored?'

'Aleida Guevara is answering your question in her foreword. She must have written that for people like you.' She proceeded to the bathroom. Disha continued to leaf through the book.

When she came back from the bathroom, Disha's gaze was on Che's portraits hanging on the wall. Her eyes finally settled on a new picture sparkling in the red glow of revolution.

'Where is this from?' she questioned Aparajitha. 'This wasn't here yesterday.' Disha moved closer to the picture.

'I downloaded it with great difficulty from the Italian site Mora Bhoto.' Aparajitha was excited. 'Have you not heard about that Italian site? Bad English; but good tutorials! Their English would make us depressed. They write Bhoto for photo!'

Disha looked at Aparajitha disapprovingly. 'Oh, praise our warden!' She said. 'Did you know a college in Kerala expelled a student for having painted Che's picture on the college wall?'

'This happened in Kerala?' Aparajitha couldn't believe it. Her memories drifted to an afternoon, years ago when she was a little girl. As she was casually walking with her father, holding on to his hand, he had told her, 'One day I will take my Sarangi there; to that historic land where the soil turned red… soaked in the blood drained from the bodies of bold martyred comrades!'

She looked at him eagerly.

'Not now', Father said. 'Later, when my daughter grows big enough to understand facts.'

When she was little, Father used to talk to her in Malayalam whenever they were together and Mother, in Bengali. She was sent to a school run by a Malayali Association, to which Mother had no objection. Father wanted to name her Sarangi, a name he had carried along in his mind since the day he had met Pundit Ram Narayanji. Sarangi is the name of a musical instrument. Ram Narayanji once visited their house and stayed the whole night, playing the Sarangi. Mother was seven or eight months pregnant at the time.

'If your wife delivers a girl, you should name her Sarangi', said Ram Narayanji as he was about to leave.

The moment Ram Narayanji left, Mother said. 'I have no doubt that I will be delivering a girl and have already decided on a name – Aparajitaa. 'She will become a woman who can never be defeated by anyone.'

'No doubt Aparajitaa is a nice name', Father also agreed. 'That's the name of Ray's second movie. But if someday I happen to meet Ram Narayanji, what shall I tell him?'

Mother found a way to end the debate. 'Aparajito Sarangi'.

Father improvised it as he wrote in the Malayali Samajam school register, 'Aparajitha Sarangi'.

'It is okay to be a student in the Malalyali Samajam School. Yet Apu, you should not completely ignore Bengali literature', Mother used to advise her discreetly. 'Do you know how deep and profound Bengali literature is when compared to Malayalam?'

Mother wrote poems in her own small way in Bengali. They used to find place in the week-end pages of the leading Bengali newspaper, *Ananda Bazar Patrika*.

In the olden days, Father made frequent visits to his native village in Kerala, all alone.... When he returned, he brought innumerable new Malayalam books. But that practice stopped some time later. Although he didn't discuss the reason with anybody, Aparajitha felt that he was deeply hurt on his return from his last visit. He never discussed his native place with anyone, anymore. She thought that someday, he would reveal the reason behind that to her, but before that....

'Poor Ranbir...' Disha woke her up. 'The kid has made all the arrangements for your stay in Patiala. He has even found a Bengali cook exclusively for you...'

'What are you talking about? These things are not going to work out Disha', Aparajitha was agitated.

Disha didn't say anything in reply. She knew that there was place for only one man in Aparajitha's mind. 'Che, Ernesto Che Guevara.'

But the question was, where would she go after she submitted her thesis at the university? Mrinalda was also anxious about her future. She wouldn't go to her mother in Midnapore. That was for sure. There was no way to compel her in that matter. She had no roots in Kolkata too. So, where would she go?

'One who has been condemned by her own life!' That's how she chose to talk about herself.

Hearing that, Mrinalda would get very upset. Disputing her words strongly, he would argue, 'Who said you are condemned to be alone?' 'Who said you are alien to Kolkata? Can this great city forget Comrade Sathyadas? Sathyadas, who fought for the rickshaw-pullers of Calcutta… restoring their status as human beings.'

Mrinalda spoke a mixture of English and Hindi. But when they were alone, they spoke in Bengali.

He fished out a paper from the depth of his kurta pocket. 'Look this is the decision taken by our local committee in Midnapore. They have decided to dedicate the new Party Office Building as a memorial to Comrade Sathyadas. Wasn't the old party office building hijacked by the black sheep of the party who deserted us and switched to Trinamool?'

'Can the party forget Comrade Sathyadas and his family?'

'Family?' Aparajitha was bitter. 'Does something like that still exist for Comrade Sathyadas?'

Mrinalda remained quiet for a while. He waited for her to calm down after the emotional display and asked softly, 'Can the Party write off your mother who lived for twenty-seven years as his shadow, so easily? What's wrong if a helpless lady accepts a way opened in front of her, in the face of adversity? – That too, a Party Comrade, Comrade Subodh. Don't you know he found his place in her heart through his songs?'

Very often Disha found Mrinalda's interventions amazing. With such a balanced mind, he could resolve conflicts! He had a special aptitude to do that. He discerned issues from different angles, weighing pros and cons to analyse the situation and finally came up with startling solutions.

Mrinalda's father was a stern railway officer… a chronic bachelor…a loner and a traveler. He never thought of marriage or a family till he reached his fifties. He travelled frequently to escape the monotony and drudgery of the life of a recluse. It was during one such journey that Mrinalda's mother walked into his life. She was younger than him by twenty years. That was the time when Mrinal Sen's famous movie *Bhuvan Shome* was released. The hero of the movie was also a stern railway officer like Mrinalda's father. Like Mrinalda's father, he also was in the habit of undertaking long and distant journeys to indulge in his one and only hobby – bird hunting, which saved him from the boredom of his lonely life. Into his life also came a young woman named Gauri. (Mrinalda's mother's name was not Gauri.) Watching the movie, Mrinalda's father got obsessed by the idea that it was his life that Mrinal Sen had portrayed in his movie and from that time, he became a passionate fan of Sen movies.

Mrinalda was born much later. When the baby was born, the father didn't think twice. Carrying the baby, he boarded the first train to Calcutta. Keeping the baby on his lap, Mrinal Sen blessed him placing both his hands on his head, and named him after himself.

Mrinalda also became a fan of Mrinal Sen. But among the Sen movies, his favorite was the second one titled *Akaasher Neeche* meaning 'Below the Sky'. There was a reason for that. The movie was the projection of Sen's thoughts as a communist. The movie was themed after the tumultuous 1930s in Calcutta.

Wanglu, a young man from China reaches the streets of Calcutta to sell silk and falls in love with Basanti, a young communist activist. When Basanti is jailed, he also joins the Communist Party. Later, when Japan attacks China, Wanglu returns to his country and joins the People's Movement against Japan.

'In the history of Indian cinema, this movie has an unbreakable record. Do you know what it is?' Mrinalda would ask, answering the question himself. 'The first movie banned by the Government of India.' Even now he watches that movie on YouTube.

Besides being an alumnus of the campus, he was also a guide and 'big brother' to everybody. He spent some time in the campus as a research fellow. When he got fed up with research, he turned his attention to labour in the unorganised sector in Bengal.

Mrinalda had left that day after announcing that he would find a solution for Aparajitha's problems in the meeting to be held in the evening in Ranbir's hostel room. He reached Ranbir's room before anyone. Ranbir opened two bottles of beer and emptied them into three glasses. Mrinalda did not participate in such celebrations. He kept his distance from all kind of fun and extravaganza. His wardrobe consisted of merely two or three pairs of cotton dresses… loose long kurtas which he washed and ironed himself. He never combed his hair... still the casually unkempt hair made him look charismatic. He shaved only when there was a minimum of six or seven days' stubble on his face.

'Apu, I have come with a solution to your problem', he said as soon as he saw her. 'I have arranged a room for you in one of the standard working women's hostels in Calcutta and a job too. For the time being, that will meet your rent and other expenses.'

'But I am not going to Calcutta', Apu insisted. 'I know that every grain of sand in Calcutta carries my father's memories…

the smell of his sweat. It's not that I want to leave Calcutta forever and go and live elsewhere. But, now I can't help it. Mother's new life in Midnapore.... Somebody in father's place... the moment she started living with that music composer, she stopped being my mother!'

He saw her eyes moistening. Disha came into the room at that time.

'Thank you, Brother', Disha picked up the beer glass. 'I was dying to empty a sea of beer at the thought of going back home. The taste of Mother's special fish curry was haunting me the whole of last night.'

'You lucky Disha', a small smile flashed on Aparajitha's lips. 'One should be a bit lucky for all that, isn't it Mrinalda?'

Mrinalda felt a need to put an end to that conversation then and there, lest Aparajitha got more hurt.

'Oh, I had one more reason for coming here... to remind you of the campus discussions on Sunday. How are the preparations going on?'

'A peep into the future: Spreading tentacles of fascism – from Allende and Neruda, ending in the martyrdom of Che', said Disha. 'It's Apu who took the pain to bring it into some shape, working on it day and night for quite some time now.'

'Where is the draft you have prepared?' Mrinalda looked at Apu lovingly.

'Oh, I forgot to bring it. Give me a minute...' Aparajitha got up.

Mrinalda kept regarding her with delight as she walked away.

'Let me be frank', Mrinal said looking at Disha. 'There is one quality in her that you lack. Do you know what it is?

Commitment! Comrade Sathyadas's daughter alone can have that quality by default.'

'But can I ask you something Mrinalda?' Ranbir picked up the third glass of beer kept in front of Disha, toasting her health. 'How did that quality help a committed comrade like Sathyadas, who ended up so pathetically, after having lived a whole lifetime for the Movement and society?'

'Exactly', Disha agreed. 'What did Comrade Sathyadas achieve ultimately?'

'Friends', Mrinalda responded. 'What one achieves is not the agenda of a real communist. Comrade Sathyadas never aspired to achieve anything.... He considered himself just as another human being among billions of deprived human beings on this earth. And it was only for them that he lived.'

'At the end, he accepted martyrdom fighting against the corporate giants and mafias, by committing himself to a hunger strike unto death.'

Mrinalda didn't respond to that. He continued to look at Aparajitha walking and fading away in the dull moonlight.

'Comrade would have achieved something, had he got an opportunity to live for some more time.'

'Had he got an opportunity?' Disha and Ranbir asked together. 'Was it not the hunger strike demanding appropriate laws for bridling the water mafia and corporates that caused his untimely death?'

Disha tried to recollect that scene.

Two years ago, Comrade Sathyadas, who was seriously fatigued on the seventh day of his hunger strike, was forcibly transferred to a private hospital from the venue of the agitation, by the police. Lying on the hospital bed, he succumbed to the lull of medicines fed through his veins and drifted off into permanent sleep. Waiting for him to wake up, Disha was also sitting along with Aparajitha by the side of his bed. Leaving them in their acute misery, without turning back, he had set off on his final journey.

'That was not a natural death', Mrinalda looked at both of them.

'What was it then?' Disha's pulse raced.

'Murder!' Mrinalda said. 'Comrade Sathyadas was murdered.'

His voice broke. After a while he said, 'That's where the indications are leading us. For the time being, Aparajitha need not know this. One misfortune after another! She may not be able to withstand this bad news.'

Disha and Ranbir looked at each other. 'Mrinalda, who is behind this? Is it the water mafia?'

'We don't know. We have to find out', he said. 'Party comrades are planning to demand a full-fledged investigation.'

Mrinalda was lost in thought for some time and then suddenly looked at Disha. 'Disha, can't you take her to your home town, along with you?'

'Will she come if I ask?' Disha was skeptical.

'She will go', Mrinalda was sure.

Bolivian Wilderness

The sound of gunshots stopped. Settling on the palm trees, crows let loose a wail in chorus.

Rain clouds remained frozen in the sky.

Somewhere in the distance dogs howled.

Comrade Sekharan slowly opened his eyes. The air was filled with the acrid smell of blood. His memory seemed to have been blocked by a screen of dark smoke emitted by the guns.

Sound of heavy boots stomping on the ground, kicking up dust which had almost settled after the mayhem.

That was the time Sekharan remembered. He was surrounded by bodies. Shot down comrades were scattered all over the place. Agonised whimpering and stirrings could be heard everywhere. Sekharan tried to get up but his body did not cooperate. Blood oozed from a wound just below his left collar bone. It burned as if his chest had been pierced through. He remembered being shot when he was aiming the spear at DSP Vaidyanatha Iyer.

'Who is lying next to me?' he extended his hand, to turn the face of his neighbour. 'Isn't this Comrade Raman Kunju?' Bloodshot eyes stared at him.

'Comrade...Comrade....', Sekharan tried to call out to him as loudly as possible. There was no response. 'Comrade Raman Kunju should not be dead...', Sekharan hoped fervently. He tried to move towards Raman Kunju. As he released the face, the lifeless head buckled. A line of black ants crawling from the nose made their way to the clotted blood on the lips.

'Comrade!' Sekharan called once again. 'Are you gone?'

Sekharan's wails were stuck in his throat. Pain seeped through his chest. He wanted to scream loudly. If only someone would help him to get up!

'Water...water...!'

He heard someone whimpering behind him. Sekharan tried to rise, and turn his head in that direction, but in vain because his chest denied any kind of support to make such a movement possible.

'Water please...a drop of water....' Again, he heard the sound of whimpering. Sekharan figured out whose voice it was. Comrade Ananthan Veli Vasu. Next to him was Comrade Bhaskaran, who was also bleeding profusely.

Stomping sound of boots came closer.

'Will the soldiers help us to get up', Sekharan thought wishfully. 'After all, are they also not humans?'

'There, something is moving out there', the soldiers came closer.

Comrade Vasu was still whimpering, begging for water. The two army men halted near Raman Kunju. Stretching out, Sekharan sneaked a glance through his half-opened eyes to see what was happening.

'Pierce him and see whether he is dead', the man with a gun fixed to his belt bellowed raucously.

'Yes Sir.' His subordinate bent down and picked up the spear that belonged to Raman Kunju. He straightened up and thrust the deadly weapon through his naval. The spear-head pierced through the motionless body.

'Ok. This guy is dead', said the officer. The other man kicked the body aside.

'What about this guy?' The officer stomped on Sekharan's stomach with his booted leg, squeezing his intestines. Sekharan went into shock due to the unbearable pain! Still, he didn't move a muscle. Holding his breath and suppressing the pain, Sekharan remained motionless, like a corpse.

As the soldier aimed at his naval with the spear, the officer drew his gun and said, 'No need…he will die. The bullet has gone deep into his chest.'

'Look at this guy', he pointed towards Vasu who was still begging for water.

'Oh, you want water?' the officer howled at him, waving the gun. 'Pull him up and make him stand straight', he shouted at his deputy.

The deputy pulled him up with one hand. Vasu had a bullet that had gone into his right shoulder. Blood coursed from the shoulder to his chest. His body swayed as the deputy tried to steady him.

'What is your name?' He pointed his gun.

'Vasu', whispered the Comrade.

'You pig, what did you come here for?'

Vasu kept quiet.

The officer became more abusive. 'You wretch, why are you quiet? Has your tongue gone down your throat?' He bent his leg and thrust his knees into Vasu's naval. Vasu writhed in pain and sat on the ground.

'Speak up, you rogue, why did you come here?' The officer slapped him.

'To go to Cherthala', Vasu whimpered.

'Get this scoundrel out of this place', the officer shouted to his deputy. 'Dump him in the boat.'

The deputy immediately lifted Vasu up, holding him by his nape. 'Move on you rogue!'

'Don't take me anywhere', Vasu screamed in defiance. 'Shoot me down too, you murderers...!'

'You dirty bastard', the officer pointed his gun at Vasu. 'Shut your stinking mouth.'

The officer emptied his gun directly at Vasu's forehead. As the bullets hit him, Vasu spat on the face of the officer. The officer's face was splattered with blood and phlegm. One more gunshot.... This time it hit him in the throat. Comrade Vasu bent forward and dropped dead.

His anger not subsiding, the officer roared, 'Don't leave a single communist rogue alive. Kill, roast and bury them deep'.

Comrade Sekharan was lying down, holding his breath. He knew, one move and he would be killed. They were making sure that all the injured were dead, by thrusting bayonets into the bodies. Beyond three or four corpses Sekharan saw three bodies shot – but not yet dead. He could see them from the corner of his eyes. One was making an effort to get up. The soldiers rushed to the man and hammered him with the handle of their guns. He fell backward, to be beaten to death like a stray dog.

Soldiers were now moving in a different direction. Sekharan was startled to sense a slight movement beside him. One of the corpses was trying to move. He was actually not dead. It was Comrade Kochappi Kunjan who had been positioned in their central defensive line. He was lying motionless. His face was covered in blood.

'Don't move', Sekharan whispered. 'They will shoot.'

'The army has gone to the other side', Kochappi turned around. 'Try to crawl fast and move out otherwise they will burn all of us down en masse.'

Comrade Sekharan crawled forward slowly. A chunk of flesh ripped off by the bullet was hanging below his shoulders and obstructing his forward movement.

'Please tear this off', Sekharan told Kochappi as he reached him. 'I cannot move an inch with this hanging out.' He looked at the hanging flesh. 'The pain is excruciating. I will hold it with my teeth. You rip it out.'

Sekharan closed his eyes, holding the hanging flesh between his teeth. Kochappi ripped it off in one go.

'Oh…ouch….' Sekharan writhed in pain. Blood streamed out of the wound. Ignoring the pain, he crawled forward. He could feel his limbs growing weak. Kochappi tried to help him and moved forward.

When they reached the bushes by the pond, Kochappi alerted Sekharan, tapping him on his back. 'Make no sound… lie as if dead…the army is searching the pond.'

Sekharan could see through the bushes. Some fifty odd bodies were scattered in the pond, clinging to the spears tightly held in their fists. There were dead and living ones among them. The army was in the process of driving bayonets into them and making sure that no one was left alive. Those who screamed as the bayonets pierced into them were pulled out and flung on to the bank of the pond. Those who were almost dead were beaten to death with the barrels of the guns and dumped back into the pond.

Kochappi and Sekharan were lying face down on the ground, as if they were dead. Sekharan remained motionless. He was finding it difficult to move with the gnawing pain. Kochappi seemed to have not been shot. The soldiers came out of the pond and started shooting at the coconut trees. Several tender coconuts dropped from the trees and they started feasting on them.

'Come on get up', Kochappi said. 'Let's move on our knees… hiding behind those bushes we can try and get into that hut.'

'Oh no…I can't get up', Sekharan wailed. Kochappi came to his knees and carrying Sekharan on his shoulders, managed to make it to the hut. There were some fifteen people inside the hut. Most of them had hidden behind the hut at the time of the shootout. Sekharan collapsed on the ground. Someone dripped some water remaining in a cup on to his dried lips.

'Kochappi, you have given us away', an old man hiding inside the hut cried in anguish. 'Seeing both of you entering the hut, those murderers are coming here. They will not leave any of us alive.'

Kochappi got up to see what was happening outside. He saw the army encircling their shelter. 'Come out everyone; the hut is going to be set on fire.' They stood pointing the guns towards the hut.

'All of you stay put', Kochappi told the comrades. 'I will face them.'

Opening the door made of woven dried palm leaves, Kochappi stepped outside, inflating his chest and throwing up his fists shouting loudly '*Inquilab Zindabad,* martyrs Zindabad'.

Crack of the gun! …was it the sound of Kochappi roaring that hit their ears?

Comrade Sekharan listened hard for the sound of death.

Niranjan stopped the bike. The mud road ended there. Aparajitha got down with her camera and note pad. Chitran was waiting for them on the road-side. 'We have to cut across three or four plots. After the Vayalar shootout, the army stomped to the Olathala camp through this way. Only seven or eight comrades died in these premises', said Chitran.

'I read that in KC George's book', said Aparajitha. 'They had constructed deep trenches on three sides of the camp. When the army started to fire, comrades sat inside the trenches with their heads down. No one came out till the army stopped firing. The gunshots stopped soon. Comrades drove the army away, hurling stones at them.'

'What you can see there is the Kanisseri property', Chitran pointed ahead of him.

'Hey! Brother Shamsuddin!' He called out to the people in the house. A man came out of the house. He stood by the side of the pond in front of the house.

'This is that pond', Chitran said. 'Twelve years ago, Shamsuddin bought this property. When he tried to clean up the pond, skeletons and skulls surfaced. And Shamsuddin stopped cleaning. This is the resting place of the Comrades from Olathala.'

'There are certain places where time hangs heavy', Aparajitha thought. 'Here in the depths of this pond, time seems to stand suspended in remembrance of those martyrs who departed to eternity unrecognised – the martyrs who gave up their lives in their effort to rewrite history!' Aparajitha stood there in silence.

A long-nosed truck came from the north side honking and halted at the junction.

Vasu Asaan peeped out of his tea shop. Two soldiers carrying heavy trunks got down from the truck. Leaving a trail of exhaust fumes, the truck lept forward. Occupants of the truck lifted the curtains of tarpaulin and gazed at the two who crossed the road. They walked towards the tea shop. The breeze made a hissing sound, brushing against their stiffly starched olive green uniforms of the British Indian Army. The one with a loftier appearance, walking in front, greedily eyed the sweetmeats neatly arranged in the glass shuttered almirah. Vasu Asaan sharpened his sight and pricked up his ears.

'Asaan, can't you recognise me? I am Soman from our locality, Soman Nair', he opened the glass almirah, picked up a sweet and bit into it.

'What, our Soman?' Vasu Asaan was stunned. 'I did not recognise you at all. O boy, you have changed a lot!'

'Um… after eating all that beef and pork and bloating up… ok, give us two strong teas.' Soman removed his cap and massaged his head. 'Along with that, give us some of those sweet snacks too. Are you okay with that Kumar?' He turned to his companion.

'Um…' Kumaran cracked his knuckles.

Vasu Asaan bent backwards, mixing the tea by transferring it from one glass to another in a perfect line forming the shape of a bow.

'Is sugar available in your place?' Vasu Asaan enquired while filling two glasses. 'We are going through a famine from the time war broke out. No rice, no clothes, not even kerosene is available. Chronic starvation… what kind of a time are we going through?' he lamented.

'So, there is no sugar in the tea?' Kumaran made a face.

'Where from? I have forgotten the days when sugar was available!' Vasu Asaan kept the snacks on banana leaves. 'Now a days, the practice here is to apply very spicy chilly chutney on the tongue and swig the boiling hot black coffee in one go, as the burning sensation seeps down to the anus.'

'I could do well with a few more edibles.' Kumaran eyed the glass almirah. The Ruling King trapped in a photo frame stared at him from behind the almirah.

Vasu Asaan emptied the snacks from the tray.

The soldiers attacked the snacks.

War!

The soldiers wiped their mouths after finishing their war with the snacks and got up. Soman Nair fished out a British rupee from his pocket and offered it to Vasu Asaan.

'Not five or ten, more than ten thousand people are rumoured to have perished starving', Asaan jingled the coins in the money box. 'And this data pertains only to our Cherthala taluk.'

'Ten thousand was long ago', Soman Nair picked up his trunk. 'The count of the dead has crossed over twenty-one thousand according to the report of Servants of India Society... I read it in the paper.'

'But... have you left the Army?' Vasu Asaan asked hesitantly.

'Um...yes...we left the Army', the soldiers got ready to leave.

'Then, what's next?'

'Oh, hereafter we will be hanging around here. We have to start looking for some work.'

'What sort of work is available in this village?' Vasu Asaan shrugged.

'Who knows?' They walked down the steps.

'In that case, what happened to all those from our village who joined the Army?' Vasu Asaan looked at them worried.

'All are coming back, my dear Asaan', Soman Nair turned back. 'As soon as the war got over, they discharged everyone. All feel that it's better to die in one's own land rather than in unknown far away countries – even if we have to starve here.'

'Oh, that also is true', Vasu Asaan walked back inside.

From Olathala, Niranjan proceeded to Thykkal. He stopped the bike under an Elanji flower tree. Dinar had promised to wait for them there. Niranjan had appointed Dinar to prepare a reading list for Aparajitha's project and make the books available to her.

Niranjan parked the bike under the tree. 'He promised to wait for us here.'

The old Elanji tree, decked with freshly blossomed flowers all over the branches stood in the centre of the carpet formed by fallen flowers, spreading heady fragrance. She bent down and picked up a handful of flowers.

Niranjan drew his mobile from his pocket.

'Just smell….' She brought the flowers close to his nose. 'What a heady fragrance!'

The fragrance reminded her of the first gift of love Che had given to Aleida.

'Comrade, if I ask you a question, can you answer me?' she quizzed him.

'What was the first gift of love that Che gave Aleida?'

He thought for a while. 'Communist Manifesto?'

'No….'

'Das Capital?'

'Oh please, don't make poor Che so unromantic!' She chided him. 'If you don't know, say pass.'

'Say pass? No…let me think for some more time.'

He started his bike.

She watched him flying away lovingly. He is not the one to yield. Disha had only complaints about him.

'Look at him roaming around even after completing B Tech. Even after getting an offer from an MNC in the campus selection, he didn't bother to take it up. He used to be an active member in the Party Federation in the initial days of his professional college life. But then, gradually…. Party comrades complained to Mother many times. He never even bothered to step into the local committee office. After all, ours is a family with Party heritage. He doesn't even think of that. Not because he is not a rebel. Rather, he has more rebellion in him than what's required. That's the problem. You must go into his room and take an inventory of his books. His room is filled with profound books on communism from all over the world. I don't know how he managed to get them. Where does he get the money to buy them? Looks like he is in some other world and doesn't belong to this!'

'In which world is he?' That was something Aparajitha also wanted to know.

He came back flying. 'Come, let's go. Dinar has gone directly to Swadeshabhimani Library.'

Aparajitha sat on the pillion.

'Did you get the answer?' she asked him. 'If not, say pass.'

He didn't seem to hear her in the roar of the motor bike.

Did Che's gift to Aleida March have the fragrance of Elanji flowers?

That tiny perfume bottle which had the colour of a red rose.

'Flower de Rica!'

How long would Aleida have kept the bottle safely with her?

Wouldn't that fragrance have lingered in her life even after its contents evaporated like the lasting memories he had left in her life?

How fulfilling their love life was! She tried to reflect. It didn't matter how long it had lasted. That may not be the measuring unit of intimate love. Love might have been condensed into a brief moment, intensifying its quality.

Where did Che walk away at the peak of Aleida's love? Wouldn't she have spent the rest of her life waiting for his return?

Niranjan resembled Che a lot. He must have been aware of that and made it more conspicuous by deliberately copying Che's casual hair style and sporting a similar beard and mustache. Earlier on, Disha had made a mention of that but it was only after seeing him in person that their striking resemblance became evident to Aparajitha.

She had met him on the second day of her arrival from Delhi. He had also returned home after a long journey.

As they heard the roar of his motor bike from the mud road approaching their house, Disha announced, 'That must be Comrade Che'.

Niranjan parked the bike in front of the house.

'Hi Comrade', Aparajitha waved at him.

'Hi!' he responded as he parked the bike.

Though she had spoken to Niranjan many times over the phone, this was the first time they were meeting in person. Disha had shown her his photo when her brother was a teenager without a mustache. In the photo, he resembled Che as he appeared on the cover page of the book her father had gifted her.

'I will definitely make a movie on Che someday', she said. 'At that time, I won't have to spend much time searching for an actor. Disha, I am booking him right now.' Aparajitha could see him blushing through his facial hair.

'OK, I am ready.' He extended his hand. 'You can make the advance payment now.'

She captured his rough fingers in her hands.

'Where is Alberto Granado?' She asked. 'Or, was Comrade Che drifting around all alone on the bike?'

Warmth from his fingers seeped through her soft fingers.

'Comrade, you haven't replied to me', Disha said assuming the seriousness of an elder sister. 'Where were you roaming around?'

'Mother said, you keep taking off on your bike. Are you in the process of writing a new motorcycle diary?'

Without responding, he walked inside, swirling the key chain on his fingers. Disha looked at Mother instinctively.

Swadeshabhimani. The Patriot is the name of the library in the Thekkummuri village, named after the great leader Ramakrishna Pillai. It's now more than half a century old. Recently, Niranjan and his friends had taken over its management. The building was old. A moth-eaten portrait of Swadeshabhimani Ramakrishna Pillai, adorned with a plastic flower garland, hung on the wall of the front toom.

'A publisher who made it his business to critique every injustice committed by the ruling class', Niranjan introduced Ramakrishna Pillai to Aparajitha. 'He was, of course, punished for his forthrightness. They sent him to exile. It was he who translated the biography of Karl Max in an Indian language.'

Aparajitha looked at the portrait of the brave publisher in admiration and commented: 'But his dress does not match that of an editor in exile. Overcoat and tie! Malayalees are still prisoners of a colonial mindset. Bengalis are not like that, despite the fact that Calcutta was the brain centre of the British Raj.'

Dinar ushered her in. The premises smelt of decaying old books and wooden almirah*s*. In a corner there was an almirah labeled 'Punnapra-Vayalar'. In it, there were some very old books which were about to crumble to dust along with a few newer books. She leafed through them.

Dinar came with a bunch of old newspapers and said, 'These are the reports on Punnapra-Vayalar struggle written by the journalist C Unni Raja and published by the Party's official newspaper.'

He handed over the papers to her.

One banner read:

*People's Age.*17 November 1946.

'Devil's Raj continues in Travancore.'

Along with the report was Sir CP's caricature and Unni Raja's byline. The report was from Bombay.

'You know, the Party had its headquarters in Bombay those days', Dinar said.

Aparajitha went through the report narrating the horrendous days after the Vayalar shootout.

Sir CP rationed food. The activists and their supporters were denied rations. Only those who could produce a certificate from the Village Officer, vouching for their character were to be given the benefit.

News dated 1 November 1946: Popular writer Ponkunnam Varkey has been taken into custody for fictionalising the hardships suffered by the people of Travancore. This was followed by details of other arrest warrants; writers P Kesavadev, Thakazhi Sivasankara Pillai, Kuttippuram Krishna Pillai. In fact, writings of Thakazhi and Dev had infuriated the Diwan.

Looking at the books, Aparajitha moved around the room. In one corner, there were about six almirahs. On the shutters of one of them was written in crimson red, 'Marxism, Leninism and Maoism'. Most of the books in the almirah were new titles in English.

'This is the first thing we did after taking over the Library… procure new titles', said Niranjan.

'Very good', Aparajitha smiled. 'You made my mission easier.'

'Looks like, it's only to serve my purpose that time has entrusted you with this Library', said Aparajitha.

'Time has in store definite tasks for each one of us', Niranjan said. 'Our mission is only to carry out those tasks. And our task now is to take forward the mission initiated by Che.'

'True', Aparajitha thought. 'How carefully does time organise everything for us!'

Suddenly struck by a thought she turned back and looked at Niranjan. Did she get an imperceptible glimpse of the Bolivian wilderness in his 'Che' persona?

The Legendary Land

Kochhappi stood, closing his eyes and thrusting his chest forward to receive the bullets. Right in front of him was the Naib Subedar, his gun tauntingly moving up and down his throat.

'One, two, three.'

Sound of a blast that shattered the ear drum. Kochhappi collapsed to the ground. The soldiers roared in laughter. The Naib had aimed the shots at the sky.

'You good for nothing worm', Naib lifted Kochhappi from the ground, holding him by his nape. 'Did you think that I will finish you off in one shot? Your guts are a bit on the higher level. We will finish you off inch by inch. You son of an ass, call out your *inquilab* once again.'

He jabbed his finger into the cavity at the bottom of Kochhappi's neck.

'Umm… call out your *inquilab*', he stripped off Kochhappi's mundu, forcing him to bend his legs and thrust his knees into his groin. Kochhappi shrieked in pain.

'Not enjoying the treatment.., are you? Go ahead and break every bone in his body', the Naib ordered his men. 'Not only has he not been hit by a bullet, he has not even been affected by the smoke.'

He hurled Kochhappi to his men. They pounced on him like a pack of wolves. Kochhappi's screams pierced through the smoke and soared over the violent landscape.

'Stop the beating', another army official who passed by, told them. 'Dump him in that boat.'

They dragged Kochhappi to the boat. They lifted up Sekharan and Kittan Asaan. Sekharan screamed in agonising pain. Kittan Asaan was from Menassery. His landlord had evicted him from his hut and gutted it. He had come to the camp famished, looking for some food.

They lifted Sekharan, holding his legs and hands. The bullet stuck inside caused him excruciating pain. 'Why can't you just finish me off in one go?' Sekharan cursed them. 'I am not able to bear this pain.'

'But we are not going to kill you', they said. 'We are trying to extract the bullet. If the pain is unbearable, we will loosen our grip.'

Sekharan thought they were teasing him. But they actually loosened their hold and Sekharan felt better. On their way, there were corpses still bleeding and holding on to their spears tightly. The soldiers kept jumping over the corpses. Here and there three or four corpses were stacked together. Pieces of bones lay scattered around. Eagles and crows feasted over the corpses. Dogs fought over chunks of flesh. One soldier shot at a pack of dogs. Howling, they scattered.

Sekharan looked at the mud reddened with blood. He couldn't recognise anyone because their faces were smeared with blood and mud. Bullets had hit most of them on their chests. Sekharan felt proud of them because no one had fled to evade death. Knowing that they were all going to die, the patriots had exposed their chests to the bullets.

'*Lal Salam Comrades, Lal Salam!*' Unconsciously Sekharan chanted and the effort made him writhe in pain.

'Shut your mouth and stop your slogans!' One of the bearers admonished him. 'Do you want to be shot dead?'

They reached the boat. Kochhappi was lying in the center of the boat in a pool of blood, wearing nothing but a muddy blood-stained loin cloth. Blood gushed out of his ears. Sekharan was made to sit with the wounded in the center. Those not wounded were made to sit around them. Blood gushing out of the wounds pooled in the middle.

The sky became dark. Water birds started settling for the night. The men from the King's army started talking in hushed tones.

'What's the time?'

'May be a quarter to seven.'

'How many would have died?'

'Around five hundred; Who bothered to take a count!'

'What about the other camps?'

'Who knows? Those who have gone there have not come back you see...'

'But this is outrageous...'

'Speak softly; if someone hears, your cap won't be on your head!'

'That's okay. I am going to quit the army. I cannot do this work anymore.'

'Are you people not hungry?' Three men came near them with a few coconuts and a sickle.

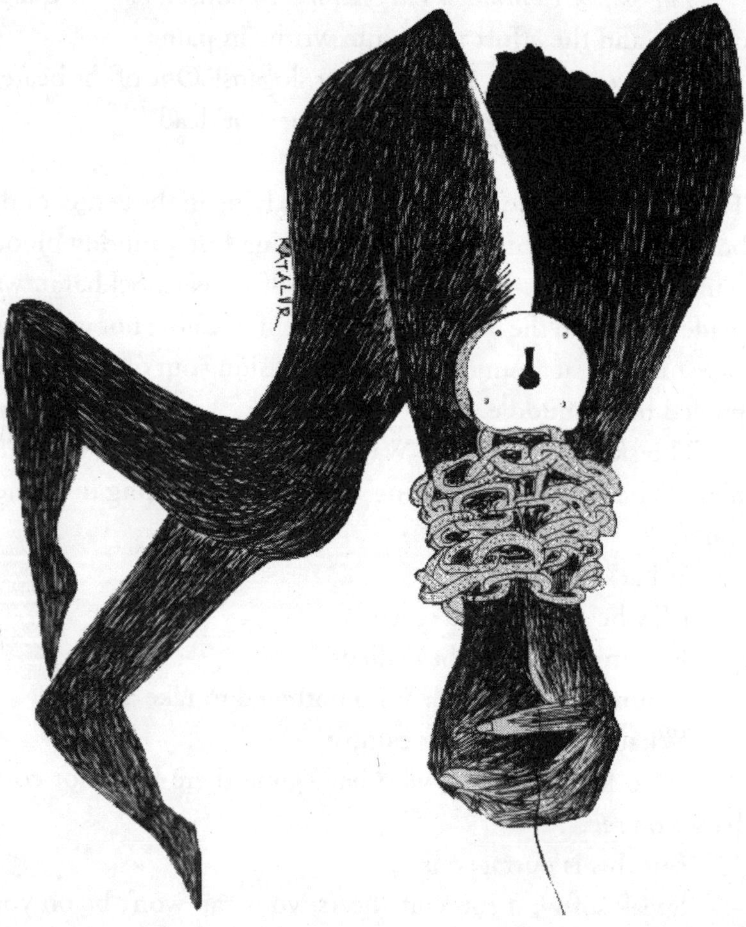

'Oh, some good use for their weapons', one said. 'This was taken from a woman. Even after dying, how firmly she was holding this. It was a very difficult task to pull it out of her fist.'

Scattering the coconut pieces on an old carpet, the soldiers started devouring the pieces. Seeing them eating, Kittan Aasan, who was famished, looked at them, ravenous.

'See, even at the time of death how greedy he is', the man holding the sickle said. He flung three or four pieces to the center of the boat. It fell into the blood pooled there. Kittan Aasan looked at it greedily, but seeing the pieces falling into the blood he lowered his head.

'You mangy dog, lick and eat it.' The man with the sickle stood up. 'Even if it has fallen into your shit, I will make you eat it.'

He caught hold of Aasan's nape and lowered his face to the pooled blood. Then he pulled his hair and brought his face up. There was a piece of coconut in between his teeth dripping blood.

'Ha! Ha! Ha!' he celebrated his victory.

'Oh, please stop it Nadar...' one of them felt disgusted. 'Don't you have even an iota of human feelings....'

'You can say all that', Nadar retorted. 'These are traitors... unpatriotic enough to fight against our beloved King with spears. The communist rogues....' He spat on their faces.

'So, instead of paddy seeds, you are going to sow communism in our fields, isn't it?'

The boat had taken them to Cherthala Government Guest House. The place was overflowing with the army. By seven o'clock, a lorry transferred them to the Cherthala lockup. Inspector Koshy in his stiff and ironed uniform and cross belt was anxiously waiting to receive them in front of the station.

'So, you are "Stalin's army" in Vayalar Moscow?' he growled at them. They were made to sit in front of the station in a circle. He stomped his boot, 'I will grind all of you into a smooth paste.'

He stopped as he reached behind Narappan. 'So, you were not hit by the bullets?' He caught him by his hair and made him stand up. 'What's your name?'

'Narappan.' The word meant a person made of fiber.

'Narappan? I will pound you and shred you into fibers.' Koshy bent his knees and kicked Narappan on his lower back. Poor Narappan writhed like a worm. Koshy dropped him, and squashing him with his booted leg, ordered the policemen around.

'You guys, instead of watching the show, start dealing with them. Their wailings should be heard in the guest house. Then there are four or five of their leaders in our cells... let them also hear.'

Two policemen opened the lockup. Comrade NSP Panikkar and advocate Kumaran came out.

Three more lorry loads of victims were brought in. Soldiers pulled them out and flung them on the ground. Koshy started his cruel entertainment. Prisoners' wails pierced the roof of the police station and hit the sky.

'Totally, how many of these scoundrels are to be hanged?' Koshy rubbed his hands together.

'Totally two hundred and twelve', said Head Constable Narapilla.

'Lock them in three cells.'

'There will not be enough space sir', said the Head, scratching his head.

'Then make them sleep on your mother's chest.' Koshy bristled in rage. 'You fool of an ass, crush them in whatever space is available.'

Three lockups which could not accommodate more than ten each were stuffed with ten times the capacity. 'Not a single one should make a movement. All of you settle down without any commotion.' The policemen locked the door.

The cell stank. Sekharan felt sick. It was a cell where a leper criminal had been locked up. Including Sekharan and the criminal, ninety-eight people were stuffed in it. The criminal was sitting in a corner. Ants crawled over his leftover lunch. Flies swarmed around a dirt container used for excreting which stank.

In those days Aparajitha was in the throes of writing. She was moving back and forth through the lines appearing on the monitor. In the background of the uprising, should it be an enquiry forward or should it be backward, or should it move in both directions?

Disha walked in with a glass of buttermilk.

'How is it progressing?'

'Here you are', she pushed the laptop towards Disha. 'I showed it to Niranjan. He liked it.'

'He will like it', Disha said. 'The very word revolution is enough for him to like it. He has Kunjunni Grandpa's genes. Didn't I tell you how Grandpa handled a Sub-Inspector who came to search our house and was knocked down with an iron rod?' Disha handed over the buttermilk to Aparajitha. 'Mother prepared it especially for you, adding crushed lemon leaves.'

Apu drank it greedily and said, 'It tastes better than what they sell in the streets of Mathura.'

'Oh, I didn't tell you. Mrinalda called. He wanted to know whether I liked the special fish curry Mother prepares.'

Disha didn't hear that. She was absorbed in a pair of mynahs perched on the tree in the courtyard. Her mind drifted to the Delhi campus where the mynahs were darker in colour. Their beaks were more yellowish.

'Hey, where are you?' Aparajitha patted her shoulder.

'Oh, I wandered off…to the Campus.' Disha came back. She was like that. Even during serious discussions in the campus, she would drift off into a dream world.

Ranbir used to say, 'when we are breaking our head analysing and critiquing Manmohan Singh's New liberal policies and neocolonial fascism, she is not anywhere here.'

Retorting, Disha would say, 'Didn't Marx daydream? Didn't Fidel Castro daydream? Why the objection to a village girl like me daydreaming?'

'One has to dream.' Mrinalda would intervene. 'Especially young people like you. Today's dreams are tomorrow's realities. But Disha, if you keep drifting off into your dream world every now and then, what will happen?'

'Sometimes descend to the earth too…', Ranbir would tease her.

'Mrinalda and Ranbir should have been here', Aparajitha said smiling. 'They would have knocked you down to reality.'

'Shall I tell you the truth Sarangi….' Disha ran her fingers through her hair. That is how she addressed her sometimes, especially when she wanted to irritate her. She loved to see Aparajitha's fair face turning red and the thin veins on her face become visible.

'I have still not left the campus totally. My mind is still there. Mrinalda, Ranbir, Sharmila, Pavanendu….'

Aparajitha looked at her slyly. Had her face turned red? Had she spun a subtle bridge of gossamer to Ranbir even without his knowledge? Why was she hesitant to disclose that? And he is in a different dream world toying with a dream that will never come true, Aparajitha thought.

'I have forgotten something there', Disha continued. 'That's what my mind says. I am still searching for it.'

'Am I also searching for something?' Aparajitha thought. 'Not in the campus… but in this battlefield.'

Her life seemed to be a big tree with its roots running in Kerala and Bengal. It may be in Delhi campus too. But she was not in love with Delhi nor with Calcutta.

'I am also searching', she said. 'But am not sure whether I will be able to discover that. As the days go by, it remains as an unanswered question. In Delhi you said that the moment we reach our home State, we will be able to discover my roots. But so far….'

'What I told you is true', Disha tried to convince her. 'Niranjan is on the job meticulously. Yesterday also, he brought some Vayalar comrades here who wanted to get some information from you. Unfortunately, you were not here.'

'What information do I have to give them?' Aparajitha asked helplessly.

'Nothing…?' Disha asked. 'Try to recollect…some hints Father would have given you in between discussions…'

'Nothing….' Aparajitha lowered her head. She tried to dig into her memories to uncover any hints Father might have dropped, including his last reminder in Rajiv Chowk before he disappeared in the crowd of the metro without any results.

Disha was in deep thought. The way Aparajitha happened to be in Kerala along with her after long long discussions in the campus – looked like Aparajitha definitely has some mission here. Every person has a mission in life. But most of them return without realising that. Few who realise that, reach the cross roads and get stuck. At the end, life ends up as a quiz question asked to a fool!

Red-crested Bird

They were on their way to the last of the sand hills.

The Vaka tree planted by Disha in memory of Comrade Anakhashayan was on the top of that hill. She had gone there long ago as a little girl along with her friends in a children's group. Disha still remembered those days. Wild fruit-bearing trees had grown on the slopes of the hill. Fallen fruits formed a dry fruit carpet on the ground. While the boys climbed the trees, she and her friends got busy looking for berries growing on small shrubs which painted the hills green.

It was when they were resting after lunch, that Kochhu Raghavan Master told them the story of Comrade Anakhashayan. It was not exactly a story but the history of a youth – Nakhashayan, a page highlighted in red in the history of the Punnapra-Vayalar uprising.

'Disha, where are you heading to?' Walking and walking, Aparajitha had lost patience. 'Haven't we been walking for a long time?'

They had walked a long distance – by the paddy fields, jumping over narrow canals, going past narrow mud roads, through thickets, uncultivated lands and so on.

'Just a little more', Disha said encouragingly.

'My legs are sinking into the sand', Aparajitha complained. 'Had I known the way was going to be like this, I would have worn my canvas shoes.'

'It was not like this in the olden days', Disha said apologetically. 'You know how much the landscape has changed. Wherever you turned you could see only vast expanses of white sand. Hills blanketed by thickets of cashew trees.... Green weeds spread on the surface of narrow streams...small bridges across the streams made of split palm tree trunks....'

'When we walked on the narrow bund roads between the paddy fields, crab shells jingled under our feet. The shells looked like tiny cowries, greenish brown in colour. Tiny crabs swam in the canal along with tiny prawns. Looks like all these species have become extinct.'

'I have come here very late, haven't I? Should have come here a little earlier', Aparajitha said stepping carefully on a narrow bridge of slit palmyra trunk stretching across a narrow canal.

'We should have come here before we were born', said Disha. 'Do you know how beautiful the seashore used to be? Mother told me. The land mafia scrapped out all the sand hills. Paddy fields were filled. Green thickets vanished.'

'What a pity', Aparajitha whispered sadly, plucking a beautiful wild flower.

'Here there used to be a big pond. There, a little farther away, there was a sand hill. On the bank of the pond was a huge tree bearing wild fruits, dotted with a number of cavities on its trunk. A variety of birds nestled in those holes...woodpeckers, mynahs and other birds could be seen flying back and forth carrying food for their chicks. At the bottom was the place reserved for waterfowl. During summer vacations we children came here to swim in the pond. One day when we were swimming, we saw a huge snake wading through the weeds. We stopped swimming here since that day.'

'Unbelievable!' said Aparajitha, trying to visualise the pond, the old tree, aloe vera thickets and the snake wading through the weeds.

'While flattening those sand hills, the land mafia covered that pond too.'

'But was it not the Diwan's army who filled the pond with corpses?' Aparajitha thought aloud.

'No, they were burnt', Disha corrected her. 'Not only the corpses, but also the people who were still alive. On the second day of the shootout, they doused the bodies in petrol and burnt them. Do you know how Grandpa Kunjunni escaped from the slaughter?'

Aparajitha looked at her.

'That was an event!' Disha excitedly began to tell the story. 'Grandpa pretended to be dead when the killer army came by. His face was all covered in blood. He was lucky that they didn't stab him with the bayonet to test whether he was alive. They thought he was really dead. The army left when it was dusk, and Grandpa started crawling away painfully. The bullet had hit him on one of his thighs. On the way, he found a tapping knife. He made an incision on his thigh with that knife and extracted the bullet. Blood gushed out of the wound and he became unconscious. He was found by the comrades who happened to come by and carried him to the nearest indigenous medical centre.'

'Grandma was visiting her home town Muhamma at that time. She was three months pregnant. On hearing the news of the shootout, she managed to reach Vayalar in two days, desperate to know Grandpa's whereabouts. Someone told her that he was shot. Screaming loudly, she rushed to the venue of the shootout.'

'Then?' Aparajitha asked curiously.

'Dakshayani...That was the name of my grandmother. Everyone called her Dashikutty. She used to look exactly like me. My father used to say jokingly that I am her – reborn. The same nature, mannerisms and sternness....'

'Actually, Father had named me Dashi in memory of Grandma. At the time of admission to school, Mr Kymal, one of the teachers, asked my father, "Why don't we swap the alphabets shifting 'A' from this side and replacing it with 'I' from the other side, changing her name to Disha? That will be trendier."'

'That's how my name became Disha in English. Kymal sir was the member of the Teacher's Association. So, my father didn't object to the suggestion. Still, as long as he lived, he called me Dashi. Mother also calls me by the same name whenever she is in a mood to pet me.'

'Then?' Aparajitha became impatient....

'Then...then....' Disha seemed to be visualising those scenes.

'Gods in Heaven! What has happened to my husband...?' Grandma kept screaming and running.

'Where are you going, Dashikutty?' Her neighbour, Kathyamma came to ask.

'I don't know what's happening. My Goddess…!' mourned Grandma, 'I am going to the place of the shootout. Only after reaching home, I learnt that there has been no news of my husband for two days.'

'I heard that your husband was shot and there was no further news', said Kathyamma. 'But you don't go there all alone. The place is full of army men. I will escort you. These are strange days….' Kathyamma started walking along with her.

The ground where the shootout took place was filled with soldiers. One could see them from afar. Masking their face with thick cloth, the soldiers and scavengers were searching for dead bodies. Breeze from the backwaters carried the stench of decaying bodies.

'Oh, what a smell!' Kathyamma felt nauseous. 'I cannot move one step forward. I will stand here. You go and search for your husband.'

'You may go Kathy chechi', said Grandma. 'That you escorted me this far itself makes me feel mighty grateful.'

Grandma kept running towards the scene of the massacre. She was not even aware of the obnoxious smell of decaying bodies. Scavengers were heaping dead bodies together in different parts of the ground. Greedy dogs ran around feasting on the corpses in spite of the soldiers chasing them out. Eagles, having satiated their hunger, settled on the coconut trees. Dashi Grandma stood under a coconut tree.

Scavengers covered the heap of bodies with dry leaves. Someone came with a black can and emptied the contents on the heap.

'Move out', he shouted at the onlookers. 'The flames will devour you.'

Another man flung a burning torch on the heap. Flames leapt as high as the coconut trees and the eagles resting on them took flight.

Dashi Grandma couldn't withstand the scene any more. Blazing flames, bursts of sparks, stench of burning dead bodies.... She thought Kunjunni Grandpa's face was popping up from the flames....

'Burn me also...burn the baby in my stomach also...I don't want to live any more...', Dashi Grandma screamed loudly. By the time the men hurried towards her, she had fainted.

'Then what happened?' Aparajitha looked at Disha.

'What's to happen?' Disha said. 'When Kunjunni Grandpa regained his consciousness, he came back home.'

'Even now no one knows how many people perished in the Vayalar shootout', said Aparajitha.

'Some historical researchers have estimated the causality in the Punnapra-Vayalar shootout at around 2,500', Disha tried to recollect.

'Oh, not so many', Aparajitha said. 'The British Secret Service of those days claimed that it was 2,000. Historian Robin Jeffrey reported in *The Hindu* newspaper that the number was 7,000. The Government put the tally around 190. KC George in his book says the number was around 500.'

'I wish I could journey back to those days, Sarangi...If only I could get two wings to fly backward in time!' Disha said, thinking wishfully.

'Like the time machine in HG Wells?' Aparajitha looked at her.

'Truly', Disha said, 'after hearing Anakhashayan's story'.

Aparajitha spread her hands like wings. 'Let me also fly backward along with Anakhashayan… through him, we shall witness those soul splitting scenes.'

Disha sat in the shade of the lone tree on the top of the sand hill. Kochhu Raghavan master was narrating the story of Anakhashayan.

'Not exactly story, but history', said Kochhu Raghavan master.

Anakhashayan was an adolescent like you. There is a place called Menassery near Vayalar. His house was there. His father was working in a nearby coir factory as a mat weaver. Poor Anakhashayan could not go to school like you. He had to struggle to complete his studies even till fourth standard. The family was always in poverty. So Anakhashayan also started working in the factory along with his father. He was only twelve-years-old at that time. He knew every nook and corner of his village. There was no place he had not visited in the village nor did any event take place there of which he was unaware. His young mind was deeply affected by the way things were in his village.

In those days, working class families of tenants lived in lonely thatched houses erected in the farm lands owned by the rich landlords. Each tenant was allotted one to one and half acres of land to take care of. The tenant could cultivate only bananas in such small tenements, but the yield always belonged to the owner of the land.

'Has any one of you read the famous poem *A Bunch of Bananas* written by Changambuzha? Those who have, please raise their hands.' Kochhu Raghavan Master looked around.

'I have read sir', Disha said raising her hands.

'What is the name of the tenant in that poem?' Raghavan Master asked.

'Chathan Pulayan, sir', Disha said excitedly, meaning a scheduled caste man by name Chathan.

'Smart girl!' Master complimented her. 'I am going to give you a prize for that.'

'In those days the landlords never allowed the tenants to even lay a line of stones in front of their houses.' Raghavan Master continued his story. Manager of the landlord visited the farm once in two months to pluck the coconuts. Tenant women were made to carry coconut-filled baskets on their head to the landlord's house. The tenant had to de-shell the coconuts, slice them into pieces and dry them in the hot sun. Then the women carried the dried coconut to the markets located in distant places. Tenants were not allowed to ask wages for all this labour. At times, the landlords would give them something very meager as a token of kindness or generosity, otherwise nothing.

In Anakhashayan's hut, which was surrounded by high-yielding paddy fields and coconut farms, the family starved for days together.

'Are we not eligible for a small share of the paddy for which we toil so much, for our own food? Can't we pluck tender coconuts from the trees which we look after?' He asked his mother one night when he was unable to bear the gnawing hunger.

'Don't be presumptuous lad… let not the landlord hear what you say', his mother scolded him in hushed tones. 'All this property belongs to the landlord. We are only their tenants.

What right do we have on their yields? If our landlords ask us to vacate this place, we are bound to do that.'

From that day Anakhashayan started to learn the names of landlords in the village by heart.

Anakottil Kartha

Kattiyattu Sivarama Panikkar

Pattathil Velayudhan Kartha

Parayee Tharakans

ACM Anthraper

Azhikkal Antony

Pooppalli Kaimal.

He also learned that a few landlords owned the entire farming land in the village. 'How can the land belong to a few landlords alone? Is this land not the common property of all the people, birds, animals and the entire creation?'

The question boiled in Anakhashayan's head without an answer.

One day as he was returning from the mat factory along with his father, he asked this question to his father.

'We continue to remain poor, in spite of all our hard work. We are never able to come up in life. At the end of the day, what we get is only starvation and suffering. Whereas people like our landlords who never do any work, are always rich and live happily. Why is it that we are not able to lead a better life?'

'That's our fate', his father restricted his reply to three small words in a resigned tone. Then silently, he continued to walk on, with downcast eyes.

Anakhashayan asked the same question to Comrade Prabhakaran who was another factory worker.

'All these feudal lords are exploiting you, me and all the labourers. Whether we work in the paddy fields, coconut farms or factories, they cheat us of our wages and enjoy the fruits of our hard work', said Prabhakaran, seething within.

'Can't we demand our wages?' he asked.

'Oh, it was because he demanded his rightful wages, that our Comrade Kochhappan was beaten by the goons of the employer blue and black till his backbone broke and now-a-days he is attending even to nature's calls lying on the mat.'

Anakhashayan kept quiet for a while. He was thinking. How many labourers are there in the coir factory? If all of them stood together, what could the employer's goons do? Take for example, the sticks in a broom. It's easy to break a single stick at a time. But can a whole broom be broken at a time?

'Comrade, can't we organise ourselves together and fight?' He asked Comrade Prabhakaran, stunning him. 'Can't we stand united and fight for our rights?'

The reason why Prabhakaran was stunned was because, till then the lad had never called him Comrade. He always addressed him as 'big brother'. When the lad called him 'Comrade', red flowers blossomed in the big brother's heart. He drew him close and hugged him. 'You are a genuine comrade my boy!... A real communist comrade!'

Prabhakaran took him to a senior comrade by the name Padmanabhan.

'Isn't this the son of Kanasseri Raman?' Comrade Padmanabhan looked at Prabhakaran.

'Hmm...' Prabhakaran nodded.

'Do you know… his father is missing since yesterday?' Padmanabhan looked at Anakhashayan. 'I got the information just now. Are you not aware of it?' He looked at Anakhashayan.

'People say that your father is absconding – fearing an attack from the goons of his employer.'

'Comrade, this lad is gutsy.' It was Prabhakaran who answered Padmanabhan. 'He will be an asset to our movement.'

Anakhashayan was filled with fear. Father did not return home after work. They all thought he would report for work at the factory the next day. But he didn't turn up. What would have made him go into hiding, away from his native place?

His poor father who did not even have the guts to look into somebody's eyes when he spoke; his poor father who didn't have the nerve to rough talk anyone; his father who never blamed anyone for his starvation; his poor father who found solace in leaving everything to fate; his father who worked hard even after factory timings.

'Since last week, Raman has been working over-time', Padmanabhan clarified. 'When he was not paid his overtime wages, he asked his supervisor. When the supervisor abused him, Raman also lost his temper and answered back. Is it not well known that even the harmless rat snake will strike if it is made desperate?'

'But how can that be a reason for running away from his native place and family?' Prabhakaran was skeptical.

'From yesterday evening, goons of the factory owner are hunting for him. Poor fellow! He must be petrified', said Padmanabhan. 'You take this lad inside and get him some food. He must be famished.'

'Come.' Prabhakaran took his hand.

'No comrade', said Anakhashayan. 'I have to return home. Mother and my siblings will be worried. Let me go.'

Snatching his hands from Prabhakaran's hold, he ran towards his house.

A spark of fire was burning inside his mind. Will father run away from the village without uttering a word to his family? Or is it possible that, last night the goons had…? He felt his legs giving away under him. He found himself unable to reach his house as if an iron chain had been fastened around his legs. His heart was pounding.

'Father, my dear Father! Gods in Heavens! What has happened to my Father?' Unable to take a single step forward Anakhashayan fainted.

'It is from here that the story of Anakhashayan turning into a rebel starts', Raghavan master continued. 'Not story, history. This is the history of the fourteen-year-old Anakhashayan, who bravely faced Sir CP's army, spreading his shoulders and thrusting his chest forward, like Abhimanyu in the story of Mahabharata. The story of the fourteen-year-old, who was trapped within a circle of army men who shot him down.'

Kochu Raghavan Master ran his eyes over each and every one who was in the gathering.

'History…. Sir, we want to hear the entire story of Anakhashayan', the children insisted excitedly.

'I will tell you', Master straightened himself.

They had reached the foot of the sand hill.

Can you see that Sizzling Tree?' Disha pointed to the top of the hill. 'That was the tree we planted in memory of Anakhashayan. It was that tree which saved this sand hill from the clutches of the sand mafia. When they came with the JCBs to flatten the hill, the villagers organised and stopped them in the name of Anakhashayan.' Aparajitha looked around. A lone sand hill! There were still wild trees on the slopes of the sand hill...palm trees...aloe vera thickets...other flowering wild plants... 'This hill has a name now', Disha said. 'Anakhan Hill – that's how people call it.' A red-crested bird landed on the Sizzling Tree atop the Anakhan hill.

What Anakhashayan Saw

Disha liked the way the story was narrated through Anakhashayan's eyes. She was getting glimpses of those days through him. Through him she flew back to those days.

The red-crested bird hid somewhere at the top of her Sizzling Tree. Six or seven small birds peeped through the branches.

'Sarangi, look there', Disha drew her attention. 'The tree is full of buds.'

Aparajitha looked up. The Gulmohar tree was getting ready to flower.

'This is the first time my tree is blooming.' Disha hugged the tree.

'How do you know? It may have bloomed earlier also', Aparajitha argued. 'After all, you were not here for the past three-four years.'

'My very own Sizzling Tree, blooming without my knowledge? Impossible!' Disha didn't like the idea of her tree blooming without her knowing. 'I have never missed visiting my tree even once during any of my home town holidays.'

She was gazing at the tree, scarlet all over with red flowers hiding the green leaves; the fallen flowers seemed to be giving her a red-carpet welcome.

'I have to share this good news with all my friends in our children's group. This calls for a celebration. Though most of them have relocated to different places far and near. Shouldn't all of us have a reunion when the tree blossoms in all its glory? My God! Where can I locate Kochhu Raghavan Master?'

Kochhu Raghavan Master was slightly crazy. Once in a while, he used to withdraw into a shell, not interacting with anyone, silently sitting in the staff room with downcast eyes, avoiding his classes.

A short man of four feet, clad in a sparkling starched stiff white mundu and shirt, he walked like a white stork through the paddy fields. Some unruly children hiding behind bushes would call out, 'White stork treading through the paddy fields', hearing which the poor teacher broke into tears.

Aparajitha sat under the tree and looked around. Down the slopes of the hill, cashew thickets formed mini forests. Countless bats hung from the tree branches, with their heads down as if in meditation. A canal skirted the hill. The side of the canal was hedged with casurina thickets. In the dried paddy fields, there were green patches of vegetables like cucumber and greens.

'I am waiting for the cucumbers to ripen. Mother makes a pudding with ripe cucumber, grated coconut and jaggery. It's so yummy.' Disha looked at Aparajitha. She was in a different world.

'What are you thinking?' Disha asked.

'What Anakhashayan might have seen and experienced', she said.

Raman walked fast carrying a long piece of split bamboo with an iron hook. Anakhashayan walked behind him, holding the other end of the bamboo and carrying a sack bigger than him on his shoulders. A mango tree close to the boundary of the paddy fields belonging to the landlord had yielded an unusual bounty of fruits this time. When ripe, they tasted sweeter than honey. The bat menace was on the high, feasting on the ripe mangoes without leaving much for human consumption. The farm manager had instructed Raman to pluck the last of the mangoes by evening. For years Raman was responsible for plucking the mangoes. He would climb on the tree and shake the branches till the fruits dropped down. Anakhashayan would pick up all the mangoes and fill the sack. He would feast on ripe mangoes before the manager arrived on the scene. Hurling the seeds far away, he would have a wash in the canal to remove the last traces of mango juice stuck to his face and body.

'Come fast', Raman told him. 'Loosen your grip on the bamboo split or else its sharp fibers will cut through your palm.'

As soon as he heard that, Anakhashayan loosened his grip on the bamboo. Tightening the small piece of cloth wrapped around his waist he started walking fast. They had to walk another furlong to reach the end of the paddy fields.

As they entered the village road, they saw Kochhu Kuttanasan racing towards them, panting. He was a teacher in the local primary school for children from the lower caste. Anakhashayan was also his student.

'Where are you going in such a hurry?' Raman inquired.

'So, you don't know anything?' Kochhu Kuttanasan stood panting. Raman was perplexed.

'You know that young girl Kochhu Thanka, who left her house to elope with our toddy tapper Koman Danavan? She has been buried up to her neck in the mud there.'

'At whose instance?'

'None other than those in authority', said Kuttanasan. 'Who else can do that?'

'Who?' Raman asked. 'Her husband?'

'Poor Koman! He is not even aware of this! He has gone to work.'

'Then who else could have done it?'

'The landlord Kalluveettil Kunjachhan and his goons.'

Anakhashayan couldn't understand anything.

'Come on, let's hurry to the scene', Kuttanasan prompted Raman. 'If all of us stand together and act, we can save the girl.'

'Oh, aren't these people empowered to punish and kill us?' Raman was reluctant to go. 'What can we do about it?'

'It's time you changed your way of thinking Raman', Asaan admonished him. 'It is this cowardice that is keeping us of the lower caste from coming up in life. Are you coming or not?'

Raman was still hesitant. If he didn't finish plucking the mangoes by evening he would get into trouble with the manager. It was horrible to even imagine what would happen then. As Asaan moved away, Raman collected his accessories and proceeded to the mango tree. But Anakhashayan flung the sack on the ground and ran after Asaan.

Raman didn't call him back. He picked up the sack and continued to walk. He may have thought, 'Oh, he is of the new generation!'

Kalluveettil Kunjachhan was a small-time landlord in the neighboring locality. He had become a landlord by exploiting the labourers and harassing the poor. He had a gang of five-six goondas to carry out his orders. He himself was strong enough to fight a group of four to five people, all by himself. His rule was that there should be no woman in the neighbourhood who he hadn't enjoyed. And the women who had to surrender to him used to whisper discreetly, 'Oh, he is a man of iron. He must be drawing all that energy from the meat of the black cats he eats once in a month.'

One day, when Kunjacchan was passing by the paddy fields where labour women were engaged in agricultural activities, he heard someone singing melodiously.

Sita is the daughter of King Janakan
Who was abducted by the demon king Ravanan.

'Who is singing there?' he asked his escorts. 'I have never heard this song before in our paddy fields.'

His eyes scanned the women at work. A dark young woman as sharp as a sickle was leading the song.

'Who is she?'

'She is the one who eloped with the toddy tapper Danavan from Muhamma district', said one of his servants walking behind him.

He had never seen that kind of a woman in the vicinity. Though dark, she was charming, with copious breasts and shapely buttocks. Her features were sharp, and the thick curly hair enhanced her looks!

'Though Danavan is a Theeya, she is from Pulaya, the untouchable caste', explained the informer. 'Therefore, Danavan's family did not allow her inside their house. Now she and Danavan are living in Pindalan Nanu's hut, who is also an untouchable.'

'You ask Danavan to come and see me', Kunjachhan told the man. 'Tell him that this Kunjachhan will provide him with a hut to live. He doesn't have to go to far off places looking for work. He can extract toddy from my coconut trees.'

His servile men looked at each other and they knew what Kunjaacchan was scheming. They also knew that it would not be easy to fulfill Kunjachhan's wishful dreams because Danavan was a dare-devil type of person. And he loved this girl very much, which made her leave her own family and live with him.

However, Danavan became the tenant of Kunjachhan. On the fifth day he was deputed to work in a distant farm as the worker originally assigned to work there had fallen sick. At first, he expressed his disquiet because his young wife would be all alone in the hut at night, in case he was unable to return home by nightfall.

'So what?' asked Kunjachhan's manager. 'You will get double the wages as well as the expenses to go up and down.'

Finally Danavan left, after arranging with the family next door to give Thanka company at night. As soon as he left, Kunjachhan summoned Thanka to his barn on the pretext of getting some work done. Only when she reached the barn did she realise that she had been trapped because she was all alone with no other workers around. She broke into a sprint through the palm trees like a wild chick fleeing away on seeing a hunter. Unfortunately, she was spotted by Kunjachhan who was on his way to the barn.

'Bring that black *koyel* (nightingale) to my granary', Kunjachhan guffawed. 'Let me see whether I can make her sing.'

Kunjachhan walked up and down restlessly in his empty store house waiting for the woman.

She was petrified when the goons brought her forcefully to the presence of Kunjachhan. Till midday, he went on cracking jokes to make her feel comfortable, sipping country liquor now and then. He made her fry fish smeared with spices and soft cook yam along with crushed chilies.

Kunjacchan was very particular that the women he chased should be bold and aggressive. He felt that the fun lay in taming and conquering them. If they were still found resisting, then Kunjachhan would change his tone and use force to make them surrender.

'Now sing that song', Kunjachhan drew her close to him. She wriggled out of his hold.

'Hey, why do you resist like that?' he said. 'I am not going to eat you up. It's only because I like your song that I want you to sing. After listening to your song, I will personally drop you back home.'

'Truly?' she asked.

'Of course', he said tricking her. 'I always keep my promises.'

'Ok, then I will sing', she agreed. She moved to the corner of the room and started singing melodiously.

Sita is the daughter of King Janakan
Was she not the one abducted by Ravanan?
Why did Ravanan abduct Sita?
Why did King Rama go to war?

'Good, good', Kunjachhan clapped his hands. 'Do you know what Ravanan wanted to do with Sita? Come close to me…I will show you.'

His extended his hands to reach her waist. She tried to dodge him and run out of the room. But all the doors to the room were secured from the outside. She started howling and screaming as loudly as possible.

'However loud you cry, no one will come here to rescue you', he said roaring with laughter. 'If you resist too much you will see my true colours. If you behave tactfully, it will be for your own good. Both of you, you and your husband, will enjoy the generosity of this rich man. If not, your husband who has gone to a faraway place like Koman islet to tap toddy will never come back.'

As she heard that, she collapsed on the floor, mentally exhausted and the rich man's hands lifted her bodily.

Anakhashayan, after running for a while behind Kochhu Kuttanasan, reached a small crowd of about fifty. All stood stunned, holding their breath. He waded through the crowd and reached the forefront to stand shocked by the gruesome sight. What Kuttanasan had reported was true. Danavan's wife was buried neck deep in a pit. She was screaming aloud, looking at the people. He was surprised that no one took a step forward to rescue her.

'Asaane', he waded back and asked Kuttanasan, 'Shall we go and help her out of that pit?'

'Can't you see the rich man's goons standing there with weapons?' He squeezed his ears. 'You keep quiet.'

'We will all go together', Anakhashayan argued with Asaan. 'Didn't you say if we all stand together….'

'Can't you keep quiet?' Asaan scolded him in hushed tones.

Anakhashayan withdrew behind the crowd. That scene was burning in his mind. Danavan's wife screaming her head off, buried neck-deep in a pit….

'Oh, why is that girl being tortured like this?' An old woman came running and screamed. 'What did she do to be tortured like this? Poor thing, she is two months pregnant. Will Danavan put up with this kind of atrocity done to his wife?' 'What? Don't you know the full story?' another woman asked in hushed tones. 'Danavan's wife bit off the rich man's private part.'

'Oh! In the name of God! What am I hearing?' The old woman wailed.

Anakhashayan couldn't follow much. Why did Danavan's wife bite the private part of the rich man? In the first place, how did the rich man let her do that?

'God knows what will happen when Danavan comes back!' said another woman. 'She is his sweetheart and he has forsaken his parents, family and life to live with her. Can he ever bear this?'

Danavan's wife was howling pathetically. 'Danavan Chetta, please come fast and rescue me.'

'There is no point in our standing and watching the scene without questioning this', said a young man from behind. 'Just because there is no law and order, nor any authority to control such atrocities, can people who assume power do anything they want?'

He walked forward. Kochhu Kuttanasan and a few others followed him.

Before they could advance more than four or five steps, someone guffawed.

'Let those dogs loose on these idiots.'

The small group stopped indecisively. The hounds were seen bolting forward. People ran in different directions. They heard a blood-curdling screech from the woman.

Later, they came to know that Danavan who had gone toddy-tapping to Koman Beach never returned home.

'Kochhu Neelandan's story is more tragic', Disha continued. 'Kochhu Neelandan was the tenant of Vettakkal Kochha. The Kochhas were immigrants from Jerusalem who had settled in the seashore village. They lasted for three generations there. Kochhu Neelandan was the tenant of the senior-most Kochha of the first generation.'

The Sixty-first Virgin

Vettakkal was the family name of Kochha who was a Jew by birth, and a descendent of Hillel who lived 100 years before Christ. When Romans ruined the Synagogue in Jerusalem in AD 68, about 10,000 Jews displaced from their homeland reached Kodungallur in Kerala, India, by sea in ten boats seeking asylum.

They settled in Kodungallur and nearby localities like Mala, Palayoor and then further on and migrated to localities like Cochin, via Chavakkad, Madayee and Panthalalyni. They were the ancestors of Kochha.

The inflow of Jews continued for a long time. They brought along with them magic lanterns which could be lit without wicks and oil. They were studded with sparkling diamonds and colourful precious stones, which lit up the premises. The sparkle of diamonds and precious stones studded inside the lanterns glimmered through the chimney throwing bright light everywhere. Somehow, these lanterns found their way to the custody of Kochha. Kochha gifted them to the then King of Cochin who was dumbfounded, as they illuminated the royal rooms and corridors of the palace.

Amazed and extremely pleased with the treasured magic lamps, the King gifted vast areas of land to Kochha free of taxes, as an expression of his goodwill.

The Order in writing ran as follows:

'Ownership of land measuring the length equivalent to the length of a thread of standard size, made out of an oxen's entire skin, is being conferred in the name of Kochha free of cost and exempted from land tax.'

Historians copied the full text as under:

> Kochha who belongs to the Vettakkal house has placed as a bequest magic lanterns studded with diamonds which can be lit without oil and wicks, at the sacred feet of His Majesty, the King of Cochin, in lieu of which his Majesty wishes to express his pleasure by allowing him property rights on vast areas of land, boundaries of which cannot be seen or measured, to be enjoyed by Kochha of the present time as well as his future generations, till the time the sun, moon and universe exist, free of cost and exempted from taxes due to the royal family.

That was how Vettakkal Kochha became the head of the seashore.

Local youths composed and rendered a song based on this folklore:

Somewhere from the distant lands beyond the seven seas
Vettakkal Kochha got a magic lantern
Turning dark nights into daylight
Kochha bestowed the lantern at the feet of the King of Cochin

The King got fascinated by the lantern
And Kochha got lands without boundaries.

Thus, self-appointing himself as the head of the locality, Kochha introduced a new custom in his land.

When a local youth got married, he had to bring his bride to Kochha's second mansion and report his attendance. Kochha's manager would receive the newly-weds and provide them with a grand feast on plantain leaves.

Every day, Kochha had his lunch at the family mansion and proceeded to his second mansion for his siesta. That was an unbroken practice. The bride and groom were to wait for him at the gatehouse to offer a coin along with betel leaves and areca nuts at his feet as a token of respect. Soon Kochha made his way to the bedroom and lay flat on his four-poster bed, chewing betel leaves along with areca nut and lime. Veronica, wife of his manager Aeron, would stand near him with a polished spittoon made of German silver to receive streams of spit spat out by him, as the chewing progressed.

However, on a day when a new bride reported, that particular task was assigned to her. So, Veronica would hand over the polished spittoon to her and accompany her to Kochha's bed. Then the fun started for Kochha. Veronica would have already briefed the bride as to how she was expected to conduct herself in the presence of Kochha, where obedience was the key factor. So when Kochha ordered her to bend down, she bent down, when he asked her to stand straight, she stood straight, when he asked her to strip off her clothes, she did so, and as his strong hands explored her body, she lay down without making any movements of resistance. If she didn't behave, Kochha would get mad. He would lift her with one hand and fling her on the bed. The tender young girl, as delicate as a flower bud, would wriggle like a fish out of water. Veronica, standing behind the curtains, would get excited watching the erotic scenes.

If Kochha was satisfied with the girl, Veronica would come to know of that from the movements in the bedroom, which would be relayed to her husband Aeron standing outside. The groom would be paid a certain amount of lease money, with which he had to leave the place. After that, till Kochha was satiated with her services, the new bride would remain in the second mansion as a piece of jewelry kept as surety for the money paid to her groom. After a week, the bride would go back to her hut to join her husband along with paddy, pulses, coconuts and clothing for a year.

In a ledger maintained by Aeron, he jotted down the details of the virgin brides enjoyed by Kochha, along with the date and year.

The first virgin: Veronica, bride of Aeron.

The second virgin: Kochhu Theresa, bride of Kochhu Autha, house name: Kurisumoodu.

Third virgin: Kalyani, bride of Vasu, house name: Vazhicherel.

The tenth virgin.........

....

....

The sixty first virgin: Kunchu Neely, bride of Neelandan.

Kochhu Neelandan had met Kunju Neely while he was undergoing a course in martial arts, in the school of *kalarippayattu* in a far away locality. Beautiful, with long black hair, tall and slender, she was a relative of his guru, the head of the school. A girl orphaned in childhood – she was too bold for a woman – that was his impression about her. She had mastered the entire course of martial art and all the eighteen techniques of using swords, shields, knives and other weapons for fighting and defending. Neelandan stayed in the school for two weeks during which period he screwed up his courage and proposed to her three times. At the third time, without thinking about their past or future, she left the school with him after taking permission from the guru, convincing him that she was going to visit a distant relative, who lived far away.

From the moment Kochha saw her disembarking from the boat, his pulse rose at a steady rate. He had a sudden impulse to devour her. He waited for a while for her to come with the spittoon but contrary to the standing practice, she didn't turn up.

'The girl is defiant and confrontational', his manager Aeron reported. 'She has mastered all the eighteen techniques in martial arts but doesn't seem to be very mature and practical. She is overly arrogant.'

When he heard that, Kochha felt as though a round metallic shield was spinning violently in his belly. He too had been to a martial art school, learnt a few of the techniques and had developed a fascination for bold girls who trained in martial arts and possessed supple and flexible bodies. His excitement found no bounds when Neely came within his reach, like a dream coming true.

'Don't do anything to subdue her', Kochha instructed his manager as he wanted a woman full of spirits. 'I want her as the fireball she is. Try to cajole and lure her. Pay her husband whatever he asks and send him off.'

'Okay', Aeron bowed his head.

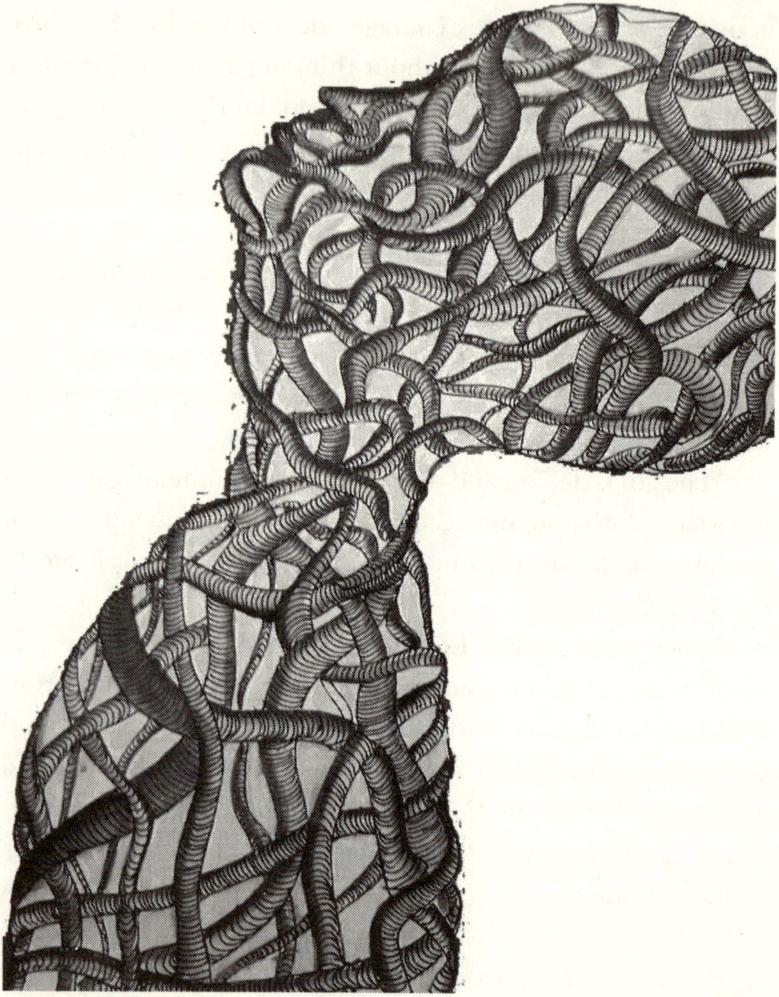

He knew that the forthcoming days were going to be full of celebrations. After the Veronica wave, this was the first time his master was so fascinated with a woman. The servants reaped the benefits of the situation when the boss was in an extremely good mood and in high spirits which made him more generous. He watched his wife standing close to his master, fanning him with a hand-made fan of *Ramacham.*

Kochha was tossing and turning on the bed as his desires kept tormenting him. Aeron came in with a glassful of foreign liquor, mixed with tender coconut water. Kochha didn't even glance at the glass.

'Maybe his burning desire for her is more intoxicating than the liquor', Veronica surmised.

'Aeron, where are you?' Terminating his afternoon rest, Kochha called out, walking towards the boat. Aeron heard the summons and hurried to his master. He was standing near the boat, resting one of his legs on its frame.

'You ask Veronica to take charge of her. I will come back early in the evening.'

Looking at the young girl greedily and folding his long mundu around the waist, he sat in the boat majestically. Aeron knew clearly what he was expected to do.

'Come girl', Veronica came out and called her. 'He will come back later. You come here and sit. We will chit chat for a while.'

She looked at Kochhu Neelandan. He was fervently praying that Kochha would not like his wife. In the midst of prayers, he promised his powerful God 'the Saint in Athungal' to light a packet of candles in front of him. He now suspected that even the Saint had been brainwashed by Kochha, who was a Jew.

'I will not come', said Neely to Veronica. Turning to her husband, she said, 'you come with me. We are going to our hut.'

'How can we do that? This is the custom followed in this land.' Neelandan tried to explain helplessly. 'If the Master takes a liking for you....'

'Why didn't you tell me this before?' Neely asked him.

'Because...because...' Neelandan stuttered. 'Why can't you close your eyes for a while Neely?' He pleaded.

'Did you propose to me for Kochha's sake or your sake?' Neely was defiant and looked at him in disgust.

Kochhu Neelandan had no answer.

'If I spend a week with him and become pregnant, whose baby will that be – Kochha's or yours?' she continued to question him.

'Of course, mine', Kochhu Neelandan said without any doubt. 'It will grow as our child.'

Neely wanted to fling some obscenities at him but controlled her tongue, seeing his sad eyes.

'Kunju Neely, we have no other options.' Kochhu Neelandan's voice cracked. 'If we confront him, master will kill me first and after satisfying his desires, he will chase you out to the street. Whether you fight or not, you will have to surrender to him.'

'That will not happen if you can be man enough to fight along with me', he saw her eyes spitting fire. 'Without my consent, even the most powerful man will not be able to touch a hair of mine. If death is inevitable, let both of us fight and die.'

'What's the delay lad?' Aeron growled at them. 'Didn't you hear Veronica calling her? Do you want Master himself to invite you with gifts ceremoniously?'

'No Kunju Neely', Kochhu Neelandan grimaced. 'I cannot fight or argue with the Master. You just close your eyes and submit to him for a while. Thereafter, both of us can live together peacefully.'

Aeron came out to the courtyard and eyed them, spitting into the garden.

'Please go Kunju Neely', Neelandan pleaded with his wife. 'I will come back to pick you up as soon as Aeron intimates me.'

'Why do you want to come back?' Kunju Neely had fire in her eyes, 'To enjoy the leftovers?'

'You go', he turned to leave.

'You disgraceful eunuch!' she spat fire. 'Never ever should I see you again!'

When Veronica took her hands, she was left with no more thoughts. Without even turning back to her husband, she went inside the house with her.

Veronica stripped off her clothes and soaked her in oil, massaged and kneaded her body with her strong hands. She filled the small cavities in her leg, hands and waistline with warm oil, in a continuous stream. Neely never asked why she was being pampered with such niceties. She felt that she had to consciously submit herself to all the new experiences to meet some unknown purpose.

Veronica applied a herbal paste of ground gram and soap nut powder on her body to remove the excess oil and washed it away in a stream of water poured out from pots. After patting her body dry with a towel, she applied a fragrant cream bought from overseas on her curly hair and combed it till it shone. She made her lie down on a swing cot, stark naked spreading her legs and passed fragrant herbal smoke into her private parts. Veronica went on chatting throughout the session, while Neely remained silent. Veronica combed her hair, braided and adorned it with a string of fresh jasmine flowers which breathed and spread a heady fragrance in the room. She applied black kohl in her eyes and sprinkled rose water on all her joints. She draped a cloth above her breasts, the shape of which amazed even Veronica despite being a woman.

When Kochha entered the room, all groomed up in fine clothes smelling of heady perfumes, she was reclining on the swing cot, lost in the euphoria of the new comforts she found herself in. A lustful Kochha seated himself on the cot with all the passion of a lover and picked up her hand and laid it on his lap. His fingers caressed her forehead and neck and crawled downwards. When they reached the knot of the cloth draped around her bosom, she opened her eyes.

'Stop.... Before you untie that', she pushed aside the fat fingers crawling all over her body. 'We have to discuss and settle certain conditions.'

Taken aback, Kochha looked at her in disbelief. That was the first time a slave girl was expressing her defiance so boldly before him.

She repeated the same question she had asked her husband, to Kochha.

'If I spend a week with you and I become pregnant ... whom will the child call "father"? You or Kochhu Neelandan?'

'Of course, your man', Kochha said as a matter of fact. 'It will call your man "father."'

'What kind of justice is that?' She got up.

'Then what should be the justice, you tell me?' Kochha grew impatient.

'The baby born from my womb should call its father "father"' she said.

'You girl, what rubbish is this? That is not the practice of this village', Kochha raged.

'But after all, aren't all the rules and practices of the village made by you, the rich and powerful, to serve your purposes? And we, the poor beings, are forced to follow them?'

'You impertinent woman! No woman has ever spoken to this Vettakkal Kochha in such a vein.' Kochha lost all his control. 'You better control your tongue and lie down there quietly.'

Kochha forcibly undid the knot on her cloth and tried to spread her legs. She wriggled out of his clutches and sprang up with a sharp knife that was cleverly hidden somewhere in her clothes. Kochha got flabbergasted on being confronted by her vicious nakedness. She was blazing like a lighted torch.

'You will not touch this body of mine as long as I am alive', her knife poised threateningly she said. 'I am a woman who has mastered martial arts. In one move, I will thrust this knife into my belly and kill myself.'

Kochha looked at her with concern and pleaded, 'No... please...no.'

She stood there firmly like a lioness in rage.

'You just tell me what you want me to do.' For the first time, Kochha surrendered in front of a woman.

'You should vouch on your holy scriptures', she ordered, 'that you will not live against the tenets of Jehovah. You should repeat what I am telling you.'

Kochha looked at her in shock. Being a Jew, their scriptures were irrevocable and divine to him. Jehovah was the only god of Jews. How did she know all this? he thought admiringly. He decided he should not lose a woman like Neely. Such women entered one's life only once.

'You should not let her go.' Nestling in his mind, Solomon whispered to him, 'If you value her as the most precious one in your life, she will take you to heights of ecstasy. If you embrace her, she will respect you. She will be a fine garland adorning your hair. She will make a good crown on your head.'

'Not only for now, she should be mine forever', Kochha surmised. 'She is not just any woman. A woman like her is a rare creation of God, which happens only once in a while. How many virgin girls had come and gone in his life. How thrilling it used to be for him to watch those girls screaming and wriggling like hunted helpless creatures when he thrust himself through their virginity. But he found Kunju Neely all the more exciting with her dare-devil nature. No one had ever resisted him or fascinated him this way. Kunju Neely is the only real woman, he thought. She is the virgin of all virgins.'

'Aeron...oh, Aeron'. Kochha came out of the room and called out for his manager. 'Have you taken a bath today? If so, go to my residence and bring the Holy Book of Scriptures immediately.'

Aeron was surprised. What is the need for the Holy Book at this time of the day? Veronica gestured ignorance with her palms. 'The Master would have fallen flat for her', she thought. She had foreseen that possibility when she soaked Neely in the oils and massaged her. Neely could be a double-edged sword, but at the same time she was also a bunch of ripe grapes ready to be harvested.

Aeron came back with the Holy Book. It was written on scrolls made out of the fine skin of sheep. The Book had been preserved and maintained through generations. Kochha opened the Holy Book and waited for orders from Kunju Neely, who was sitting stark naked arms crossed over her breasts, resting her legs one upon the other, in the corner of the cot. The knife was still menacingly poised in her left fist.

'What is the oath you want me to take?' Kochha asked impatiently.

'The child born out of Kunju Neely's pregnancy', she said 'will call Vettakkal Kochha "father". I promise, promise, promise...okay...repeat.'

Kochha repeated.

'Okay, what next?' he asked.

Kochhu Neely phrased out the next condition. Kochha repeated.

I promise in the name of Jehovah that now onwards other than Kunju Neely, no woman from the bonded labour class will step into the second mansion of Kochha...Kunju Neely will remain the queen of this palace... In the name of Jehovah, I promise, promise, promise.'

'What's next?' Kochha looked at her.

'The share of Neelandan', she continued, 'a yielding farm and paddy fields of sown area of five bushels.'

'Why so much?' Kochha was hesitant.

'That much is required', she was adamant. 'Though he is not manly and a coward – wasn't he the one who married me and brought me here?'

Kochha agreed to that also.

'I need you for the rest of my life and I am willing to sacrifice anything for that', said Kochha.

Thereafter, from the second floor of the mansion, Kochha took a flight to the seventh cloud along with Neely.

On the third day, people spotted a two-three-day old rotten dead body hanging from a cashew tree a little away from Kochha's second mansion. He had not changed his clothes from the day he had left his wife with Kochha. People came to know about the body when they found crows and eagles raising mayhem around the place.

Thus, Neely became the mistress of Vettakkal Kochha. She accompanied him on his routine boat rides in the evenings in the vast expanse of the backwaters.

Veronica re-wrote the entries in the register which maintained the accounts of virgin molestation.

'The sixty first and the last virgin – Neely, wife of Kochhu Neelandan: Outstanding performance.'

'Was Kochhu Neelandan murdered or did he commit suicide?' Aparajitha looked at Disha.

'Poor man', Disha responded without hesitation, 'He would have taken his own life because of mental torture.'

'Can't it be Aeron who did away with him, knowing that he would come back to Kochha, demanding his wife?'

'Why do you suspect that?' Disha asked.

'Was he not wearing the same dress he had on, when he came to drop Neely at Kochha's residence?' Then the dead body was spotted in the cashew bush close to the second mansion. He had said, he would come back when Aeron summoned him to take back his bride. That would mean that he didn't go back to his hut, which was far away. If he had left the place alive, he would have come back to claim his wife. After all, he would have been desperately in love with her which had made him bold enough to abscond with her from the martial art school. Aeron, knowing what was playing in Kochha's mind, would have ...'

'...finished him off', Disha filled in.

'Poor man! Ultimately the loss was Neelandan's.' Aparajitha's heart went out to him.

'But more pathetic was Neely's fate', Disha corrected.

'Neely's? How is that possible?' she looked at Disha.

'Hm... After six or seven months, she became pregnant. Kochha's fascination for her died. In fact, he got fed up with her. Aeron paddled her in a boat through the backwaters and dumped her in the sea. The fishermen who had reached the seashore early in the morning spotted her. Her mouth was gagged with coconut fiber, her hands and legs were tied with ropes and she was unconscious. Before the big waves rolled her away into the depths of the sea, they brought her to the safe seashore. People said she was seen roaming in the seashore without knowing where to go. Then, one day, they saw her body swept ashore. Her eyes were gauged by the fish, cheeks were bitten by the sea turtles and nipples were nibbled away by the seagulls.'

'Vettakkal Kochha offered a carton of candles in the synagogue in the form of penalty for having taken an oath in the name of the Holy Scriptures.'

Once again, a bride and groom reported at the gate of the second mansion to pay respect to Kochha. Veronica opened the register of virgin molestation:

'The sixty second virgin.........'

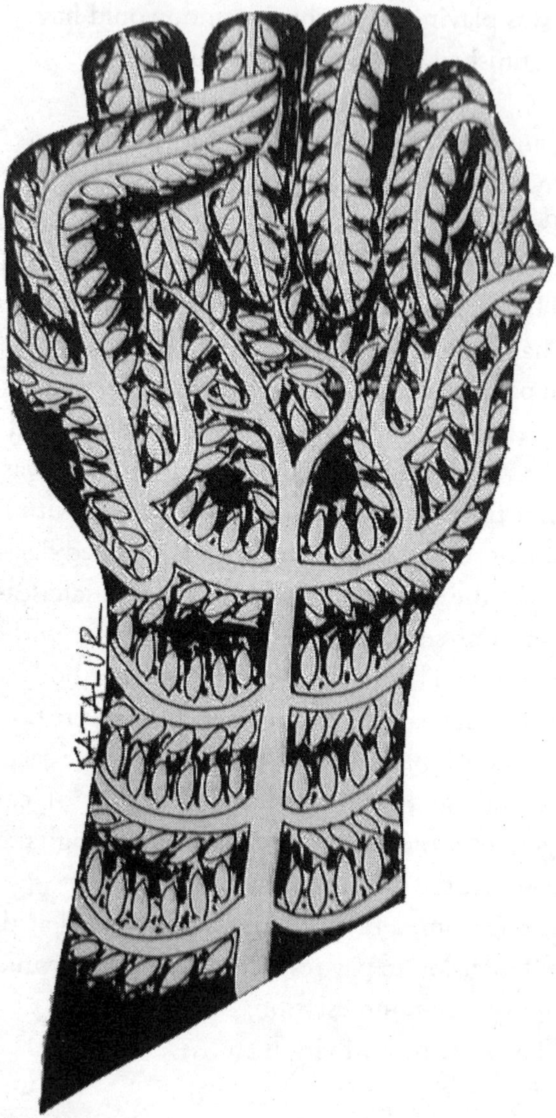
KATALUR

Hail to the Saviour

Che peered at her from the cover page of the *Bolivian Diary*. He was sitting with the book kept open in his lap in a hideout formed by the branches of a tree in the dense Bolivian forest.

'Aleida', Che called looking at her.

'No, I am not Aleida, I am Aparajitha.'

'Okay, Aparajitha, where are you now?'

'I am freezing in this Delhi winter', she said. 'Can't you see this heavy thermal wear?'

Che detached the gun from his shoulders, polished it and started taking aim at something through the trees.

'Are you in a dream world?' Che enquired.

'Umm...' she said. 'I am watching the glorious arrival of the red sun...I am dreaming of the red flag hoisted at the top of the Red Fort.'

'If not today, tomorrow', Che was confident. 'Time will make it inevitable.'

'You are right. If not today, tomorrow', she repeated. 'In India, a time will come when Communism will triumph;

I keep dreaming of it. It is sure to happen in the near future.'

'What do you mean?' Che looked at her. 'Communism cannot be implanted. It should sprout spontaneously.'

Che pulled the trigger. Birds nestled on the trees scattered in the sky with a wail of protest.

'Those poor birds', she said, 'They would have been petrified.'

Che looked at her and smiled teasingly.

'At times I feel you are very cruel', she expressed her disapproval.

'Cruel! Me?'

'Didn't you kill that puppy', she grimaced, 'that too, by twisting its head?'

'Are you referring to Khabak?' He tried to explain, 'Poor thing.... If he barks and throws tantrums at the most inappropriate times, what can be done about it? We were in the middle of an operation to capture the Military General Sanchez Mascaras and the occasion demanded absolute silence. So, when Khabak let loose his tantrums, there was no other option but to silence him.'

'His final struggle to wriggle out', she seethed, 'It was pathetic.'

'In his journey to reach the goal, a rebel's heart cannot afford to relent', suddenly Che's voice became Niranjan's. He was climbing down from the tree with a gun hanging from his shoulders. Then Che turned into Niranjan. He came closer to her. His hot breath brushed her upper lip.

'The red sun is to emerge shortly.' Only she could hear his whisper. 'It's time to hoist the red flag at Red Fort.'

'Is that true?' she asked.

Without answering, he walked away in a hurry through the dense forest.

'What is this? Dreaming in the broad daylight?' Disha walked in.

'Niranjan', Aparajitha looked around.

'Niranjan?' Disha teased her, 'He is not anywhere here.'

'He was here, in my dream; there was a gun in his hand….' Aparajitha got up.

'Niranjan? …with a gun?' Disha burst out laughing. Suddenly she became serious. 'He should have been here yesterday. It is two weeks since he left. Did he give you any hints about his plans?'

Aparajitha shook her head. A dark shadow spread over Disha's face.

'But he is not alone. Dinar is also with him, isn't it?' Aparajitha turned the pages of the book in her hand with disinterest. 'Guys will come back from their roaming, the moment they have spent all their money.'

'But', Disha's face turned dark, 'He is alone. I called Dinar. He too doesn't know his whereabouts.'

'Is he having an affair?' Aparajitha asked her hesitantly.

'What made you think like that?' Disha looked at her.

'Nothing dear', Aparajitha tried to duck out of the gaffe. 'I just asked.'

'Not possible', Disha ruled it out. 'If he was, he would have definitely told me.'

'Then…some other activities…I mean….'

'He never used to be like this', Aparajitha heard a mild tremor in Disha's voice. 'But now I feel…I feel he is getting misguided these days. Somewhere, something is amiss…. He doesn't seem to be on the right track.'

'Come on', Aparajitha held her close. 'Chill...no need to worry dear. You often tell me about your Kunjunni Grandpa. He would have inherited his genes.'

Kunjunni Grandpa was a bold person who had attended the first meeting of the youth, organised against the rich and feudal lords in a village called Ottappunna. Disha recollected those stories narrated by her father, sitting on the easy chair stretching out his legs.

The meeting was jointly organised by Comrade CG Sadasivan and Comrade CK Kumara Panicker, the then leading comrades.

Clad in a white cotton mundu, which was folded and tied above the knees, and an unbuttoned shirt to let the body cool from the scorching heat of the sun, with a sweat band made of thorthu mundu around his head, Panicker ran around, organising men and material for the function. From the way he was dressed, he looked like an eminent personality of the village. He belonged to the Panavalli village and was the grandson of the prominent Ayurveda doctor Krishnan. In those days, any Congress meeting in the area commenced only after the melodious recitation of a song written by him.

Move on, move on my fellow men,
We have no one unholy or unclean among us
We are all born after one great father
And let us brothers be bold and
Move on the same path holding our hands together.

'From the time he was in the State Congress, your Grandpa knew CG.'

He was a bold leader. Tall and thin in stature, upright in thinking, CG never bent his knees in front of anybody. He was the elected leader of the Congress party in Cherthala. He was not very happy with the functioning of the party those days. That was the time Comrade Krishna Pillai visited Cherthala. He was the personification of the word 'Comrade' and while all the Communist Party members used to prefix Comrade before their names, Krishna Pillai used to be known as just 'Comrade'. He was the one who enrolled CG in the Communist Party.

In those days, without the presence of a powerful person from the upper caste, the poor labourers did not dare to attend party meetings. They were terrified. They were afraid that the goons of the rich landlords and the police would not leave them alone. There were so many CIDs in the village who would carry information to the powerful against the poor of the working class.

So, there was a need for a role model, a powerful and bold leader from the upper echelons to motivate and embolden them.

'In Muhamma village, we used to have such a person. He was the Grandpa of our Comrade Susheela (born to the famous Ezhava *kalari* family, Cheerappanchira).'

He was a member of the *Praja Sabha,* an association for the people. Whenever they wanted to organise a worker's meeting, the leaders used to request his presence to give them confidence to participate. He used to come to the locality, galloping on his horse and assure the villagers, 'Yes, I am also with you, I support anything that is meant for the common good. No one needs to be afraid. I am here to support you.'

That was enough to embolden them.

'We needed someone like that in Vayalar too.'

There was a feudal home by the name Kunthirisseri Cheriya Kunnel, which belonged to the Ezhava community. Kumara Panicker was the central pillar of that feudal family.

Kumara Panicker in those days was well known for his expertise in martial arts and an iron nerve to confront anyone. He came to public life when the locality was fighting against the centuries-old barbaric practice of untouchability, which meant that a member of the lower caste could not associate with the upper caste by touch or even sight. The fight against this practice turned into physical violence which was initiated by the first slap on the face of the upper-class male members by Kumara Panicker. This was followed by the next slap from Grandpa Kunjunni, and thereafter by other members of the rebel group who believed that such condemnable practices could be stopped only by defiling the upper caste men by touching them through a slap on the face.

In the meanwhile, the Second World War broke out and coir factories which formed a major component of the industrial sector ran out of jobs. Jobless workers joined the army and went to Assam... forty three out of forty five workers went to Assam. The three left were president Avira Tharakan, vice president CG Sadasivan and Grandpa Kunjunni. When Comrade Krishna Pillai came to Cherthala personally to form a Communist Party Cell, its proposed secretary, Comrade KN Keshavan was also getting ready to go to Assam.

'That's because he has no means to survive', CG said. 'Somehow we have to stop Comrade Keshavan from going to Assam.'

Comrade Krishna Pillai, along with CO Mathew, decided to visit the famous feudal house to which Kumara Panicker belonged. It was Grandpa Kunjunni who went along with them as a guide. They had to cross seven or eight canals which skirted the farm house and then joined together to merge with the backwaters. To cross the canals, they had to use bridges made of split coconut trunks. The closest bridge brought them to the gate house of the huge house which had its roofing made of braided coconut fronds. The gatehouse itself was grand, with sculptures carved on the wood work. There were two more gatehouses flanking the main gate house. When VVIPs visited the family, they were seated in the big gatehouse which was furnished with wooden easy chairs, a brass container with betel leaves, areca nuts and lime. By the side of the half-wall, a brass vessel filled with clean water was kept for visitors to wash their feet and face after long walks in bare feet in the hot sun through muddy roads. Hand-made fans made of the blades of palm trees were made available for the use of visitors.

The big gatehouse always seemed ready to receive visitors. After the gatehouse, on the south-east side of the main house was a big cattle shed which housed six or seven milch cows. Heaps of straw used as the fodder for cattle rose high like small hills by the side of the cattle shed. On the north-west side was the kitchen with an open well by its side from which water could be drawn using a pulley and rope. Inmates of the house could view through the wooden bars of a window to see whether any visitors had arrived at the gate house. Wasn't the entire complex rummaged by Sir CP's army after the shootout in Vayalar? Wasn't the entire house complex pulled down and the ruins buried under water which was filled in the basement to form a pond, by the army to get even with the Communist Party and Kumara Panicker?

'I will narrate that story to my Dashi Kutty another day', Father had assured Disha, calling her by her pet name. Next day father continued....

Kumara Panicker had observed Comrade Krishna Pillai approaching from a distance itself. A dark young man, tall, and slender, with a broad face, strong and firm jaw bones, long chiseled nose, eyes sparkling with energy and a smile perpetually hidden in a corner of his lips. His thick unruly hair defied the efforts of oil and comb. Though, somehow it was combed backward, a few strands kept falling on his broad forehead. He was clad in a white mundu, folded above the knees for easy walking. His brisk walk, with hands crossed at the back, reflected his inner confidence.

Comrade CG introduced Comrade Krishna Pillai to Kumara Panicker. At first sight, Kumara Panicker developed a deep respect for the great Comrade. Unfolding his mundu to its full length, as a sign of respect to Kumara Panicker, Comrade Pillai folded his hands and greeted him. His dark face turned bright when he smiled, exposing his strong and perfect rows of white teeth.

No doubt he is a humble iron man, thought Kumara Panicker. It was not for nothing that people referred to him as the Comrade of all Comrades, meaning a person living up to all the expectations of being a comrade.

After lunch they sat for a discussion in the main gate house.

Comrade Krishna Pillai started to explain. 'You must be aware that after the arrival of CP Ramaswamy Iyer as Diwan, atrocities against the working class and poor people have gone up by the day. What's happening in Alappuzha for instance... Without consulting anybody, they cut down the wages of the factory workers by sixty per cent. When a few of the workers challenged this action, CP's police let loose a reign of terror on them, beating them down mercilessly. They didn't even spare the peaceful workers who were also tortured inhumanly. Bava, a worker in the William Gudekkar Company, was beaten black and blue till he was incapacitated and could no longer work for a living. That poor man, along with his wife who was about to deliver the sixth child, and his five children ultimately died of starvation. The police assaulted a few comrades fatally and dumped them in the canal with bleeding wounds on their heads. The blood stain in front of the South Police Station has still not dried up. It's not going to dry up too, because it is the blood drained from the labour class.'

'Now take the case of rickshaw pullers. Have you not seen the poor men pulling the two-wheeled carts, with fat rich people sitting on rhem? And then they are paid peanuts for their backbreaking service. If they demand their rightful wages, the police drag them to the station and assault them till their limbs break. I have seen the workers walking on the bridge after being beaten up by the police. They barge into the houses of the poor working class, arrest the men and molest their wives in front of them. At the police station, the torture continues using clubs, butt of the guns, bent knees, boots soled with horseshoe, round granite stones and the like. So barbaric and uncivilised are the police that they urinate into the mouths of people who beg for water. Into the mouth of a comrade who was writhing with tooth ache, one Assistant Circle Inspector lifted his Khaki shorts and stuck his... well it is so difficult to explain all this.... Just imagine, all these indignities are happening in the police lockup. The prisoners are not permitted to go out to attend to nature's call. A bucket is kept inside the cell which when filled with pee and shit, has to be carried outside by the comrades themselves for emptying and cleaning for re-use.'

'Our mission is to unite all these workers, the lower castes, untouchables and the deprived under one red flag to fight against such injustices and inhuman practices. For that purpose, it is important that capable people like Kumara Panicker come forward to organise a cell of the Communist Party now and here. We don't have to turn back anymore and brood over our shortcomings. I can tell you one thing for sure; tomorrow's world will belong to the hard-working labour class.'

Kumara Panicker felt that what he had heard were not words but flames of a fire which encircled him. He could feel the heat of the air which emitted from the furnace that was this man seated in front of him, personification of the impending inevitable revolution. His eyes were blazing, yet his manner was gentle and polite. He spoke confidently and his diction was simple and effective.

Kumara Panicker, who never stood before anyone, got up in reverence and drew Krishna Pillai closer to him. Keeping his hands on his shoulders, he embraced the Comrade with deep affection.

'Comrade, you can go ahead with confidence', he said. 'Henceforth, my people and I will be with you.'

'To begin with, we have to make sure that Comrade Keshavan does not join the army and leave for Assam', said CG. 'We should find work for him here, without having to go anywhere. I entrust that task to Kumara Panicker.'

'Leave that to me', said Kumara Panicker. 'I will take care of that.'

Kumara Panicker kept his promise. He arranged a job for Keshavan in the nearby teashop. He also helped his mother to set up a small working unit to make coir out of coconut fiber by providing them with necessary raw materials like outer shells of the coconuts for dehusking and later twisting the softened fiber into coir ropes. Keshavan's mother ran her household with the money she got from the sale of her product.

In the locality of Ottappunna, CG hoisted the red flag in front of a gathering. After saluting the flag, Comrade Keshavan spoke about the plans and proceedings. CG rendered his welcoming song melodiously, followed by a bold and inspiring speech. Panicker was never a speaker but he presented his insights briefly in four to five lines.

CG's composition ran like this:

Come forward my brethren
Let your legs not falter
Keep firm steps forward
Police beatings and firings
Assaults and massacres may make you halt
Yet move on forward without fear
To open a fair and fear free new life for all of us
Surge forward...forward...forward.

As CG finished his rendition, one among the audience, Kumaran leapt forward, throwing his fists up and calling out:

Feudalism be damned, capitalism be damned
Inquilab Zindabad, Inquilab Zindabad.

Kumaran was screeching as if his throat would explode. Agitated comrades and industrial and farm workers repeated the slogan, throwing their fists up. Kumaran, who could not even stand straight, leapt skyward, screaming louder than everybody. It was just a week ago that he had been assaulted by the landlord's supervisor while he was trenching the ground for planting a coconut tree. The supervisor, Kunjuttan, was a distant relative of Kumaran. He was also employed by the landlord who provided him with three meals a day and covered other expenses for keeping the workers under his thumb. On account of asthma, Kumaran was unable to work continuously in the field. He had to stop working often as he gasped for breath. It was on one such occasion that Kunjuttan had assaulted him.

In the midst of his sobs, Kumaran asked his relative, 'What did I do to be assaulted like this?'

The irritated supervisor folded his leg and drove his knee into his belly, saying, 'You vermin, have you grown up enough to question the higher-ups?'

Kumaran collapsed in the trench. He couldn't urinate for the next three days.

Kumaran could not supress his anguish. He continued to shout:

Let feudalism be damned…let capitalism be damned.
Inquilab Zindabad, Inquilab Zindabad
We are no more slaves …we cannot be controlled
We will fight firmly and confidently
Inquilab Zindabad, Inquilab, Zindabad.

That night Kumaran passed away broken-hearted.

Before the smoke in Kumaran's pyre settled down the workers got together. 'We should not let this go just like that.'

'It's only because there is no one to challenge or question them, these goons are acting according to their own sweet will.' It was Grandpa Kunjunni's outburst from the crowd.

'Should we act on a sudden impulse?' Some of the workers were skeptical. 'Should we not weigh the pros and cons of the outcome before we act? Shouldn't we consider that we are confronting the powerful lot?'

'Our Comrade is more powerful than them. As long as Comrade is our leader, who are we afraid of?' Grandpa raised his voice. All the young men knew that Grandpa was referring to Comrade Krishna Pillai. Under his leadership they were an energised lot.

'Should we not wait for the pyre to burn out Kunjunni?' Comrade Vasu tried to pacify Grandpa. He was the eldest among them and Grandpa was the youngest. 'Then we will discuss an action plan.'

That was the social practice in those days. Till the pyre burnt down completely, the dear and near of the departed hung around close by. Suddenly flames blazed from the middle part of the pyre. Since Kumaran was a thin person, it didn't take much time for the ritual to be over.

'Come on', Grandpa lit a torch made of coconut fronds.

'Should we not wait for daybreak Kunjunni', Comrade Vasu tried to stop him.

'Right now, who all are willing to accompany me?' Kunjunni asked, raising the torch above his head. 'Even if there is nobody, I will go alone and question him.'

The red light from the torch fell on the faces one by one.

'We will come.' Some six or seven young men came forward.

'Um...that's enough', said Kunjunni. 'Only those who are men enough need come with me. Others will learn their lessons for cowardice in due course of time when they are beaten down by the goons of the landlords.'

Taking the lead, Kunjunni and the young volunteers lit their torches and walked ahead through the paddy fields.

Muttalan Kunjuttan had his house in a plot leased to him by the landlord.

'Kunjuttan...hoi...Kunjuttan!' Kunjunni shouted. 'You come out.'

His companions looked slightly jittery. They knew that six or seven people were not good enough to confront Kunjuttan. He was as strong as a wild ox. There was no sound from inside. Kunjunni mounted the verandah and banged on the iron door with his legs.

'If you are a man...', Kunjunni repeated his threat.

The strong iron door didn't give in. In fact, the whole house was made of strong old tempered teak wood that no one could break into.

'Please, he is not here', a weak soft voice came from inside. 'It has been more than three days since he has come here. He does not even care for his small children.'

Kunjunni came out of the verandah.

'We can judge from that voice that what she says is not a lie. Then where shall we look for him?'

'There is a place where we can look for Muttalan', one of the men volunteered. 'He is likely to be in the house of the elephant keeper Keshavan. I have heard people murmuring slyly that he is having an illicit relationship with Keshavan's wife. I saw Keshavan leaving his house to attend a temple function far away from here, and he is not likely to be home for a few days. His house is also at a distance from here.'

'Let's not waste time', Kunjunni started walking in that direction.

Kunjunni tore down Keshavan's door made of palm leaves with one kick. Inside the hut, by the red light of the torch they could see Muttalan and Keshavan's wife sleeping together, locked to each other unclad.

'Disgusting!' Kunjunni threw one mundu from the clothes line over the woman to cover her nakedness. Kunjuttan, who was in deep sleep, woke up and looked around as if in a trance.

'Before he is up, tie his legs and hands', Kunjunni gave instructions to his companions. Shouting obscenities, Kunjuttan tried to wriggle out from their grip. Stretching his strong legs, he tried to kick them. Keshavan's wife got up struggling to cover herself with the mundu.

'You disgusting woman!' Kunjunni accosted her. 'When your husband is not in the house...you...' He spat at her in vehemence.

'Not because I wanted to', she moaned. 'If I don't submit, this wild cheetah will tear my husband apart and leave me orphaned on the street...I am scared of that...'

'You bitch', Muttalan Kunjuttan snarled at her.

By that time, Muttalan was tied up and incapacitated. He screeched like a demon and struggled to free himself. Kunjunni and company carried him unceremoniously and dumped him at the foot of the pyre.

'Do you know whose body is burning here?' Kunjunni kicked him on the belly. Kunjuttan's hands, tied together, reached out to the spot where it hurt. 'It is the body of Kumaran whom you kicked brutally while he was working hard in the farm. We will not leave you till you offer apologies to Kumaran, prostrate naked in front of his pyre and pay him respect.'

Kunjuttan looked around. In front of him was the burning pyre. Around him were red eyes burning holes through him in the red light of the torch. They were well armed with iron clubs, machetes and other deadly weapons.

'Cut him into pieces and dump him into the pyre of Kumaran.' All turned around to see from where the voice came. It was

Vasu, who was standing with the axe he had used to cut down the mango tree to prepare the pyre.

'Once again let me warn you, if your hands fall on any one of us…' Grandpa Kunjunni raised his legs….

Muttalan Kunjuttan folded his hands and whimpered like a dog, 'Please...Don't kill me'.

Comrades threw their fists up and roared, *Inquilab Zindabad.*

Fish that Couldn't be Netted

Anakhashayan was sprinting in panic. He kept asking whomever he met on his way, 'Did anyone see our Comrade Prabhakaran?'

Prabhakaran was busy watching the children playing a game known as Sayoo on the village road near a temple. The game Sayoo is played on a nine-square board drawn on the ground. In the middle square a big circle is also drawn with two eyes, a nose and a mouth representing Sayoo. In the squares around Sayoo, numbers from 0 to 100 are written. A round heavy disc made of ball nut is rolled on the squares carrying specific numbers. If the ball lands in the center square, then Sayoo wins 100 points and the player loses 100. If it lands on the square with 100, the player wins 100 points.

One of the boys, Dinakaran, was taking aim at the square where he wanted the disc to land. Dinakaran was the nephew of Comrade Prabhakaran and son of his brother Vasavan. Vasavan was thrilled to see the disc entering and falling in the square 100 without straying anywhere. Not even once had it been swallowed by Sayoo!

'Oh, my score has reached 950 and if I score another fifty, I will make it to 1000', Dinakaran shouted in excitement.

'Our Dinakaran is going to win the seventh time too', Vasavan told Prabhakaran without being able to contain his excitement. His highest opponent, Viswambharan was trailing behind with just 230 points and Peethambaran had less than 100.

Sayoo swallowed the disc when both of them played and they lost 100 points each.

That was the time when Narayanan came by. Narayanan was the grandfather of Viswambharan. He couldn't tolerate Dinakaran leading in the game against his grandson.

'If this goes on at this rate, your son will outsmart even Velumooppan', he said referring to the owner of the factory where both Vasavan and he worked. 'Pity the factory owner! Don't ruin the livelihood of the poor man', he said sarcastically.

Vasavan was truly irritated. But he knew he couldn't retort because Narayanan was the supervisor in the factory and poor Vasavan was just a worker under him. Narayanan was in-charge of the export division which made four crores per annum. It could reach eight or twelve crores too. Vasavan knew he could not express his irritation because, as of now he had the privilege of working on the machines in the factory. If he rubbed his supervisor the wrong way, he knew he would be deputed to do meaner tasks like carrying big bundles of coir rope on his head from distant corners of the factory premises, which was extremely difficult and unpleasant.

'But this is just a game and there is no money involved', said Prabhakaran. 'After all, these are only lines drawn on the mud.'

'Still… even at this age, his target is nothing but hundred', the supervisor's jealousy spilled over. 'He is just a chick which has not even hatched out of the egg!' He sarcastically commented. 'You needn't go to the coir factory; your son will mint whatever you need.'

'How is it possible? It's just a game. What's your problem?' Prabhakaran could not contain his temper. 'You hate to see, even one among the lot, being smart and coming up, isn't it? When the poor workers struggle with hard work, you pocket the profit without even paying them their rightful wages. Is that a good practice?'

'What did I say to annoy you so much?' the supervisor withdrew. 'This is ridiculous!'

'Middlemen like you are as dangerous and treacherous as the two-headed catfish.' Prabhakaran let loose his temper. 'When you are in the midst of water snakes, you will bring up your hood and when among fish, you will swim with your fins.'

'Come lad', the supervisor dragged his grandson and walked off without continuing the debate.

'You shouldn't have offended the supervisor', Vasavan's face was pale. 'He will make my life miserable in the factory. He is a cobra.'

'If the job goes, let it go', Prabhakaran said. 'This is not the only factory and job provider in the locality.'

'Oh, it's easy for you to talk', Vasavan started walking away with downcast eyes. 'Only when one is without a job and is forced to suffer from starvation, does he know the value of a regular job.'

That was the time Anakhashayan arrived at the scene running, panting and panicky.

'What's going on here Comrade Prabhakaran', he asked. 'Is this the time to watch and enjoy a kids' game?'

'What's it?' Prabhakaran knew instinctively that something had gone wrong.

'Come with me, I will explain the matter on the way', said the lad.

Prabhakaran didn't think for a second. He started walking with him swiftly.

'Comrade, we have to go a long way', said Anakhashayan. 'We will have to go faster.'

'Where are we going?' Prabhakaran found it difficult to catch up with the boy.

'Kadakkarappally.'

'Tell me what the matter is, boy, without making me more anxious', said Prabhakaran.

'You know our Pakkaran?'

'Yes of course! What happened to our Pakkaran?'

'Goons of Pattathil Kartha....' The boy was panting

'Goons of Pattathil Kartha?'

'I will tell you. Now let's walk faster', Anakhashayan panted.

The harvest season had commenced in disharmony and arguments. The first disagreement was on the rightful share of paddy yield due to workmen. From time immemorial, the practice was to give one bunch of paddy cuttings to the workmen. When the grains were separated, it would measure up to about two bushels of paddy. This time, the landlords held a meeting and decided that the workmen need not be given their share. The union of the agriculture workmen insisted that this practice should not be stopped. Though the police intervened, the farmworkers stood together. No farmworker was willing to get into the paddy fields for harvesting. Finally, the landlords had to relent.

The president of the Travancore Landlords' Association was one Anthrapper who had his lavish bungalow on the banks of Vayalar backwaters. That was where the landlords used to get together and hold discussions over liquor and sumptuous food.

'Is it a right strategy to leave these men unbridled?' Kochhu Narayana Kartha addressed all the members. 'Step by step, they have started going overboard. Now the demand is to share one fifth of the produce, rather than the one tenth as per the standing arrangement. If their atrocities go on like this, where will we end up? All of us should decide unanimously that we will not allow a single untouchable caste person to work in our paddy fields or farms. Let them all die of starvation without wages.'

'Then who will work in the farms and paddy fields? Can we work? Isn't their strength and skill working against us?' asked George Peter.

'We should put an end to that kind of monopoly over skill enjoyed by them', said Pattathil Kartha. 'We have others like Mappilas, Nairs and so on, who are equally poor. We should train them to do the work. They will remain servile and loyal to us.'

'That's a good idea', agreed Anakottil Kartha. 'We will train their young women also to sow, harvest and thrash.'

'That's really a practical solution', agreed the president. 'Henceforth we should be more alert. I have discussed the issues with the Deputy Special Police. He will be coming here within a couple of days. The police are with us. We have to get a few of those rebels arrested and implicate them in various cases. All of us should file written complaints against them in the police station. Even the government and Diwan are bent on suppressing the trade union and communists, who should, no doubt be done away with. The only way is to suppress them ruthlessly.'

'Leave that to us', said goon Narayanan, rolling up his sleeves. Narayanan belonged to the Matheparamban house and after retiring from army service he was back home. Now he was the self-appointed leader of the local goons.

'There will be no need for the police or army. We are more than enough.' Narayanan looked at his gang members Raman and Kurukkal with confidence. 'Then we have these two also', he referred to Chandrappan and Krishnappan, who had just joined them.

'We have a strong gang of forty men who are well versed in street fighting.'

'It's time we exterminated a few of these communists', Raman looked directly into the bloodshot eyes of Narayanan.

'The first one to be finished off will be that Kumara Panicker.' Krishnappan swirled a knife in his hand. 'Finish him with one quick stab.'

'Yes, yes', Chandrappan and Kurukkal chorused. 'We should finish at least four or five others too.'

By afternoon, an emergency meeting of the local Nair community was summoned wherein an agenda was tabled by Advocate Padmanabha Menon along with the resolution reading as under:

> It is hereby decided that no labourers belonging to lower castes like Ezhava and untouchable classes like Pulayas as well as members of the Agricultural Workers Union be allowed in the farms and

> agriculture fields for work. Lesser fortunate minority communities and castes like Christians and Nairs belonging to poorer sections should start training themselves for carrying out such agricultural tasks. This Committee has decided to contribute forty shovels and sixty baskets to cater to the training needs. But only those Ezhava and Pulayas, who are members of the Royal Loyalists Association, sponsored by Narayana Kartha, can be hired for agricultural activities.

The resolution was seconded by Sivarama Panikkar and passed unanimously.

On the second day after the meeting, Kartha's premise was vibrant with farm women threshing. Alongside, harvesting also continued in the fields. It was required to thresh and separate grains from the stalks soon after harvesting and store them in the granary, failing which the paddy grains would sprout and become unsuitable for consumption.

Threshing was done in a specially arranged area in the courtyard. A square frame of split palm tree firmly tied to four wooden pillars formed the threshing area. A mat was spread to keep bundles of paddy stalks for threshing and separating the grains. Men and women holding on to the frame of split palm fixed on the top, threshed the bundles in rhythm. As threshing speeds up, women unknowingly thrust back their buttocks rotating them in a rhythm. Leaning on a coconut tree, Chandrappan was watching this scene with great interest. His eyes roamed around the third threshing group where Pakkaran's sister Kochhu Paru was at work. Though younger than Pakkaran, her well-developed body gave her an older look. Pitch black in colour, with large black eyes and a well-shaped bust line, she was simply stunning. She had recently attained puberty and Pakkaran's attention was always on her, as a guardian after his father passed away succumbing to tuberculosis.

'Why do you want to suffer like this, standing in the hot sun, respected Sir?' Pakkaran ventured to ask Chandrappan with unconcealed sarcasm, 'while people like us are forced to go through this ordeal for our livelihood.'

As they heard this, the women burst out laughing. The enraged Chandrappan went near the third threshing group and snarled at the women.

'Instead of laughing, why don't you do your work?' He pawed the buttocks of Kochhu Paru. 'Let me see how good you are at threshing.'

Seeing that, Pakkaran leapt like a leopard to pounce on Chandrappan. His fellow workmen stopped him.

'Big man', he accosted Chandrappan, 'Don't you dare touch her body.'

Kochhu Paru hid her face with her palms and ran towards a vacant corner of the workplace, with tears rolling down her face. Chandrappan left the premises as if nothing had happened.

In the evening after threshing, the landlord's manager came to measure the quantity of paddy kept ready to be transferred to the granary. As per the existing norms, the workmen were entitled to one tenth of the produce. Besides, a small quantity of paddy left over after measuring was also the entitlement of the workers. When the workmen were about to gather the scattered grains, Chandrappan walked in.

'The leftover paddy need not be given to the workers.' He kicked the grains aside. Then the manager scooped the same from the ground and added it to the share of the landlord.

'Okay, don't leave anything for us.' Pakkaran pulled out the mat. Grains stuck to the mat scattered on the ground. 'There are a few more grains on the ground. You can wipe that up and fill your granary.' His voice cracked and eyes brimmed with tears.

'Who is that arrogant fellow speaking with so much of insolence?' The landlord Pattathil Kartha called out from the southern verandah. Then there was no delay. Chandrappan and the man in charge of measuring grabbed Pakkaran and tied him to the coconut tree.

'Beat him till his arrogance comes down!' Kartha lifted and folded his sweeping mundu above the knees, as if in preparation for performing a kalarippayattu, picked up a cane and ran down the verandah.

'You fill your stomach eating the rice from my land and dare to challenge my decisions! I will see to it that your arrogance is brought down today.' Pakkaran, who was tied to the coconut tree, was beaten black and blue by Kartha.

The frightened farmworkers stood in small groups watching the scary scene. His sister Kochhu Paru screamed and rolled on the ground, her fists pounding on her chest.

'Beat him to pulp and finish him off', Kartha ordered.

Chandrappan took over with great enthusiasm when his turn came. Pakkaran writhed in pain. He screamed his guts out as blood splashed out of his mouth. Even then Chandrappan was not in a mood to stop.

'Please sir, that's enough. If you do not stop, he will die', women screamed.

'Do whatever you want to do with me. But please don't beat my brother any more Sir', Kochhu Paru collapsed at the feet of Chandrappan.

'Okay, stop', Kartha walked towards the verandah. 'But that doesn't mean that we should relent. Don't give him a drop of water. Let him remain tied to the coconut tree till morning.'

Chandrappan stopped beating and wiped the sweat off his forehead.

'Go and take a dip in the pond', said a woman's voice from inside the house. 'After all, haven't you been touching that untouchable while beating him – the lower caste vermin who eats the flesh of rats, mice and bandicoots!'

The moment Chandrappan heard that, he pulled out a thorthu from the clothes line and walked across the compound to the pond and dived into it. At daybreak, he thought, Pakkaran should be entrusted to the police, after filing a false case. Then Paru will be easy to handle. The image of her inviting body with her mundu folded and tied up exposing her naked legs, busily threshing the paddy stalks, haunted him. He could not erase the image of her two taunting buttocks swinging in the rhythm of threshing. A tender untouchable girl! Her body had developed so beautifully, with the food provided by the landlord's family. Who else other than the members of that family had the right to enjoy that body?

He had to wait till the police took custody of her handcuffed brother, to force her to the work shed behind the house where he would....Chandrappan dived into the pond and splashed and immersed himself in the water like a wild ox to suppress his libido.

It was dusk by the time Prabhakaran and Anakhashayan reached the place of violence. Both of them visited the hutments of farm workers in the vicinity and organised them in a group. The poor tenants and agricultural workers of Pattathil Kartha, who were hanging around not knowing what to do, also joined the group willingly.

'Are you sure that you also won't be in the same situation that Pakkaran is in now?' Prabhakaran addressed all of them, 'if you wish that such a thing should not happen to you, stay united and come with us.'

The workers looked at each other. Then they stood firmly behind both the leaders, extending Prabhakaran and Anakhashayan their unstinted support.

'Come, each one pick up a torch', Prabhakaran instructed, 'Also remember to carry four or five sickles and machetes.'

Prabhakaran lighted a torch made of a bunch of long dried palm leaves, using a match box. The next one lighted his torch from Prabhakaran's lighted torch. All of them passed on the flame from one torch to another. The lighted torch procession progressed through narrow village mud roads and farms. Pattathil Kartha was strolling leisurely on the eastern verandah of his huge house. The roaring, torch-bearing procession entered his house by the northern gate. A petrified Kartha stopped walking, staring at the progressing army of farmworkers dumbfounded.

'Chandrappa…Krishanappa…' he called out in panic. No one came out of the house.

'What are you up to?' he accosted the procession with whatever courage he could muster. 'Do you think there is no one here to control you?'

Without bothering to reply to him, the torch-holding army moved on to the western courtyard of the house.

All the windows overlooking the western verandah were shut abruptly by someone inside.

Pakkaran, tied to the tree with his legs up and head hanging down, was semiconscious. Two or three grains of rice were stuck to his bleeding lips. It looked like, someone in the house had taken pity on him and tried to feed him. Anakhashayan undid the rope binding Pakkaran. Pakkaran fell on the ground motionless, as if he were a corpse. The workers carried him on their shoulders and came out of the house. The western verandah remained empty. Through a small slit between the window shutters, a number of eyes watched the procession leaving the house with Pakkaran.

Pakkaran was totally incapacitated. They decided to take him to the nearest village doctor before dawn.

At the break of dawn, all the men left the settlement where Pakkaran lived, to go to their daily jobs. By afternoon, the women were forced to come out of their huts hearing a loud roar. Armed with swordsticks and daggers, goons started rummaging the place under the leadership of Kurukkal. Kurukkal was a distant relative of Pattathil Kartha.

'Where is Pakkaran?' He snarled at the women and gave a murderous call. 'Wherever you try to hide him I will smoke him out and drive this knife into his stomach and draw out his intestine...come out if you have the guts.'

Frightened women and children screamed and howled in desperation.

'All of you go and search inside',' Kurukkal ordered his henchmen.

The goons barged into the huts, terrorising women.

'Those rascals released him last night', Chandrappan came running and panting. 'If you don't find him here, bring that whore, his sister. Then he will come there on his own.'

'Alright, then bring her here. If she doesn't come, drag her', Kurukkal ordered.

The goons dragged Kochhu Paru and dumped her at the feet of Kurukkal. The poor girl pounded on her chest and wailed.

'Respected master, we have not done anything wrong knowingly….'

'You have grown haughty after eating the food given away as charity by the Pattathil family. We own you, body and soul and have all the rights to deal with you in any way we like.' Kurukkal tore her blouse, using the sharp end of the blade fixed to his swordstick.

Chandrappan eyed her breasts greedily as she tried to cover her nakedness with her hands. As she moved her legs, her shapely thighs became visible.

'Instead of enjoying the scene, you rascals, carry her and follow me.' Chandrappan folded his mundu above the knees.

As the goons made an attempt to lift her up, Kochhu Paru's neighbour Karambi leapt towards them with a sickle.

'No one touches her', Karambi warned. 'No one can touch her as long as I am alive. I am the one who brought up this motherless girl, putting her to sleep on my shoulders. Come on all of you women, come with your sickles.'

The women didn't hesitate further. With sickles held high, they gathered behind Karambi, one by one.

'Come, let's go.' Chandrappan realised that they were not in safe waters.

'Some day, you will come into our hands', Kurukkal said, looking daggers at Kochhu Paru.

'Get lost, you scoundrel', Karambi shouted in uncontrollable rage. Women charged towards Kurukkal, their sickles waving threatningly. He broke into a sprint and ran for dear life.

Chandrappan stood by the canal in utter disappointment. The fish had been almost trapped in the net, but had slipped out. Now it would be impossible to catch it again. Times were changing. The slaves were growing defiant. It was that adolescent boy from Menasseri who had emboldened them and made the situation bad, in the night taking away Pakkaran. He should be nipped in the budding stage itself.

Mrinalda was on the phone that afternoon. He had made it a practice to call them at least once a week without fail. Ranbir also called now and then. He had left for Patiala. A new batch of students had taken over the campus.

'This time Federation has taken it up as a challenge to win back the Union', Mrinalda became eloquent. 'We lost it two years ago. Come back to power after correcting the lapses; is that not the policy of the Federation?'

'That apart', Mrinalda asked softly, 'is she around?'

'No', Disha replied, 'She is going through the pain of delivering her thoughts – in the process of re-writing history; all the time busy writing behind closed doors. She doesn't even bother to eat properly and keeps skipping lunch. To me it looks like, this book project has gone into her head. I didn't expect so much of creativity and commitment from her.'

'How is her writing?' Mrinalda asked. 'We should translate that into Bengali. It's easy to market the theme here. The impact of the Tebhaga struggle in Bengal and the Punnapra-Vayalar uprising in Kerala are similar. These events have helped the Communist Party to grow deep roots in both the States. Unfortunately, the Telangana struggle did not go so much in favour of the Communist Party there. If that struggle had led to a full-fledged revolution as had happened in Bengal and Kerala, it would have re-written the history of our party.' Mrinalda paused. 'Actually, I called you in a different context; ...re-investigation of the death of Comrade Sathyadas.'

'Oh Mrinalda, what happened?' Disha grew anxious.

'The Sub Divisional Magistrate has ordered to exhume the body for a detailed re-examination.'

'After a lapse of so much of time...', Disha was skeptical.

'If it was murder, evidences will be hidden somewhere... even if the re-examination of the body is delayed.' Mrinalda said.

'Mrinalda, how long will it take?' Disha asked.

'Maximum two to three weeks', he continued, 'Disha, what I want to tell you is that let Aparajitha not be informed of this now. Its better she is not aware of this. It will upset her mind now. Let her continue writing. Then Disha, I want to alert you on something else. They will send notices to the family members to be present at the time of exhumation. I have informed her mother. She will be present. Notice addressed to Aparajitha will go to her Midnapore address. By chance, if it is redirected to the

Campus and from there to your address...I want you to keep it away from her.'

When Disha turned, after keeping the phone back on the cradle, she looked straight into Aparajitha's eyes. Had she been standing behind her all this time, walking in softly like a cat?

'Why are you looking like a ghost, seeing me?'

'Oh nothing', Disha was unsure what to tell her, 'when I saw you suddenly behind me...'

'It was Mrinalda, wasn't it?' She bent down and picked up the phone.

Fork-tailed Silverfish

Punnasseri Padmanabhan came to Alappuzha town when he had no means to survive in his village. He wandered along the streets for a long time. Then he got a job of carrying coir bundles in Darragh Smail. He then moved on to another job – that of flattening iron rods in D'cruz. Later he learnt to weave and became a skilled weaver. After becoming a weaver of mats, he began to stay in the hotel belonging to the manager, in the east of Shavakottapalam. One day during lunch time, he heard people whispering that there was going to be a meeting. A comrade was arriving to form a Communist Party cell in the town.

Padmanabhan had only heard of him but not seen him yet, so he decided to go to the meeting. Somehow Padmanabhan reached the meeting place. He could see someone addressing the gathering. Next to him in the chair was seated another person. In the front row there were Govindan Mooppan, VK

Karunakaran, Divakaran Asaan, Chandrasenan, TA Kumaran and some others, listening keenly to the speech.

Padmanabhan stood a little away.

Comrade stopped the speech and asked, 'Who is that?'

The audience looked back and Divakaran Asaan recognised him. 'Is that you Padmanabhan? Why are you standing there? Come forward and sit.'

Padmanabhan hesitantly moved forward.

'He is a labourer in the mat weaving factory', Divakaran told the others.

'Young communist, do sit down', the comrade pointed to a seat.

Padmanabhan sat there. The comrade began from where he had stopped.

'So, what was I saying ... In Travancore, to establish a responsible rule, the Kerala Congress Socialist Party under AK Gopalan has decided to support Travancore State Congress to initiate a movement.'

'Earlier also we have joined hands with Congress in such matters. We protested jointly to release Manabendra Nath Roy from jail. The British had locked up the man for twelve years. He is the one who stood for workers rights, they accused him of terrorism and sedition.'

'Weren't the British forced to kneel down before our joint protest and let him free? Just like that – if we move forward together, we can fight against Sir CP's torture agenda. For that, we are opening Party cells almost everywhere. The last edition of *Prabhatham* carries the new rules.'

Comrade took *Prabhatham* from the table and gave it to Divakaran Asaan.

'Party is moving in a new direction. From now onwards, the party needs more members who can work for it. Others can act as supporting members; they can attend party meetings, voice their opinions, but they will not be able to vote. The working members should chart beforehand what activity they are going to pursue to take the party forward.

'We are raising our voice to remove the ban on the Communist Party. In a democratic nation, any party has the right to perform their activities with freedom.

'From now onwards we will be working towards that. Our campaign should be made powerful.'

Just as one comrade ended his speech, the one sitting next to him got up.

'British rule and monarchy should be shattered and replaced with a responsible rule. The bourgeoisie should be uprooted. Shackles of slavery should be broken down. For that we may sometimes have to face death. If we are born, we have to die once. So, let it be for our nation, for the well being of people around us. Dipping our hands in our own blood, we should take the oath, "Our goal is the liberation of our country."'

Comorades' voices echoed all over the meeting ground. Padmanabhan, returning to the hotel room at night, pricked the tip of his finger with a needle and dipping a pen in the blood oozing out from it, he wrote 'My goal is the liberation of our nation'.

Someone knocked at the door.

Padmanabhan was a little confused. It may be the police. They might have heard about the meeting.

Those who were members of the union and those who attended the meeting were all in the CID's lookout list. Again, the knocking continued. At last Padmanabhan opened the door. It was not the police; KV Pathrose and PK Padmanabhan were at the door. There was a pile of books in KV Pathrose' hand. From the pile, Padmanabhan took one and gave it to him.

'*What is Communism?* The price is eight anas.'

Padmanabhan opened the drawer and picked an eight ana coin.

Pathrose's eyes fell on the piece of paper on the table. Pathrose extended his hands and drew Padmanabhan close to him. 'From today onwards, you are not simply Padmanabhan, but Comrade PG Padmanabhan.'

Niranjan had reached home very late the previous night.

Disha had tried to contact him several times on his mobile. But it was switched off. She was woken up at midnight by the whirr of his motorbike. As she opened the door, she was shocked to see the state in which he had arrived. He was unkempt and smelled of sweat, as if he had not taken bath or changed clothes for days together, as though he was coming from a guerrilla camp. He went directly into his room, without even looking at her.

Disha was offended by her brother's indifference. 'You know how many days it has been since he left the house without informing anyone about his plans or whereabouts. Is it possible for the family to write him off just like that and allow him to stray around like a bullock let loose? Is he not the only male member of this family? Is he not responsible to run the family? Let it be daybreak. I am really going to give him a piece of my mind.'

She couldn't go back to sleep after that and spent the night weeping for a long time, leaning against the wall.

'My poor mother! She is so innocent. She may not be able to understand him, but I am here, elder to him by at least two years. He can at least tell me what's on his mind. Mother is sick, worrying about his future and safety. She has never known happiness in her entire life. Even when Father was alive, Mother led a life of turmoil.'

Disha had told Aparajitha about their life. Disha's mother Malini was a teacher in the local primary school.

'Father was a full-time party worker. Mother's admiration for this very epitome of vigor, the young, bold, dynamic and versatile leader of the village, culminated in love and ended up in marriage without the approval of both the families. Immediately after the marriage, Father became the Party's local committee member.'

When Indira Gandhi declared emergency in 1976, Kerala was ruled by the Right Wing of the Communist Party in alliance with the Congress. That was the time when the Left Wing of the Communist Party used to publicly insult the Right Wing as 'wagging tails'.

One day, when Home Minister Karunakaran was travelling by the State car on the national highway, her father and his friends jumped in front of the car with black flags as a sign of protest. Instead of proceeding to Ernakulum, the car was diverted to Cherthala guest house; the guest house from where DSP Vaidyanatha Iyer and others had secretly planned to shoot the rebels in Vayalar. It was from Cherthala guest house that the army boats embarked on their historical expedition to the Vayalar camp by the backwaters.

By midnight on that day, police came home searching for Father. The Party had got news of their imminent visit to arrest

Father and had stopped him from going home. Even Mother didn't have a clue about his whereabouts. The police party searched for him in every nook and corner of the house and confirming that he was not around, instructed Mother to close the door and left.

After a while, there was a knock on the door again. Mother saw the police through the window.

'Woman open the door', the Inspector yelled.

Mother opened the door without any hesitation. The police forced themselves inside the house.

'Where have you kept your man hiding?' The Inspector gave her a tight slap which left her spinning.

It so happened that the police had heard some movements in the attic as they were leaving the house. They heard some more noise coming from the attic. Two policemen got ready to climb up. Mother also thought that without her knowledge, Father had sneaked into the house and was hiding in the attic. Thinking of his plight if he were to be caught by the police, mother folded her hands and begged the Inspector, 'Respected sir, please don't torture my husband.'

That infuriated the Inspector more. He thought that she had been deliberately misleading them, knowing that her husband was in the attic.

He slapped her again and kicked her in her stomach. Mother fainted in a pool of blood. The police left the house after catching a bandicoot from the attic.

Father sneaked home a few times to see Mother after she was discharged from the hospital. During one such visit, he was caught by the police. The police tortured him in the Cherthala lockup, fracturing three of his ribs. People passing by could hear his screams of agony from the lockup.

By the time Father came back from jail after Emergency was revoked, Mother's world had turned silent; her ears totally damaged by the slaps of the police.

Disha's eyes turned moist.... Music left mother's world forever.

Mother who used to anxiously wait for the Malayalam song programme *Ranjini* on radio. Mother loved the Malayalam songs on Radio Ceylon.

She used to write to *Akashvani* regularly to broadcast her favourite songs.

Father had gifted Mother, who loved Jesudas's Malayalam songs, a gramophone player. The player turned rusty without anyone to use it.

'After the police torture, Mother who was three months' pregnant suffered a miscarriage.' 'After that she suffered three more miscarriages on account of police atrocities.'

Disha had come out of her fifth pregnancy. 'By then Mother's world of music had become totally silent...no sound of music... no sound of chirping birds...no sound of whispering leaves... no musical note of the breeze.... As she drifted into the world of silence, mother resigned her teaching job. Now she lip-reads to understand what we talk to her.'

'Disha', Aparajitha said, 'Please don't fight with Niranjan. I will try to talk to him. I will try to find out what's on his mind.'

'Do you think he is going to open up, the moment you start talking to him?' Disha asked skeptically. 'No, how much ever you try; he is not going to divulge anything. His ways are not what you perceive them to be....'

'Cool down my girl.' Aparajitha patted her shoulders. 'Leave him to me.'

It was an afternoon. The sun had started slanting towards the west. The day was in the process of rolling the carpet woven and spread out by the sunlight. Niranjan and Aparajitha had trudged up the Anakhan Hill. The Vaka tree was full of buds.

'It won't take many days for the tree to be in full bloom', Aparajitha's eyes widened as she thought of the tree turning scarlet.

The sea breeze from the west caressed them. The wind carrying the fragrance of screw pine flowers nestled in his unkempt hair and on the stubble on his face.

She sat on the tree resting her head on a branch, listening to Rabindra Sangeet rendered by Indrani Sen, daughter of the Bengali singer Sumitra Sen and student of Debabrata Biswas, on the iPod.

Father used to have a large collection of Tagore songs by Debabrata Biswas; LP gramophone records of olden days. Debabrata Biswas used to stay in a rented flat in southern Calcutta. The moment he reached the flat, Father would enter the kitchen. 'Deb Da', that was how Father, used to address him, would have prepared some special dish for him. Father often used to reminisce about those days…evenings soaked in music… his party songs used to intoxicate the party workers. As the party was divided into two, Deb Da distanced himself from both the wings. Still, he remained a staunch Communist till he died.

'Is this why you brought me here, saying that you have something to discuss with me?' Niranjan looked askance at her. He was sitting in the shadow of the tree, resting his palm on the ground. 'If it was for listening to music sitting on the tree, you should have come alone. Why bring me along?'

'But, from the moment we came, you have been reading', Aparajitha retorted. 'So, I thought I will listen to Rabindra Sangeet.'

Niranjan closed the thick book with a red cover page by Jon Lee Anderson and remarked, '*Che Guevara: Life of a Revolutionary*. Excellent work.'

He lay down on the ground looking at the sky, watching a piece of cloud drifting away alone.

'Who is riding pillion on Alberto Granado's Norton motor bike?' Niranjan got talking. 'Is that Ernesto Guevara?'

'My iPod is full of poems', he continued. 'Almost all the poems are written by ONV and Satchidanandan. Do you want to listen to the poems of revolution written by ONV, based on the Vayalar shootout?'

He started reciting loudly:

Oh the brilliant flame lit by history
You are the inspiration for today
To win a beautiful 'tomorrow'...
To win a new world of tomorrow.

'But that's not how it begins', she tried to correct him. 'Kerala's Paris Commune...That's Vayalar ...Salute Vayalar...that's how it starts.'

'Paris Commune', he repeated. '...the revolution, through which the working class captured power for the first time in the world.'

'People's socialist democratic rule' lasted for seventy-one days, symbolic of France's defeat in the Franco-Prussian war.

Luis Napoleon the third had to bend his knees in front of Prussian Chancellor Bismarck. After the war, the country faced widespread famine and unemployment. People were dragged out of their houses to the streets. Supported by the national guards, people came together to confront the army, to form the Paris Commune. The result was an explosion of democracy, freedom and human creativity unparalleled in history up to that point.

Although the Commune lasted only seventy days and was drowned in blood by the French ruling class, its example has inspired workers in revolutionary struggles across the world ever since.

Around thirty thousand people lost their lives. About ten thousand people were captured as prisoners.

She had heard about the Paris Commune for the first time during a campus discussion. As soon as the discussion ended, she settled in front of the computer. Google searched all over the world and presented reports and pictures on the monitor. She was astounded looking at the results; around 1,980,000 results! As she touched the images, Google poured out a rain of views which made her aghast. Her attention was pivoted on a black and white picture of the fighters in the forefront of the uprising. Surprisingly, the colour of the flags alone held by them was red. Written on them was:

'Vive la Commune.'

'Vive la Commune', she hummed.

'...Vive la France.'

He looked at her with interest.

'They are the lines of a rebel song', Aparajitha explained. 'A French song published by Eugene chatline to celebrate the 100-year anniversary of the Paris Commune. They had also released an album to commemorate the day. This song is included in that.'

'Eugene chatline – I have not heard of such a chatline.'

'Even Google does not seem to be aware of it', she said. 'I searched Wikipedia also. No trace of it there too.'

'May be Eugene would have been someone like our own poets, ONV Kurup or Satchidanandan.... A faith.... After all is that not the core of everything?...Faith!'

'Isn't that an advertisement slogan?'

'Umm...the language betrays the depth of words!' he commented.

'Faith is like a peacock feather kept hidden inside the pages of a book', Aparajitha tried to stretch her imagination. 'It breeds on its own in happy moments! In sadness its eyes shut....'

'Wow! That's really appreciable.'

'The lines are Satchidanandan's', Aparajitha said.

'Great! Were you doing a PhD programme in Malayalam from Bengal?' Niranjan teased her.

'Oh no', she laughed. 'These are all my father's legacies. Father had three or four shelves full of Malayalam books, both old and new. He made me read almost all of them. To compensate that, Mother made me read Bengali literature.'

'Father was a great reader', Aparajitha continued. 'He would have been one of the first few in India to read *One Hundred Years of Solitude,* the novel by Marquez published in 1967. The book had somehow reached Safdar Hashmi. Father was also a part of the Jana Natya Manch, the cultural movement, for a few days. Safdar Hashmi died in a New Delhi hospital following a murder attempt on *Janam* activists the previous day by anti-social elements patronised by the ruling party's vested interests while performing "Halla Bol" in Jhandapur, Sahibabad.'

'Father was in Delhi when Hashmi was murdered on 2 January 1989, the day I was born. Knowing that Mother had been hospitalised in Calcutta and I was born, he was getting ready to board a train from Delhi to Calcutta. That was the time the news of Hashmi's death reached him. He postponed his travel plans to see me by four days....'

'Oh, that may not be the reason', Niranjan teased. 'He would have intuitively known what an abominable daughter has been born to him.'

'You sadist...' Aparajitha pounced on him and squeezed his neck, 'Do you know how much my father loved me?'

'Oh, sorry, sorry, my apologies.' Niranjan cried out. 'Leave my poor neck alone. I was just joking.'

'Ok, I am leaving you for now', she said. He sat there looking like a kid.

'Did you get hurt?' she ran her fingers through his hair.

'Even Dashi chechi was like this before....' he started to say something and stopped.

'So what happened now?' she asked.

'Oh, nothing', he looked into her eyes, moist with affection.

'Her mind is so full of worries about you my dear boy.'

'Why?' He sat up.

'Your sudden trips without telling anyone where you can be reached, your mobile which is always either switched off or out of range, your vagabond lifestyle – all these are worrying her. Can't you tell her where you are going and when you will be returning?'

'Why is she so adamant that she should know all this?' he asked, irritated. 'I am not a kid. If I were employed, would they be able to track my whereabouts all the time?'

'That's exactly the problem', She explained. 'You are not even trying for a job. You got a campus placement but you rejected the offer. Remember, you are the only male member in that family. Is it not your responsibility to take care of your family? Are you not supposed to take responsibility for them?'

He remained silent.

'Niranjan', she asked. 'In truth what is your hidden mission? I get a feeling that you have some connection with…'

'Umm…' he stared at her. 'What do you mean?'

'Tell me…' she continued, 'are you in some kind of trouble?'

Without responding to her questions, he got up and climbed down the hill and disappeared in the cashew bushes.

'Niranjan', she ran after him into the Bolivian wilderness.

Disha went to the library directly. Dinar was stacking the publications for compiling and binding. The reading room was occupied by seven-eight known and unknown people.

'Where are our friends?' Disha asked, entering the room.

'I didn't know he was coming here', Dinar replied. 'But, is he back after his expeditions?'

'Yes, yes…he is back home', Disha was not very happy. 'Both of them left together in the afternoon. They told me that they were planning to come here. She wanted to search for old newspapers. Where else can she find them?'

Disha felt that somebody was watching and listening to her from behind the book shelves. Two eyes were drilling holes in her through the gaps between the books. As she looked towards those eyes, they retreated.

'But I haven't seen them here. He hasn't called me so far', Dinar expressed his disquiet.

'How is that possible?' Disha couldn't conceal her anger and spoke a little loudly. 'He came yesterday at midnight. I cannot understand what he is up to.'

'Hush...' Dinar suddenly kept one of his fingers on his lips. His eyes moved to the gap between the books. Disha felt something was wrong.

'Oh, I forgot', Dinar changed the subject. 'Our Bengali friend had asked me to reserve the book *Comrade* written by TVK. The book is a firework about Comrade Krishna Pillai, his life history. It has been lying around here all these years and it's only now that I could lay my hands on it.'

Dinar lifted up an ancient book which was almost crumbling. 'Doesn't look like this can be carried outside, see, it is already turning into powder.'

'True', Disha looked at the book. The pages were coming out loose from the binding.

'Do you want to hear something amazing?' Dinar was excited. 'You know our first Prime Minister Jawaharlal Nehru? He rode pillion on our Comrade Krishna Pillai's bicycle.'

'Is it true?' Disha looked at him in disbelief.

'It's true alright.' Dinar insisted. 'Will our comrade TVK write fiction when it comes to such historical truths? That was when Nehru visited Calicut beach to deliver a speech. The whole place was so crowded that Nehru couldn't be driven in a car. So, he rode pillion on Krishna Pillai's bicycle. Remember? In those days our Comrade was in the Congress party. See look here....'s

He transferred the book to her hands. Three or four silverfish from the loose pages crawled on to her fingers.

'Oops…' as she shook her hands vigorously to shake off the silverfish, *Comrade* fell flat on the floor transforming into a heap of paper bits. Dinar's face grew angry.

'I must blame myself only for trusting you with the book', he said bending down. 'After all, they were only silverfish and not cobras, why were you so scared that you dropped the precious book and destroyed it?'

'Sorry', Disha's face turned red.

'Half of the book has turned into powder now.' Dinar was sour. 'It is okay, there must be a broom in the work area. Please bring it and clean up the place.'

'Oh! So that's my punishment', Disha asked and turned to the work area.

'Umm...You may consider it a punishment.' Dinar accompanied her to the work area.

'Ok, I want to tell you something', Dinar said in hushed tones. 'You should be careful while talking', he looked behind through the corner of his eyes. 'That guy is a special branch police'

'Who?'

'The one who is standing behind the bookshelf; He is from a village close by. Nowadays, he hangs around here on the pretext of searching for books.'

'In what way does it concern me', Disha was brusque. 'Let him search for books.'

'No, that's not the issue', Dinar explained. 'He is enquiring about Niranjan.'

'About Niranjan? What for?' Suddenly she was worried.

'He hasn't asked me...but asked our Sathyanesan', Dinar continued in hushed tones. 'I will explain to you in detail later.'

He went back to the book shelves, carrying the broom. Disha stood there dumbfounded. She couldn't take one step forward... rooted as if her legs had been chained. She felt a blast in her chest.

'Is there anything unperceivable in Niranjan's ways these days?' Disha thought. She had been thinking like that for quite a few days now. There seemed to be no affection in his eyes. He looked at her as if she were a foe. He treated Mother in the same way. She had been observing that from the day she returned from Delhi. She did know who Sathyanesan was. He was the local barber. His saloon was the pulse of the village. Why should he enquire about Niranjan from Sathyanesan? If what Dinar mentioned is true, why has the detective been hanging around here for four-five days?

She again shook her hands. A few more silverfish crawled freely on her hands.

Paddy Fields Hedged by Kasithumba

Comrade Prabhakaran came running and panting just as Anakhashayan and his elder brother were finishing the roofing work of their hut. They slid down the roof and landed right in front of Prabhakaran, startling him.

'My God! You gave me the shock of my life', said a rattled Prabhakaran who only then realised that they were working on the roof. 'All right, is your work complete?'

'Not yet', said Anakhashayan, 'There is some more trimming and finishing work left. But why have you come here in such a panic? What's the matter?'

'We have to go to a place', said Prabhakaran. 'Quickly finish your work. I will wait here in the shade.'

'But how can we finish it in such a hurry?' asked Anakhashayan. 'The hut will not look nice.'

'You have to finish the work fast', said Prabhakaran. 'The matter is serious.'

'What is this serious matter?' Anakhashayan slipped the sickle into his waist band and came closer to Prabhakaran, 'Is it confidential?'

'I don't know all that', replied Prabhakaran. 'Comrade Karunan's son came and informed me that we have to meet Comrade Padmanabhan immediately.'

'In that case, we will start off right away.' He looked at his brother and said, 'I think you can trim the fronds and give the final touch better than me'.

'I have done most of the roofing work', said his brother. 'But I am not good at trimming and giving the finishing touches. That needs some expert hands.'

Two people came with a long and narrow strip of split bamboo to level and trim the fronds evenly.

'Both of you come and help us' Raghavan told them.

They held the strip closer to the hanging ends of the fronds. Anakhashayan trimmed the edges neatly and with expertise, running the sickle along the length of the wooden plank. Prabhakaran looked at him with admiration.

'This is really a skilled job', said an amazed Prabhakaran. 'One ought to make a mention of that.'

'I learned this from Father. He used to do it better. Watching him doing the job itself was a big delight', said Anakhashayan.

'That reminds me', Prabhakaran said. 'Any news about your father? Have you heard from the workers who came from Muhamma village for whitewashing ...?'

'Yes, we too heard from the workers who came for whitewashing the joint family house of Chullikkat... that after running away from here, Father stayed in his sister's house in Muhamma.'

'Oh, that's good news', said Prabhakaran with relief. 'At least he is alive.'

'But we don't know where he went from there', said Anakhashayan. 'Maybe, he is wandering around.'

'Oh, then he will come back home after his safari' Prabhakaran tried to comfort them.

'Umm... Not likely in this birth', Anakhashayan retorted. 'How will he do that? He had to run away from here for his dear life.'

Anakhashayan changed his clothes and left, along with Prabhakaran.

Comrade Padmanabhan was walking up and down in the veranda of his house, when Prabhakaran and Anakhashayan sprinted through the paddy fields and reached there. Hearing their footfalls on dry leaves, Padmanabhan looked at them.

'Oh, so you have come.' Padmanabhan stopped walking. 'Where were you all this time? I had sent Comrade Karunan to look for you.'

'What's the matter comrade?' Prabhakaran became anxious.

'So, you don't know about all the chaos that's happening?' Padmanabhan grilled them with his eyes.

'Karunan's son came and told me that you were looking for me and that the matter was serious. But I don't know what exactly the problem is', Comrade Prabhakaran confessed. 'I went to Kanasseri village immediately to fetch Anakhashayan and both of us are here now.'

'Oh stop it', Padmanabhan spoke irritatedly. 'Why do you drag this little fellow with you all the time? When I call you to discuss serious matters, why do you take it as kid's stuff?'

Anakhashayan looked at Prabhakaran meekly. From the beginning, Comrade Padmanabhan had expressed his disapproval on involving a teenager like him in discussions and activities.

'Shall I go back?' Anakhashayan prodded Prabhakaran.

'Though he looks small in size, he is a very knowledgeable person', Prabhakaran spoke for Anakhashayan. 'On that day, when Bhaskaran was tied up and tortured by the goons of the landlord…'

'Enough, enough…' Comrade Padmanabhan was more irritated.

'Is there any news about your father?' He looked at Anakhashayan.

'The talk is that he is still alive', Prabhakaran answered. Anakhashayan nodded in the affirmative.

'Okay, if you are hungry, go inside and eat something. You may find cooked tapioca and smashed chilly chutney in the kitchen.'

Smoldering in frustration, Anakhashayan turned back and walked towards the fencing.

'Why did you ask me to come?' queried Prabhakaran, watching the offended Anakhashayan walking away.

'The matter is serious', Padmanabhan replied in a heavy tone. 'A few of our comrades have been tied down and assaulted by the goons of the landlord Kattiyadan and subsequently handed over to police custody. We cannot take this lightly. The union has decided to take over this case. You must immediately leave for Alungal where the incident took place. A few of our comrades are already there. I have made arrangements to report the incident to our comrades Panicker and Bhaskaran.'

When Prabhakaran came out of the house, he saw Anakhashayan waiting for him at the fencing.

'You also come with me', Prabhakaran told him.

'I don't want to come', Anakhashayan said with unconcealed annoyance. 'I get irritated with the way he talks.'

'Sometimes, he behaves like itching plants. Are you not aware of that?' Prabhakaran said soothingly. 'You don't have to take it seriously. He is actually a kind-hearted person. Sometimes when he acts impulsively you may find it offending, but that's temporary.'

Prabhakaran held Anakhashayan close, wrapping his arms around his shoulders. 'Come, let's go fast.'

'Oh, this is similar to what they did to Pakkaran', Anakhashayan said as they cut across the paddy fields.

'All these landlords behave the same way', said Prabhakaran. 'Did you know, they have enrolled the goon Matheparamban also in their association? And goons Krishnappan and Chandrappan are already related to the Pattathil house. They are staying with their step- father Pattathil Kartha. All the time, they roam around the village with towels twisted and tied around their heads, and machetes in their sheaths tucked to their waist, the typical dress code of a goon. They molest good-looking women working in the fields and farms, the moment they get a chance even in daylight. At night they creep into their huts and violate them which often results in an illegitimate pregnancy. The poor women don't open their mouths, fearing for their dear life. Even their husbands maintain silence as their lives are also at risk. There is no one to control them. Even the police force is scared of them.'

'They should be chopped into pieces', Anakhashayan's young blood boiled.

'Umm...you go there to cut them into pieces', Prabhakaran mocked him. 'They will make themselves available to you to get cut into pieces!'

Both of them went directly to Pakkaran's hut. His sister Kochhu Paru peeped outside. Her expressive eyes brightened, the moment she saw Anakhashayan. She moved behind the door made of braided coconut fronds as a matter of respect.

'Please don't stand outside, come on in and take a seat. My brother has gone to take bath in the pond. He will be here soon', she said with great reverence.

'Oh, no, that's not right. We will wait here', said Anakhashayan.

Pakkaran came back, toweling his hair dry.

'Hello, when did you come? Come on in and be seated', Pakkaran was delighted to see them.

Kochhu Paru brought cooked tapioca and smashed chilly chutney in three plates and black coffee in three mud cups.

'The coffee is not sweetened at all', Pakkaran warned them. 'There is simply no sugar available in this village. You can apply some ground hot chutney on your tongue and take a sip of the hot coffee. That way it will become tastier. That's how we all manage.'

Kochhu Paru stood at a distance respectfully and eyed Anakhashayan through the corner of her eyes. He was their saviour when her brother was ruthlessly beaten by goon Chandrappan. From that moment she had been toying with a wish. One day, when no one is around when Anakhashayan comes, she would address him as 'Comrade' and pay her respects.

It was during this Onam season that everyone had witnessed Anakhashayan's expertise in traditional archery. His shots hit the target 'the onam wheel', a moving wheel made of banana stem, all the three times.

The village astrologer Rayappan and friends celebrated his talents, composing a song sung to rhythm.

Why have you come here teenager?
This is a game of adults with perfect aim
Why should a teenager without even a moustache come to compete?
Only to get ashamed by losing the game.

Kannappan rolled the wheel in great speed, which was struck by the arrow shot by Anakhashayan, making the wheel spin like a top. Arrows shot by his competitors didn't even get close to the moving wheel. His excited team members lifted Anakhashayan and held him high. The landlord presented the trophy to the winner; one pot full of country liquor and one spike of bananas.

Astrologer Rayappan went on teasing Anakhashayan, 'In a country of noseless people, a King with half a nose.'

Anakhashayan devoured the cooked tapioca along with the hot chilly chutney with relish.

'The cooked tapioca was so delicious', he complimented her.

'Oh, what is there to talk about it so much', her brother Pakkaran said, trying to dismiss her culinary skill. 'That's because of the quality of the tapioca. It would be delicious even if we cooked it.'

'Not only that, the smashed chilly chutney also is equally delicious', Anakhashayan said.

'Oh, that's because the green chilly is so spicy', said her brother.

Anakhashayan sneaked a look at Kochhu Paru. She was standing behind the door made of braided coconut fronds, trying to suppress a smile, covering her mouth with her hand.

'Had she been taller, Kochhu Paru would have been more noticeable than Kaithara Pappy.' Pappy, who was twenty years old, was considered most beautiful among the slave working class women. 'But Kochhu Paru is still a girl and will grow taller. At that time Kochuu Paru will be the most beautiful girl among them', thought Anakhashayan.

Anakhashayan often felt that Comrade Prabhakaran had a crush on Kaithara Pappy. Otherwise, why not take the short-cut to his house from the coir factory rather than the longer route skirting Pappy's house every evening? Pappy's courtyard was full of colourful flowering plants like hibiscus, poppies, marigold, jasmine and the like. Most of the evenings, Pappy would be engaged in cutting grass for her cows from paddy fields where blue kasithumba flowers bloomed. Otherwise she would be having a lively conversation with her pet black cow called Karambi. If not that, she would be threading marigold flowers into a beautiful garland. The moment Prabhakaran's head became visible, walking through the paddy fields she would lift her head to throw a glance at him. Looking at her sideways, Comrade Prabhakaran would walk past Pappy. Not even once had he spoken to her.

There was a well-known story about a guy by name Theeyattu Unni who used to sit for hours together behind the bamboo thickets to listen to Pappy's melodious songs while replanting paddy shoots in the fields. He sat there mesmerised, watching her work to the rhythm of the melody. He wasn't aware of a black rat snake crawling into the bamboo clusters. When it coiled around his legs, he sprang up and threw himself in front of the women working in the paddy fields. The women ragged him, saying that he was attending to nature's call behind the bamboo cluster when the rat snake coiled around him. He turned red in shame.

'If you like her so much, why don't you ask her directly?' Anakhashayan asked Comrade Prabhakaran.

'You really don't know how sharp her sickle is', Comrade said. 'What will happen if she cuts me into pieces on hearing my proposition?'

'Once when fish vendor Showri made a pass at her, slapping her buttock, she charged at him with her sickle. People say no grass has sprouted on the path he took on that day, chased by Pappy with her sickle. That's the kind of woman she is.'

The make-shift door moved a little and Kochhu Paru came out to gather the vessels used for serving the food and looked at Anakhashayan.

'It was very delicious, and I am full', he complimented her once again.

'Okay, we didn't tell you the reason for this visit', Comrade Prabhakaran said licking his fingers. 'The tapioca was so tasty that we forgot why we came here.'

'Oh, I thought I will tell you leisurely, after the food', said Pakkaran.

'The incident took place yesterday afternoon', he started off. 'The practice is that those workers who thresh the paddy are responsible for bringing mats to spread the grains.' Fifteen-year-old Parameswaran came with two mats. Mat space was not sufficient, and the landlord insisted that the work be continued only after a third mat was brought.

'But we don't have another mat at home', said Parameswaran, tears welling up in his eyes. 'Where will I go for another mat?'

The landlord was offended by the direct insolence in the boy's question. As he sprang up to assault the boy, Parameswaran bolted and broke into a sprint. The landlord's son, Gangappan, chased him, caught him and tied him to a coconut tree. The landlord whacked him till his wrath subsided. Then the son took over. The beaten and bleeding Parameswaran was totally immobile for four hours.

The trade union members brought Parameswaran's mother Manikkam, to question the landlord.

'What was my son's offence that you beat him up like this Master?' a heart-broken Manikkam asked the landlord, folding her hands. 'Though we are poor, we have been bringing up our son like the apple of our eye.'

'We have to know one way or the other....' Parameswaran's relative Hariappan, who was a member of the Farming Workers Union, came forward.

'What is it that you want to know?' the landlord said furiously. 'Are you all under the impression that you have the right to talk any nonsense standing in my courtyard?'

Hearing that, the union leaders who had remained in the rear, came forward.

'Landlords are not entitled to talk insolently to the working committee. Our policy is an eye for eye and tooth for tooth.'

'Oho! So, all of you have grown up enough to talk to me in this way? Then I want to see how you will get away with this...'

The landlord turned to Manikkam, 'Why are you standing here gaping at me? Didn't I ask you to get lost?'

Manikkam started sweating, as her conscience interfered with her thoughts inconveniently. After all, he was the God who had been providing them with food for generations. The blood running through her and her children's veins was the blessing of the landlord. She entwined her hand with Hariaapan's and tried to plead. 'Please, let's go.' Aghast, union members looked at each other.

'You guys…', the landlord turned to them, 'don't you have any plans to leave? If his mother is not concerned about him, why are you hanging around here?'

'This is not an issue concerning Parameswaran alone.' One of the union members faced the landlord. 'This concerns all of us, the farm workers. And the union is planning to handle these issues as "our issues". If you hurt one of us, it will apply to all of us and we are not going to hold our hands and remain dumb witnesses to such unjustifiable incidents. You better remember that.'

It was Shanmugham who had attended two meetings presided by Comrade Krishna Pillai who delivered this short and crisp speech.

'Oh, so you are trying to terrorise me?' The landlord went inside his house. 'I would like to see how you are going to do that.'

Inside the house, the landlord's relative Sivarama Panikkar, who was the headmaster of the Cherthala English Medium High School, was sitting majestically with his legs crossed and smearing fragrant lime on the tender betel leaves to be chewed along with tobacco. He had dropped in to say hello to his brother-in-law, on his way back from the school. Next to him was the Village Officer Kumara Kartha. He was also a relative.

'Didn't you hear their threats?' the landlord addressed both of them.

'But what you did was a little high-handed. That boy is sick and weak', said the headmaster. 'See if you can talk nicely and disperse the crowd. We will see the rest later.'

The Village Officer came out of the house and addressed the crowd, 'For the time being, let go whatever happened.

We will see that it's not repeated in future. Let there be no violence now.'

'Ok, now we will leave', Shanmugam said. 'We too need to have some discussions. We will come back after that.'

The workers walked away.

'Look at their arrogance', the landlord was smouldering.

'Yes. I heard', said Panikkar lifting the brass spittoon. 'Is the harvesting over?'

'Almost. Only the western side has to be covered', said the landlord.

'Don't finish the work tomorrow', Panikkar advised the landlord.

'Then?' the landlord asked skeptically.

'Give some reason and stop the work until day after tomorrow afternoon', Panikkar continued. 'Tell them they can do the rest the day after tomorrow. Let all the workers get into the paddy fields day after tomorrow. It's not desirable to leave them scot free. We have to convince them that this land has its own rules and rulers.'

'But for that purpose, do we have to put a hold on the work?' the landlord was still in two minds.

'Yes, it's a must', Panikkar got up twirling his white towel before hanging it on his shoulders. 'Should I give an account of the fest that's going to happen the day after, now itself? Let me go and see Iyer.'

He was referring to DSP Vaidyanatha Iyer.

'The fest will be grand!' the landlord was exhilarated, thinking of the events of the next two days.

As planned, harvesting was put on hold the next afternoon with an announcement from Raman, the landlord's manager.

'By day after the harvesting season is getting over. Without fail, all of you must be present for work.'

Harvesting started early on the day-after morning. By 10 am three police vans, full of police and reserve police, were rolled into the location.

'You don't have to worry about the police or army', Raman assured the workers. 'Landlord will take care of everything.' Workers became engrossed in their work without any apprehension.

Goon Narayanan arrived at the scene, with his team. The police rounded up the workers to make sure that no one escaped.

'We have been cheated', Shanmugham cried out, 'all of you run.'

Leaving the harvested stalks in the paddy fields, the workers started to run. The police and the goondas started chasing them. Sixteen of them were caught and brought to the landlord's house with their hands tied up.

'How is the fest?' Panikkar laughed, looking at the landlord.

'Fantastic' replied the landlord, pleased immensely. 'What is lacking is only fireworks.'

'Oh, we will overcome that shortage now', said goon Narayanan. 'Tie them up and start beating them. Leave them in the hot sun till evening.'

'Oh, here comes Raman with a few more', the landlord said appreciatively. The police, goons and Raman together had rounded up about eight more workers.

'Where did you get these from?' asked goon Krishnappan.

'They were working in the farms', said Raman proudly. 'Smarties made us run hell of a lot. It was very difficult to catch them. But the police and the goons got them.'

'Alright; let's not wait', said Krishnappan.

Panikkar was reclining on an easy chair, extending his legs to full length. Kartha took a seat next to him. Women and children of the family took their place near the windows to watch the drama to be staged outside.

'Look there, he is the leader', Chandrappan pointed his finger at Shanmugham.

'Oh, are you the one who launched an attack on Pattathil house along with your goon gang?' One of the police constables slapped Shanmugam on his face.

Shanmugham was flabbergasted. He knew immediately that the police had fabricated a false case against him and his friends.

'It's a fact that when an innocent teenager was assaulted, I came here to question… but it was not to….

'You scoundrel, who are you to question and challenge; are you one of the ruling English?' He swung his club and pounded on Shanmugam's head. Shanmugam went into shock. He couldn't speak or react.

'People like him should be beaten with peduncles dipped in shit', said goon Narayanan who picked up a thorny stick from the cow dung pit and handed it over to Krishnappa. The police constable retreated.

'What did you say yesterday, standing here, in this courtyard? That your union will intervene? Where is your union?' Krishnappa struck Shanmugam on his face with the stinking stick. 'Since when have you been emboldened to talk like this?'

Shanumgam's face, mouth and body were all dabbed with cow dung and he writhed in pain.

In the burning sun, the police and goons continued to whack the labourers till afternoon.

'Okay, now you stop for the time being', Headmaster Panikkar told them. 'You can continue the fun after lunch.'

On the verandah the servants served meals on plantain leaves for the policemen and the goondas.

The workers were made to lie down on the ground.

'They should not be given even water to drink', Manager Raman shouted indignantly. 'The ungrateful were fed on our tender coconuts and gruel for generations. They have forgotten all that.'

'Umm...now they have been emboldened to question us', Panikkar put back the towel on his shoulders after shaking it vigorously.

By seven in the evening Comrade Prabhakaran, Anakhashayan and Pakkaran along with seven other comrades reached the police station and hid behind a few trees. Three police vans rolled in with sixteen arrested workers including Shanmugam. The Inspector came running in excitement. He caught each of the arrested ones by their hair, bent them and hit them on their back with his elbow. Then he pushed them forcefully inside the lockup, making their heads hit the wall.

'Go, your leaders will give you company in the cells', he growled.

'Who all are inside?' Comrades asked Prabhakaran in subdued tones.

'Comrades PK Madhavan, Sreedharan, Ramakrishnan and NSP Panikkar', someone answered.

'Look there, Inspector Koshy is coming out', Pakkaran prodded the others. 'Let's not be seen by him.'

The policemen stood erect and saluted as Koshy approached them. 'Tonight, all of you have work.' Koshy stood in front of them inserting his hands in his trouser pockets and expanding his chest proudly.

'All of you have to be in Kadakkarapalli Thikkal village. Search all huts threadbare. Don't mind whether the occupants are women or girls. By morning there should not be any hut left. Tear them down and set fire to them.'

'Comrade Pakkaraan, didn't you hear that?' Anakhashayan was petrified.

A spark of fire lit Comrade Prabhakaran's mind also. Kaithara Pappy raised her head from the midst of the fields where the Kashithumba flowered.

'Let's inform the Comrade', Prabhakaran said hurriedly.

Night started to spread its net slowly. The police vans came alive abruptly.

'Come on. Let's go soon.' Pakkaran was restless at the thought of Kochu Paru being alone in her hut.

When the Crops are Ripe

Clinging to the iron bars of the lockup, Shanmugham had managed a semi sitting position. There was no place to rest his head anywhere. The cell was packed with comrades like cattle packed for slaughter in a slaughter house. Inspector Koshy's vicious strike on the spine sent flashes of lightening to his brain and his whole body pulsated in intense pain.

Inspector Koshy was restlessly walking up and down in the police station, rubbing his palms together as if he were very badly in need of a victim to bash up. He stomped his booted legs on the floor and at times shouted at the occupants of the lockup.

The police brought in two more comrades tied and incapacitated. They were Comrade OM Abubekker who was a member of the coconut-pluckers' union and Comrade AK Paraman who was a member of the coir factory workers' union.

Police constables hurled the two comrades at Koshy's feet.

'You mangy dog!' He stomped on the abdomen of Comrade Paraman and dug his boots deep into the victim. Then he bent down and picked up Comrade Abubekkar with one hand and held him high, suspended in the air and hit him on his stomach with the other fisted hand. Comrade Abubekkar grimaced in pain.

'Where the hell are your leaders?' Looking at the lockup, the Inspector showered obscenities on them. 'In which warehouse are they hiding? Ask them to come here and see what's going on.'

He tightened his grip around Comrade Abubekkar's neck. The emaciated comrade wriggled under his hands, struggling for breath. 'This is the *Garudan Thookam* performed by police officers. Were you not the one who was shouting slogans against the Diwan's rule? Diwanji, who was sitting in his administrative office a mile away, heard you. Your paper reported that Diwanji hid in a mustard seed fearing all of you. If you have the guts, call out your slogan once again.'

The moment the Inspector loosened his grip, Comrade Abubekkar shouted using all his energy.

'Let Diwan's rule go to hell. Let Sir CP's rotten administration go to hell. Let the rule of violence go to hell.'

In spite of being beaten to within an inch of their lives, the comrades locked in the cells repeated the slogans in unison. The sound hit the walls of the police station and reverberated. Police constables scattered outside the station stormed inside. Inspector Koshy flung Abubekker on the floor and booted him.

'Get that rascal outside', the Inspector pointed at Shanmugham.

'Where is head constable Narapillai?'

'Sir', a heavily built man with thick mustache came forward and saluted the Inspector. He was head constable Narapillai, whose expertise was in fabricating false cases.

'Where is your club? You can start your special technique.'

'Tie up that scoundrel', Narapilla yelled at the police constables. His breath stank of liquor. He was so drunk that a whole bottle of liquor could be extracted by squeezing his nose.

The police pulled Shanmugam out of the lockup and dragged him to the yard. They tied his hands tightly to a wooden bench and kept his legs stretched, exposing the soles. His mouth was stuffed with an old cloth.

Head constable Narayanan Pillai came with his club. The sight of his defenseless, hapless victim excited him; his mustache bristled and eyes spit fire. The liquor in his stomach activated the animal instincts in his brain.

'You mangy dog…!' he again showered obscenities and started bashing Shanmugam's sole with all his strength. Shanmugam wriggled in pain, unable to even cry out, as his mouth was stuffed.

'Beat him till your club breaks into pieces and his ankle is smashed into smithereens.' Inspector Koshy guffawed. 'He should never be able to go anywhere on his feet and shout slogans.'

Comrade Shanmugam's sole started bleeding and blood splattered making designs on the wall. A comrade who was watching the scene fainted. The club went up and down on Shanmugam for some time. The old cloth stuffed into his mouth fell off and a horrifying animal shriek pierced the skies.

Narapillai's hands went up again in fury.

'Enough, enough', a few constables watching the scene said in unison, appalled at the cruelty and took hold of Narapilla's hands. 'How can one be so inhuman?'

Inspector Koshy did not relish the interference and rolled his eyes at the policemen.

Unnikandan saluted the inspector and begged his pardon.

Inspector Koshy grunted harshly; stomped his booted legs on the floor and stormed out on his motor cycle without any particular destination in mind. Shanmugam fainted on the floor exhausted.

At the crack of dawn, policemen unlocked the cell and shouted.

'Get out all of you, and attend to your toilet needs. Don't mess up and stink up the cell.'

There were five or six local constables and a few from the reserve police carrying guns to herd them. Two comrades carried Shanmugham out. His legs were swollen and he couldn't keep them on the floor.

'No need for him to go out', said the policemen. 'We will keep a tin which he can use temporarily. You have to take the responsibility of emptying it and keeping it clean.'

Rest of the workers were herded to the banks of the canal. They were given five minutes each to attend to their morning chore one by one, on the same spot. They were not even allowed to move to a different spot.

'Hey, time is over', said a constable. 'Now get into that water, wash yourself and also your face and come back. We won't give you a drop of water for this purpose.'

'That's not possible', Comrade Paraman objected. 'We can't wash our face in that dirty water. We need clean water, tooth powder or a mango leaf to clean up our teeth and mouth. We are also human beings, don't forget that.'

Hearing that, one constable charged forward, dragged him by his hair and dipped his face in the disgusting water of the canal and snarled, 'Since when did you start deserving these luxuries? If you open your mouth again, we will make a pulp of you.'

'What comrade said is right', said Comrade Abubekker. 'None of you should wash your face in this dirty water.'

All the comrades stood up. The police hit them with the handle of their guns. They yelled at them and forced them to sit down. A few of them were forced to drink the dirty water. They kicked them on their backs and some of them fell into the water.

'What did we do to deserve this kind of a cruel treatment?' one of the comrades expressed his mental agony. 'What's our offence? Is it because we challenged the goons for beating up a teenager from among us?'

The constable caught him by his throat, 'Who are you to question us?' 'There is nobody to ask us even if we kill you. After all you are worthless vermin, worms which can be crushed under our feet.'

In front of the lockup a small group of constables stood with granites to receive them when they came back.

'So, you all want to clean your teeth? But you need to have teeth in your mouth for that, isn't it?'

They punched them on their face with the stones.

Outside the station, three police vans came to a stop. There was a shrill wail from the prisoners in the vans. Comrade Paraman lifted his bleeding face to see what was happening. The reserve police hurled more prisoners out of the van, kicking and punching them.

Pakkaran was standing in the shade of the big hog plum tree laden with plums that stood on the banks of the paddy fields. Kochhu Paru had spotted a bunch of ripe plums hanging from the top of the tree. Pakkaran was trying to hit them with stones. But his stones didn't reach anywhere near the target.

'Oh, I can't do this anymore', he lost his patience. 'My arms are hurting.' Kochhu Paru was disappointed.

'Oh, here comes the right person for this', Pakkaran said as he saw Anakhashayan approaching. 'I was just thinking of him.'

'What's the matter?' asked Anakhashayan as he came close.

Kochhu Paru looked at him hopefully and pointed her finger to the top of the hog plum tree. 'Oh, that's a little high. Sticks won't help. We need big granite stones', said Anakhashayan.

'Look here, is this enough?' Kochhu Paru came with a granite stone.

'This is a bit small. Still, we will try.' He stretched his palm out to her. While transferring the stone, her hands grazed his fingers accidently.

Anakhashayan closed his eyes and aimed at the plums. All he could see was the moist lips of Kochhu Paru, anxious to devour the plums.

The plums are at least ten feet high, he thought, if, in three attempts at least one plum does not fall, I am not a man! He flung up the stone with all his strength. Instead of one, three plums fell at Kochhu Paru's feet.

'Hey, where were you?' Anakhashayan turned around to see Comrade Prabhakaran. 'I was looking for you everywhere.'

Prabhakaran looked pale.

'In Katakkarapalli and Mataikka areas, the police and goondas have gotten out of control and are committing atrocities. They barged into the hutments of poor people, cleaned up all their rations and wages, and arrested and dumped many innocent men in the lockup without any provocation. Women and children are roaming in panic, without even a change of clothes. Oh, look, Comrade Karunan is coming!'

Anakhashayan watched Karunan approaching fast. Karunan was a beedi worker in the local market.

'Don't stand where men discuss things, go inside the hut', Pakkaran reprimanded Kochhu Paru. She was busy licking the hard seed of the plum after eating the fleshy pulp. Sneaking a glance at Anakhashayan, she went inside the hut.

'Did you know', Karunan panted, 'yesterday, in Vettakkal and Veeyathara localities, the police and the goondas attacked the villagers. The entire community was forced to leave their premises. This evening the party committee and trade unions are holding a meeting. If we don't retaliate, we won't be able to lead a decent life. They are molesting and raping young women in front of their men and beating up children and aged mothers. The men who resisted were beaten to pulp and carried away to the police station.'

Before Karunan could finish, they heard the sound of a crowd approaching.

As they turned, they saw the goons Matheparamban Narayanan, Nalukettungal Raman and a lot of others on the road. Trailing behind them was a line of small children. Raman was holding a megaphone in his hand. Men and women came out of their huts to see what was going on.

'Look there', Pakkaran nudged Anakhashayan. Matheparamban Narayanan had rolled up his sleeves and had his hands crossed behind his back. As he turned towards the megaphone, Anakhashayan saw a deadly machete in his hands.

'All of you gather here, listen and try to understand', Raman announced through the megaphone. 'The most respected feudal lord Pattathil Kochhu Nanu Kartha wishes to tell everyone who is loyal to the King of Travancore, to join the Federation of people who are loyal to the royalty by paying the membership fee of one rupee. Whoever thus becomes a member of the federation will be looked after by His Majesty, the King. They will not be touched by the police or army if they show the receipt for having paid the membership. Come forward. Become a member of the Federation today itself.'

Matheparamban Narayanan looked at the crowd with his bloodshot eyes and made another announcement which was louder than the megaphone.

'This is for everyone; all of you are expected to join the Federation for people who respect His Majesty, the King of Travancore.'

It sounded like a threat.

The megaphone group walked past.

'So the police and army have taken a joint decision. Now or never', Karunan found his voice again. 'We cannot remain silent any more. We have to raise this issue in the meeting this evening.'

'We should', Prabhakaran agreed.

When Karunan left, Prabhakaran got worried as he thought of Kaithara Pappy. She lived all alone. There was only the namesake company of an old woman at night. That did not help much. No one knew when the army would barge in. The strength of her sickle may not work in front of the armed police and army. Before that, a way-out had to be thought of. After a lot of thinking, he found that there was only one solution. But he was doubtful if she would agree to that.

'I was thinking', reluctantly he opened the subject to Anakhashayan, 'Why don't we bring Pappy over here?'

'Where?' Anakhashayan looked a bit confused.

'To Pakkaran's aunt, Karambiamma's house. Kochhu Paru will keep her company. Besides, we have our own people in the surrounding eight to nine huts to protect them.'

Anakhashayan conveyed that to Pakkaran and he found it feasible.

'So have you decided to bring her over here? Will you be able to convince her to come with you?' Anakhashayan asked doubtfully.

God only knows whether she will agree, Prabhakaran thought. That's the kind of person she is. She is the type who will not let anyone take charge of her. Still, he should try calling her.

On his way to the meeting venue that evening, he took a deviation to Pappy's house through paddy fields hedged by kasithumba plants in full bloom. Pappy was not to be seen either in the small farming area or in the flower garden which looked freshly watered. Her cow was feasting upon the lush green grass at the base of the coconut tree which was still wet.

'Hi, what's the news?' Prabhakaran turned around to see from where the disembodied voice came and realised that it was from the pond in the paddy field. But there was no one in the pond too. Marottis (a wild variety of almond), fallen from the ten meter tall tree were floating all over the surface of the pond.

'Look up...here', someone called out. Prabhakaran looked up.

Folding the edge of her mundu well above her knees, with legs hanging to both sides of the branch of the tall tree, she was sitting there holding a long stick tied to a sickle, plucking the fruits expertly.

'What is the reason for your visit?' she enquired. 'Come on, tell me.'

'But how can I explain with you on the top of the tree and me down here?' Prabhakaran managed to speak. 'It's a serious matter.'

'What is this serious matter?' she asked as she tried to pluck another fruit. It landed on Prabhakaran's shoulder, which hurt but he didn't flinch.

But Pappy noticed it. 'Oh, these fruits have no control over where they fall. Please move away from the tree or it will fall right on your head and hurt you. There is no point in regretting afterwards.'

Prabhakaran felt insulted and humiliated. She has no sense of propriety. She should know that I am a man and that is no way to talk to me. When she peeped at me as I walked along, I thought that she was warming up towards me. But now she is so indifferent. Does she just think of me as any other person? He wondered.

'If you cannot tell me standing down there, why don't you climb up', Pappy invited him. A crudely made ladder was leaning against the tree. 'You can come up using that. Otherwise you will have to wait till I finish plucking all the fruits. I can hear you even when you talk from there. But you don't want to do that. So, you climb up and come.'

Prabhakaran had no idea as to how to tell her what he had come to say. Had she come down, he could have begun with other subjects and then told her. He was trembling from the moment he had seen her. This was the first time he had spoken to her. How is it possible to present such a serious matter so casually? He didn't know what to do.

'In that case, I will come some other time', Prabhakaran got ready to leave.

'If you could wait for a while, I will treat you to a cup of sugarless tea', she offered. 'After all, you have come all the way to tell me something.'

Prabhakaran stood there indecisively. He had to go a long way to the venue of the meeting. It was beyond the Pudukkotta hill, where Gurudevan had installed a mirror as a deity in a temple. But sugarless tea fixed by Pappy was holding him back. He could not take one step ahead, in spite of what his mind was insisting he do.

'No, please let me go', His tongue said, but his feet refused to move.

'In that case please get going', she said concentrating on the bunch of fruits she was trying to pluck.

As Prabhakaran dragged himself forward reluctantly, Pappy's song floated to his ears.

Oh my dear parrot maiden, what was that matter you wanted to tell me?
When the crops are ripe for harvest

Show me your strength to come, cut and take away the stalks full of grains…

Thathayyam, chimi, thattinam thinthayetharo….

The song chained Prabhakaran's feet to the ground. He could not go.

Bespectacled Cobra

As he lay on the verandah of his Ayurveda clinic on his easy chair, Vaidyan Kumaran's ears picked up a harvest song. He could visualise young labour girls hailing from untouchable lower castes, singing and working in the paddy fields, standing in knee deep water.

Our Goddess Mari poured out rains,
Paddy fields are full with rain water
Paddy fields are ploughed and seeds sown
Hi! Omala, Chenthila, Mala, Cheru Kannamma, Kali, Karambi, Chatha, Chadaya,
All men and women of lower birth, please come and line up for work
It's time to replant the paddy seedlings.

How the paddy fields transformed into a stage for singing and dancing! In Kumaran's mind, the thoughts created hatred against communists. The party and unions jointly ruined the harmony which prevailed between the landlords and labourers. They injected poison into the minds of the labour class, who were leading a contented life surviving just on watered gruel. The labourers who lowered their eyes meekly, even when the landlords bashed them up, had started talking back. Landlords had to face a lot of problems during the harvest season this year.

'Where will all this end?' the Vaidyan pondered uneasily, thinking of the communists barging unauthorised into the paddy fields owned by the local Thirumala Temple Management and forcibly harvesting the yield. The docile temple management was so petrified that they couldn't raise a word against them. The rich temple had large cultivated areas, fetching more than ten thousand bushels of paddy during one season. The communists had forcefully entered an area of three hundred bushels and harvested it. The Landlords' Association had arranged their own labour to harvest the crops belonging to the temple property. It was while they were at work that the communists had barged in.

The Vaidyan had sent a telegram to the Diwan on the same day, on behalf of the temple authorities.

The Diwan had immediately issued orders to the Deputy Inspector General, who in turn, issued orders written right on the back of the same telegram reading, 'Depute a battalion of armed police to camp at the premises till the harvesting season is over.'

Next day early morning, a van full of armed police and another van full of unarmed police arrived. They camped in the school building belonging to the temple authorities. They encircled the periphery of the paddy fields, ready with their clubs and guns. The moment the workers engaged by the temple authorities moved on to the paddy fields, the workers union members also barged in.

'We are the people who sowed the seeds standing in knee deep water. So, it is our right to harvest the yield. No one can stop us', one Cheruman youth declared.

'How insolent the working class has become...' the Vaidyan thought in disgust. 'Where is the rule that only those who sowed the seeds can harvest the yield?'

Listening to the worker's union leaders, a police inspector from the armed police came forward and asked the temple authorities, 'Is this true, what these people are claiming?'

The temple manager said, 'I am not aware of these people working here'.

'If you people have worked here, do you have any proof?' The inspector challenged the trade union leaders. 'If you have proof, bring it here, otherwise clear out from here.'

'The proof is on our hands, respected sir, we don't have to bring it from anywhere', said Kandan Pulayan. Extending both his hands, he said, 'Look at our hands and look at their hands and see where you find the calluses, which is proof in itself that we do hard work in farms and paddy fields with shovels throughout our life.'

All the trade union workers extended their hands to show the calluses formed in their palms.

'Master, now you take a look at their hands', Kandan Pulayan requested the Inspector.

'All of you show me your hands', the Inspector ordered the workers brought in by the temple management.

The workers stood uncertain, not knowing what to do.

'Why don't you all have calluses in your palms?' The Inspector squeezed the hands of one worker.

'We do, respected master', said one of them, 'but not because of holding the shovels like agricultural workers'.

'Then?' the Inspector queried.

'We have calluses formed by holding knives.'

'How do you get calluses by holding knives?' the Inspector asked again.

'When we work in the coir factory, we have to keep cutting the coir to make coir mats, so we get calluses from holding the knives continuously.'

'In that case are you not the workers working in these fields regularly?' the Inspector asked in disappointment.

Workmen looked at each other and said, 'We are the workers of the nearby coir factory. Factory management instructed us to work here today. That's the reason why we are here. We are not familiar with harvesting work… we can just manage.'

The Inspector looked daggers at the Thirumala Temple president. 'Is it for this that we have been summoned here?' he asked.

The president sat down on the paddy field wearily, his hands supporting his head head.

'Ok, only those who know how to harvest can start working in the field', the Inspector ordered helplessly. 'Rest of you may clear out without obstructing the work.'

The Union leadership was bent on humiliating the landlords in front of the general public. Kumaran was infuriated; sending a telegram to Diwan and getting his orders against the agricultural workers, all turned out to be futile. Times were changing. He sighed sadly. Laying limply on the easy chair, he stared at the main road reminiscing about agricultural activities.

Twice a year paddy was cultivated. August-September was the harvesting season. Sowing started in the month of April-May after the paddy fields were ploughed.

The soil was prepared by mechanical agitation of various types, such as digging, stirring, and overturning. Male labourers went through back-breaking work during those days.

Seeds of two varieties of paddy, *Mundakan* and *Virippu* were mixed thoroughly and sown in the paddy fields. Now it was the turn of the women. Three weeks following germination, the six to eight-inch stalks were picked and replanted in a backbreaking manual procedure. Before that, they were also engaged to pick weeds, heaps of which were kept in an inverted position in the paddy fields. These weeds were then decomposed in the water pooled in the paddy fields to become manure.

By June-July, the Virippu paddy would start blooming. By August they would be ripe enough to be harvested. The head of the Virippu plants along with the Mundakan plants were cut together at the harvest. The stubs of Virippu decomposed in the rains and became manure for the Mundakan plants. Mundakan plants grew healthy and produced abundant crops. When the rains started in October, there would be another round of weeding. Harvest season started for Mundakan around November-December.

Then it was the turn of the vegetables. Paddy fields became farming lands for banana and vegetables like white and yellow pumpkin, bitter gourd, snake gourd, lady's finger and spinach and so on. A temporary pond was dug in the middle of the paddy fields to water the vegetable plants.

Twined around the banana plants, deadly cobras would sit in meditation. One such meditating cobra stung the right hand of the farm labourer Chami for waking it, Kumaran reminisced.

Chami had gone to cut the banana bunch, unaware of the presence of the cobra coiled around the plant. Chami was brought to Kumaran's father, Vaidyan Neelandan for treatment. It was believed that if Neelandan Vaidyan looked sternly at a snake bite victim, the venom would get drained off on its own. He tried his level best. He mixed some medicine in milk and poured it down his throat. He extracted the juice of different leaves and poured it into his nostrils. Again, he made a paste of different leaves and mixing it in cow's urine applied it on the wound. Nothing seemed to work. It was almost twenty-four hours. Chami turned blue and stiff with the venom, and lay in a coma on the verandah of the vaidyan's house. Spit and froth streamed out of his mouth. His young wife, heavily pregnant, rolled on the ground lamenting in agony.

'The sting is deadly and no one can save him', said the physician. 'The snake would have thought that he is being attacked and has used all his might in injecting the venom. He is alive only because of my medicines. Now it's beyond my powers. There is only one solution. We should call the cobra here by chanting mantras and make him draw back his own poison through the wound. But I don't practice such witchcraft. It is an unpardonable sin. It will bring disaster to my family.'

Chami's wife rolled on the ground, 'Please someone save my husband…I don't have anyone'.

'Try to summon the culprit snake, oh great physician', the crowd gathered around beseeched in chorus. 'Can't you see his young wife rolling on the ground? Who will look after her?'

'There can be multiple disasters if I do that', the reluctant Vaidyan said. 'You still want me to do it?'

'Um….' It was from his teenaged-son Kumaran. He was curious to know about the culprit snake being summoned by mantras and being forced to surrender.

'Didn't you hear your son?' his neighbour Sivaraman asked. 'Only if the boy can witness such miracles happening can he learn from that and practice it later after your time, isn't it?'

'Okay.' Father got up and gave instructions, 'Take Chami to the serpent shrine and lay him on the ground. Keep a lighted brass lamp filled with oil to the brim at his feet. Then keep some flowers and tulsi leaves on a banana leaf. No one should hang around in the vicinity. He (meaning the snake) will come in full rage'.

It was dusk. Darkness spread everywhere.

'Come with the chest of medicines', his father instructed Kumaran. He was clad in a red mundu. He wore a long piece of red cloth as Brahma sutra across his torso.

'You should never disclose what happens here to anyone', warned his father.

Father sat by the head of the snake victim and started chanting mantras. The chanting went on for a long time. A little later than midnight, the moon also set and whatever moonlight was there also faded. Wild cocks and hens clucked relentlessly. Somewhere in the distance foxes howled. As sleep nestled in Kumaran's eyes, his eyelids grew heavy.

He opened his eyes in the morning listening to the voices of the people who had gathered there.

'There is a dead cobra on the steps of the shrine', he heard someone saying.

He got up and ran to see the steps. It was true.

'The serpent killed itself by striking its head on the stone steps', informed Sivaraman.

'But where is Chami the victim?' he enquired.

'Oh, Chami is up. Can't you see him resting under the tree?' Sivaraman pointed his fingers.

'We did not expect him to come back to life. We should make a shrine for Vaidyan Neelandan.'

'Where is my father?' Young Kumaran looked around.

'He has gone home to sleep after last night.'

Kumaran ran towards the house. His father was lying flat on the ground. As soon as he saw Kumaran, he gestured him to come closer. Kumaran went near him.

'Did my son learn everything about how to call back the striking snake?' His father caressed his hair. Kumaran couldn't remember anything; even the time when he slipped into sound sleep.

'Good you slept', Father said, 'Good you didn't learn the process. It's not a chaste karma'.

Father's hands moved down from his shoulders. They crawled towards the wooden cot and started striking up and down. His body arched like a bow. Like a serpent standing on the tip of its tail father's body sprang up.

'Father', Kumaran screamed. Father didn't hear him. His eyes focused on the roof, he appeared like a serpent. Black blood streamed out of his mouth.

Old scenes that had dimmed in the smoky memory lane started flashing back one by one. How fast time travels! Kumaran was stunned. He looked at his wrinkled hands. Everything was changing. Deadly cobras have started avenging past wrongs. Would the monarchy also come to an end? No. Impossible! Kumaran tried to comfort himself. Can the country be without a King and a Diwan to rule? He couldn't think of such a possibility. Vaidyan Kumaran was also a small-scale landlord.

'This is my ancestral property hard earned by my father, grandfather and ancestors generations ago. It is my responsibility to maintain it till my last breath', he thought.

Kumaran was in great mental stress after Kochhu Kunjan Asaan warned him about the possibility where the country could move into anarchy. Kochhu Kunjan Asaan was a communist to the core. Asaan and Kumaran were classmates in the Sanskrit school. More than that, they were close friends too. Other than Asaan, no communists had permission to enter the Vaidyan's property. He was extremely loyal to the monarch. He was also known to the Diwan. That was how he had become a member of the Maharaja's vigilance committee. Whenever the Police Inspectors got a posting to that locality, they would go and meet him first before meeting anybody else. It was a practice they all followed.

Asaan was very excited when he spoke about the Bolshevik revolution in Russia. A revolution lead by the Communist Party, which had organised the industrial workers and farmers under one banner. They usurped the throne of the emperor and took control of the government. They distributed vast lands owned by the landlords to poor farming communities.

'It was Lenin who had taken a major initiative in this endeavor', said Asaan. 'The revolution took place in October 1917. That's the reason why the Revolution is named as October Revolution. Kumaran, you just wait and see. An October Revolution will take place here too. If not today, tomorrow. The farming and agricultural land will belong to the community of people who work on it.'

'Oh, this can't be true', Kumaran said vehemently. 'Nothing like an October Revolution could happen here.'

Asaan produced a book in Hindi and thumped through the pages depicting the pictures of Lenin, Trotsky and others who were leading the working class there.

'Oh! So it's true?' Kumaran was jittery. 'Time will not always move in the direction we expect.'

'Time has its own pace and direction', Asaan said philosophically. 'Like a river it may flow in different directions and convert dry deserts into wet lands.'

Asaan's forecast pierced the Vaidyan's heart like sharp iron nails. He couldn't bear to imagine a time when the King and Diwan would be stripped of their powers.

'Nothing should be allowed to thwart the King's rule, Diwan's administration or the feudal system', Kumaran swore loudly. 'There is only one way to achieve that. The striking venomous snakes should be made to draw back the venom. Maybe, I should send a telegram to Diwanji today itself.'

'Which snake's matter are you referring to?' Vishuvappan who was rolling *beedis*, a kind of rural cigarette, sitting in front of the verandah asked.

'The venomous Communist snakes', the Vaidyan said putting his feet up.

'Who? Our CK and CI', Vishuvappan asked while crushing the tobacco in between his fingers for the beedi.

'They are all just water snakes. But the real snakes are different, and not one or two.'

Vishuvappan knew whom the Vaidyan was referring to… Comrades Krishna Pillai, PT Punnoose, TV Thomas, R Sugathan, KV Pathrose… the list was long.

Now and then, when the vaidyan was frustrated, he would mutter to himself…'These are the guys who are the most venomous and who should be done away with. They are the rascals who are destroying the peaceful existence in the country. That R Sukhian, the comfort lover….' That's how the Vaidyan refered to Comrade R Sugathan.

Mentally, Vishuvappan supported all of them but he had never expressed his thoughts aloud. If the good Vaidyan knew what he really thought, he knew, he would be kicked out of his working space on the verandah.

The workers from the coir factory next door visited the Vaidyan's pharmacy to enjoy the herbal concoction specially brewed for them by the physician to make them energetic after the day's hard work. Habitual consumers would invariably visit the pharmacy punctually on a daily basis to enjoy this treat. Thereafter, they would buy a bundle of small beedis from Vishuvappan which would work out to at least 200 numbers a day. This was his daily income and he was not willing to thwart the arrangement.

'Oh look here', Vishuvappan got excited, 'before you even finished your sentence the army vans are here'.

Two vans rolled a large number of armed policemen into the nearby coir factory.

'That's not the army, it's the reserve police.' The Vaidyan corrected Vishuvappan.

'Will there be any trouble if the army comes?' Vishuvappan was cutting the leaf for rolling the beedis.

'Trouble for whom?' the Vaidyan asked. 'The army will shoot down all the communist goons. Then what is the trouble? What do you know about the Iyer from Mylapore who is our Diwan? What a superb brain he has got! No one in the Iyer community is dumb. Don't you know this brainy Iyer will never allow those communists to play the fool with him?'

The physician sat on his easy chair with his feet up, full of confidence.

The speeding police vans halted in front of the office of the Coir Factory Workers' Union. Sub-Inspector Raman Kutty Nair sprang out of the van, shaking the ground. His eagle eyes rested on the red flag flying high in front of the building.

'Come out all of you', he snarled at his subordinates. 'Four or five of you must charge into the office on the pretext of searching the premises. By then, I will climb up and tear that flag down and fling it on their faces. If they try to attack me, you should encircle them with your guns. Not even a single red flag should be seen in the vicinity of Cherthala district by tomorrow morning. That's the order from the top.'

Raman Kutty Nair was hefty and gigantic; a fair healthy-complexioned Nair aristocrat with a terrorising mustache who commanded much respect from the onlookers. Earlier, he belonged to the horse wing of the army of the Maharajah and was closely connected to the power center in the palace. As the connection extended to a female in the royal family, he was dismissed from the King's employment. Subsequently, he joined the police force.

As the first squad of police barged into the union office, Raman Kutty Nair marched towards the guava tree on which the red flag was hoisted. As the heavy boots stomped on the ground, he sensed a small movement which made him alert and reluctant to advance. The workmen sat there with bowed heads and downcast eyes. As the police approached, they sat up on their knees and started shouting slogans:

Never, never, never will we part with this flag
This flag is our existence
If you are bold enough, come closer.

The sub-inspector looked at the the sea of faces. No leaders were to be seen. All were ordinary workers of lower ranks. Maybe it is not enough to cane and chase them out. At the sight of the rifles only they will scoot, he thought.

'We have come here to remove this flag. Without creating obstacles in doing our duty you should disperse peacefully.' As Raman Nair delivered his orders roughly, he heard a sound of roaring waves.

The sound came from thousands of workmen approaching from the paddy fields like roaring waves of the sea. The factory compound was soon filled with slogan-shouting workers.

'Didn't you hear the orders?' A policeman tried to terrorise them with a gun. 'Move away from the flag.'

'This is our flag', Kunjachhan, a farm worker, came forward, 'you are the people who should move out'.

'Insolent dog! How dare you challenge us?' He pointed his gun towards him. 'With one click I will finish you off.'

'Then finish me', Kunjachhan leapt forward and forced the gun out of his hands.

'Don't let him go easily', the workers shouted together and approached the sub-inspector.

'Oh, president, please come fast', a panicked sub-inspector ran inside the party office and pleaded. The party president, CK Kumara Panicker, was inside the party office.

'But have you not come here to take off that flag?' CK kidded him. 'Why don't you finish that work?'

'President Sir, this time you have to help me out', the sub-inspector pleaded with folded hands.

'Do you know they are about ten thousand?' CK said. 'Having heard that you are planning to remove the flag, they have assembled here. That red flag is their life force. As long as they are alive, they won't let you take it away. It would be better for you to give up that mission.'

'Outside, the workers are holding the policemen captives', the policeman told the party president. 'They won't leave them free till you instruct them.'

'Okay, you may go for the time being', CK warned the policemen. 'You have made a small mistake without knowing our strength, isn't it inspector? Henceforth if you come here to remove the flag, you will know the real strength of the workers.'

The police vacated the premises in a hurry.

Around eight o'clock in the evening, Inspector Koshy, escorted by a few constables, stood in front of the Beedi Workers Union Office. The moment the union secretary Ramachandran came out, the Inspector showered him with obscenities and swore, 'I will see to it that your flag is torn into bits and pieces and make your leaders wear those bits as loin cloth'. He rolled up his sleeves and guffawed. 'You may tell your president, if there is a tomorrow, I will be here at nine o'clock in the morning to tear off that flag in front of your office.'

The hour needle of the clock in the union office waited for Koshy to come for many more hours beyond nine o'clock. Koshy didn't turn up!

'Can the government be humiliated any further?' The feudal lord Kattiyatt Sivarama Panikkar looked at Assistant Commissioner of Police Anthrapper in disgust. 'What else could it mean when the police force deputed to take away the flag comes back like meek squirrels without accomplishing the task? Why are they equipped with clubs and guns? Things cannot be allowed to progress the way they are moving now. As soon as Iyer Sahib comes over, he should be briefed about what's actually going on.'

The dining table in the bungalow on the lake shore was laid with delicious items of food. Pearl spotted fish fry, seer fish fry, delicious oyster fry, fish mango curry, spicy Kerala chicken curry and other mouth-watering dishes. The cook poured a bottle of special malt whisky into six or seven glasses. Instead of adding water, the liquor was mixed with tender coconut water.

The discussions continued while the discussants, all the leading landlords of the area, enjoyed the sumptuous food.

'The party leaders seem to be taking dare-devil decisions', said Parai Tharakan. 'The situation has turned so bad only after that Krishna Pillai made his entry into Alappuzha. Now, leagued with him are others like that Punnoose,

TV Thomas, Vaidyan Varghese, and that scoundrel Sugathan. Did you know, Diwanji got that Sugathan arrested and dumped him in a cell? That was for protesting against the "American Model". Now the police force will subdue his arrogance. Another guy here, that CG Sadashivan, is absconding on being alerted about the arrest warrant on him. I am sure even he will be smoked out by Diwanji's police. It has been heard that in Alappuzha also, many leaders have been arrested like PT Punnoose, Shankaranarayanan Thampi and Simon Asaan under the Domestic Security Act. They will have to remain there for quite some time eating bland wheat balls.'

'This is not enough; they have to put cuffs on that Krishna Pillai.'

'What business has this Krishna Pillai got here', asked Peter George, sipping his glass and tossing a piece of roasted oyster into his mouth, 'Isn't he an outsider?'

'A Nair who has no roots here or in the other world…', said Kimal. 'He is a native of Vaikom. He was a server in a tea shop on the western side of the temple. Once when I went there, he served me coffee.'

'Is that so?' asked Kartha. 'So, the revolution started from the tea cup….'

There was talk that Krishna Pillai worked as a server in a tea shop. Kimal had pulled a fast one based on that. Who would bother even if he bragged that Krishna Pillai had served him tea!

'Now I will tell you something which most of you are not aware of. His brother-in-law was an accountant in a dealers' shop in Alappuzha. Twice he got him jobs in two different coir factories. He didn't stay.'

'Even otherwise how can lazy people make a living on hard work?' laughed Kimal. Is that not the reason for more and more people joining the party?'

'Okay, is this Krishna Pillai a high class Nair or a low class Nair?' asked Kartha.

'Oh, he is a high class Nair. His father and ancestors were all aristocrats', said Advocate Padmanabhan. 'He was a vagabond right from his youth and spent a number of years in North India. He came back during the Vaikom hunger strike days.* He would have been around twenty-one years at that time. He can speak Hindi fluently.'

'Oh, that reminds me', said Kartha. 'God in Vaikom temple was the tenant of landlord Nambiadiri.' (Meaning that the land where the temple stood belonged to this rich landlord.)

'Hats off to Nambiadiri', said Kimal. 'Remember the way he raised a barbed wire barricade to stop low caste people from entering the temple? Didn't he dab lime into the eyes of the guy who promoted the cause of the untouchables?'

'Did you forget the Congressman Kunju Krishna Pillai who was beaten black and blue by the goons?' asked Kartha.

'Oh, that was what I was about to say', said advocate Padmanabhan. 'Do you know who fought and chased out those goons?'

'Who?' They looked at each other.

'This very same Krishna Pillai', said the advocate. 'So, his revolution started from the temple...a good start....'

'So, the advocate is on his side or our side?' Anthrapper burst into laughter.

* The agitation was to demand that people of all cases are allowed access to roads to temples and entry of all castes into temples.

'Should that be doubted', the advocate raised his glass and said cheers. 'But one fact we all have to admit. He is damn bold. I know that personally.'

Advocate closed his eyes and swallowed the contents of his glass.

'It was an incident I witnessed on the verandah of Alappuzha High Court. Our firebrand Inspector Sathyanesan had brought a low-ranking communist comrade in cuffs. He kicked him on his belly with his knees. He was very close to the Diwan you see, and could never stand communists.'

'Umm....' said the Advocate. 'When the inspector raised his legs once again, a man caught hold of his hand strongly. Don't you dare touch him again. Remember, this is a Court. The Inspector was stunned.'

A vintage car came roaring and halted in the front yard. The chatter stopped abruptly.

Anthrapper bolted upright. 'Swamy....'

'DSP Vaidyanatha Iyer...'

'The issue of deputing the army...', Kattiyadan whispered into Antrapper's ears.

'Umm...' Anthrapper murmured.

Everyone got up and stood in deference. The DSP entered with an escort of police officials on all the four sides.

'Is it possible to forget those days so easily?' Comrade Vasu's memories remained intact even at the age of eighty-nine.

'I was twenty-one years old. When the atrocities of goons and police became unbearable, we young people organised a meeting at the market place. Goon Narayanan had let loose a reign of terror in the locality, including molesting and raping young women.'

'Now it is not possible to keep quiet. We have to retaliate', said the young comrade Krishnan.

All the young men agreed to that.

'Do you have the courage to retaliate?' asked Comrade CK Bhaskaran.

'We are ready', all of us said together.

'Then cut that Matheparamban's arms and bring them here', said the senior comrade. 'Let those hands not be available to him to agonise and trouble our men and women.'

'That was like a war front', recollected Comrade Vasu. 'The procession started with fifty people. I walked in front holding the red flag. As we progressed, more and more young men joined us. The procession moved towards Matheparamban's house, shouting slogans. As we reached the neighbouring houses someone shouted, "Here goes Matheparamban's right hand, Raman."'

Raman had finished his lunch and was sitting on his verandah when he heard the slogan-shouting.

'End feudalism.... End Matheparamban's hooliganism.'

Raman sprinted and reached Mathew's house. People shouted from the procession.

'Don't leave him... He is the villain who is inflicting all these atrocities on us.'

'He was the one behind that fourteen-year-old lad being tied to the coconut tree and assaulted cruelly.'

'He is the spy of the police.'

Raman rushed into the unfinished kitchen in Mathew's house and bolted it from the inside.

Mathew's petrified family screamed in chorus. Raman was holding a metallic ring ready to strike the enemy at any time. Somebody broke open the kitchen door using an axe and Raman came close to striking him, calling out obscenities. The mob got more infuriated. Someone took a long iron bar and struck him. They heard a ear-piercing shriek from Raman.

'The party men killed Raman.' People ran around shouting. Actually, Raman was not dead. Beaten up by people all over, he lay there in coma in a pool of blood.

'Without wasting time, lets go and finish off Matheparamban before he escapes.'

The procession moved on to the well-constructed house which stood on a hill top.

His gigantic body smeared with oil all over, Matheparamban stood at the entrance of his house holding two machetes menacingly. The mob got slightly jittery at the sight of him.

'Whoever is man enough to confront me come forward', he bragged. No one said anything for a while. Comrades looked at each other and waited.

'If you have no guts, give me way', a powerful voice said from behind.

Wrestler Comrade Keshavan waded through the crowd and came forward unarmed. Seeing him, more people came forward.

'I will stab you and remove your intestine.' Matheparamban waved his machete and tried to terrorise them.

Then, Matheparamban stepped back and made three somersaults, leaped and broke into a sprint. No one saw him anymore in the vicinity.

Raman was transferred to the hospital where he died.

That night, Matheparamban stabbed three workers, one of whom died; then he went straight to the police camp.

The same night the Vaidyan sent a telegram to the Diwan.

'Situation worse in Cherthala; Request army be deployed.'

He couldn't get a wink of sleep that night. Those who killed Raman could kill others too. There is no safety for the rich and landlords. Before that, all spectacled vipers should be exterminated en masse, he mumbled to himself.

The Vaidyan tossed and turned on the bed, straining his ears for the sound of army trucks.

The Net Spread in Vacuum

Disha came very late from the library. As soon as she came, she walked into Aparajitha's room.

'Where were both of you? Do you know I looked for you everywhere?' she said.

'We were on Anakhan hill', said Aparajitha.

'Then where is Niranjan?' asked Disha.

'I don't know.'

'But didn't both of you go together?' Disha got anxious. 'What happened to you?'

'Oh, a mild headache', Aparajitha tried to evade her.

'Did Mrinalda call you?' Disha asked.

She didn't respond.

He had called Disha while she was returning from the library.

'I have good news, not for you, but Aparajitha. She is going to get a brother or sister. Her mother called me. But doctors have asked her to be careful because it is a high-risk pregnancy, considering her age....'

'Mrinalda', Disha asked him, 'Why is she taking such a risk at this age?'

'She also needs someone in her loneliness you see... her only daughter....'

'Can you blame Aparajitha for that?' Disha tried to defend her friend.

'Rights and wrongs are to be decided by circumstances', said Mrinalda. 'You should tell Aparajitha when she is composed. It may give her some happiness.'

'You should forgive me Mrinalda', Disha said. 'I cannot tell her this.'

Would he have called her later? Sometimes Mrinalda had no sense of timing, thought Disha.

As Disha left, Aparajitha settled in front of her laptop but she was not in a mood for writing.

'What happened?' she tried to recollect. 'Like two fish caught up in a net of delusion?'

Niranjan, where did he go? She thought. He too seemed to be in a trance.

It had happened while they were traversing between awareness and illusion on a fragile bridge made of flimsy twine. While trekking to Anakhan hill, he told her about his dream to visit Santa Clara to see Che's memorial where his remains were kept.

'Would you like to join me?' he had asked.

She thought he was joking and said, 'Why not? I am ready'.

'I am serious, no kidding.' He was looking very serious. His eyes glowed intensely. She saw a reflection of the cover page of Jon Lee Anderson's book in his eyes.

KATALUR

'Don't ask me when, where, how etc… but I will be going for sure… one of these days… to Cuba, Chile, Bolivia, Peru… to the heights of Machhu Pichhu…. Have you not read that poem written by Neruda?'

'From air to air like an empty net…' she hummed.

'Canto General …The Heights of Machu Pichhu'….

'You're a genius…' he held her fingers tightly. 'Do you remember the last lines?'

'Cling to my body like a magnet…' he recited.

'Hasten to my veins and my mouth…

Speak through my words and my blood…'

'I have translated the verse.... Do you want to hear?'

'Like Neruda I will also travel through the nervous system of the earth…from air to air… through an empty net which has nothing to collect.'

Disha knocked on the door.

'Has your headache subsided?'

'Umm...'

Amma entered in wet clothes after her bath and opened the door of the home shrine where the family ancestors were worshipped.

'Today is the New Moon, the night of ancestors…' Disha explained.

Mother kept a few ripe mango leaves and split spine of coconut leaves and water in the shrine.

–'Mango leaves are for cleaning the teeth; split spines for cleaning their tongues and water for rinsing their mouths – it is for the ancestors.' Disha explained.

Disha presented a long list of ancestors including her grandpa Kunjunni and Dashi grandma, ending with her father.

'Was your father not a communist?' Aparajitha looked surprised.

'So what...?' she asked. 'After death all are the same. Here, in most of the party families, they commemorate the day of ancestors.'

Aparajitha laughed.

'You don't have to laugh', said Disha. 'We are remembering your father too....That's why Mother called you...'

'My father?' Aparajitha was surprised again.

'A day to remember those who are dead; that's all', said Disha.

But I remember him every day... always, Aparajitha thought.

Amma came out of the shrine and went to the kitchen. She came back with the favourite sweetmeats of each ancestor and kept them in the shrine and closed the door.

'Did you forget the favourite item of Grandpa Kunjunni?' Disha asked. '*Maraneer*, liquor extracted from coconut trees?'

'Oh no no...it's there in the verandah', Amma told Disha. 'Go and get it.'

Disha brought in a small pot. Aparajitha peeped into it.

'It is toddy', Disha explained. 'Grandpa used to take it every evening. He had earmarked two coconut trees for tapping, exclusively for his consumption.'

Amma kept the pot of liquor and a few tender coconuts with the top portion chopped off, ready for drinking, in the shrine and closed the door.

'Meditate on your father and stand in front of the shrine', Disha told her.

Aparajitha closed her eyes. Her father's face became visible to her inner eyes.

'How long it has been since I have seen my baby with black teeth', he was asking her.

'My father', Aparajitha brought her hands together. 'Is there something called soul?'

Her eyes brimmed.

'My God, I forgot to keep the dish which was your father's favourite!' Mother said in a panicked voice. 'Can't you help me Disha, once in a while on occasions like this?'

Disha was lost in thought at the mention of Father's favourite dish. She remembered that night on which Mother had prepared his favourite dish and had waited for Father to come back home after his night classes at the library.

That evening, Father had told them stories sitting on the verandah. Mother sat on the arm of the chair leaning on to him, removing the tangles in her hair.

'This place was known as Karappuram in olden days, meaning the area left by the sea when it retreated.' Those days Karappuram and Purakkad were two distinct countries, separated by a huge sandbar running miles together from south to north. Next to Purakkad was Chembakassery. Karappuram was a part of the kingdom of Cochin. On the west was the sea and on the eastern side were backwaters known as Vembanattu Kayal.

Initially, Karappuram belonged to the Chembakassery Royal family. In a terrifying war, the Dutch captain Delany fought for the Travancore King, Marthanda Varma, and defeated the King of Chembakassery. Purakkad was subsequently given to the Cochin royal family who were friendly with Chembakassery. Under the Chembakassery royal family, there were nine chieftains who ruled the country. Eight of them were Nairs who were disloyal to the King and soon became the dependents of the Cochin royal family. But Malur Thandan, a non-Nair who belonged to the toddy-tapping community, stood firmly besides the King of Chembakassery, declaring, 'I will be loyal to my King who continues to be the King of Chembakassery'.

Thandan was a bold fighter who had mastered all the eighteen techniques of martial arts. In those days, only the aristocratic women had the right to clothe their torso in public. Thandan declared that women from lower classes should cover their body properly when they came into public places. The Cochin King said 'no' and insisted customs should remain status quo.

Thandan advised everyone that they should not be servile and docile. The King insisted that they continue like that. The King warned that a fine of 101 gold coins would be imposed on whoever defied his orders. Thandan declared that no such fine could be imposed.

Fed up with the insolence of Thandan, the King tried to make the Portuguese his allies to conquer him. Knowing Thandan's valour, the Portuguese withdrew. So, the King decided to kill him through deceit. He hired two assassins to perform the task. Kurup, who specialised in killing and Menon, for his assistance. They waited for an opportunity to carry out their task.

Thandan used to come out to the front yard of his house to wash his hands and rinse his mouth after dinner. His daughter would accompany him with water filled in a brass vessel. On one new moon day the killers waited for him to appear, hiding behind a bush at night. As he bent down to rinse his mouth, the blade of a sword flashed and Thandan's head rolled on the ground separated from his torso. They immediately fled with the head to submit the same at the feet of the King as a token of their valor. A highly pleased King rewarded them with the entire area of Karappuram. 'All these landlords have such histories of deceit behind their making.'

'Our ancestors, the *Ezhavas*, came from Ceylon from where they brought coconut trees to Kerala. They also brought Ayurveda, the ancient medical science to Kerala. They were experts in farming also. All this raised their status as the highest caste in Kerala in those days.'

Mother made a face, reading his lips.

'Look!' Father teased her as usual. 'She made that face only because she is from the Nair caste and thinks that she is a high-class Nair. But after getting married to a Theeyya like me, the Nairs don't entertain her; and she is finding it difficult to mix with my people also.'

'Okay, what do you want for dinner today?' Mother changed the subject. 'Kanji, dry fish fry and ground roasted red chilly chutney?'

'Oh, Mother, can't you change your permanent menu once in a while?'

'That's right', Father said. 'How long it has been Malini, since you made *Kadalapidiyan* (dish made of *channa* dal, gram)?'

'That's true', Disha agreed.

'Thank God, you told me at least now', said Mother. 'Let me soak the channa.'

'Our ancestors, the Theeyyas were Buddhists when they came here from Ceylon.' It was a noble caste. Subsequently, Sankaracharya cult superseded and brought them down from their status in the social order. Those who resisted were beheaded, their property confiscated, and the survivours made slaves.

'Who did that?' Disha had bristled.

'Outsiders who came from the North...the Aryans', Father continued. 'They barged into the peaceful Buddhist Viharas at night, holding blazing torches, and beheaded the Buddhists. Then they went around their shrines carrying the severed heads on round plates. It's in memory of those events, that even now, in Kerala we have this practice of going around our temples, carrying brass plates with lighted lamps on it.'

'Do you know the Buddhist temples are all designed as circular structures? Look at the ancient temples which exist even now. They are all circular in structure. They all are the old Buddhist temples.'

'Now also, if something untoward happens, we call out *Ayyo*... don't we? Why is that?' Father asked.

'The name of the God of Death is *Ayyo*, isn't it?' Mother said.

'Dear Malini', Father said, 'that was another game plan of the Aryans. *Ayyan* means Buddha. Our people used to consider Him as their father. The Aryans interpreted the word *Ayyo* as the name of the Death God's mother and *Ayyan* as *Kalan* the God of Death. These all are the politics employed by invaders when they come barging into a new place'.

There was no Alappuzha district before 1947. All this land was part of Kollam district. 'Finally, when Raja Keshavadas came as Diwan, Karappuram was annexed to the Kingdom of Travancore.' He was looking for a suitable place to build a sea port and discovered Karappuram, which was at that time a marshy land. Karappuram was renamed as Alappuzha, meaning the land of rivers. Diwan Keshavadas became Raja Keshavadas and was renowned as the builder of Alappuzha.

'He built a network of rivers and canals to facilitate smooth transfer of goods to the newly-constructed port.' In the new sea port, ships came from Gujarat and other northern cities. Rice came from Andhra, salt and clothes came from Bombay and in turn our hill products and spices were exported to distant countries by our ships. It was after six decades that the first coir factory of Alappuzha came into being, Darragh Smail Company of the Irish American James Darragh. He brought from the West, spindles to weave coir carpets and other coir items. He was followed by Aspinwall, William Gudekar, Volkart Brothers, Bombay Company, Madhura Company and so on.

All the factories belonged to the Whites except the Alappuzha Coir Company which belonged to local people. There were around twenty-seven large companies. They bought farms and engaged agricultural workers from the locality as workmen to work in those factories. To slave drive them, they brought supervisors. Every day by 7.30 am the first siren would go and by eight am at the third siren the factory work would commence in full swing. Tall chimneys spat out dark clouds of smoke into the sky.

'Child labour was used for winding unending lengths of coir in the spindles for a pittance, a quarter of a rupee.' Wages for extra work done by the children was pocketed by the supervisors. There were no wages for drying the coir standing in blazing hot sun, filling water in the dye tanks or loading the products into the trucks, which was considered as a part of the child labour.

Workmen toiled on millions of spinning wheels and spindles for a daily wage of half a rupee.

Thus, Alappuzha became the city of industrial workers. Inside the factory sheds, the supervisors reined them with their barbaric rules, extracting work till night. Wages were neither given in full nor on time. 'Any workman who dared to ask for wages was showered with obscenities.'

Disha remembered having read the story of Kunjachhan, who was the supervisor in William Gudekkar Company. The supervisor would walk up and down in the factory yard, staring and terrifying the factory workers. The workers had to collect their weekly wages from his house. His wife would hang a cluster of bananas on the verandah. When the workmen arrived, she would give them four bananas whether they wanted it or not. Kunjachhan would deduct four annas, quarter of a rupee towards the cost of the bananas which would be given to his wife separately, while the market rate would be two bananas for one anna. If the workman declined the bananas, the supervisor would impose some kind of a fine on him at the work place.

One day singer Kittappa hummed a song while turning the spinning wheel. He was made to pay a fine of three rupees; one rupee for each word.

'In those days, the industrial workers were not organised you see', Father continued. 'It took another six decades for them to organise. The supervisor of the Empire Company, Bawa, who himself had been a worker earlier, organised a labour meeting of workers, the first of its kind, in the market ground to form the first labour union. Later, it became the Travancore

Labour Association. The Union provided a reading room, library and night classes for the workers. They published a newspaper also by the name *Industrial Worker*. Do you know who taught English in the night classes? – Our Comrade R Sugathan.'

'Later, the Alappuzha workers went on a strike and took out a procession. Do you know who organised that? – Our writer, P Keshavadev, the one who wrote the two books, *Odayil Ninnu* and *Ayalkar*. In those days, he was the secretary of the Union. He was a writer, so he wanted to bring an element of drama into the event. Exactly at 10.30 am, a firework exploded in the vicinity and at that moment the spinning wheels stopped. The workmen left the factory and moved into the streets.'

They came from different localities lead by their leaders, and all the processions met at the meeting ground which became an ocean of humanity. Alappuzha town reverberated with the excitement of the working class who shouted slogans.

Capitalists, pay wages for our work.
Not beatings and death.
Capitalists, we are not slaves henceforth.
We are the fighting working class.

The slogans were coined by R Sugathan. The workers repeated them. However, the strike was not much of a success. Finally, it was decided to present the problems to the food provider, His Highness the King of Travancore. Fifty of them set off from Alappuzha to Thiruvananthapuram on foot. Diwan Habeebullah banned the procession. All the fifty were arrested, sent to jail and beaten up savagely – the blessings of the King!

'After that came Comrade Krishna Pillai. Once he took over the Association, there was a transformation in the line of thinking and it became a rebel organisation.'

That was the first time a red flag was hoisted in Travancore. On the red cloth Simon Asaan painted the sickle and hammer with lime and hoisted the flag to the accompaniment of slogans:

Let the red flag fly higher and higher
Let the red flag soar up in air higher and higher
Let it keep flying higher and higher
All over the world.

The comrades saluted the red flag to the accompaniment of an orchestra. Thirteen resolutions were passed on that day starting with minimum wages.

A minimum wage of rupees thirty for the workers, for eight hours of work in a day

But did the authorities or capitalists agree to do that? No!

Instead, they cut down the wages and assaulted those who protested, using the police and goons.... Finally, it became evident that there was no other alternative but to organise a strike all over the land. Sir CP passed an order to suppress the strike call. Leaders like Comrade Sugathan and other workers skipped work. Coir factories stood still. Workers led a procession to the police station, demanding release of their leaders. 'The first martyr of the struggle for the rights of the working class died a horrible death. He was beaten to death by the police... Comrade Bawa.'

Mother came outside to the front verandah.

'This is an institution nurtured by the blood and sacrifices of countless comrades', Father continued emotionally. 'Those who sprouted in fire will not fade away in sunlight.'

'Malini', Father called out, 'please give me my shirt and mundu. Fetch my umbrella too. It looks like it's going to rain'.

'Where are you going at this time of the day?' Amma looked unhappy.

'Just till the party office. I have some work', said Father.

Mother came with the shirt and said, 'Please come soon or your dinner will go cold'.

'Where is the kid?' Father enquired about Niranjan.

'He slept long ago', Amma said.

'So soon?' asked Father. 'Ask him to concentrate on his studies. I couldn't make much of my life, having spent my entire life building up the party, but in future days, one will have to work keeping in view one's own life.'

'Why do you tell all this now?' Disha grimaced. 'There are so many party men here who have made enough for their lives. But you didn't want to do that.'

Father had looked at her sternly. 'There will be people like that also; you know that petty bourgeois culture has spread in the party to an undesirable level.'

'The needs of party workers are no longer restricted to small things like black tea, snacks and rolled beedi. That period has come to an end Father', she said. 'You are the only one who is stuck to that time.'

Father started to walk. When he reached the gate, he stopped and turned back and asked her, 'Have you read Liu Shaoqi's book, *How to become a Good Communist*? A copy is in my wooden almirah. In that it says….' Without completing the sentence, he walked away.

As he walked away, it started raining. It became a storm. High speed winds uprooted the huge mango tree in the courtyard.

The cows started mooing in terror. A few tiles from the roof top flew away. The rain didn't cease at all. Mother waited for Father to serve him his favourite dish. He didn't turn up. Around midnight, party colleagues brought his body home. He had fainted while talking to his party comrades at the party office. They carried him to the hospital but before reaching there....

Father had been talking to them in a vehement tone...borrowing Liu Shaoqi's words...:

'We should not try to correct our lapses with further lapses. We have to firmly stand by the side of "right and justice" to correct the lapses, uncompromisingly. It is true that some of our comrades are indulging in wrong activities against the party's ideologies. They are making the party a tool to meet their vested interests. There is an old Chinese proverb. "If a sharp knife makes a wound on our body it will heal. But the wound inflicted to the minds through sharp words will never heal." A few of our senior colleagues are dragging our internal problems to the streets for cheap propaganda. They have to remember one thing. The party is our mother. It's that mother they are ...', his words had broken. He had collapsed on to the floor....

Mother opened the door of the shrine and came out.

'The turn of the ancestors is over', said Disha. 'Now it is our turn, the turn of the living.'

Mother brought each of the items out.

'First take Grandpa's favourite item', Disha hurried. 'If Niranjan comes we won't get a drop.'

She poured the liquor into two glasses and raised a toast, 'cheers'.

'We can have Father's favourite dish as a starter. It's a good combination.'

Red Sea Changing Its Course

Thirty comrades from different parts of the State met secretly in the house of Comrade PG Padmanabhan in Pathirapalli. The meeting was on the occasion of the visit of charismatic communist leaders, AK Gopalan and PK Kunjambu. Both of them were in hiding from the police and participated in meetings under false names. Comrade Gopalan was in the midst of taking a class for the farm workers:

'Farm workers should unite. They are the wealth creators of the society, the village and the country. They are the people who convert the land into a goldmine. They have the right to get the value for their sweat and contribution towards wealth creation, not as a token of generosity from the landlords but as their birthright. It has now become necessary for the labour class to have an organisation to take up the challenges of fighting for their rights. As the first step, we are proposing to assign you to different batches to go to different parts of Kuttanad like Kainakari, Mangombu, Pulinkunnu, Chambakulam,

Nedumudi, Kavalam, Nilamberur, Eera, Cherukara and other localities for impressing upon them the need for formation of such an organisation. Each of you will be given one *chakram* (money coin prevalent in those days). Remember that this is being given to you to facilitate transforming our toiling brethren from ignorance to a knowledgeable society and making them capable of running the government machinery of our country.'

Suddenly Comrade Gopalan became silent and looked at the entrance and asked, 'Who is that?' Someone was there at the entrance. In those days, CIDs were moving in disguise in order to know the movements of the party. A weak lean man came near the fence. Something was seen weighing down the pouch of his mundu. He came and sat down at the back row. He took something from the pouch and began to chew. PG Padmanabhan came near him and asked, 'What are you eating alone. We are also hungry'. He was shocked when he saw that he had been eating the oil cake given to cattle. The man told PG that he was a farmer who had come all the way from Kommadi. As he was too weak, no one called him for work. He had been starving for the past three-four days. He had somehow managed to get some oil cake that day.

PG helped him to get up and offered him some rice gruel. Comrade's eyes watered. 'This is the condition of our poor farmers who work in the fields.' He wiped his tears.

Kuttanad – the rice bowl of Kerala – in those days used to be owned by four or five rich feudal families known as Murikkan, Mangombu, Kavalakkan and Chale represented by a man called Panikkar.

Comrade PG Padmanabhan read out the names of workers detailed for each place. They were MT Chandrasenan,

NSP Panikkar, VS Achuthanandan CK Keshavan, MK Sukumaran, R Thankappan….

'All of you should go in batches to these places', said AKG. 'You have to work as a Committee in Kuttanad.'

'But we are not familiar with all those localities', Thankappan, expressing his doubts, said. 'Where will we stay?'

It was Comrade Kunjambu who replied to that question. 'After all, you are going to meet human beings. Will there not be farm workers like you there? You have to go to their houses and make them understand. They will understand what you are talking about. Blood will recognise blood!'

And blood did recognise blood.

It was about three years before the Punnapra-Vayalar Uprising that the Communist Party started getting rooted there. During war time, price of food grains shot up. Agricultural workers demanded paddy as wages instead of money. By then, workers had established Communist Party cells in major areas like Kinakeri, Kavalam and Thakazhi. They christened their organisation as Thiruvithamkoor Agricultural Workers Union and elected Comrade Vaidyan TK Varghese as its president.

Head of the feudal family Mangombu was walking on the narrow road dividing the agricultural fields. His manager, another Raman Nair, was trailing behind him. There were other servants holding the brass container containing betel leaves, areca nuts, lime and tobacco and mud pots filled with cool tender coconut water sprinkled with herbs to quench the master's thirst.

'So harvesting is going on in full swing, isn't it?' he asked his manager.

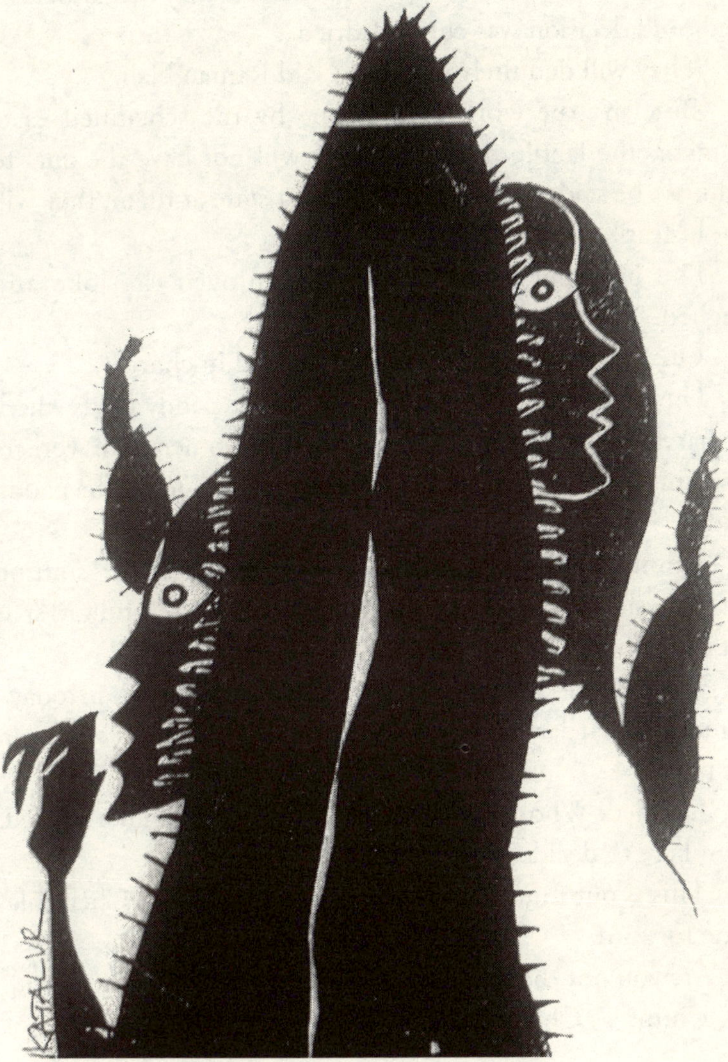

'Yes, of course', Raman Nair responded immediately, 'but there is a small dispute regarding the settlement of wages. The Union has intervened'.

'There is no question of giving whatever they demand.' The landlord's decision was cut-and-dried.

'They will definitely demand', said Raman Nair.

'But isn't the work being done by the scheduled caste women?' the landlord asked. 'They will not have the guts to fight us', he said confidently. 'If we just stare at them, they will piss in fear!'

The manager and the servants enjoyed the joke and laughed.

'Oh, yes, yes...that's true', they replied in chorus.

The landlord and company reached the paddy fields where the harvesting was going on. As soon as the women farm workers saw him, they stopped their work and stepped out of the paddy fields.

'Umm...what's happening...all of you... together?' spitting out the residue of betel leaves from his mouth, the landlord spat out a question.

'We have decided to demand your final decision today.' Karambi, their leader, gestured as if sharpening the sickle on her palm.

'Decided? Who decides? What decision?' the landlord yelled. 'I am here to decide these things.'

'This is our union's decision.' Another woman, Chenthila, came forward.

'Are you not the daughter of Karatha?'

'Umm...', Chenthila said.

The landlord looked her up and down. He did not know when the young girl had blossomed into a beautiful young woman.

'You give her whatever she wants', he murmured into the manager's ears.

'Umm....' The manager had got the message.

'By evening have your bath, deck up and come and see me', Raman Nair whispered the message into Chenthila's ears.

'Why should I come alone?' The young woman responded in great spirits. 'In that case, all of us will take bath, deck ourselves and come together to meet with you.'

This girl seemed to be a spicy chilly. The feudal lord was impressed by her confidence. Oh, how I wish the sun sets in the west at the earliest! He thought.

'We can go into other matters only after settling the paddy-based wages', said Kannamma, another woman. 'Is the feudal master going to give us his decision now and here?' she asked.

'I am not willing to give you a final decision,' the lord was firm. 'Who here is bold enough to demand a decision from me, while standing in my paddy fields? I would like to see how far you will go.'

'In that case, we will continue the harvesting only after a decision has been taken', Karambi tucked her sickle in her waist.

There was a movement in the center of the abundant paddy fields where the plants heavy with grains were bent towards the ground. The landlord and his manager looked in that direction. A group of union volunteers, with red bands tied around their waists, stood scattered in the fields. They stood up swirling their wooden staffs, as if unaware of what was going on between the landlord and the workwomen.

'Water...Rama water...', the petrified landlord asked his manager. The manager offered the mud pot containing coconut water to his master. Before he could take it to his lips, Chenthila came forward and snatched the pot.

'Are you going to give us your decision now or not?' She tightened her grip on the mud pot. 'You can enjoy the coconut water after that.'

The landlord sat on the mud road running between the paddy fields. He felt faint. Everything around him seemed to be swirling.

'How can master become so weak?' Chenthila chided him. 'Are we not to meet in the evening? Isn't it so, Manager Sir?' She looked at the manager coyly. The women suppressed their giggles.

'Raman Nair', the master called out to his manager, '...settle the matter in any possible way'.

Hearing that, the thrilled volunteers shouted, 'Long live worker's unity'. The women workers also joined the chorus.

'In that case master, you can now drink your coconut water.' Chenthila lowered the mud pot to his lips and chided, 'What time in the evening would you like me to visit you, master? Please finalise that too.' The landlord couldn't find his tongue to answer that.

The decision was uniformly implemented covering the entire agricultural region of Kuttanad.

The Farming Workers' Union started making preparations for celebrating their first annual day at a location called Mampuzhakary, nearby. Red flags fluttered from big and small boats drifting in the backwaters and rivers moving towards the venue. Armies of farm workers holding red flags marched towards Mampuzhakary in full enthusiasm. Mampuzhakary was soon converted into a red sea, boosting up their confidence. Leaders like PT Punnoose, K George and CS Gopalapillai arrived at the battle field, transmitting energy to inspire the followers.

President Varghese Vaidyan called out to them in gusto through a megaphone:

'Landlords, exploiters, can you hear your death knell now? Come to Mampuzhakary to see the power of workers. It's time for all of you to realise the mountains of food grains you are hoarding in your granaries come from the relentless efforts of these workers working day and night, living in their humble huts. Be warned, these workers will demolish your mansions....'

Varghese Vaidyan paused, hearing the sounds of approaching police boots. As he turned around, he saw a high-ranking police officer escorted by a group of armed policemen. He fished out a paper from his khaki trousers and handed it over to Varghese Vaidyan.

'What is this?' Vaidyan stared into the eyes of the police officer.

'Ban order', the officer informed him. 'This is an order banning this function, issued by the Kollam District Magistrate. All of you have to disperse immediately.'

'If we don't...?' Vaidyan challenged the police officer.

'We will have to use force and make arrests.'

'In that case arrest us.' Vaidyan pushed the police officer with force.

The police force pounced on him, holding their guns.

The police officer stopped them. 'No, we are surrounded by a red sea.'

The workers turned into roaring waves, shouting slogans against the police force.

The police officer said firmly to Vaidyan, 'You have to respect the orders and disperse immediately.'

'The ban order is only within Kollam District, isn't it', asked TP Punnoose.

'Umm...' said the police officer.

'We have to discuss this among us', said Punnoose.

After a short discussion, he said, 'All right, we will respect the ban order. The police officer is decent. Let's not have any unnecessary confrontation'.

'We will all meet at Koduppunna Padanilam.' Varghese Vaidyan announced through his megaphone, 'All of you please march towards Padanilam'.

Padanilam was situated three miles away, in Kottayam District. Leaving the police behind, the red sea started flowing towards Padanilam.

From the boats, men and women challenged the police. 'It is okay... if it is to be in Padanilam let it be in Padanilam. Come and fight with us.'s

The police stood unsure of what to do, watching the flow of humanity.

It was abozut three months earlier that the fishermen in Cherthala had decided to form a union. Prior to that Ambalapuzha Fishermen's Union had come into being. They were active on the seashores; Vattayaal, Vadakkal and Punnapra. Simon Asaan was the one who took lead in these activities. His house was to the west of the Vattayaal Church. He was a teacher in the church school, teaching scriptures.

The church came to know that he was mixing divine directives with communism and an angry priest dismissed him from his services saying, 'You Satan, you should not be seen in this churchyard... people like you will be damned forever.'

Thus Vattayaal Simon stepped down from the church and proceeded to Vattayaal beach. The beach was empty. He lay down there with his head resting on his arm as a pillow. Nicolas's son Benjamin chanced to pass that way. Nicolas was a VIP of the seashore.

'I heard from my father that you are going to be expelled by the church.' Benjamin came near Simon, 'Why do you get involved in such prohibited activities?'

'What is this prohibited activity?' Simon asked.

'Communism', the boy said. 'What did you mean by saying that Jesus Christ is a communist in the Sunday class?'

'Oh, what's wrong in that?' Simon asked.

'It's not correct to say that Jesus Christ is a communist', the boy was vehement.

'Umm...That may be true', Simon said. 'There was no Communist Party in those days, you see.'

'Had it been there?' The boy got curious.

'Jesus would have marched through the streets in Jerusalem holding a red flag. Was he not the one who got the fake clergy and fraud nobility whipped? Didn't he demolish their churches? Didn't he uplift the oppressed and liberate the chained? Didn't he give food to the famished and resurrect the dead? Didn't he stand against the malpractices of the wicked? Now, you tell me, what's the difference between the communists and Jesus Christ?'

'Oh, if we see from that angle, what you say is correct', Benjamin was in a fix. 'But still....'

'Are you aware of the intentions behind the activities of these church authorities, hand in glove with Mudalalis like your father? Are they not exploiting the poor fishing workmen – who risk even their lives while making a living by venturing out in the stormy seas – using religion as a whip? Are they not robbing these already poor men of their meager income for subsistence, pushing them into absolute poverty? Are they not precipitating violence among people? Do you remember what triggered off that unrest in the seashore sometime back? You were all small kids those days. The Church vicar made the bell boy summon all the believers to the churchyard by ringing the emergency bells and instructed them to attack the Muslim community members living in the vicinity with whatever weapons available to them in the name of God. Do you know how many Muslims died, as the fishermen in their drunken stupor immediately obeyed those orders?'

'What was the reason for such an atrocity?' Benjamin enquired.

'Some of the hoodlums passed some obscene comments on a few Christian women who were crossing the bridge near the burial ground. They might have been Muslims. But how can one hold the entire Muslim community, who lead a decent life, responsible for the offence? Which God said that humans should fight and kill each other? If Jesus was to return to the present times, he would whip his own church men for this offence!'

'If we look at things from this angle, what you say is also correct', Benjamin said getting up from the bench, ready to walk away. 'If I continue to sit here, I also may not feel like stepping inside the Church. Let that not happen. It's better for me to leave now. Ok, bye.'

Simon Anthony continued to lie on the beach and stare at the sea. He felt that it was time to save the fisherfolk from these exploitations by making them aware of their own plight and rights. He decided that he would make them literate as and when he got time and convince them about their rights.

'You have to learn to read and write', he told those who didn't even know how to calculate the selling price of a fish, 'only then you will have freedom from this bondage'.

Thus, Simon Antony became Simon Asaan, meaning Simon, the teacher. It was during those days that Comrade AV Kunjambu was offered the Communist Party membership. There were two Communist Party members from the Latin Catholic community; Simon Asaan and KV Pathrose.

In those days all fishing equipment including the boats and fishing nets belonged to Mudalalis hailing from the seashore. Only they had the authority to decide who could go fishing in their boats. They fixed the price for the catch. From that price, fifty per cent belonged to the Mudalali towards the rent for the boat and net; then the Church claimed a certain percentage, as offerings to the Church followed by the share of the chief of the community. The workers got only whatever was left after that, may be some twenty per cent. If the net got damaged, the workers had to mend it. Once all the computations were over, the workers would end up as debtors again, despite all their hard work.

The boats set off to the deep sea, either early in morning or late in the evening. If it was in the evening some of the owners of the boats would come to the seashore to find out who had gone to the sea in his boat. Once the boat faded away in the distance and dusk set in, they entered the huts of those with good looking young wives. If they resisted, the women were threatened, 'your husband who has gone into the deep seas will lose his job... your family will starve… your husband may even be killed and thrown into the sea….'

So that was what happened to Chethikkaran Yaakov. He was well-known for his strong and iron body. He could pull out a boat stuck deep in the sand on the seashore with just one hand. He was strong enough to drag a huge hairy shark from the deep sea ashore, tied to the ridge of the boat. The moment he entered a boat he would be the unquestionable anchor.

As the keys in her keyboard started moving to weave the story of Yaakov, Mrinalda's phone came.

'How have you been doing?' he asked in Bengali.

'Umm… Ok', she replied.

'Ranbir is a little unhappy that you are not responding to his calls', said Mrinalda.

It was true. Ranbir had called several times. She had not answered his calls deliberately.

'I would have been busy writing', she said.

'His number would have been in the list of missed calls', Mrinalda was annoyed. 'Couldn't you have called him back?'

'I intended to call him back', she said.

'No, no, you are deliberately avoiding him. Where are you trying to abscond?'

'Abscond?' she laughed. 'Don't you know Mrinalda, that I don't have a place even to abscond to?'

Mrinalda became silent.

Ranbir was still walking over the delicate bridge of love. She knew that. That was the reason why she decided not to encourage him.

His love had sprouted in the tears at the time of the final farewell to Comrade Sathyadas. After returning from the cemetery, he had tapped on her shoulders and consoled her saying, 'Aparajitha (that was how he addressed her), don't ever feel that you are alone. Henceforth I will be with you forever.'

'I know, not only you, all of you are with me...but my father...' her voice cracked. She covered her face with her hands.

'Aparajitha', he took hold of her hands. 'I mean....'

She looked at him with tears misting her eyes. His eyes were sparkling with love which had been triggered off by her misery; the agony at the unexpected departure of her father.

Later, when she was passing by the hostel 'Tapati', where he lived, he climbed down the steps and approached her.

'Aparajitha wait...', he came close, 'wait, I want to talk to you.'

She stopped. 'Make it fast. I am in a hurry.'

'I messaged you several times', he said, 'I need a reply.'

'Let's be good friends', she said. 'That's my reply.'

'You should call him', Mrinalda continued on the phone.

'What for?' She laughed. 'He is eccentric!'

'I am telling you this because Comrade Sathyadas was my guide too', Mrinalda said. 'He will be able to provide you with a good life. As you know, his family is well known in Patiala. Besides, ideologically both of you ....'

'Mrinalda, I am in the midst of trying to recognise the soil under my feet... let me complete that', she laughed.

'Oh, your roots!' Mrinalda reflected 'Were you able to discover them?'

'No traces so far', she said in disappointment. 'I have lost my hopes. Who knows Comrade Sathyadas in this village? His roots were pulled out from this soil long ago. My hopes are also uprooted.'

'Those roots cannot be uprooted', Mrinalda said. 'You will be able to discover them. May you accomplish it at the earliest!'

She thanked him. He disconnected the phone.

She woke up the keys on the keyboard to give life to the crucified love of Yaakov and Rosa Kutty.

Shark that Cuts Across the Waves

His was love at first sight when he met Rosa Kutty at the famous Athungal Church, where Yaakov played the clarinet. Clad in a white skirt reaching till her ankles and covering her head with a snow white net, as she glided towards the shade of the ornate umbrella with pearls hanging from it, Yaakov's melody flapped its wings and soared high up into the sky through the tiny holes in the clarinet. Rosa Kutty sneaked a glance through the corner of her eye at Yaakov attired in the glittering robes of the church orchestra.

Rosa Kutty was the daughter of Ouseph Marakkar. His elder daughter was married to a boy from the nearby village. Rosa Kutty, who was next, took care of the household when Marakkar went to the outer seas for fishing. The youngest was a son who was a small kid. Yaakov tried to persuade Rosa Kutty to be his wife and go along with him. Rosa Kutty was also happy about getting married to him; but she was reluctant to leave her father and kid brother in their village to start a family with Yaakov in another distant village. Yaakov was also in two minds about leaving his village but since there was no other alternative, he decided to do so. Ouseph Marakkar also gave his consent for the marriage. They decided to have the betrothal ceremony on the Sunday before Palm Sunday.

As Rosa Kutty was returning from the church, she saw Yaakov approaching from a distance. She waited for him under a berry tree. 'What's in this packet?' Rosa Kutty saw the gift pack he was holding.

'Oh, this is for my Rosa Kutty', Yaakov said, 'Will you please stretch your hands for me?'

'Why?' Rosa Kutty blushed.

'Give me your hands.'

Rosa Kutty extended her hands. As he opened the packet, glass bangles jingled and he slipped them on to her hands

'They are fabulous', Rosa Kutty looked at the bangles.

'Shouldn't we break them?' Yaakov asked her mischievously.

'Get lost!' Rosa Kutty waved her hands in fake anger.

'After the betrothal, I will come by your house', Yaakov said. 'I cannot wait till the marriage.'

'When?' Rosa Kutty asked.

'When your father leaves for the sea', he said.

'At night?'

'Um…'

'No way', she said. 'I won't open the door. All that cannot happen now. We will wait for the wedding to be over.'

She ran away swinging her hands and jingling the glass bangles.

Later in the evening, Ouseph Marakkar reached the seashore to take off to the sea. As he was pushing the boat into the water, the owner of the boat, Anthappan Mudalali came to the beach.

'Oho… ho, you have become a big person now... Ouseph', he mocked at the fisherman.

Ouseph looked puzzled, not knowing what the Mudalali had in his mind.

'It was the church priest who gave me the news about the betrothal of your daughter Rosa Kutty', said the Mudalali. 'Even after working on my boat, you didn't even bother to tell me.'

Ouseph didn't reply.

'Just think, here in this locality itself how many strong, bold and eligible young men are there to marry her!' Mudalali expressed his disquiet. 'Still, your daughter liked an outsider only. Anyway, if you need any cash for the function, do come to me. You don't have to consider that amount as a loan.'

A spark of fire burnt a hole in Ouseph's heart. He stood rooted to the seashore, unable to move.

'Anthrayose', he beckoned his neighbour, 'Keep an eye on my hut till I come back from the sea.'

As usual, Anthrayose nodded and expressed his willingness.

It's time to stop the night work, Ouseph thought. 'I should opt for day work till Rosa Kutty's wedding.' He pushed his boat into the water and hopped on to it and stood firmly at the rudder. Anthappan Mudalali watched the boat slicing the waves and vanishing into the horizons with Ouseph at the helm.

Keeping an eye on the sea waves moving towards the west, Ouseph Marakkar kept glancing back at the shore where Anthappan Mudali was standing still, lost in thought. As the boat entered the outer sea, he ran into Yaakov who was expertly gliding his boat against the dominant south-west wind. It was a New Moon night. On such nights, the sea turns violent with huge waves hurling the boats. Still, Yaakov maneuvered his boat smartly, cutting across the waves in great speed.

'He will take care of Rosa Kutty like a treasure', Ouseph complimented himself for having found a good bridegroom for his daughter.

Anthrayose, Ouseph's friend and neighbour, sat in front of the house in guard till Rosa Kutty finished her dinner and spread her mat for sleeping. The moment her younger brother saw the spread mat, he lay down and started snoring.

At midnight Rosa Kutty was woken up by a continuous knock on the door.

'Who is that?' she asked.

'It's me. Open the door', someone said softly.

'Who?' Rosa Kutty was in doubt. Could that be Yaakov? She remembered him asking her whether he could visit her at night.

'Is that Yaakov?' she asked.

'Umm....' Outside, from the darkness she heard a hum.

'But our engagement is still not over, how can we....?'

'You open the door Rosa Kutty', the voice repeated in hushed tones.

'What is this Yaakov, at this untimely hour?'

As she opened the door slightly, she saw Anthappan Mudalali with a lighted torch in his hand, reeking of stale liquor.

Immediately she tried to close the door, but he barged into the room and covered her mouth. Two of his accomplices tied her hands and legs. They carried her to an empty boat lying on the seashore. When she opened her mouth to scream, they tied her mouth. She tried to wriggle out of their clutches when Anthappan entered the boat. He scanned her body with his torch. Fear made her mute. 'Let this Anthappan Mudalali see your body properly Rosa Kutty.'

He ran the torch light from her head to toe. 'Just ask your elder sister Elikutty. She could leave this shore only after giving me my rightful share. Have you ever looked at the face of her child carefully? Do you know whose face the child resembles? Your father also knows this. I had an eye on you from the time you were as tiny as a fish. Do you know the rule of this shore? Whatever a rich man deserves as a right, it should be given to him. Whatever a saint deserves, that should be given to him!'

A huge wave pushed its way to the shore. Anthappan freed his hands, flinging his torch on the sand and made her still, using both his hands. Her crushed glass bangles scattered on the floor of the boat. Wild breeze whistled. Her gut-wrenching screams for Yaakov echoed on the seashore as the Mudalali's thick black lips hushed her.

As Yaakov came ashore the next day, he heard about his fiancée's fate. He rushed to her house. It was locked. He went near the boat and looked inside, sobbing with a broken heart, at the sight of the crushed bangle pieces. 'Why did you break them, you devil of a man… why did you blight my woman?' He became a whirlwind and rushed to the storage sheds and boats belonging to the Mudalali and set them ablaze. People who lived on the seashore crowded in excitement to watch the flames leap high. Snatching an oar, Yaakov ran to the Mudalali's house. 'If you are man enough, come out; you the one born of Satan', Yaakov challenged. The Mudalali did not step out. On the second day, the waves swept ashore the bruised and busted body of Yaakov; like the body of a gigantic sword fish.

The labour union convened its first meeting on this seashore. The fishermen decided not to go fishing that day. The landlord Antony also received a crudely-printed notice of the meeting. By evening, around two hundred workers assembled at the seashore. Antony and his goons surrounded the workmen and flung fine sand on their faces. As the attack came abruptly, with the sand blinding them, they ran helter-skelter. Thus, the first attempt to convene a labour union meeting was thwarted.

After a week, the meeting was convened again at the same venue. Thousands of workers assembled. This time they came armed with long ores and challenged, 'If a fistfight is the need of the hour, we have come prepared for that too. These hands callused by holding the ores for years are indeed very powerful'. There was no sign of Antony and his men.

A long array of frontline leaders spoke at the gathering. By the time the last of the speakers finished his speech, a cycle rickshaw halted on the road leading to the seashore. That was the first time the labourers of the seashore were getting to see TV Thomas. He advanced forward to address them in the midst of an uproar of slogans, Inquilab Zindabad.

'Landlords and church authorities are holding you in captivity. Who is fixing the market price of the fish you bring to the market in abundance from the sea, risking your lives? Who is fixing the price for your labour? – you or those in power? My dear brothers, you are being exploited for generations. Does this sea belong to the bourgeois landlords? No. Does this wealth of fish belong to the bourgeois? Absolutely not. Is there anyone paying a price for the fish that belong to the sea? Not at all. So, when does the fish acquire a value in price? It happens when you bring your harvest of fish ashore, risking your lives, toiling and fighting with the waves in the sea. So, can't you see that it is your labour that is being priced when a price is fixed for fish?'

TV Thomas paused and looked around. The fishermen looked at each other.

'Is it the price of the fish or the price for your efforts?' Simon Asaan repeated the question.

Suddenly, as if a flash or inner realisation hit them, they roared, 'For our hard work'.

'Yes' TV said. 'That price is rightfully yours. You are the inheritors of the sea, inheritors incapacitated by the bourgeois and church authorities who stop you from enjoying it. You, the fishermen should rise above this bourgeois class and fight with them with the same spirit and bravery with which you fight with the sea waves.'

TV's speech enthralled the workers.

'Henceforth, we will fix the price of our catch in the market', Simon Asaan announced. 'Workers who stay back ashore will safeguard the houses of those who go for work in the outer seas.'

Fishermen roared in excitement, Inquilab Zindabad, 'Hail the Fishermen's Union'.

Red flags formed crimson lines on the seashore.

'There is a specialty about the sea here', said Vasudevan Master. 'It is the abundant supply of prawns from Kayamkulam to Palli canal, from north to south. Have you not read the famous

Malayalam novel *Chemmeen*, meaning prawns? It is explained in that book....'

Aparajitha recollected Karuthamma and Parikutty, the hero and heroine of the novel. She recollected the sharp camera eyes of Marcus Bartley. She remembered the film editor Hrishikesh Mukherjee. She remembered Salil Da, the music director of the movie. She remembered the lyrics of the wonderful song rendered by the famous singer Manna Dey. She had watched the movie along with her father when she was a kid long long ago in Calcutta, and again in Delhi with her friends.

Vasudevan Master walked through the crowd at the seashore.

'During the monsoon months, the sea is in turmoil and has an uncontrollable temper', he continued, 'but as autumn sets in, she becomes docile. That is when shoals of prawns glide in. We can figure out its arrival with the smell of mud spreading on the shore. It is the harvesting time for fish like prawn, mackerel, sardine and the like. They don't stay in one part of the sea for a long time. It has taken at least twenty years for them to come back.'

He stood looking at the sea.

On the seashore among the crowd of *chakara*, Aparajitha looked for the characters of the novel – Chempan Kunju, Parikutty, Palani, Karuthamma....

Modern fishing boats and country boats drifted on the surface of the sea. On the shore, peddlers and makeshift eateries were crowded with people. Brokers and truck drivers stood waiting for the arrival of the fishing boats.

'In olden days, during chakara time, they used to construct temporary storage sheds all over the seashore. The bourgeois used to buy the whole catch, dry and stock them in these storage sheds. Rich traders from Cochin, known as Settus, would reach the seashore to buy the stocked fish for exporting to Ceylon, Rangoon and Singapore. Nowadays, the moment a boat nears the shore, truck drivers bargain for the entire catch and flee away with the same.'

'Then what does the fisherman get?' Aparajitha asked.

'All that is leftover, the same now as it was in olden days.' Vasudevan Master smiled ruefully.

'The exploited never recognise the changes in the wardrobe of the exploiter', she told herself.

Disha looked at her.

'Oh, that is a Bengali proverb', explained Aparajitha.

Knight on a Chessboard

Lords of ill-gotten wealth
Get ready for a shock
Get ready for a horror

Anakhashayan was walking on the village road singing loudly. His elder brother Chathu was also with him. Chathu was Anakhashayan's second elder brother, Raghavan being the eldest of the brothers. Though Chathu was older to Anakhashayan, he was a tiny boy whom Anakhashayan could carry around. Weak lungs and severe respiratory problems had stunted his normal growth. It was unbearable to watch him struggling for breath when the lungs struck work, especially on the full moon and new moon days when all health disorders took a bad turn. Anakhashayan used to move away from the house, unable to watch his brother suffering. Chathu used to dread the darkness of the night and the moonlight in the sky. As the moon rose high in the sky, his breath staggered with phlegm ...like pigeons.

'Gods in heavens! How can I bear to watch this agony!' their mother, Kali Kutty would start beating on her breast in helplessness.

It was during the Onam festival day that a sharp piece of broken glass had pierced his foot. During the festival this year, it was Chathu who played the role of Maveli, the mythological emperor who visited his old empire once in a year on Onam day. Last year it was Anakhashayan who had played Maveli. Suddenly he had grown tall like a coconut tree and the villagers found Chathu more appropriate to play the role.

'If Anakhashayan is to play the role, we won't have sufficient grass to weave the garment', said Pavithran, an opinionated leader in the village. The costume for the role was made of woven wild grass grown in the village and they felt Chathu was the right size to wear the same this time. So, attired in the costume and holding an umbrella made of palm tree leaves, Chathu was going around the village as the emperor paying visits to his subjects. A group of singers preceded him, singing the Onam song

'Maveli has arrived… as he comes once every year… he has come to enjoy the Onam feast…'

As the song reached its climax, Chathu lost himself in excitement and danced over the sand dunes from where a hidden treacherous glass piece pierced his feet. Whatever money had been collected as donations for the function was paid to the village vaidyan for Chathu's treatment.

They tried all sorts of herbal and traditional medicinal treatments which did not help. The wound remained septic and the vaidyan suggested that the boy be taken to the local dispensary. Anakhashayan carried him on his shoulders to the dispensary where the compounder administered an injection in Chathu's buttock. Anakhashayan was surprised that the wound on the leg was healed by an injection in the buttocks. The swelling on the foot subsided. The wound was surgically cleaned and dressed. Chathu could manage to walk to the dispensary by the time the dressing had to be changed for the second time. Now they were walking back from the dispensary after attending to the wound the third time.

Anakhashayan moved on to the next song:

We are not slaves any more
No one can dictate to us any more
We will fight with firm feet...

'Do you know who composed these lyrics, brother Chathu?' Anakhashayan asked his brother.

'You only tell me', said Chathu, who was not very well informed about such worldly matters.

'Oh, this is written by our Comrade', said Anakhashayan. 'I was not aware of that. It was Comrade Bhaskaran who told me this when I participated in the procession in Ponnamveli (a nearby village).'

'Oh, who is this Comrade?' Chathu asked innocently.

'Hey, you are irritating me now. I will hurl you into that canal.' Anakhashayan was infuriated. 'You are asking which Comrade? Which comrade do we refer to as Comrade without adding the name? Comrade Krishna Pillai! Who else could that be?'

Chathu did not know anything about the workers' struggles in the neighbourhood. Because of his frailty, he never ventured out of their house much. Till then, he had not even attended a single party meeting.

'Poor thing, has just got a brief respite from his illness!' Anakhashayan was overcome by sympathy for his elder brother. 'Oh, I said that just out of a sudden irritation. Please don't feel hurt', he told Chathu.

'Even otherwise, why would I feel hurt?' Chathu laughed 'Don't I know you are a little short-tempered?'

They kept walking and finally reached the canal.

'Oh, where is the palm tree bridge which was here when we came? Who removed it?' Anakhashayan stood hesitatingly, wondering how to cut across the canal without the bridge. The canal was about six feet wide. The current in the waist deep water was forceful. They would definitely get wet if they walked across the canal. Anakhashayan looked around.

At a little distance on the other side of the canal, Chandy Anthrapper, owner of the surrounding property and his manager Showryan Mappila were supervising the work of a few farm workers who were digging round cavities under the coconut trees.

'Hello Showryan Mappila, what happened to the palm bridge which was here when we went this way?'Anakhashayan queried.

'Who the hell are you to question me, you low-born?' Showryan raised his head.

'What sort of talk is this?' Anakhashayan spoke in anguish. 'That bridge has been in this place from the time we were school-going kids. This is a public road used by the people here.'

'All that was in the olden days', Showryan Mappila guffawed. 'Now onwards, we cannot allow Communist hooligans to use this road which runs through the property of Anthrapper.'

'Oh, please don't talk like that Showryan Mappila....' Anakhashayan mellowed. 'Are not Communists also human beings? Besides, see his leg. We just bandaged it. It should not get wet.'

'In that case carry him on your head and cross the water', Showryan Mappila teased them.

'You don't have to tell me that.' Anakhashyan removed his waist cloth and tied it around his head. He raised Chathu to his shoulders and started wading through the water, taking each step carefully. Slowly he got across the canal safely.

'Chandy Anthrapper, this is cruel', Anakhashayan addressed the property owner while untying the cloth he had tied around his head and tying the same around his waist. 'This land has not been brought from England by your ancestors. Remember, people like us will still be hanging around.'

'How did you address him?' Showryan Mappila was in a rage. 'You better address him respectfully as Chandyachha (Father Chandy). Should someone teach you how to address the elite?'

'Should I be addressing him achha?' Anakhashayan said sarcastically. 'Then what will I call my own father? Should I call him Anthrapper?'

'Uhh, being so insolent?' Mappila moved towards him menacingly. 'Better call him Chandyachha'

'Please do what they want you to do', Chathu was petrified, 'otherwise they will beat you.'

'Chathu brother, you go home.' Anakhashayan folded his mundu. 'I have a few words for him.'

'Tie him down', Anthrapper accosted his workers, 'look at his insolence…'

The workers ran towards the canal.

'Anakha, run!' Chathu was jittery. He ran, dragging his ailing leg.

'In that case, come and tie me down', Anakhashayan started cutting across the canal thrusting his chest forward.

Chathu sprinted as fast as he could, announcing to everyone what was happening on the way. 'Our Anakhan is being tied down and beaten up by Chandy Anthrapper, on the banks of the canal. All of you please go and save him.'

Their elder brother Raghavan assembled a few youngsters from the neighbourhood and rushed to the spot. Chathu also went along, dragging his incapacitated leg.

Raghavan and friends were stunned to see what was happening there. Chandy's goon and manager, Showryan Mappila was tied to a coconut tree nearby. Anakhashayan was monitoring the workers who were fixing the coconut tree bridge across the canal.

'Now, I want to see who will dare to remove this bridge', Anakhashayan challenged.

'You scoundrel…' Showryan Mappila shrieked in anger.

Anakhashayan went near him menacingly, holding his hand up ready to strike Mappila.

'Hey, don't you dare do that', said Mappila grimacing.

Anakhashayan squashed his chin between his fingers.

'I don't want to do anything now, considering your age', Anakhashayan said gritting his teeth, 'but in future, if you commit any such an atrocity, you will get to know the true nature of Anakhashayan.'

'Are you not a worker in that coir factory belonging to Madhavan Manager?' Chandy Anthrapper shouted from a safe distance, 'don't act too insolent. I will see to it that you lose your job.'

'Get lost you fatso', Anakhashayan turned towards him. Chandy disappeared from the scene in a flash.

'We are leaving now', Anakhashayan told the workmen. 'When your hands are free, let him loose', he said, referring to Showryan Mappila who was still bound to the tree.

Aparajitha was sitting in front of the laptop, running her fingers on the keyboard. Niranjan passed by.

'Hey', she called out.

He paused.

'Why acting so stiff these days?' She asked him seriously. 'As if you don't even see me.'

'Oh, nothing.' He shrugged.

'Hey, don't run away man', she said.

He continued to walk hesitatingly.

'I am very sorry for what happened that day', he said.

'Oh, is it not a little late to make that statement?' she laughed.

'Sorry', He repeated.

'C'mon, leave it.' She kept the keyboard aside. 'Are they all not matters of the past? After all, are we all not humans? Is this body not made of sinews and bones? Things can happen unknowingly. We didn't do anything knowingly, isn't it?'

'Had it been knowingly?' he asked.

'You mean…' she came to her feet.

'Hey, nothing.' He tried to evade her.

'No, there's something', she got close to him. 'You are hiding something.'

'No, I want to tell you everything', he said, 'but not now'.

'Niranjan', she enclosed his fingers in her hands. 'You can tell me anything. I always think that both of us are on the same wavelength.'

'I know that', he said, 'but….'

She led him inside.

'On that day, in a kind of shock, I also acted crazy…. I am also sorry.' She sat on the stairs leading to the first floor and looked up at the ancient wooden ceiling of the room.

'Am I not the reason for that?' he asked, taking a seat on a lower step of the stairs.

'Not only you, me too.'

'I am not sure', he said. 'Nowadays I lose my composure while facing you. My sister can read my face very easily. So can my mother….'

'What's there in it?' she laughed 'Are you not a follower of Che? You can apply guerrilla war strategy in love too.'

He looked at her sceptically. He felt that he could not read her mind, however hard he tried. Her words moved like the knights on a chess board, never straight.

Niranjan, I know you are in love with me…I can feel it; he felt she was telling him.

'Let me go', he tried to get up, 'before Disha and mother get here'.

'They will be late', she said. 'Your face… it's like the Bolivian forest. Its wilderness is camouflaging everything unbeknown to you.'

'Is that so?'

She nodded.

'Except in front of me', she said later. 'Maybe because at times, I also turn into a Bolivian forest.'

'True', he said. 'Often I also think about you like that… a Da Vinci Code which cannot be cracked so easily.'

'Have you been able to decipher the code?' she looked at him.

'I am trying to…', he said. 'I am sure I will be able to do that.'

'Not only you, no one can do that.' She rested her face on his shoulders. 'I prefer to be a migrating bird... without a place to nestle...'

'Niranjan, I am so fond of you', she told herself. 'I like your face resembling Che, and your attitude akin to his... your commitment to Economics... your intense youth... Niraṇjan I am aware of your destination and the routes you will take to reach there. But I have lost my sense of direction... I am not sure of my routes.'

'Niranjan, didn't you mention a trip to Santa Clara?'Aparajitha found her voice. 'I am ready to go with you...en route Cuba, Chile, Peru to the heights of Machu Pichhu.... That also could be one of the transitory destinations of this migrating bird.'

'But right now, I have a different travel plan', he said.

'Where to?'

'To Bastar... to study the tribal communities in Bastar', he said, 'to study their lives and the setbacks inflicted on them as an impact of the mainstream politics.'

'Are you going all alone?' She looked at him sceptically.

'This is not a mission that can be carried out all alone', he said.

'Did you discuss with Disha and Mother?' she turned his face towards her. 'Do you have their consent?'

'I didn't... I know they will not give their consent.'

'Then how can you...?'

'I will still go... without telling anyone... like my usual trips... they are used to all that now', he said firmly.

'Niranjan, you are far away from the world of realities', she said. 'Life is not what you are witnessing now. You are still in a dream world.'

'When the young man Ernesto Guevara started travelling on Alberto's bike, he was also dreaming; the dream that transformed him into Che Guevara.' He came to his feet, 'This Bastar trip is just between the two of us. A third person should not come to know of it.'

She didn't respond to that, instead watched him mounting his bike and riding away out of sight. She was thinking of Che's visit to Aleida and the children in disguise, prior to embarking on the Bolivian mission. Ranbir had presented her that book on her birthday; *Evocation*, memories of Aleida.

> 'Aleida', Che told her, 'Tomorrow I am taking off to Bolivia. I hope, this time, you are aware of the intensity of my mission. Before I leave, both of us must spend some time together along with our children. We should have lunch together. They should not come to know that I am their Papa. They won't be able to recognise me. I will be in the disguise of a sixty-year-old Uruguayan. You should tell them that I am their Papa's friend. None other than you should recognise me. Come to the park in the city along with them. I want to spend my time with them till late evening.'
>
> Aleida made it to the park along with the children early in the morning. The old Uruguayan was already there waiting for them. 'If there were no children, I also would have accompanied you.' Aleida whispered in his ears. 'I remember those good old days when I was active in the urban underground movement during the revolutionary war in Cuba and our first time in the Escambray Mountains.'
>
> 'Aleida', Che whispered, 'I also wish you could be with me now'.
>
> 'I will be with you… like a shadow', Aleida said endearingly.
>
> 'Aleida, our children are rushing towards us… you must introduce me to them', said Che.
>
> 'Do you know who this is? This is Papa's friend, Ramon Uncle.'

> The children started playing with Papa's friend. They ran around the park. In the excitement, seven-year-old Aleida hit her head and hurt herself. One should have seen Uncle Ramon's concern. He seated the girl on his lap and nursed her bruise. After a while, the girl reported to her mother, 'You know how uncle likes me? Like the way Papa likes me.' Camilo also said the same. 'When I sat close to him, I could get the smell of Papa's sweat.' How fast he had figured that out. At the time of departure, when the three-year-old Celia kissed him on his cheeks, one could see Che's eyes filling. Tiny Ernesto looked at his Papa with stars shining in his eyes.

Che knew and valued the depth of human relationships, she thought; but Niranjan was not aware of it. His impending journey to Bastar.... Aparajitha thought of Disha's and Mother's brimming eyes.

How can she not alert Disha about his Bastar mission?

Is it true? ...This mission?

Mystery gripped her.

Seven Army Trucks

The Raman murder case was getting hotter by the day.

'Countrymen, are you aware that the manager of Kattiyatt, Nalukettungal Raman has been brutally murdered by the Communist activists', Krishnappan and his group members announced through a megaphone. 'Respected Countrymen, isolate the Communist varmins, finish off all the Communist activists… long live the feudal system… long live the royal King….'

As the group with the megaphone reached in front of the tourist bungalow, where police sub inspector Raman Kutty Nair, a few reserve police inspectors and four to five landlords including Anthrapper were waiting for someone, both Krishnappan and his friend Chandrappan untied their mundu, letting them flow down to their full length, touching their ankles, as a mark of respect to the authority.

'Kuttappan, are you able to sleep peacefully at night?' landlord Kattiyadan asked. 'To be honest, I am not able to sleep. How do we know when they are going to attack us with their long spears? They entered some Nair's house in Kadakkarappally and stabbed the people in the house late in the night. They can gatecrash into our houses at any time. CID Kochhu Pillai came and warned us that we have to be alert.'

A police truck rolled into the courtyard of the tourist bungalow. Kattiyadan turned his head to see who the visitor was. It was Inspector Koshy. 'Are they about to arrive?' Anthrapper asked Koshy authoritatively.

'They have left Alappuzha', Koshy sounded very meek. 'Just half an hour more. They are directly heading towards the Boy's School.'

Deputy Superintendent of Police Shri Vaidyanatha Iyer and Assistant Superintendent of Police Achyuthan were coming to hold discussions with the landlords regarding future plans, following special instructions of the Diwan.

'Alright', Landlord Kattiyadan looked at Anthrapper, 'then shall we proceed to the school?'

'Either way, there should be a final decision today. As things are progressing, it is not safe to let these Communists be free anymore', Anthrapper said, turning to Inspector Koshy.

'By eight, the army will arrive', Inspector Koshy reported. 'Where will they stay on their arrival?'

'Umm... I have already discussed that with Swamy', Anthrapper said, raising his head and looking towards the Inspector.

'Is it?' Koshy enquired.

'Haven't arrangements been made for the soldiers to stay in the factory shed Nanu?' Anthrapper asked.

'Yes sir', Raman Kutty Nair said coming to attention position.

'An eye for an eye and tooth for the tooth', Kattiyadan spread his chest. 'Have you not heard of the Law of Retaliation?'

'Eye for an eye, tooth for a tooth', inspector Koshy translated the law into Malayalam. 'The army won't remain quiet during the night. Captain Prasad called me over the phone. He was asking whether any sprightly Theeyya or Pulaya woman would be available. I said, "master please come over and we can just crash in. Ha ha ha!"'

'So tonight, the police and army men will have no sleep?' Anthrapper let out a vulgar laugh.

'How can they?' Koshy roared with laughter.

'We have to put an end to the entire class of people exactly the way Marthanda Varma did with Ettuveetil Pillai.'

'We have to avenge Raman.' Kattiyadan spoke, gritting his teeth.

'But we have already avenged him', Sub Inspector Raman Kutty Nair interrupted. 'Among the two whom the landlord Matheparamban killed, one was a Pulaya from the untouchable community.'

'How can you compare that incident with what King Marthanda Varma did?' The landlord expressed his annoyance.

Inspector Koshy looked harshly at Raman Kutty Nair.

'Sir', Raman Kutty Nair came to attention again.

'Then where is Matheparamban?' asked Pattathil Kartha who was standing slightly aloof.

'He is in our camp along with the police', Koshy replied.

'That's good', Kartha nodded. 'After all, you won't have to worry about his safety when he is there.'

'Raman's dead body…', Raman Kutty Nair was about to ask something.

Kattiyadan figured out what he had in his mind. 'That must be lying around by the side of the canal', the landlord said in disgust. 'Who wants to see the body which has been torn apart and wrapped up in an old mat after the inquest?'

'The dead are gone, no point in wasting any more time on them', said Anthrapper. 'Come on; let's proceed without any delay.'

What an insensitive class without an iota of human feelings, Raman Kutty Nair thought.

Kattiyadan climbed down from the verandah.

That night, seven truck full of soldiers disembarked at Kadakkarappally.

'Enquiries made after the struggle! Some of them have taken a blind view, leaving the truth behind', Dinar said as he handed over the books.

'Oh, I just finished the book, *Cheated Venaad*', Aparajitha said. 'Sreekandan Nair alleges that Communists have initiated a fake revolution. Doesn't that also belong to this category?'

'Sreekandan Nair, who had accompanied Comrade TV for conciliatory talks with Sir CP, should not have written that', Dinar looked in the direction of the approaching footfalls. It was Disha.

'Who is this? Dinar…' She tried to conceal a smile in the corner of her lips. 'Did you run into our Comrade?'

'To tell you the truth, I have no news at all', Dinar replied. 'I came here hoping to see him.'

'That police constable whom we met the other day…' Disha looked at him pointedly.

'Oh, while enquiring about the library', Dinar tried to recollect, 'he might have asked about two or three of us who frequent it… that's all.'

'Hm... in case you happen to see him on the way, tell him to come home before midnight.'

'She acts and talks as if we have done something wrong', Dinar grimaced as Disha disappeared.

'She is all tensed up', Aparajitha tried to defend Disha.

'Why?' Dinar couldn't understand her tension.

'Oh...', Aparajitha looked at him through the corner of her eyes, trying to read his face, which was impassive.

'Again, the Bolivian wilderness!' she returned to her keyboard with a deep sigh.

Comrades CK Kumara Panicker, KC Velayudhan, Nagappan, Sreedharan, Raman Kutty, Sekharan and others had assembled in a ground closer to the family house of Kunthirisseri for a discussion.

'Look there, can you see some more people coming?' Sekharan pointed to the approaching group of people, 'Panicker sir, they are coming here'.

'Okay, let them come', Kumara Panicker said.

'They don't seem to have had a wink of sleep last night', Velayudhan said, 'weren't they running for their lives with whatever belongings they could gather?'

Farmer women carrying their infant children from nearby villages like Kadakkarappally, Vettakkal and Menasseri who had to desert their home and hearth, stood scattered in the ground. There were also aged men and women who did not possess even a change of clothes.

'But where is the granddaughter of Cheera grandmother?' asked Comrade Nagappan, '– that sprightly girl who was always in the forefront of processions along with Kaithara Pappy, shouting slogans with voices reaching the skies?'

'I don't know anything my master', Cheeramma, who was exhausted and sitting under a coconut tree, replied. She had a walking stick crudely cut out from the branch of a tree.

'Where is my granddaughter?' Cheeramma turned to her friend Karambi, 'Did you see her going anywhere?'

'The Army took her away forcibly in their truck', Karambi said in a hushed tone.

'Don't say that aloud. Let the grandmother not hear', said Nagappan, 'she will never stop screaming'.

'They have taken away other young women too.' A young mother carrying her infant baby on her hips whimpered. 'They didn't take us away, maybe because we were holding our young infants, but instead, in front of our husbands....' Her eyes were bloodshot after hours of crying... her blouse was torn and torso bare... and her voice trembled.

'Not one or two guys... but three or four of them... drunk and reckless....' The young woman trembled.

'They took away all our household possessions, our poultry, goats...everything....'

'They emptied even our ration rice... they whacked our men black and blue. We sprinted away as fast as we could to save our lives.'

'Ten to fourteen of our huts were gutted by the police and army.'

'There were local goons also assisting the police and army. They were the ones who set the huts on fire.'

A small boy came sprinting and pulled out a letter hidden in his mundu and handed it over to Kumara Panicker.

'Who sent this?' CK looked at him, 'your face doesn't seem to be familiar in this area.'

'I was told not to explain all that. Everything is written in that letter', he said coolly. 'Somebody entrusted me with that, to be delivered to you. I must rush.'

He disappeared.

Panicker opened the letter.

'Be careful. At the secret discussions held in the Boy's School, it was decided to do away with Comrade CK.'

'Whose letter is that?' asked Velayudhan in a whisper.

'It's not from the party', CK said. 'It could be someone who is secretly in our favour.'

'What's the news?' KC was anxious.

'First Regulation has been announced.' CK folded the letter and tucked it into his mundu. 'Red flag banned. Shouting Inquilab also has been banned. Meetings and processions are banned', CK lied. These were things he had wanted to disclose to his comrades earlier. But he did not want to bring down the confidence level of his comrades by letting them know about the threat to his life.

Anyway, I have to die one day, thought CK. Will anyone try to hide in a mustard seed to escape death? It may be more meaningful and worthwhile to get killed while trying to change this bad state of affairs in my country.

'Now, what about the fate of these poor people, who have been forced to move out of their dwellings without any belongings?' asked Comrade Raman Kutty.

'There is plenty of paddy in the granary', Kumara Panicker said confidently. 'Also, we have high-yielding coconut trees on our property. It's enough if we have a few people to help us with cooking. Knowing CP's ways, it seems that the worst is yet to come. At any rate those who take shelter in Kunthirisseri tharavadu need not starve.'

From the family home a servant came panting and said, 'From Muhamma, Comrades NK Ayyappan, Madhavan and Karunakaran have come to see you. They took the road on the western side of the property to avoid being seen by anyone.'

'Ask them to come to the gate house', CK started for the gate house along with KC Velayudhan and Sekharan.

'Things have gone from bad to worse in Kanichu Kulangara, Muhamma, Kanji Kuzhi and Mararikulam villages', Comrade Ayyappan reported. 'The police lockups have been packed with comrades who are being tortured to the core. We can hear their screams from the nearby roads. It will not be possible for us to carry on like this anymore. We need an immediate solution.'

'A lot of people will have to sacrifice their lives in this struggle', said CK, trying to keep his face expressionless, 'then only these atrocities will come to an end'.

'We are ready to die for our movement', Comrade Madhavan's hands curled into fists. 'There is no question of surrendering the movement on the face of CP's arrogance.'

'Don't we all have to die some day?' CK asked. 'Let's do that in a manly way. Anyway, let me go to Alappuzha. Our Comrade EMS is camping in Pathrose's house. Let me meet both of them. Then we will decide.'

Three-four men came running into the front yard of the big house.

'What happened?' KC Velayudhan came to his feet.

'Wife of the toddy tapper Manikkan, who is eight months pregnant, was molested and raped by three-four soldiers. She is lying unconscious over there.'

'Remove her immediately to a hospital.' Kumara Panicker handed over two British rupees to Comrade Sekharan. 'Sekharan and Raman Kutty, both of you go with them.'

Pakkaran had dropped his sister Kochhu Paru at their aunt's residence in Koipuram, which was a safer place. While returning home he saw Prabhakaran running towards him.

'Pappy has not been seen since last night.' Prabhakaran was agitated. 'People say she has been abducted by the army.'

'The soldiers?' Pakkaran also felt jittery. He was relieved that he had dropped his sister at his aunt's place.

'Whole of last night, the police, army and local goons were running wild in the locality. I went there to bring Pappy to the safety of my house. But on my way, I heard that...' Prabhakaran's voice choked.

'Where did the men take her?' Pakkaran questioned.

'They did not take her to the police station. Four of five of them had knocked on her door. She leaped out holding her sickle, ready to strike. But as she saw the men holding rifles, she started running. They ran behind her and caught her by the side of the canal bund. There are people who heard her screaming while struggling to get out of their hold.' Prabhakaran sat down as if his knees had given up.

'They would have taken her to that market place in Ponnamveli', Pakkaran tried to make a guess. 'Shall we go there and take a look at the place?'

'There the whole place is crowded with the army', Prabhakaran said hopelessly. 'No one can access that place.'

'Shouldn't you have brought Pappy here earlier when you knew that it was risky for her to stay in her locality?' Pakkaran reprimanded Prabhakaran.

Pakkaran is right, Prabhakaran thought. I should have persuaded her to leave that place when I went there earlier. But how could I have done that? How could I have spoken to her when she was among those women singing and playing?

In the afternoon, Prabhakaran had been to her place, walking through the lovely kasithumba flowers blooming on the sides of the paddy fields. Her cow was feasting on the fertile grass growing under the coconut tree. Colourful firecracker flowers bloomed in her small garden invitingly. The moment the cow saw Prabhakaran approaching, she stopped eating and stretched her neck towards him. Prabhakaran had stroked her under the neck fondly. She stuck out her rough tongue and licked his hairy hands. Prabhakaran brought his face closer to her forehead, adorned by a red circle of vermillion paste applied by Pappy.

'OK dear, where is your foster mother?' Prabhakaran asked her.

The cow turned her face to the northern neighbouring plot and called out to Pappy in a long moo.

As if in reply, a folksong rose from the northern neighbourhood.

Are you coming to pick flowers early in the morning?

Prabhakaran went to see what was happening. Pappy and friends were engaged in a game. Prabhakaran stood hiding behind a tree and watched them. The women had divided themselves into two groups of five and stood shoulder to shoulder holding their hands. The two teams faced each other on both sides of a straight line drawn in between. One team had Pappy standing in the middle and on the other side was Mara, a neighbourhood girl. They were moving in rhythm with their steps in unison to the tune of the song.

Whom do you need from among us…?

Mara and her team danced forward singing

We need your Pappy this morning…

Pappy was looking the most beautiful, in a red blouse with her sweeping colourful mundu tucked to her waistline neatly and a red dot adorning her forehead in between her eyebrows. Among them she had the perfect rhythm and movements. Hidden behind the bush Prabhakaran gazed at her without being able to take his eyes off.

'Who will come and take us away early morning….' Pappy and group came forward singing.

'Someone will come from distant lands and he will take you away…' Mara teased and sang.

'Then where is "the one" who has come to take away Pappy…' singing, Pappy's team came forward holding and shaking the bunch of grass in their hands.

'The "one" is there standing behind the bush', Mara and group pointed their fingers towards the bush laughing.

Prabhakaran was embarrassed. Had they seen him hiding behind the bush? He felt ashamed. Prabhakaran quietly moved out. As he was walking back to the exit, the women sang in chorus again.

Would you like to pick the flowers early morning…

Whom would you like to pick to meet your requirements?

The women have not seen me, thought Prabhakaran. He should have waited till the game was over and persuaded Pappy to go along with him to a safer place. Prabhakaran felt a heavy weight on his chest.

Pappy will come back, he thought. Pappy will wriggle out of the army's hands and come back. No man can touch her body alive. That is Pappy. Even if something happens, he will still make her come back to him.

Comrade Karunan came along sprinting. 'They have imprisoned her on a boat and have taken her to the Tourist Bungalow. She bit the hand of an army officer in the barracks. The whole place is swarming with armed men. No one can go near the place.'

'Comrade Karunan, what can we do now?' Prabhakaran stared at the sky above hopelessly.

A Big Toad

The stormtroopers passed the ayurvedic clinic of Kumaran Vaidyar on their way to the Cherthala Boy's School playground. Seated on the front verandah, Vishuvappan craned his neck to see what was happening on the road with great fear in his heart. This was the first time he was seeing an army.

Relaxing on the easy chair in the verandah, Vaidyan Kumaran started bragging, 'The moment this Kumaran Vaidyar sent a telegram, the army descended on this road from nowhere. Did you see the troops?'

'Yes, yes…', said a stunned Vishuvappan. Continuing to cut the palm leaves to shape into beedis Vishuvappan responded, 'Isn't this the result of your close connections with our great administrator, the Diwanji?'

'Yeah…. At least now you have taken note of that…', said Kumaran Vaidyar trying to stretch his aging neck with jutting veins to hold his head high

'Oh, everyone in this country knows about that', said Vishuvappan as he stuffed the crushed tobacco into the palm leaf cuttings, and started rolling the beedis.

It was known among the villagers that the army was deployed on the explicit request of the landlords Anthrapper and Kattiyatt Sivarama Panikkar who had held discussions with Diwanji in person. Diwanji had halted at the palace in Alappuzha to personally study the situation and gather firsthand information. Inspector General of Police, Parthasarathy Aiyangar, and Army Commander Parameswaran Pillai were with him during the discussions. They had also summoned Anthrapper and Kattiyadan. Vishuvappan had heard the union members also discussing the matter. Still, he wondered how to tell the Vaidyan the truth.

'Our third-rate locals want to lock horns with the brainy.... Now we are going to see the Cherthala fireworks…' the Vaidyan laughed, shaking all over.

'But will the army shoot down the Communists? Are they also not the subjects of the beloved King?' asked Vishuvappan.

'If not for shooting them down, why do you think they have deployed the army, you fool?' the Vaidyan growled. 'The army will not let a single Communist be alive; you will see them perishing once and for all.'

School children raised a mayhem, seeing the army with its gun battery rolling into the school ground and tried to crowd around. Uniformed men stretched their legs, alighted from the vehicles and screamed, 'clear the road, you asses, if you don't want to be crushed by the army vehicles….'

The stormtroopers proceeded to Vayalar village and went around the Siva temple in the center of the village, running through the temple pond. The soldiers addressed the stunned villagers, 'Did you all see? This can travel by land as well as water. Did you see the barrel of this canon?' They turned the barrel toward the crowd, 'in one shot ten to a hundred of you can be killed. Not one will remain alive.'

The villagers backtracked the moment they heard the threat.

As the battery reached in front of the Ponnamvelii Beedi shop in the village, it stopped. The men turned the canon towards the shop. All the sixteen workers working in the beedi factory put down their shallow baskets containing their accessories and fled.

The battery also halted in front of the coir factory where the union had its office. The troopers terrorised the workers, 'If you are not willing to work and be docile, you will be shot down. If you care for your dear lives, you better behave. Be informed, in case you are not aware; if you try to organise and demonstrate, none of you will remain alive....'

Comrade CK Bhaskaran stepped out of the office and stood in front of the canon, thrusting his chest forward. 'Don't ever dream that you can bring down the working class to its knees by flashing your canons. Don't be under the illusion that the working class can be crushed down under the feet of the unscrupulous feudal lords. If you have guts, let your first bullet drill my chest.'

Comrade unbuttoned his shirt, 'Come on, shoot'.

'Yes, if you want to shoot us...' all the workers standing on the sides of the road came forward spreading their chests and encircled the battery.

The soldiers lowered the barrel in apprehension.

'Leave them', said Comrade Bhaskaran, 'At least now they have understood who we are.'

People hooted and whistled; the King's army lowered its guns.

By four in the evening, two vans full of reserve police halted in front of the union office. They roared and barged into the office and pounced on the five comrades who were present there. They smashed tables, chairs and other furniture. A police jeep rolled in, menacingly. Inspector Koshy leapt out of it and stood near the flag post.

'Pull down that damn red flag', he roared. One policeman climbed on to the flag post and tore down the fluttering flag. As it collapsed on the ground, Inspector Koshy stomped on it shouting, 'the damned red flag. Hereafter, not a single red flag should be seen flying in this land'. The comrades, with bleeding heads, were driven away to the police station. A few more police vans rolled into the Ponnamveli market place. Police looted the shops and chased everyone who was there.

One group of policemen rushed to the clinic of Vaidyan Keshavan. It was rumoured that he was a Communist sympathiser.

'Come on, ransack his clinic', Inspector Koshy ordered, barging into the clinic. Vaidyan Kochuraman was bandaging the fractured bones of Comrade Paraman who had been subjected to police torture. As he was handing over a package of medicines to Paraman's son Kunjumani, Inspector Koshy's elbow smashed on to the backbone of the healer.

'Aiyoo...' the Vaidyan fell down and writhed in pain.

As Koshy poised his booted leg to land on the Vaidyan's back, Kunjumani screamed.

'Fellow men, all of you please come running and save the Vaidyan who is being killed.'

Koshy turned to Kunjumani, 'You son of a whore, not yet hatched from the egg… still acting smart!'

Inspector Koshy held him by his collar and hurled him into the jeep. As soon as he landed in the jeep, the boy chanted 'Inquilab Zindabad, Inquilab, and Zindabad'.

He didn't know the meaning of 'Inquilab' but he knew it was a rescue mantra for people like him. He hauled up the Vaidyan, who had also been dumped into the same jeep

Bottles in the shattered almirah cracked and spilled medicines ran on the road.

Pappy couldn't figure out where she and the other women were being forcibly taken from the Ponnamveli military camp. Her hands were crossed and tied firmly behind. Her friends Mara and the granddaughter of grandmother Cheera were also with her in the army truck. The three of them were dumped together in a dark cell in the military camp. As she was about to close her eyes, she heard Mara's gut-wrenching scream. She was being dragged away by three or four men. As her hands moved along, looking for the granddaughter of Cheeramma, Pappy found that she too was missing. She heard the thud of three pairs of booted legs walking through the verandah and entering the cell.

'Are you not Kaithara Pappy?' One flashed a light on her face.

'Are you not the one who shouted slogans, swirling your sickle in your hands?'

She did not respond. She could not open her eyes due to the brightness of the flash light.

'Oh ho… is she a communist?'

'She is not what she appears to be. She is gutsy. Her story is very interesting. After hearing that, our Captain Saab is so excited... he wants to be the first one to enjoy her.'

'Oh, that means you are a smart one, isn't it?' one of the soldiers came close to her.

She scrambled to the corner of the cell.

'So, prove your smartness to our Captain, thereafter a few of us will also be waiting for you....'

They rolled in laughter.

'No!' she screamed in anguish, 'don't you dare touch me!'

'Come here you bitch!' The soldier caught hold of her bodily, 'You dare to try your tricks on army men?'

From the sitting posture, she kicked him on his shin. He had not expected that.

'Tie her down, this whore', he grimaced.

'Behave, you bitch', holding her by her arms and legs they dragged her out of the cell. As they moved into the darkness, she felt someone's fingers squeezing her breasts. She bit him hard on his arm and he loosened his grip in pain. Immediately she ducked into the darkness and made her escape. They chased her.

Kaithara Pappy knew every nook and corner of the village even in darkness.

She knew that once she crossed the coir factory, she could reach the paddy fields. She used to frequent the place almost every day to gather green grass for her cow. She used to work for daily wages during the harvest seasons in those paddy fields. Slipping out of the grip of the soldiers, she sprinted through the paddy fields. The men groped in the darkness. As she went on running, she was confronted by a flash light. A few other men were busy catching frogs in the fields.

'Oh, look! ...a big toad!' they circled her. 'Catch her before she leaps.' She bent down and scooped up a fistful of fine sand and then started running through the knee-deep canal.

Unfortunately, she got trapped in a net tied in the canal for trapping fish.

'So, finally, you are trapped in our net', the soldiers were exhilarated.

A boat wading through the water weeds brought her in front of a bungalow. They dragged her out of the boat and carried her into the bungalow. A few men stood on the lush green lawn in front of the bungalow, busy in discussion. Stomping heavily on the ground, her abductors saluted one among them. Making rings of smoke from the cigarette resting on his lips, he looked at her.

'Is this that horny shark?' he asked, sipping a yellow liquid from a glass.

'Yes sir', the soldiers stood in attention.

'Get her washed thoroughly, removing the scales on her skin and make her lie on the bed.' His eyes surveyed her from top to bottom, 'You are not bad. I will come to you after two more pegs of this'. He held his glass high. 'I want to enjoy watching you wriggle.'

'Ha, ha, ha', they laughed.

'Be careful', said a bald man, 'This creature will come back to life even if she is cut into pieces.'

'Oh, don't tell me. In how many ponds has this crane fished?' bragged the captain.

'Ptooey...' she spat on his face.

He snarled ferociously.

'You whore', he slapped her on the cheeks. 'Tie her hands and legs. I will subdue her arrogance this evening. Whoever wants her can queue up. After the entertainment, dump the whore in the backwaters.' Captain Prasad panted like a dog.

When Comrade Sekharan was returning from the Cherthala Hospital after admitting Manikkan's wife who was due for delivery, he heard the gut-wrenching wail of a small boy from the police station. It was not just wailing. It sounded like his death pangs. He hid himself behind the tamanu nut tree on the road side.

'Call out once again, your Inquilab.' He could hear Inspector Koshy guffawing.

The boy continued to scream 'I am being killed… they are killing me.'

After a while a police constable came out of the police station. Sekharan pulled himself back a little more behind the tree so that he wouldn't be seen. Only when he came close, Sekharan saw that it was Constable Unnikandan, whom Sekharan was familiar with. He quickly came out of his hiding place.

'What are you doing here?' The police constable enquired.

'Oh, I heard the scream of a small boy from the station.' Sekharan scratched his head.

'Come, I will tell you. It's better not to stay here', he looked at the station. 'Let's not come under the gaze of that devil', Unnikandan guided Sekharan to a side lane.

'I am tired of this job', he said, removing his peaked cap. 'Whatever is going on there cannot be acceptable to anyone's conscience. What to do with three daughters growing up? I have no other go…. But then, where are you coming from?'

Sekharan explained about the pregnant woman who was admitted to the hospital.

'Oh, isn't that the wife of that toddy tapper Manikkan?' Unnikandan wrinkled his brows. 'Was he not the one who died after a fall from the coconut tree? How come his wife has been admitted for pregnancy? Did you do anything fishy?'

'But he died only six months ago. She is gone seven months now', Sekharan tried to correct the constable.

'Oh, is that so?' The constable nodded as if he understood. 'Then, the scream of the boy you heard from the police station....'

As he was about to narrate the tale, those terrorising scenes passed through his mind.

'That boy was taken into custody along with our Vaidyan Kochhuraman. That evil Inspector slapped him on his face and asked him to shout Inquilab. As the boy obliged, he caught hold of him by his belly button and dangled him in the air. In a frenzy of pain, the boy bit him. The Inspector is striking back at the poor boy for that.'

The Inspector was not satisfied with bashing up the boy. He had turned to the constable and asked him to get the rib of a coconut tree leaf.

The constable quickly brought a few, thinking that it would be used to beat the boy.

'Lay him on the table', the Inspector grunted his orders.

The constable had a hard time doing that. The boy was wriggling in sheer agony.

The inspector pulled down the boy's knickers and squeezed his genitals. The boy screamed.

'Hold his hands and legs', he ordered, and the constable obliged. The inspector pierced the sharpened rib of the palm leaf through his urethra. The boy wriggled like a worm.

The monster went on blabbering, 'If such boys are allowed to survive and grow, nobody will be able to live in this country... they all are seeds of evil.'

The constable fled from the station, unable to bear the gruesome sight.

Aparajitha was tired. She had keyed in a lot of matter.

Disha and mother would be fast sleep, she thought.

Just as she closed the laptop and hit the bed, Mrinalda called.

'You weren't sleeping, were you?'

'Not yet', she reclined on the bed with the mobile.

'You know Hemanth Mishra, don't you?' he asked.

She tried to recollect.

'He was active in the radical left-wing debates...AISA... CPML.'

'Yeah...' she said, 'that guy with a goatee?'

'The police arrested him a few days ago for associating with the Maoists in Chhattisgarh. But that's not the issue.' His language drifted from Hindi to Bengali. 'Subsequently, the Maharashtra police arrested Professor Sai Baba of Delhi University. During interrogation, it seems Mishra disclosed his connection with Maoists. Professor was the link of the Maoists in Delhi and Hemanth was his courier.'

'Didn't ISA protest?' she asked.

'Should that be doubted?' he laughed.

'Today a protest rally was held on KG Marg in front of Maharashtra Bhavan.'

'Is ISA likely to win a landslide victory in the campus elections this time?'

'We should hope that does not happen', he said. 'The Federation is alert. Still, winds are blowing in a different direction in the campus. You know, the new generation is inclined more towards the extreme left.'

'They must have lost faith in the old stand we used to take', she said. 'We were a little late to recognise that.'

Mrinalda didn't respond.

'Oh, it's too late in the night.' He wished her good night.

That was when she found the message from Niranjan in the inbox.

'Have you gone to bed?'

'No, but now I am going to', she replied.

'I want to talk to you.' His next message said.

'Now? It's almost midnight. Go and try to catch some sleep, you kid. Let the day break', she replied.

'I am leaving for Bastar.'

'When?'

'Early in the morning'

'You didn't tell me.'

'I am calling you out to tell you.'

'What did you tell Mother and Disha?'

'What to tell them? This is just a routine trip.'

'???'

'Will you come?'

'Are you crazy, man?'

'I have to talk to you.'

'Don't trust your phone.' Suddenly she became alert. 'And go get some sleep.'

She couldn't sleep. Where is he really planning to go? Is it Bastar or some other place?

After a while someone knocked on the window shutters. She opened the shutter partly. It was Niranjan.

'What happened to you? Why don't you go, get some sleep? Don't you have to leave early in the morning?'

'I have to talk to you.' He was insistent.

'Seriously?' she was sceptical.

'Can you come out? We will sit outside for some time.'

She looked into his eyes and got up.

An Invisible Track

Anakhashayan and Pakkaran reached Ponnamveli Market early in the morning. Most of the shops were closed. The whole market area looked lifeless. Only the soldiers jostled around in a hurry. The army was camping in the coir factory and in a two-storeyed building on the north side of the market belonging to Kartha.

The tea shop owner Gopalan had locked his shop. He was afraid the army and policemen would loot him by forcing him to give food items on credit.

The tailor Kochhanian Pillai kept his shop half-open and was busy with his sewing machine which produced a thud… thud…noise that sounded like deep sighs.

Vaidyan Keshavan's pharmacy remained closed. Remains of the medicines thrown out from the ransacked shop left black marks on the walls and steps. The provision stores next door, which had earlier been looted by the police and King's army, also remained closed as there was nothing left to sell.

Kunjan Nair, a platform vendor, showcased his commodities; A few packets of Passing Show cigarettes, three or four plastic containers which had the picture of Charminar pillars stuck on them containing numerous homemade goodies in different shapes and flavours like ginger sweet and sesame seed balls soaked in jaggery syrup. Pakkaran bought one anna worth of sweets.

'Why are you guys hanging around here?' asked Kunjan Nair, 'Aren't you all party men? If you fall under their gaze, they will lock you behind bars. Don't complain later that I didn't warn you.'

'We came to the tailor shop to find out if he has stitched my shirt', said Pakkaran.

'Do you know where they took all those people whom they abducted?' Pakkaran asked wanting to find out Pappy's whereabouts. He had spent the last two days in depression, withdrawn from everybody, without food or sleep.

'Oh!' Kunjan Nair shrugged. 'I heard that the Vaidyan was beaten black and blue. Then the boy has been hospitalised, being unable to urinate. His private part is swollen… the devils!'

'What about those young women who were abducted?' asked Pakkaran.

'Oh!' Kunjan Nair shrugged again, 'who cares about those scheduled-caste farming women? But they seem to have struck gold. Haven't they been abducted by great bullocks? They will satiate the women in every way… after all, the men have been fed with only fish and meat. Isn't that enough for the women to just comply…?'

Pakkaran was furious. He wanted to smash Kunjan Nair's head. But his sister Kochhu Paru whispered in his head, 'Don't, Pakkaran brother, leave it.'

'Come along', Anakhashayan dragged Pakkaran by hand towards the tailor's shop.

Tailor Kochhanian Pillai was slogging away on the sewing machine. Royal monarch Shri Chittira Thirunal gazed at them through the glass of the framed portrait fixed on the wall right above the tailor.

Kochhanian Pillai peeped at them through his thick lenses. 'Oh, I have not finished stitching your shirt. Look there. I have already cut the material and kept it ready for stitching.' Anakhashayan's eyes followed the direction of his fat nose.

'When are we going to get this? We were planning to wear it for Onam. Now it is more than a month since Onam.'

The red cloth had been purchased with the money Mother had saved for stitching shirts for Pakkaran, his brother Raghavan, Comrade Prabhakaran and himself. 'Oh, this work will be over by today', the tailor pointed to the work he was doing. 'You come back the day after tomorrow', he said while pushing the cloth under the needle. 'But is it safe now to wear this red shirt and walk around? I am just asking because I don't know. Has not Sir CP banned red flags, Inquilab and anything red?'

Anakhashayan had an uncontrollable urge to give a fitting reply when Pakkaran prodded him in his ribs. 'Look there….'

In the market junction, two Hindustan-48 cars pulled to the curb. Landlords Kattiyadan, Pattathil Kartha, Anthrapper, Parayitharakan, Kalluveettil Kunjachhan, Azhikkal Antony, George Peter, Kuttappan Kymal and Anakottil Kochhu Narayana Kartha stepped out from the cars.

The tailor stopped stitching and peeped outside. 'The ruling King's loyalists are taking a procession to Cherthala', he said.

'Oh, look, Matheparamban Narayanan is standing there', Pakkaran pointed his finger in that direction. Attired in a police uniform, khaki trousers, coat and hat and holding a sword stick, Matheparamban alighted from the police vehicle. His goon squad consisting of Krishnappan, Chandrappan, Kurukkal, Sankunni and others had already formed a line. Matheparamban took his position at the head of the line, holding his sword stick. Behind him, Kurukkal positioned himself, wearing Khaki shorts and a white-sleeved banian, holding a dagger, followed by Krishnappan and Chandrappan.

A police van roared in. Inspector Koshy leapt out of it.

'Okay, so let's start', he looked at Anthrapper. 'One police van will lead the procession. One will be at the tail of the procession, followed by the military trucks.'

'When all these heroes are here, why do we need police or army men?' Inspector Koshy prodded Matheparamban on his ribs.

Landlords lined up in front, followed by a few Nairs of the warrior caste, shepherded by their managers in three rows.

Two reserve policemen walked into the tailor shop. 'Okay get up, come and join the procession; you can do your work later.'

Then they moved on to Kunjan Nair's shop, 'Wind up your shop and join the procession', they told him.

Both Kochhaniyan Pillai and Kunjan Nair reluctantly stood up.

They got busy gathering everyone in the market.

'Let's not delay any more. We will start off', Kattiyadan ordered. 'You can start the invocation prayer song.'

The tailor locked his shop and joined the procession. Anakhashayan and Pakkaran hid behind the tailor shop.

Standing in attention, Matheparamban raised the sword till his nose, and rendered the inaugural song.

Vanchi bhoomi pathe, chiram vanchithabham jayikkenam
Let the royal King of Vanchi kingdom win all the battles
Vanchi Bhoomi pathe chiram
Let the royal King of Vanchi remain forever
Devadevan Bhavanennum desha sowkhyam valarthenam
Our King who is also our God should maintain his health forever
Vanchi Bhoomi pathe chiram
Let the royal King of Vanchi remain forever
Thavakamam kulam melmel shree valarnnullasikkenam
Let the lineage of the great king keep growing forever
Vanchi Bhoomi pathe chiram
Let the royal King of Vanchi remain forever
Vanchi Bhoomi pathe chiram
Let the royal King of Vanchi remain forever

'Let his highness Padmanabha Dasa Vanchi Pala Maharajah Sir Balarama Varma Kulasekhara, the crown holder',

'Let Sultan Maharajah Rama Rajah Bahadoor Shamsher Jung and Shree Chittira Thirunaal Maharaja reign forever'. Kattiyadan called out in a single breath. Matheparamban repeated the prayer and the procession started moving forward.

'Let Vanchi kingdom win the battle', Kurukkal, his strongman, bellowed. 'Long live Diwan's rule; let Sir CP rule the country forever.'

The procession moved vigorously.

Kill the Communist devils.

Communism is dangerous for the country.
Let Communism drop in the Arabian Sea.
We want Diwan's rule,
Diwan's rule is for the safety of the country.

'Feudalism is for our safety', Matheparamban screeched at the top of his voice. 'Feudalism is the safest for the country. Feudalism is the Divine Law. Let the feudal lords reign for ever.'

The procession moved on to Cherthala town four miles away.

Comrade CK Kumara Panicker and his comrades walked through narrow lanes, passing cashew thickets and tiny canals crisscrossing the rural areas. Comrades KC Velayudhan, Sreedharan and Ramankutty were also in the group. He parked his car a few miles away and started walking towards Pathrose's house because they did not want anyone to know about their visit. Pathrose's house was under surveillance by the police. Sir CP's CIDs were swarming all over the place.

'Oh, this route looks like the one leading to Kunthirisseri house', said Sreedharan as they crossed the third coconut tree bridge. 'I was told that Kakka Karunakaran is waiting for us on the way but where is he?'

'Oh, what a surprise, before you could even finish your sentence, here he is… he will live for a hundred years', CK pointed his finger towards the left. At a distance, through the areca nut trees they could see Karunakaran approaching them with his broad chest thrust forward. He was tall and well-built and walked like a military man, holding his head high. His demeanour reflected confidence.

'After being expelled from the King's army, he is constantly under surveillance', CK said.

'But why was he expelled from the army?' Ramankutty Nair couldn't digest that.

'Because he belongs to the Ezhava community', said KC Velayudhan. 'Will a Ezhava be allowed to remain in the Nair army? He locked horns with the Commander, who was a Nair. So, they expelled him.'

'Oh, where were all of you all this time?' asked Kakkachi as he came close. 'Do you know how long I have been waiting for you? I arrived from Paravoor at the crack of dawn, after meeting Comrade EMS. My neck is hurting, looking for you. Come, let's walk fast.'

Kakkachi walked in front.

'Oh, we took a different route', said KC Velayudhan, 'That's how we missed you.'

'Oh, comrade has arrived! That's good news', said CK.

'Comrade EMS reached yesterday itself. He finishes his bath before daybreak and washes his clothes himself and dries them in the sun. He spends his nights reading and writing in the light of a tiny kerosene lamp. Of and on, he visits this place to stay a couple of days. Since Mother is here to cook, there is no difficulty in providing him with meals.'

'Mother? Who is that?' KC looked at him.

'Anna Rosa Ammachi, Pathrose's mother. Even if she has to go around with begging bowls, she will manage to cook and feed everyone and then starve herself. Our comrade EMS calls her party's mother.' Kakkachi explained. 'Gruel and tapioca curry prepared by her along with smashed chilly and fried chilly chutney are a hit among the party workers.'

All the four of them walked through paddy fields and reached the thatched house. Comrade EMS was sitting inside the hut, reading a newspaper. He raised his head on hearing the footfalls.

'They are comrades from Vayalar', Kakka Karunakaran introduced them. 'Comrade CK Kumara Panicker, KC Velayudhan and....'

Comrade EMS's face lit up. He came to his feet and invited the guests to the hut.

Ammachi came to the front door and asked, 'Did all my children have something to eat?'

'Yes Mother', Kakkachi replied.

'Is that true?' she asked the guests.

'It's true, Mother. They are coming from Vayalar', Kakkachi repeated.

'Alright. Pathrose will be home soon.' She went inside.

Comrade Pathrose had gone to the reading room in a nearby locality to conduct party classes.

'Did you hear that?' Kakkachi turned to CK. 'She herself is famished, still she enquires whether we all had anything to eat.'

'There is a mother like this in Vayalar also', CK told Kakkachi 'Our mother....'

Comrade EMS nodded. 'Yes, yes.'

'Oh yes, Comrade would have met her when you came last time.'

As her fingers paused on the keyboard Disha came and sat down silently.

'Would you like to run through this?' Aparajitha raised her head from the monitor.

'Oh no, I am not in a mood.'

'What happened to ruin your mood?' Aparajitha closed her laptop.

'Can you come with me?' Disha asked. 'Let's take a stroll.'

'Oh, why not', Aparajitha came to her feet. 'Sitting all the time, I am getting rooted here.'

'Oh, what dress is this?' Aparajitha noticed Disha only then. She was in a half-skirt, its length reaching just till her knees. She looked younger by ten years.

'I found it when I was looking through Mother's almirah', Disha said adjusting the pleats. 'This is Father's last gift which he gave me on the occasion of Onam, the year he died.'

They started walking towards the paddy fields on the mud road running in between.

'Where did Niranjan go?' Disha asked abruptly.

'I don't know', replied Aparajitha.

'I know that you know.' Disha's voice was serious.

'Disha…', Aparajitha was stunned for a while.

'You really don't know?' Disha turned back and looked daggers at her. 'He spoke to you last… I have evidence…'

'That's true', said Aparajitha 'He did speak to me…but…'

'Ummm…?'

'But his mission, I am not aware of…'

'You didn't ask him… in spite of chatting with him till late in the night?' Disha asked sharply.

Aparajitha looked perplexed. 'Till late night…'

Disha guided her to the Champak tree in the southern yard, where Niranjan had taken her the previous night.

'Look there', Disha pointed towards the white sand under the Champak tree where they had left marks of having sat the previous night. 'See, the fine sand on the seashore will not hide anything.'

'Why are you getting so worked up over it?' Aparajitha got upset. 'He said he wanted to talk to me about something important and I came here. Nothing beyond that….'

'Beyond that…?' Disha looked at her. 'I didn't ask you anything of that sort. It's your life, your rules, it's up to you. All that I want to know is where he went?'

'Bastar', Aparajitha relented.

'Bastar?' Disha stood still. 'Dinar called. Niranjan left the bike near the railway station.'

Aparajitha kept quiet.

'Finally, is it resting time for La Poderosa', she wondered 'his huge motor bike running incessantly through unending tracks?'

'Let your writing not suffer on account of me', Disha said and walked back to the house.

The Diwan's Secret Moves

Koman Kochhu Kunjan Asaan reached the pharmacy, exhausted from walking in the hot sun. Vaidyan Kumaran was busy searching for something inside the pharmacy. Vishuvappan was not to be seen in the verandah. Koman Asaan sat on the wooden bench which was kept in the verandah.

He craned his neck to get an inside view and called out, 'I am here.., I am exhausted, walking in the hot sun. Can I have a dose of Dasamoolam…?' He was referring to a medical concoction made of the extraction of ten herbs and used as a remedy for fatigue.

'Oh, here you are. Where were you all this time?' The Vaidyan called out. 'I was looking for you. Come on in and give me a hand.'

Keeping a pile of papers on the bench, Koman Asaan went inside. The Vaidyan was transferring various herbal extracts and concoctions from different containers to a huge jar.

'That boy is still not in… that Vishuvappan… the one who used to sit here and roll beedis. He is not the kind of person to be late for his work. Do you know what happened yesterday? Your nephew was here to force him to take a membership in the trade union. But he didn't agree. You know he is slightly scared of me.'

'Who, my nephew Sekharan?'

'Hm… that sycophant, bootlicker of Comrade Kumara Panicker. Tell him not to play his party games on my chest.'

'That, I will tell him. All right, what are these?' Koman Asaan changed the subject.

'These? This is Dasamoolam, the ten medicinal herbs, cumin seeds, dried grapes, kurunthotti, the Mallow plant. Give me a hand with this jar.'

'Do you know what this is?' the Vaidyan tilted the jar. 'This is Vajeekaranam, the medicine to increase the libido in men…. Oh, what's the point in telling you all this.'

Koman Asaan could not understand what the Vaidyan was talking about.

'Mister, this medicine is to improve the virility in men. You, who have never been married and do not indulge in such activities, will not understand all these terminologies. Do you get it now?'

'Yes, yes', Koman Asaan nodded his head vigorously. 'But for whom are you concocting all these medicines now?'

'Oh, this has been ordered by the high-ranking army officers. The army vehicle will come now to pick it up', said the Vaidyan.

'But I still don't understand', Koman Asaan was unconvinced. 'Why do you want to mix all these medicines together?'

'Mister, they want to enjoy their evening cocktail by mixing this with their usual brandy to give it a greater kick', the Vaidyan explained. 'But I also have not heard of such a practice in the whole of my life. Seems to be some new discovery!'

'What I don't understand is', Asaan, getting more confused, asked, ' why these people need it now? Is shooting our men with those guns not enough for them?'

'That's the day-time activity', said the Vaidyan, grinning sheepishly, 'but at night it's a different story. Can't you see them running around restlessly like studs when it is dark?'

Asaan's face became red with embarrassment, 'I don't relish such jokes', he said.

'In that case let's move on', the Vaidyan said, pouring some Dasamoolam in a mud cup and handing it over to him. 'Here you are. Gulp this down.'

Asaan gulped it down in one swig.

The Vaidyan came out and sat on the easy chair in the front verandah. And Asaan sat on the wooden bench. An army truck went past.

'Okay, so CP seems to be bent on deciding one way or the other.' Asaan looked at the Vaidyan. 'Did you see the announcement issued by Comrade Keshavan under his signature?'

Asaan picked up the pile of papers he had kept on the wooden bench.

'Oh, what is this?' the Vaidyan stared at the papers.

'This is a drama script based on the book *Residual Rent* written by Comrade K Damodaran. Sekharan copied it by hand.'

Asaan pulled out a paper from the pile and read:

> There has never been an occasion in the history of our country, ridden with sufferings as it appears now. Everywhere one can see only dark pictures of starvation and suffering. One can hear only the pangs of hunger... rice not available, clothes not available, sugar

> and kerosene not available. The government is trying to confront the situation using all the weapons available in its armoury. They have banned public processions in the entire Travancore region for three months. Nowhere in the land are labour strikes allowed. Army and reserve police are kept on alert in locations like Alappuzha, Kottayam, Aluva and Punaloor. If we want to take our freedom struggle forward to its destination, we cannot remain silent any more. All political prisoners should be freed and all ban orders withdrawn. The army posted for surveillance in our various towns should be called back. We should get all the legal rights of a citizenry. To that end all of us should transcend above the narrow constraints of caste, creed and community and continue with our agitations. This is my humble request. We will definitely succeed in this endeavour.

'How does it read?' Asaan looked at the Vaidyan, 'is that not an inspiring address?'

The Vaidyan continued to gaze outside. 'We have still not recovered from the damage caused by one boycott!' The Vaidyan was referring to the three-day strike earlier in Alappuzha and Cherthala districts.

'This is not like that', Asaan said. 'This will transcend all the agitations carried out all over the country so far in theme and content.'

'That is what I am also concerned about', the Vaidyan said frowning. 'In the Cabinet, Diwanji referred to the impending strike as a national disaster. In spite of that, the government restored ration meals in Alappuzha and Cherthala.'

'Oh, even a child cannot fill its stomach with the kind of meals offered by the government', Asaan protested.

'Why are you Communists so reluctant to accept good deeds? It is not through your unions that the meal coupons are being distributed?' the Vaidyan retorted

'But it is like the food served to a prisoner before his execution.' Asaan grew emotional. 'Immediately thereafter, the army was deputed to chase the Communists and eradicate them from our land. Wait and see, at the end, there will not be a single low-caste man left alive in our country.'

'That's not a fact', the Vaidyan refuted his friend. 'I had gone for the meeting convened by the Diwan to discuss the upliftment of backward communities. It was because the two backward communities refused to come together that the meeting fizzled out.'

'Oh, that's how the jackal's intelligence works.' Asaan was irritated. 'The meeting was convened by CP in a hurry, with the intention of appointing his man Padmanabha Pillai to unite the two castes. What was the need for CP to organise this meeting in such a hurry? Definitely CP has some ulterior motives behind such games. You just wait and see. This CP can be put under the category of men like Hitler in Germany. Have you not heard of the story of Hitler who massacred the Jews en masse?'

'No, no, no', the Vaidyan was vehement in his denial. 'CP is not of that type. But if the Communists become unruly, should the police and army sit idle with their hands tied behind?'

'What is it that you are claiming? What are the crimes committed by the Communists?' Asaan raised his voice. 'In spite of so many atrocities by the police and the army, was there any resistance from the workers? Were they not putting up with all this injustice? What has been going on here for the past few months? Are not the police and army running amok doing things that can never be justified?'

'Okay, when we bring up such matters, we have to do that in context, shouldn't we?' the Vaidyan tried to justify himself.

'How long have you been going around claiming that you are an ardent Communist? Has anyone touched even a small strand of hair on your body?'

'Oh…it is only because of my survival instincts that I am managing to continue like this', Asaan retorted. 'Are you not aware of how the police chased me and how I dove into the river to escape?'

Horrifying memories of the incident flashed back in his mind.

They had all assembled in the market ground to protest against Sir CP's American Model of governance. Comrade Sugathan was the chair person. Simon Asaan, KV Pathrose and N Sreekandan Nair were very eloquent in their critique of the Model. After the meeting, a few comrades from the trade union and State Congress Gandhians had got together for a discussion.

'We don't need anything less than a responsible elected government', Comrade OA Govindan said flatly. 'Sir CP is trying to use the Model to prevent the formation of such a government. Some leaders of the State Congress Party are also supporting him. We should be alert.'

Asaan immediately understood that the Comrade was attacking the Congress leaders Pattom Thanu Pillai and TM Varghese.

'Sir CP will definitely do that and more. Who in this Travancore State doesn't know his intentions?' Comrade Sreedharan grimaced. 'Is he not making his moves to force the citizens of this land to surrender their rights at the feet of the British? We have to resist this move even at the cost of our blood and lives.'

'Nowadays, he is being referred to as the adopted son of Britain', one of the comrades reported.

'That's true', another comrade seconded, 'Aren't his moves pointing in that direction? His loyalty is not to the country but to the British.'

'Isn't that the reason for him being knighted with the title "Sir" by the British... to be instrumental in sacrificing the interests of the whole country to their advantage?' Comrade Kumaran scoffed.

'But this time, CP's calculations will fizzle out', Comrade M Krishnan said militantly, rolling up the sleeves of his shirt.

'Let's not be too optimistic', said Comrade Divakaran Asaan as he entered with a roll of newspapers.

'Are you all aware of the heated debate between the Congressmen Pattom and TV Varghese and Comrade TV? Their question was what's wrong in trying out the reforms suggested by the Diwan, in implementing the American Model. Comrade TV objected to the very suggestion vehemently. The three of them entered into a heated argument. Ultimately they blamed the Communist Party for the failure of the meeting. The wretched Brahmin is playing games holding Pattom and TM Varghese as a facade. Did you see the press notification issued by him?'

Comrade Divakaran Asaan had opened the newspaper and read:

> 'Under the absolute control of the Royal King, adult franchise and formation of a responsible government will be implemented in the kingdom of Travancore.'

'Oh, isn't that something positive?' Sreedharan asked.

'Let's not make quick judgments', said Koman Kochhu Asaan. 'Let him read the notification in full.'

Sreedharan moved closer to Divakaran Asaan and read the notification:

> Under the rule of responsible government, the King will appoint the Diwan. The Diwan will not be responsible to the body of elected representatives of the public. The Diwan can veto any decision taken by it. The Diwan will be responsible for executing any orders issued by the King. The Diwan will be an irremovable executive who will maintain the power and status of the Royal King.

Everyone looked at each other. 'Is this called the rule of a democratically-elected responsible government?' They turned to look at others accusingly.

'But this was not what the State Congress meant by the rule of a responsible government.' PS Madhavan, member of the State Congress, sought to correct the statement. 'According to the party, there was no place for a Diwan in the elected government.'

'The Diwan is very much there in the American Model. His position and power are very much like that of the American President. That's how the situation is going to be in this land too. There will be adult franchise, but the ruling government will not have any obligations to the elected representatives of the people. They may give insignificant ministerial portfolios to one or two elected people's representatives, chosen by the King and the Diwan, but they will remain inactive. This is the American Model conceptualised by Sir CP', Koman Kochhu Asaan had explained.

'This evening there is going to be a demonstration against the American Model', Divakaran Asaan had remined one and all.

'In that case, let's not waste our time here', Comrade Sreedharan got ready to leave and take the lead.

Streets in the town had become vibrant with volunteers in red and freedom fighters wearing Gandhi caps. Slogans reverberated in the air.

'Come along all countrymen, reach the battlefield, and join the struggle for our freedom.'

The procession starting from the Cemetery Bridge had moved along the roads in the town systematically. As the procession crossed each junction of four roads, the length of the procession grew bigger. The participants threw up their fists and shouted:

> Fight against baton-beatings and gunshots
>
> Hunting by police and oppression by the landlords
>
> We don't need the rule of oppressors.
>
> We don't need the rule of the Diwan.
>
> Let the rule of the oppressors be condemned.
>
> Dump American Model in the Arabian Sea.
>
> End Diwan's Rule.
>
> Down with King's Rule.

All of a sudden, police jeeps had rolled in from four sides. The procession scattered. Comrades, hit by batons, collapsed with head injuries. Koman Asaan had sprinted as fast as he could on a road which had turned red with the blood shed by the comrades, with the chasing police right behind him. It was getting dark. His thin legs kept running, not following any direction. He could hear the thuds of the police boots in the darkness.

'Don't let that thin-legged rascal escape! Smash his head with batons as soon as he falls in our hands.' He could hear the police swearing. Unconsciously, his feet had taken him to the riverside. 'Catch him', he heard the police shouting. Without thinking for a second, he had dived into the water and disappeared into the darkness.

Next day he had come to know that Comrade Sugathan and Simon Asaan had been arrested. Police had issued arrest warrants for Comrades Sreekandan Nair and KV Pathrose too. The comrades went underground.

'If not for these thin legs, you can imagine what would have happened', Koman Asaan eyed his deformed legs fondly. 'These two are the ones who saved me on that day. I owe them my life, especially considering how many people have been caught and jailed by the police since that day.'

Asaan started listing them. 'Didn't they arrest Comrades NSP and A Sreedharan on the allegation that they made instigating speeches at the Malabar Rebellion Memorial Day? They kept Comrades PT Punnoose, Shankaranarayanan Thampi and KG Madhavan under home-arrest. Didn't they arrest and put under house arrest, Congress leaders like Akkamma Cherian, RV Thomas, MM Varkey and CI Andrews who were inclined towards the left? Didn't they imprison Comrades Bhaskaran, CK Velayudhan and VK Karunakaran? How many of us were served with warrants including Comrade CG? Were they all not forced to go underground? What was their offence? Didn't the Congress leaders like C Keshavan and Sanku Pillai publicly criticise the government for its injustice?'

'In spite of knowing that it is injustice, why has the government flooded our land with army and reserve police? Have they not already banned demonstrations, processions, labour strikes and propaganda strikes? For the last nine-ten days, the police and goons of George Peter are hunting for the workers. They forcibly closed down the press that printed a notice against such barbarism. From that time, no printing press is willing to print any more of the notifications and public announcements of the Communist Party for fear of facing imminent closure. Have they not banned newspapers also from publishing news against the government moves? Are not CP's police force and the soldiers hunting for Communists and trade union leaders? In spite of all this, how can they talk about justice without an iota of human sensitivity?'

Asaan's throat went dry. He felt his whole-body giving way.

'Is there water in that pot?' he looked around.

'There it is', the Vaidyan pointed to the corner and continued. 'Most of what you said is true. But if we can maintain the right attitude, no police or army would hurt anyone.'

As Asaan moved towards the water pot, a young girl came running towards the clinic in tearing haste, screaming her guts out.

'Help, help.'

'But, who is this?' Asaan craned his neck to take a look.

'Isn't she Vishuvappan's sister?' the Vaidyan turned his head.

'Please help us', she stood in front of the clinic, beating on her chest with her hands and howling pathetically, 'The police took away my elder brother Vishuvappan....'

'Why on earth did they do that?' The Vaidyan got up in trepidation.

She stood before them and panted. 'The police and goons came to our hut early in the morning. As soon as they came, they demolished our hut. We were all sleeping in the hut. They took away my brother forcibly.' Her voice quivered. 'They seem to have beaten him and broken every bone in his body. There is no use even if we get him back alive. They have made a pulp of his body....'

The Vaidyan's face turned ashen as he looked at Asaan.

'Send a wire to your CP', Asaan taunted the Vaidyan. 'Are you not the person who wires the Diwan for every small reason?'

'Koman Asaan', Vaidyan Kumaran's voice sounded very weak, 'don't prick a corpse'.

A kettuvallam, a large boat used for carrying huge cargos in olden days and being used as house boats in the present days, was drifting slowly in the center of the Vembanattu backwaters. One of the oarsmen threw an ore into the water softly. The men who had dived into the depths of the water to scoop the seashells, surfaced. Their eyes were alert, scanning the surroundings as efficiently as the rays sent out by the lighthouse on the seashore. They stayed in the water to give alerts on the roaring yellow Dacota plane which would appear in the sky unexpectedly. The boat was occupied by leading Communist leaders, EMS Namboothiripad, KV Pathrose, KC George and a few others to strategise future programmes for ending CP's barbaric rule.

EMS tucked the newspaper *Kesari* in the wooden frame of the boat. He spoke mainly about the people of Telangana and Bengal surging forward in the freedom movement. 'When the war ended, the people in Telangana were facing the same situation which is prevailing in Travancore now. The kind of torture the landlords inflicted on the working class was horrid and inhuman. If it is the King who oppresses the people in Travancore, it is the Nizam and landlords in Hyderabad torturing the farmers. Torture and harassment have become rampant everywhere. The farmers have organised against the atrocities committed on them. They have made squads in every village. Communist

Party is under perpetual threat from the government. Though they banned the party, there is no way they can barricade the surge of people. The Communists will free the villagers from tyranny. The coming days will prove that. In Bengal, the struggle is about fixing the ratio of sharing the yield between landlords and farming workers. The people's front is demanding a new law to define the share of the landlords – for the yield that the farmers produces – to be restricted to only one third of the total yield. Waves of revolution are spreading everywhere. Was there not a discord in the air force and navy too? The unrest was demonstrated by shouting slogans like "Let imperialism perish, let the revolution triumph". Last February there was a strike in the city of Bombay. Two lakh industrial workers struck work on that day. It was the Communist Party who worked hard and stood in the forefront to lead the strike as the people surged forward. The indications are that it's time for such an action here also. In the strike in 1938, didn't about forty thousand workers from Alappuzha stand like a rock and fight relentlessly for three weeks? Who can overlook such facts? Now the strength of the organised workers has doubled. As far as I know, Sir CP Ramaswamy Iyer is an exceptionally intelligent person. But after seeing his actions against the working class in Alappuzha and Cherthala, I wonder if his capacity to think has deteriorated. His strategy is to single out Alappuzha and Cherthala – that has maximum party concentration – from the map of Travancore kingdom with a hidden agenda of eradicating the Communist Party by letting loose mindless criminals in the two localities to ruthlessly suppress the people. We remained silent in spite of being fully aware of his strategy. But now the situation has gone out of control. Comrade C Kumara Panicker has briefed me about the situation in Vayalar. In Punnapra also, the situation is getting worse. Comrade

TV also is of the same opinion. The question is, what should be the party's policy from now on?'

EMS looked at both of them.

'Armed struggle', Pathrose said. 'That's the only solution.'

'A Communist Revolution', KC George added.

Trying to pick up words in between his stammer, EMS said after a lot of thinking, 'We need a high-level summit of the party leaders to brainstorm. We have to ask Comrade Krishna Pillai also.'

EMS sat back, unfolding the newspaper. The boat slowly approached the shore.

Hideout Scattering Light

Moonlight spilled over the waves of the backwaters, kicking aside the night's black blanket. Pale frozen moonlight chased out the darkness forcing it to hide behind the casurina thickets hedging the backwaters. Lusty black cobras slithered through the veins of darkness, looking for havens of pleasure. Water chicks rudely woken up from their slumber started wailing in terror. Their wriggles ended in a helpless surrender as the cobras tightened their grip around them.

She opened her eyes to the dull light streaming into the room. Shadows on the walls danced in a frenzy around her head. Bruises set fire to her body as if she was secured with a thorny creeper. Inside her head, the earth spun like a top. Wild beetles buzzed in the ears. Kaithara Pappy rubbed her eyes and forced them open to the dull light of the night. Her body lay on the floor like the carcass of the cattle without a stitch on. Her long hair lay scattered around her. She felt her memories blocked behind a smoke screen. Her lips stank of spit and liquor and tasted of dried blood. She made an effort to lift herself off the floor with the support of her elbows, but her body didn't cooperate, as if it was chained and locked by a padlock at the midriff. She felt her body was stinking like the slush in the freshly ploughed paddy fields. Her nipples and the lower parts below the navel were on fire. As her fingers moved lower, the clotted blood coursing from her private parts between her thighs stuck to her fingers. The smell of slush and sticky blood nauseated her as her fingers ran on the marks left by the hooves of the lusty oxen who had ploughed her body.

She stared at the darkness outside through the windows. The spider spinning a web in her mind stirred a little. She remembered that it was those four soldiers who had brought her into the room. She tried to recollect her efforts to free herself from their clutches, the sickening soap smell of pots of water poured over her, the stripping off of all her clothes, and how she had bitten one man's wrist in her struggle.

'I will kill you, you whore', he had showered obscenities on her. 'It will be difficult if this whore is allowed to remain conscious. This obstinate bitch will bite and rip off our Captain.'

'We shall tie up her hands and legs and make her immobile', suggested another one.

'You dumb man, if you tie her hands and legs together, how can…' the third one abused him.

'Oh, I have a medicine for that', he pulled out a bottle of liquor tucked at his waist.

'Ptooey!' she spat on his face.

As she tried to wriggle out to make an escape, the four of them together incapacitated her and tied her to a cot. They poured liquor into her mouth forcibly. Then they violated her, taking turns. She screamed her guts out. Yet the bullocks in musth ploughed into her in a frenzy. The sharp iron point of the plough plunged into the swirls of the earth. She was unable to recollect much. The spider gnawed into the maze of her memory. Devils of fire danced in her head. She slowly got up and covering herself with a crumpled bed sheet lying on the cot, strode through the door, closing it softly behind her. She stared at the backwaters. Darkness slowly covered the corpse of the pale moonlight.

'There is no meaning in continuing this life any more', she decided. 'I should jump into this backwater and die. Let my body surface in front of their eyes.'

Her legs were giving away and steps were unsteady. She stood there holding on to the lamp post in front of the bungalow.

'You devils', she cried out in anguish. 'You devils of the funeral pyre... all of you together roast me and eat up my flesh!'

In the night, police constable Unnikandan reached the station pedalling his bicycle. He saw someone sitting on the steps.

'You rascal get up', he yelled as he got down from the cycle. 'I would have tumbled on to your head, if I had not seen you on time.'

He kept the cycle leaning against the wall, lowered the wick of the lamp and removed the muffler wrapped around his neck. There were only two police constables who had cycles in Cherthala police station. The new Hercules cycle owned by Pappan was kept under lock and key in the guard room, safe from dust and sunlight. But the old one belonging to Unnikandan could be kept anywhere. It was a gift from head constable Madanan Pillai who had been transferred to another station. One could not say it was a gift. It was a sort of settling an old loan account of twenty rupees he had borrowed from his subordinate in small amounts. Finally, in the end when he was about to leave, he made an announcement in front of everybody, 'I am gifting this cycle to you. You may keep it in my memory.'

Even when Unnikandan returned after keeping the cycle in its place, the man had not moved from his position.

'Phew, rascal, can't you hear what I said?' He removed the baton hanging on his shoulder. 'I don't like hitting or beating anyone. But if some people ask for it, what can I do? After all am I not a policeman? How can I put up with this kind of insolence?'

Unnikandan was annoyed. He stomped his foot on the ground with all his might.

'Hey man, move from my way.'

The man brought his palms together, bowed his head and made some sounds.

'Hey, who cuffed your legs like this?' Unnikandan looked at the security police who shrugged his shoulders.

'Why did they catch you?' Unnikandan turned back to him.

He blurted some sounds meekly.

'What's wrong with you? Are you a dumb mute?' the policeman prodded his bandaged chin.

In response the man again made some meek sounds.

'Oh, maybe a petty thief or a pick-pocket!' He went inside the police station.

There were eight to ten policemen sitting inside the room, leaning against the wall and scratching themselves.

'Where is that vaidyan?' he asked the head constable.

'Oh, he was allowed bail', the head constable said without lifting his head. 'As he was leaving, our Inspector sir kicked him on his shin. In his life, he will not treat any communist rascals hereafter. Ha...ha...ha.'

Unnikandan sat on the wooden bench stretching his legs.

'Who is that guy sitting on the steps with his legs cuffed?' he enquired.

'Oh, he is a trickster', said the Head, noting something on the paper he was going through. 'He is the one who has been dodging us all these days. We have decided the treatment for him. You can see now.'

Before he completed his sentence, three drunken constables entered carrying the man. They flung him on the floor in front of the lockup and started beating him with batons. Unnikandan sat there watching the scene without much feeling as it was not new to him. At each beating the victim shrunk his body into a round shape like a leech.

'You dirty pig, how dare you hoodwink the police and run around?' One constable kicked him below his naval.

He curled and urinated. Stench of urine spread everywhere.

'Enough, enough', Unnikandan intervened. 'If you continue to torture him, he will die in the lockup.'

'You don't know what type of a criminal he is', said the Head, irritated by the interference. 'During the last trade union strike, he threw a spear at our ASP Chandrasekhar.'

'Is that so?' Unnikandan lifted the man's head, holding his chin up. His ears were bleeding. Holding both his palms together, pleading, the man bent down to touch Unnikandan's feet.

'He is a skilled criminal', said another constable to Unnikandan. 'You don't interfere. I am going to make this rascal come out with the truth.' The policeman lifted the man.

'Oh, this has become a nuisance', said Unnikandan, stepping out and picking up his cycle. 'Its time to go for my night beat.' He lit the lamp on his cycle.

'Still.., was it the same guy?' He tried to recollect as he started pedalling. He tried to recall that day.

The procession holding spears, was storming towards the bridge near the burial ground. On the other side of the bridge were the police and the army, carrying guns. Assistant Superintendant of Police Chandrasekharan came forward and ordered:

'Halt!' The procession halted gruntingly.

'All of you should disperse immediately', commanded the ASP.

'We have to go ahead, give us way', said the leader heading the procession, holding his spear with its head pointed outward, ready for striking.

'If you don't disperse, we will have to open fire', threatened the ASP.

'We don't mind your gun shots', said the young comrade from the second row of the procession. 'We are not scared of your baton and gun.'

One spear came menacingly toward the ASP followed by another one. The third one came from the side of the bridge railings and Unnikandan leapt and caught it, saving the ASP from imminent death. The spears kept flying incessantly towards the police force. Somewhere from behind, a bugle was blown as an indication to start gunfire. Two constables waved the red flag to alert the police force. The ASP raised his hands above his head as a sign to start action. No one withdrew. The comrades surged forward holding the spears ready to strike. Gun shots reverberated in the air. A spear hit the shoulders of a policeman.

'Fire…fire…fire…' someone bellowed. Gunshots thundered. Police constables attacked the comrades swirling their batons. Comrades scattered.

When Unnikandan returned to the bridge, the gunshots had stopped. After the comrades dispersed there was a deathly silence. There was a comrade whose right leg and hand had been shot, and he was bleeding to death. As the ASP went near him, he sent a jet of blood from his mouth towards the ASP's face. Curling his left hand into a fist, he screamed. 'Let the revolution triumph, let Sir CP's police be damned.'

The ASP had removed his cap and stood before his body with bowed head. Unnikandan could not sleep that night. The moment he closed his eyes, the man's scream echoed in his ears.

As he was returning from his night round, a police jeep braked in front of him. Policemen seated inside craned their heads.

'So, your curse worked. That poor fellow died.'

'Didn't all of you together beat that poor dumb creature to death?' Unnikandan wanted to….

Instead, he thought, the one who died has gone forever. There is no need to anger one's colleagues. When a policeman is in a crisis, only his colleagues will be there to support him.

'Get into the jeep', beckoned his colleagues.

'Where are we going?'

'To the backwaters; if we move him now, no one will come to know.'

Unnikandan locked his cycle with a chain and padlock and got into the jeep.

In the afternoon, Dinar came to the house with two of the party comrades from Vayalar. A meeting had been scheduled for that evening in Vedikunnil to deliberate on the celebrations of Punnapra-Vayalar Martyrdom Day.

Party leaders from Vayalar were also attending the meeting.

'If we can reach there a bit early, we can acquaint you with the party leaders…', Dinar said.

Aparajitha turned to the Desabhimani Calendar on the wall. 27 October was indeed fast approaching.

'But who are these leaders whom we have still not met?' she asked, closing the book she was reading.

Dinar looked at the book. It was titled, *The Scapegoat and the Spearman* by KV Pathrose.

'Oh, that's true', said Dinar 'Comrades Vasu, Karunakaran, Gangadharan and Raghavan; yes, we have met them all. But I thought we could meet them in a group.'

'That's true.' Aparajitha admitted.

'Are you going to Muhamma tomorrow, to meet Comrade Karunakaran? You can also see the historical bridge in Mararikulam', said Dinar.

'Didn't a horrendous shootout take place there, while demolishing the bridge?'

'I would also like to see the place in Punnapra, where Aplon Auraj lived', Aparajitha added. 'The old police camp was his house. Was it not from there that everything started?'

'It did not start from there', an old comrade corrected. 'It started from the front yard of Comrade Kumaran's house. Was it not there that the comrades decided to attack the police station and capture the guns?'

'Oh, that's right', Aparajitha agreed.

The Comrades sat on the half-compound wall of the house.

'Okay, then you may get ready', Aparajitha told Dinar.

'Would you all care for something to drink?', she asked her visitors.

'Oh, no need for all that', replied Dinar.

'No, no, that's not acceptable', she walked inside.

'This verandah was the place where we all used to assemble to debate till late night and sleep during the good old days of Comrade Anandan', a senior colleague said nostalgically, running his eyes over the wooden roofing and supporting pillars.

'This is an old party family', he continued. 'The party used to conduct its cell meetings, off and on in this front yard when senior Comrade Kunchunni was alive. And remember, that was the time the party was banned. Do you know our honorable Comrade Krishna Pillai spent two days and nights here in the attic when he went into hiding?'

'Is that true?' a stunned Dinar and Aparajitha asked in unison.

'It is true', said the old comrade. 'If you don't believe me, you can check with Mr MR Nair who was working for the *Patriot*, and who is in Delhi now. I got this information from an article written by him.'

'MR Nair?' Aparajitha was further taken aback.

'Why, have you not heard of him? Maybe the new generation is not likely to know him.'

'No, I have heard my father talking about him', said Aparajitha. 'He was earlier with *Statesman.* Then he joined some news agency. He was the one and only media person in India who got the opportunity to interview the former Pakistan President, Yahya Khan, during the Indo-Pak war, on behalf of that agency.'

Disha walked in with buttermilk.

'No wonder', the excited senior comrade said as he picked up a glass, 'otherwise who would have heard of MR Nair?'

'But, how is MR Nair connected to this house?' Aparajitha asked.

'This house? Is he not a native of this place? Are his roots not here? Did he not grow up, get educated and get trained to become a journalist, from this party office?' He cleared her doubt.

Disha looked at them without knowing what was being discussed.

'Did you know? Comrade Krishna Pillai, during his exile days spent two days in this house?'

'Comrade Krishna Pillai...!' The plastic tray and glasses slipped out of her hands. 'Then why didn't anyone tell us till now?' Disha asked.

'But how was it possible to find out? They all would come in assumed names. No one would know who the person was', the senior comrade explained.

Disha still looked stunned.

'At least Comrade Anandan should have known about it', one of the comrades commented.

'That's true', said Disha. 'Father should have known about it.'

'I read this in an article written by MR Nair some three or four years ago about the underground life of Comrade Krishna Pillai in disguise.'

'Is there a way I can get hold of that article?' Aparajitha wondered.

'There is only one way I can suggest. Meet MR Nair in person and request for a copy', advised the senior.

'But one should know where he is!' Aparajitha was desperate.

'That I won't be able to tell you', the senior confessed.

'Who is this MR Nair?' Disha enquired.

'I will explain all that to you later Disha, but right now get ready to come with us.'

'Ok, we are leaving now', Dinar said. 'Both of you hire an auto and reach the meeting venue.'

'Alright', the party leaders said, 'We will meet at Vayalar.'

Aparajitha waved her hand. Disha was still lost in thought.

'The fact that Krishna Pillai was hiding in this house….' She turned to Aparajitha.

'Can that be true?'

'Could be', said Aparajitha.

'Yet, no one has mentioned it till now.'

'Didn't you hear him saying that he was here in an assumed name?'

'Still.' Disha looked at the wall from where her Grandpa Kunjunni peeped at her through a photo frame.

'Is this true, what I am hearing?' she looked into his eyes. Someone had drawn that picture very long ago. The eyes looked exactly like Niranjan's.

'If you had known this, couldn't you have told my father before you left? How thrilled he would have been to hear that.' She made a face at the photo.

How proudly Father used to narrate those stories… she tried to recollect.

Grandpa Kunjunni was also present in the procession whose destination was Kayyoor Central Jail where the Communist

Party leaders had been condemned to death. He was positioned behind Simon Asaan, who was holding a placard which said, 'Madras Governor, Please do not hang our Kayyoor Comrades'. The procession reached Kannur. By then the leaders had been hanged. It was well known that the chants of revolution rose sky-high as they went to the gallows shouting Inquilab Zindabad.*

Kunjunni Grandpa had also been a member of the reception committee appointed to receive the procession that came from Malabar to support the struggle for a 'responsible government'.

Those were the days when Sir CP had banned the Indian National Congress and the Muslim League. The whole country was in turmoil with agitations and rule-flouting, processions, police hunting and mass massacre; a large number of people who went in a procession to Thiruvanthapuram from Neyyattinkara were shot dead. There were widespread shootouts everywhere in the princely State of Travancore in which innocent people were shot down, when raging mobs turned out of control. Leaders like Pattom Thanu Pillai, TM Varghese, John Phillipose, C Keshavan and PK Kunju had been arrested and Sir CP's jails had started to overflow. Processions from Malabar lead by AKG and from Madurai lead by Pandyan were marching to Thiruvanthapuram, capital of the Travancore princely State. Police arrested AKG from Alwaye. Pandyan was beaten to death by the police in Chengotta police lockup.

On the birthday of the ruling King, a procession was organised to the royal palace under the leadership of Akkamma Cherian,

* Kayyoor is considered the cradle of agrarian revolution in Kerala. In 1940, peasants under the leadership of communists rose against local landlord.four communist leaders were found guilty and hanged by the government, One underaged rebel was given life imprisonment.

which was joined by enthusiastic youth from different parts of the State. The coir factory workers' union deputed twenty-five workers and Grandpa Kunjunni was one among them. Her father had told Disha that story many a times.

Diwan's administration had taken all precautions against anything untoward. Contrary to all the calculations made by CP, thousands of volunteers treaded through the streets, elegantly, in an organised manner. Freedom fighters wearing Gandhi cap, volunteers in red, all moved towards the western gate of the palace at the scheduled time when the King visited the royal temple, the Padmanabha Swamy Temple. The fort walls had trembled with the sound of slogans. Government authorities shook in their shoes. CP's armed police had confronted the mob. Akkamma Cherian, thrusting her chest, surged forward shouting, 'You police murderers who killed Pandyan..., shoot me down also.'

His Highness Sree Padmanabhadasa, Vanchipala Maharaja Sir Bala Rama Sekhara Kireedapathi Mannan Sulthan Maharaja Ramaraja Bhahadoor Shamsher, Jung Sree Chittira Thirunaal Maharaja, had escaped through the back gate without receiving the memorandum from the mob. The procession had then headed towards the Central Jail. Sir CP had to surrender. Under the pretext of offering a gift to the people from the Maharaja on his birthday, the doors of the jail were opened and the prisoners were given their freedom.

'We have to locate that MR Nair', said Disha.

'Yes', Aparajitha agreed.

As they were travelling to the meeting, Aparajitha was thinking. In Telangana and Nalagonda, more than two thousand villages had been taken over by the agitating mobs. Telangana had sprung up much before Punnapra, at least two years before. The Communist Party had gained strength as a people's movement right under the nose of the Nizam and Razakar rule.

The mob had surged forward towards fulfilment of the great dream of the farmers gaining ownership of the farms. Still, where did the people's movement slip up in the course of its great journey?

Wasn't Punnapra awakened by the thunder of the Communist movement in Telangana? Or was it earlier than that? She retraced the path of the revolution committed to her memory.

The Congress Socialist Party was formed in 1935 at a public meeting held in Thiruvannur in Calicut. Next year, the State Congress was born. Following a number of mass struggles, the Congress Socialist Party was declared as the Indian Communist Party in 1939, at a huge meeting in Kannur.

'What are you brooding about?' Disha asked. 'Mrinalda called twice, complaining that you are not picking up his calls.'

'There is no place for Mrinalda in my mind now', Aparajitha was irritated when Disha broke into her thoughts.

'Then who ?'

'I am too preoccupied with a road map to Punnapra-Vayalar.'

'At times, you become eccentric!'

'At times?' Aparajitha threw her head back and laughed, 'when am I not?'

Disha pinched her on her thighs and muttered, 'that auto guy will think that you are nuts'.

'Is that not a fact?' Aparajitha continued to laugh. 'Have you not heard? Writers are eccentric and enjoy bathtubs.'

Disha gave her a look.

'*Wall Street Journal* recently conducted a survey among writers to find out their way of writing. All were big and famous. You know, what is the fancy of Pulitzer Prize winner Junot Diaz? When he gets into the mood for writing, he locks himself inside the bathroom and writes. Man Booker Prize Winner Hilary Mantel rushes to the shower when her flow of thoughts gets stuck. You want to hear what Orhan Pamuk does when he gets cranky…?'

Disha's cell phone came to life.

'Oh, Mother is calling from home.' She picked up the phone.

'Wha…t? When?' Her face turned pale, nerves strained, and hands started trembling. 'Listen, quickly turn the vehicle and go back', she patted on the driver's shoulder. 'Fast!'

'What happened?' Aparajitha caught hold of her arm.

'The house is full of police', her lips quivered. 'They are searching Niranjan's room.'

'Niranjan?' Aparajitha was stunned.

'I don't know anything', Disha trembled.

Aparajitha could hear Disha's heart pounding like a drum.

The Clip is Coming

Vaidyan Kumaran came searching for Comrade Koman Kochhu Kunju Asaan who was stunned to see him crossing the split palm tree bridge across the narrow canal.

'Oh, you still remember the way to this locality?' pleasantly surprised, Asaan enquired. During their school days, both of them used to go to the primary school by this route. Once both of them reached adulthood, it was Asaan's practice to go and meet his friend at his clinic in the town. Never even once had the Vaidyan come over to his locality.

'Hey, Sekharan, quickly go and get a chair', Asaan excitedly called out to his nephew, 'See who has come.'

'Hello, who is this?' Sekharan came out and said mockingly, gazing at the sky. 'Has the crow started flying on its back? Is this not our vaidyan? Just two days ago, there was a talk in the union office that if we come to your clinic, you will break our knees. How come you are here now?'

'Is this the time to talk like this?' Asaan reprimanded his nephew and welcomed the Vaidyan. 'Come on in and have a seat.'

Sekharan brought an old mat and spread it for him on the mud floor polished with cow dung.

The healer looked gloomy. Something had gone wrong, Asaan concluded, looking at him.

'Old routes have changed. It has been quite some time since I came this side', said the Vaidyan. 'Our Nanappan's son seems to be going through some mental disorder. The astrologer says, while coming back from his work in the coir factory after the nightshift, he saw some evil spirit under the banyan tree and got a shock.'

'Then what happened?' enquired Asaan.

'I don't think it is any evil spirit or such nonsense', the Vaidyan explained. 'He happened to witness some of his co-workers being cruelly beaten up by the police constables and he was so shocked by the sight of the cracked bleeding heads that he is now sitting on his roof-top saying someone is coming to kill him.'

'How sad!' Asaan said unhappily. 'That kid used to go to school along with my Sekharan. How is he doing now?'

'I have advised them to try a herbal concoction for twenty one days', said the healer. 'Any average variety of mental disorder will be cured with that under normal circumstances. If it doesn't work, as an extreme step, I have some other treatment methods which were used by my ancestors in such cases. Any kind of incurable disorders can be cured with that treatment.'

'But you have walked a long distance to reach me', Asaan said. 'If you had sent someone for me, I would have come and met you in your clinic. Okay, what happened to that boy who was whisked away by the police?'

'Oh....' the Vaidyan lamented, wiping the sweat on his face with his upper mundu. 'The boy was beaten to a pulp.'

'What did he do to get such an extreme punishment?' Asaan asked with concern.

'Remember that young girl who came to our clinic, screaming her guts out?' the physician tried to explain, 'She is our Vishuvappan's sister. She is working in that coir factory near that temple. After her mother's death she moved into Vishuvappan's house. She happened to watch a group dance programme at the landlord's place. Fascinated, she organised some ten women to form a dance group. Problems started with that.'

'But what's wrong with that?' Asaan frowned.

'Our police CIDs (Criminal Investigation Department) visited the coir factory to enquire after the formation of the group and made a report on that. On the second day, early in the morning they barged into Vishuvappan's house looking for the girl. She was sitting in her friend's house next door. Vishuvappan refused to reveal her whereabouts to the police. That enraged them and he was taken away to the police station.'

'But why should the CID enquire about a dance group?'

'They do have some reasons uncle', Sekharan came out. 'Don't you know Comrade Meenakshi who is the one-and-only-woman member of the five-member workers union committee?'

'Oh, yes, yes...I have heard', Asaan nodded his head in the affirmative. 'The one-and-only-woman member....'

'Yes. She choreographed that folk dance, *Thiruvathira* for the celebrations at the party's annual meet.' Sekharan tried to remember that programme.

Women wearing red blouses and red flowers on their hair, standing in a circle and dancing, keeping step with the rhythm, to the tune of a song rendered by a twelve-year-old girl… *Thiruvathira* folk dance of Kerala.

The lyrics were the contribution of the on-the-spot poet Ramankutty Asaan.

Our mother land Bharatha Bhoomi also
is being looted by the dark forces of fascism
Time for us to come forward actively together,
my country men
For a long fight to save our mother land

'A thin girl like a creeper…' Sekharan tried to remember her name. 'She sang the song.'

'Oh, is this the girl who often sings at our party functions?' Asaan asked, 'Anasooya…'

'No, no', Sekharan corrected, 'Anasooya is a grown-up girl. This is a small girl… Medini… yes… Medini is her name.'

'We should invite both of them for our next annual function', Asaan proposed. 'We have to stage Keshavadev's *Karshakan*… Anasooya is ideal, she can sing as well as dance.'

'Then what about *Pattabakki*? Sekharan countered Asaan.

'Oh, we can stage that too.' Asaan turned to the Vaidyan. 'Ok, so coming back to our subject.'

'I don't think Vishuvappan is going to be of much use in the coming days', the Vaidyan said, looking very depressed. 'The injury is on the backbone. I examined him. I am sure he won't be able to sit up and roll beedis anymore.'

'Couldn't you have sent a telegram to Sir CP?'

'Are you trying to scoff me?' asked the Vaidyan, looking hurt.

'No, no, no', Asaan clarified. 'I was serious. Aren't you one of the vigilance committee members?'

'No point in talking about that now.' Kumaran looked into Asaan's eyes, 'I have already resigned from the committee.'

Asaan looked at the Vaidyan unbelievingly. 'What happened to you?'

'Enough is enough Kochhu Kunja', he muttered in disillusionment. 'I am sick and tired of the sights I have seen and the news I have heard. I am resigning from the Club of Landlords also. I cannot support murder and slaughter anymore.'

'They will make you a scapegoat', Asaan warned. 'Try to remain the same, as diplomatically as possible.'

'I know all that, my friend', said the Vaidyan. 'Even if I have to die, I can die with the satisfaction of having stood for justice. I have already decided my course of action. It's enough if you stand along with me.' Tears rolled from Kumaran's eyes. Asaan got up and hugged his friend. Holding him close to his chest, Asaan said emotionally, 'Not only I, our entire party will be with you.'

'From today I am also a Communist', said Vaidyan Kumaran. His lips quivered and Asaan's eyes turned moist.

The Vaidyan caught hold of Asaan's hands. 'I feel as if I have been relieved of a heavy weight from my chest.'

Asaan patted his hands.

Lal Salaam Vaidyare, Sekharan threw up his fist skyward and called out the Communist slogan, addressing the healer.

TheVaidyan's right hand went up involuntarily and fingers clenched to form a fist.

Asaan sat reflecting on what had been said as the Vaidyan took leave of him. Our country is in the grip of the tentacles of a fascist octopus which is tightening its hold and crushing her down. Sir CP is acting like a combination of Hitler and Mussolini.

Asaan had entered active politics during the Abstention Movement in 1932.* He was inspired by the newspaper *Kesari*, run by Balakrishna Pillai who wrote a column on the Movement every week which Asaan used to read with great interest.

CP's efforts in 1938 had all been directed towards demolishing the movement. His goon squad was entrusted with the task of handling the agitators. The goons publicly attacked Neelakandan Pillai who was the State Congress Secretary with an iron rod, resulting in a deadly head injury. The treasurer, Madhava Variyar was also attacked in a similar way. Activist Annie Mascarene's house was ransacked in the middle of the night and all their possessions were looted. A horse cavalry regiment was detailed to suppress the students' agitation. Meetings held at several places were dissolved using police and goons. They surrounded the audience and showered them with stones. The public also did not keep quiet. They fought back. They forced the police and goondas to retreat. Sir CP's iron wheels grunted against the people's agitation in favour of a responsible government. He gave orders to shoot the public twelve times in two months.

Meanwhile, people were led to the second stage of the boycott. As a prelude, in August, the State Congress leaders submitted a memorandum to the ruling King, listing out one by one the atrocities committed by Sir CP against the people. The Diwan refused to attend the meetings convened by the King for discussing the Memorandum. Mahatma Gandhi had then intervened.

* A social movement arising spontaneously among the lower castes, leading to the creation of the State Congress.

During the days of agitation for entry of the scheduled castes and tribes to the Hindu temples, Gandhi had visited Travancore in 1924-25. He was in constant communication with the Diwan regarding the situation in Travancore. Gandhi was not very happy about the memorandum and attacks on the Diwan. Senior Congress members like Pattom Thanu Pillai and TM Varghese set off to meet Gandhi to clarify the memorandum.

'Sir CP Ramaswamy Iyer is one of the eminent statesmen in India. Travancore King is a very kind ruler, always concerned about the welfare of his subjects. Your State is very lucky to have both of them at the helm of power. You should not be instrumental in denying your country the services of an excellent administrator like Sir CP. So, it would be wise on your part to withdraw the memorandum', Gandhi had advised them.

Sir CP had arrested the leaders who were responsible for submitting the memorandum and had appointed a special court to deal with the case and issued a notification to that effect. Due to Gandhi, Pattom and Varghese came back and withdrew the memorandum. The Youth League and Democratic Socialist Party had protested. The Youth League constituted an agitation committee and read out the memorandum in public.

At the end, Krishna Pillai had made a public statement. 'To withdraw the memorandum was certainly not the right action. But to maintain the unity within the Congress Party and take forward the agitation more strongly, we are putting an end to this debate.' The Comrade had saved a major split in the Congress Party by this intervention in 1938.

R Shankar had been the president of the State Congress Party in those days. His stand to withdraw the memorandum and comply with the prohibition had met with tremendous opposition within the party. The Congress working committee had met and resolved to go ahead with the agitation. One day before the agitation, Gandhi had sent a telegram. 'Hold the agitation', it had said. The radical wing of the Congress was disillusioned and had insisted on summoning a radical conference. Once again, the practical vision of Comrade Krishna Pillai had saved the situation. He had said:

'The need of the hour is unity between the left and right wings of the Congress. It is wiser to unite against the common enemy rather than split and fight on ideologies.'

On the eve of the harvest festival, CO Mathew had sent a note to Asaan: 'Tomorrow at eight in the morning wait for me near the local chapel. Keep some papers and writing ink ready, will discuss details in person.'

CO Mathew had come by car, accompanied by KC Pathrose, KK Kunjan, K Joseph and PK Padmanabhan. They had gone to the house of KP Keshavadev, Asaan recalled. Krishna Pillai had greeted them along with Keshavadev. His eyes roamed over everybody and had settled on Asaan. Then he looked at Pathrose.

'Mathew brought him along', Pathrose explained. 'His handwriting is as good as printing.'

'Um…' A smile had appeared on Comrade's lips.

'It is essential that the radicals come together urgently', Comrade had said. 'But that should be done, keeping the State Congress in one piece. It is essential to make a firm foundation from the level of the general public. We all are aware of certain questionable relationships that some of the senior Congress leaders are maintaining with the Diwan. We have to put pressure on them to commence an active agitation to take the movement forward.

We have to bring the State Congress and the people together. We have to avoid creating any situation that would lead to a split in the party, even if senior leaders like Pattom Thanu Pillai go to extremes. This is the time to surge forward unitedly.'

Comrade had listed out the different stages of the strike and their details. By evening, an outline of the plan and strategies were finalised in writing in a thirty-page document. Comrade went through the paper carefully.

While handing over the document to Pathrose, he had complimented Asaan, 'What you said is true. This handwriting is better than printing'. Comrade had extended his hand to Asaan. As he held on to that hand, the energy from his eyes travelled through Asaan like electricity.

'Next week I will be visiting Kommadi (a village panchayat block), where there will be a study class on the political importance of strikes by Comrade K Damodaran. You have to come without fail.' That was how Asaan's association with Comrade Krishna Pillai had commenced.

During the strike period of 1938, Comrade had been living in a room close to the library in Alappuzha. He had leased the premises in the name of a government official. Potty's tea shop was next door. Those were the days when the CIDs (men of the Criminal Investigation Department) of Sir CP were busy hunting for Comrade. One day, he was sitting in the tea shop waiting for the snacks he had ordered, when CID Madhavan Pillai entered the shop and took a seat opposite him. Comrade recognised him at once. The shop owner brought the snacks for Comrade.

'Get me a strong tea', the detective placed his order.

Comrade smiled at the detective, as if he knew him.

'How is the snack?' the detective asked him.

'It's a little spicy', said Comrade. 'Only when you taste you will know. Would you like to try one?'

The detective looked around nervously.

'Don't be nervous', said Comrade, 'you can take one'.

The detective picked one hesitantly.

Soon the policeman got talking: 'I am totally exhausted from the work in the past three to four days.'

'Hm…what happened?' Comrade enquired.

'A terrorist has come down from Malabar', said the detective. 'One Krishna Pillai. All these problems are his creations. Four or five of us have been trying to find out his whereabouts, but he is always in hiding. He never gets out in the daytime.'

'Do you have more details about him?' asked Krishna Pillai.

'He speaks Hindi very well. He has been to the North for a while and claims that he came back here to promote the language. But his intentions are different. He is a native of our Vaikom village.'

The shop owner came with tea for the detective. He emptied the glass in one gulp.

'How does he look?' asked Comrade.

'Don't I have to see him to know that?' said the man.

'That's true', said Comrade.

The detective looked at Comrade in confusion.

'I was saying, if you can give me some details, I would have drawn his picture.'

'Oh, you meant that', the detective noddded his head in approval. 'Still, you keep an eye open. If you come across someone with a narrow face, dark complexion, six foot, if you grow suspicious of someone….'

The detective fished out a cigarette from the bag and offered it to Comrade.

'I don't smoke after tea', Comrade refused politely.

'So long', said the detective and got up to leave.

'Unimaginable guts', Asaan reminisced, 'leading an agitation in the daytime without going into hiding. Remarkable'

'Lunch is ready', coming out of the kitchen after washing his hands, Sekharan announced, 'Come and have a seat. Let's start.'

Asaan woke up from his reverie. An appetising smell of spicy meat curry wafted through the kitchen.

'What is this? Have you cooked a non-vegetarian meal today?' Asaan enquired in surprise. 'Don't you know I am an avowed vegetarian?'

'Oh, this is not meat uncle', Sekharan laughed. 'When I got up this morning I found a few mushrooms had sprouted in the corner of our room, through the mud floor. So, I cooked it along with raw bread fruit, adding all the spices, like a meat curry. You are definitely going to like it.'

'In that case make sure that you apply some cow dung to that part of the floor', Asaan instructed, his mouth watering, 'otherwise the fungus growing inside the house will damage the floor'.

Asaan and Sekharan lived together in their ancestral home. Both of them had no other family. Apart from communism, only tasty food fascinated Asaan. Sekharan was an expert chef. He would grind nice spicy pastes on the grinding stone which added a special flavour to the curries he prepared. Still, the absence of a woman in the house was strongly felt by Asaan.

'I have remained a bachelor, a loner like this', Asaan pulled out a wooden plank and sat on it to eat. 'At least you should get married and build a family with children. Otherwise there will be no one to continue our lineage.'

'We can think about all that later', Sekharan replied while serving the food. 'There is not enough time even to attend to party work. And you are talking about getting married and setting up a family. How is it possible now? Well, all that can wait.'

'But you should remember that you are losing time, this is the right age to get married', said Asaan while dividing the heap of rice on the leaf into two parts.

When Unnikandan was about to leave the police station for his night beat, three police vehicles rolled into the front yard. As he set his leg on the pedals, he noticed three high-ranking police officers alighting from the vehicles. One among them was Deputy Superintendent of Police Vythi Iyer. He could not recognise the other two. He was petrified and jumped off the cycle, which fell down. He ran inside the police station through the backdoor.

The entire police force stood to attention. The DSP stormed inside, along with the landlords Pattathil Kartha and Kuttappan Anthrapper. All the three of them were in a drunken stupor. Inspector Koshy and SO Raman Kutty saluted them. The DSP stomped directly to the lockup.

'Bloody fool, what the hell are you doing here?' He pounced on Inspector Koshy.

'Sir', Koshy was in jitters.

'Didn't I ask you to stuff this lockup with those buggers?' He howled. 'You got only so many of them?'

'He is asking why the lockup has not been stuffed with the communists', Unnikandan muttered to the police constable standing next to him.

'Shh…' the police constable kept a finger on his lips and signed to Unnikandan to hush.

'Sir', Koshy saluted the DSP once again and said, 'we will do that latest by tomorrow sir'.

'Hm…' he grunted. 'Where are the leaders? Pull them out and whack them, right in front of us. Let these two watch and enjoy the scene', he grinned at the landlords. 'Come and have a seat.'

The DSP and the landlords took their seats. Inspector Koshy looked at the policemen and barked, 'Get them here'.

Unnikandan and the other policemen opened the lockup and lined up the prisoners in front of them.

'What's your name?' the DSP asked Comrade Prabhakaran.

'Prabhakaran.'

'Hmm…next?'

PK Madhavan.

K Das.

Sreedharan A.

CS Ramakrishnan.

OM Abubakker.

AK Paraman.

NSP Panikkar.

'Are you the NSP? You rascal!' the DSP growled.

'Yes. That's me', Comrade Panikkar stood boldly, unaffected by the threat.

'Don't you look like a soda bottle?' the DSP curled his fingers into a fist. 'Make him bend down and hit on his backbone till it fractures', he ordered the policemen.

The policemen rolled their cuffs and started the bashing. Comrades wriggled and screamed in sheer agony.

'Listen all of you', The DSP came to his feet, 'we will shoot down everyone in the Communist Party and reduce them to ashes'. The landlords also got up from their chairs.

While leaving, he turned back and threatened the comrades once again. 'Beware! These are your last few days. Get ready to die!'

'Did you hear what Master said?' Raman Kutty Nair lifted comrade Paraman and squashed him against the wall. 'All of you get ready to die. After the birthday of the Royal Highness, all of you will be gunned down to ashes.'

'Isn't the King's birthday on the seventh?' reflected Unnikandan. 'There are not many days left.'

Inspector Koshy stomped inside, after seeing off the DSP and addressed the prisoners who were in a pathetic state after the beating. 'To get you all in line, the Clip is coming from Alappuzha station.'

Unnikandan had heard of the Clip from head constable Appukuttan Pillai. It was used to torture prisoners by clutching their necks with an iron clip. As the grip tightened, the policeman would lift the man from the floor with one hand and poke the index finger of the other hand into the base of the throat and the victim suffocated.

'Stop standing idly and bash his guts', Inspector Koshy ordered the policemen, kicking Comrade Das on the shin.

Unnikandan bent his arm and hit on the backbone of Comrade PK Madhavan with his elbow. He wriggled with pain and fell on the floor, nose first. As he picked him up and lifted him again to kick on his backbone, Inspector Koshy said,

'Weren't you planning to leave early to attend to your ailing mother? You may leave now.'

Unnikandan left comrade Madhavan. Brushing away the sweat on his forehead, he removed his cap and dived into the darkness of the night.

She could only recollect her own screams, standing under the lamp post. Her legs buckled and she collapsed on to the ground. Somewhere, she could hear the panting of the hunting dogs. As the black spider stirred inside her head clogging her memory, Kaithara Pappy opened her eyes and found herself inside a locked room. Sunrays permeated through the slits on the door like needles. Her body was laid out on a mat on the cement floor, rolled in a bed sheet like a crushed shell fish.

Bootfalls outside the room. The hunting dogs entered the room. Nauseating stench of sweat and stale starch wafted through the room. A uniformed police official ran to her and pulled away the bed sheet covering her. She tried to cover her nudity by crossing her hands and legs.

'Finally, you fell into our hands only', the man gawked at her. 'Now let us also savour you.'

He pulled her legs apart and lifted her into his arms. She didn't struggle any more as there was no strength to do that and surrendered herself in a comatose state.

The Heights of Machhu Pichhu

By the time Disha and Aparajitha reached home in panic, the search was over. Two police vehicles rolled away, kicking up a cloud of dust on the mud road.

Neighbours peeped out to see what was happening. Crows raised a pandemonium, settling on the branches of trees. Disha went inside. Mother was crying, heartbroken. Aparajitha stood at the door, hesitant to get closer.

Disha sat on the bed. Mother looked at her with her red swollen eyes and wailed. 'He shouldn't have done this to you and me.'

'What did he do?' Disha asked.

'I don't know anything', Mother buried her head in the pillow.

Disha got out of the house. A few party comrades stood leaning on the wall around the well. Comrade Swamy was there.

'What happened, brother Swamy?' she asked him. 'Why did the police come? Couldn't you have asked them?'

Folding up his mundu, Comrade Swamy looked at his companions gravely. They turned their faces away.

'It is better to hear that from the police itself.' Comrade Swami lifted his chin up. 'Because it is a matter pertaining to the family of our senior comrade Anandan, we could not ignore this completely. That's why we are here. If Comrade Anandan had been alive, such annoying things wouldn't have happened.'

'What sort of annoying things?' Disha demanded.

'Young lady', he rolled up his sleeves, 'Don't act as if you don't know anything. After all, how many times have I come over here and told you not to spoil the relationship with the party. Did anyone in the family pay heed to that?'

'But you know that I was not here, brother Swamy', Disha implored. 'And as far as Mother is concerned, you know that… But what has that got to do with the present situation?'

'How does it matter?' He looked at his friends. 'Why don't you explain Ajayan?'

The young men looked at each other. Ajay was Disha's senior in college.

'How do we explain this?' said one among them. 'Didn't you also advise him a lot? Who knew this was what was playing in his mind?'

'I knew he was not on the right track.' Comrade Swamy unfolded his mundu and said. 'If my memory is correct, I told you about a question he asked me some time ago.' He turned to Ajay. 'You know, the way he snubbed me when I asked him why he was not visiting the party office?'

'He snubbed you?' Disha looked perturbed.

'Yes he did. Then he said, "you people have been trying to put this country on the right track for half a century, still have you ever thought of the twenty-seven million people living under starvation and absolute poverty?" I told him that that question was not to be addressed to our party but to the Congress and the BJP (Bharatiya Janata Party). After all, they are the people who have been running the country all these years!'

'Once he also asked me, – "Has it not been almost a hundred years since the Communist Party has been trying to bring about changes in the country, yet how far has it succeeded in its endeavour?"' – said Ajay.

'A hundred years?'

'Yes, a hundred. As a matter of fact, was it not in 1920 that the Indian Communist Party was formed in Tashkent?'

'Oh, that's true. It was on 17 October.'

'So, four or five years down the line, we will have completed one hundred years.'

'Couldn't you have listed the achievements of the party in bringing about social changes in Kerala, starting with the land reforms?' Swamy was agitated. 'What is this? Are you also trying to close your eyes to make the world look dark?'

'That was not his question comrade', Ajay tried to explain.

'How many armed struggles did the party conduct after the Calcutta Thesis? That was his question.'

'But the party had already recognised that the Calcutta Thesis was nothing but an ideologically bankrupt concept', Swamy twisted his face in distaste. 'Couldn't you have told him that the party now believes in democratic agitation tactics?'

'Whom shall I tell? Who will listen to all that?' Ajay rubbed his fingers on the half-wall.

'Okay, brother Swamy', Disha broke into their discussions. 'What shall we do now?'

'You don't need to do anything', said Swamy. 'Whatever has to be done, will be done by them.'

'By who?'

'The Police', he snapped, 'who else but the police?'

'Shall we make a move now?' He turned to his friends. 'Let them take care of themselves.'

'But brother Swamy…' Disha started to say something.

The mobile in his pocket began to ring.

'Who…?' Swamy held the phone close to his ears. 'When…? Oh…We are coming there.'

'What has happened Comrade?' Ajay appeared quite disturbed.

'Oh, because of one person, so many people are in trouble. The police have taken our Dinar into custody for interrogation. They have also closed and sealed our Swadeshabhimani library. Come on, let's go and see what's happening.'

Comrade Swamy folded his mundu and walked away with his friends.

Aparajitha came out from the room and said, 'tomorrow we both have to go to the police station'.

'Who says?'

'They told Mother.'

All the people had left. They were alone now.

'What did he do?' Disha looked at Aparajitha.

'He wouldn't have done anything', Aparajitha defended him.

'Then why the intrusion by the police?'

'After all, this is not the first time the police are raiding this house. Was it because someone did something wrong?' Aparajitha took off her spectacles and started polishing it. 'It's not easy to swim against the current. A few will have to become scapegoats. Is that not what happened to Che in Bolivia?'

'What are you trying to say?' Disha looked at her fearfully.

'What I guess…' she put on her spectacles again.

At night she sat in front of her laptop doing nothing.

She could not resume writing. She tried to call Niranjan on his mobile but it was always out of range. Deliberately she avoided calling Dinar on his phone. She was not sure if the police had released him from their custody. Mother never got up from her bed. Disha also lay next to her. Aparajitha was fed up answering the visitors who barged in.

She remembered Disha's mother picking up the holy book Ramayana on the first day of the holy month, dividing the page into two sections and reading, after skipping seven lines and seven alphabets as a ritual. The verses spoke about Lord Sri Rama getting ready for the battle. Is this an indication? Aparajitha was distressed.

She got up and opened the *Bolivian Diary* in front of the table lamp.

1 October, 1967.

Che reached a forest which was not very dense. Around forty soldiers were moving along the mountain ranges, with their guns spitting fire. They heard the last shot at noon. Albano said so, having seen five soldiers going down the mountains. The rest of Che's group then went searching for water. By nine in the night, all of them came back. One of them roasted meat for supper.

'This place is safe', Che said to himself. 'It is ideal to make an easy escape. Movements of the army also can be watched from here.' So, he decided to stay there for one more day.

'Where would Niranjan be now?' Holding the book close to her heart she prayed, 'Let him be safe wherever he is'. She closed her eyes in prayer. She didn't know whom to pray to. She wondered who would listen to her prayers. Would Aleida also have prayed for a moment?

Suddenly with a start, she skipped through the pages.

> 7 October.
>
> The Diary is coming to an end.
>
> This is the day which completes eleven months after the formation of our guerilla force. An old woman strayed into our premises to feed her goat. We had to keep her under custody. From her we got an idea of the mountain ranges. By evening we released her.
>
> We set off on our trek in the moon light. A very tedious journey indeed! We were sure that there was no point in continuing with the journey and camped around two in the night. Our hideout is about 2,000 meters above the sea level.
>
> Bolivian Diary came to an end.
>
> The next day Che was taken into custody by his opponents.

And the next day... she looked at the page in anguish. Only seven days are left.... Aparajitha closed the book. Her heart pounded madly. Her fingers trembled; throat dried up. She tilted the mud pot to drink water. The pot almost slipped off her shaky hands. Somehow, she kept holding on to it.

As she turned back, she saw Disha behind her. There were traces of dried tears on her face.

'I am not able to sleep my dear', Disha came closer.

'How is Mother?' She enquired.

'She slept.'

Aparajitha hugged her and drew her close.

'What does your mind say?' Disha asked, resting her head on Apu's shoulders.

'Don't be upset', Aparajitha patted her head.

'Will he be in any trouble?'

'No chance', Aparajitha said soothingly. 'He will come back soon.' But tears streamed down her face, falling on Disha's hair.

'You are in tears!' Disha became anxious. 'What made you cry?'

'Oh, nothing', she dried her eyes.

After Disha slept, Aparajitha went into Niranjan's room. The room had been ransacked by the police. The floor was scattered with books, papers, folders... Che's photo stuck on the wall looked gloomy. There were black and white photos of Comrade P Krishna Pillai and Bhagat Singh. She was noticing the photos for the first time. Maybe, they had always been there on the wall, but were not visible from outside. On the top of the almirah was his father's laminated photo. She sat on his bed. His scent was everywhere in the room. It engulfed her. His blanket was neatly folded and kept at the foot of the bed. She held it close to her face. She had sensed something very intimate in his scent, which had bonded her to him at their brief encounter under the tree on the Anakhan Hill. She realised much later why it captivated her. It was Comrade Sathyadas's scent; her father's scent. As a child when she slept in her father's arms, that scent would give her a sense of belonging. Niranjan had the same scent. The straight line she had drawn sometime back, from her father to herself, had now stretched till Niranjan, without her being aware.

She lay down, burying her face in the pillow, engulfed in Niranjan's scent as if she was in a trance. She woke up hearing footfalls near her. It was Disha.

'You....' She didn't ask anything further.

Aparajitha scrambled to her feet. Disha looked at her with moist eyes and wrapped her arms around her.

He interrogated her in a room away from the chaos of the police station. Disha was taken to some other room. He was the Inspector in-charge of internal security investigations. He went on questioning her left and right. Other than the table, covered by a green table cloth and two chairs there was no other furniture in the room. The only sound was the soft whir produced by a silent tape recorder doing its work. It was sucking up all his questions and her answers into its soul. After listening to her, finally he asked, 'So, you don't know anything besides what you have said so far?'

'No', she said. She was feeling nauseous at his insolent questions and bullish attitude, as if he was toying with a prey which had fallen into his paws.

'I am asking you once again, didn't he tell you where he was bound for?' Looking into her eyes, he asked her. She shook her head in the negative.

'Okay, I trust you', he said.

She had warned Disha also not to disclose anything about his trip to Bastar. They will trap him. His dreams are not meant to be shattered in a fake encounter.

Her heart throbbed at the memory of a scene in the crowded narrow streets of Ahmedabad. She remembered the protest march staged later by the students in Delhi in front of Jantar

Mantar, with their mouths covered with black cloth. She was also one among them, holding a placard of Ishrat Jahan. Later on, she came to know that one Mr Pranesh Pillai who had been shot down in the street was a Malayalee. Police had shot them down cruelly on the assumption that they were Lashkar-e-Taiba terrorists…!

'We suspect that he has gone to Bastar', he said. 'Do you have any idea about that?'

'No!' she said with a start.

He noticed the shock in her eyes.

'Why did you get startled?'

'Oh, nothing', she tried to conceal her shock.

He pulled out a paper from the folder lying on the table and extended it to her. 'See, we got this from his room.'

Her fingers trembled.

'Hm…read', he grunted.

'Communist Party of India (Maoist), Dandakaranya Zone Special Committee Press Communiqué Mahendra Karma…', she regarded him.

'Um….?' He grunted.

She continued reading.

Elimination of fascist *Salwa Judum* leader Mahendra Karma.

'It happened on 25 May last year. A group of twenty-seven people including the Congress leader Mahendra Karma was wiped out by People's Liberation Guerilla Army in an encounter. They were attacked while returning after participating in a *Parivarthan rally* (a procession for transformation) through the Bastar forests in well secured army vehicles. Thirty people including the former union minister Vidya Charan Sukla were wounded. The communiqué says that by overpowering the security personnel they confiscated arms numbering twenty-three.' The Inspector gave a lengthy explanation.

'Sir,' her lips quivered, 'What is Niranjan's connection....'

'You continue reading', he grunted again.

She glanced through the paper.

> 'The dog's death of Mahendra Karma, notorious tyrant, rapist, robber, maligned ass, corrupt... was celebrated by the entire region of Bastar. In truth, our goal was to eliminate all his accomplices in one encounter. They were all acclaimed adversaries of common people. Unfortunately, along with them a few innocent people also were killed. The *Dandakaranya* Special Zonal Committee sincerely regrets this slip up. We take responsibility for these murders.'

The remaining part of the communiqué contained the profile of Mahendra Karma. He was born in a feudal family although he claimed to be a tribal leader. His family history was an account of atrocities committed on the tribals for generations. He became a member of the All-India Students Federation when he was a law student and a member of the legislature in 1978, contesting on the ticket of the Communist Party of India. Next time, when the party denied him a ticket, he resigned and joined the Congress Party. Subsequently, he became a member of Parliament and later a minister in Madhya Pradesh. Thereafter, when Chhattisgarh was formed, he became a minister there too. He conspired with mafia gangs to smuggle timber worth millions of rupees from Bastar's forests. He was instrumental in using the police support for evacuating tribal families from their villages for formation of an iron and steel company in the private sector. He formed an organisation known as *Salwa Judum* to confront the Maoists who volunteered to protect the tribals from his atrocities. In Gondi language *Salwa Judum* meant 'cleaning hunt' an anti-rebel movement against Maoists. Hundreds of tribals were hunted and taken under police custody. They raped tribal women and burnt down their huts. 'As a last measure we had to eliminate him. Our red salute to the People's Liberation Guerilla Army.'

'What do you feel?' he regarded her.

'Sir, what's the crime in killing a criminal like Mahendra Karma?'

He didn't expect that.

'Are you a Maoist?'

'No sir', she shook her head, 'I am a humanist.'

'Then why that question?' He demanded.

'I feel that what they have done is right.' She said with conviction.

'We have a judiciary to decide what is wrong and what is right. What we want to know is not whether killing Mahendra Karma is right or wrong.' His voice became stern. 'We want to know what Niranjan's connection is with this incident. How did this document reach his hands?'

'Sir, isn't this just a newspaper report?' she tried to defend Niranjan.

'That may be true.' His eyes became alert. 'But why didn't this reach you or me?'

She had no reply.

'Something is rotten in the state of Denmark!' He twisted his lips in contempt. 'Isn't that an old cliché?'

'Sir, but I don't think Niranjan has any....'

'Leave that to me', he came to his feet, 'after all that's our job. In case he calls, in case you get any indication about his whereabouts, you are to inform us.' He stared at her fixedly. 'Even if you don't, we will come to know. And if that happens, you know, it will be very unpleasant?'

He came out of the room along with her. Disha was waiting outside. Her face had turned dark.

'Both of you can leave for the time being', he said.

'Both of you will be under our observation. We will have to meet again.'

'Sir', Aparajitha pleaded. 'That Dinar is a poor guy. He doesn't know anything.'

'Hm...', he muttered sternly.

As they walked along the road Disha said, 'they are torturing Dinar'.

'Did you see?'

'Hm...' Disha replied. But she didn't want to explain what she saw in the lockup. She had seen it through the window bars. They had stripped him off except for the underpants and he was lying on the floor with his hands tied behind. She saw him writhing in pain as their boots landed on his naval. She couldn't control herself and screamed out. At that time, a fat woman came running to her... her fingers ran over the black thick finger mark on her cheek.

'Did they find out anything from you', Aparajitha felt the mark on Disha's cheeks.

'No', Her eyes were swollen. 'And from you...?'

'Me?' Aparajitha laughed. 'George Orwell's Thought Police will have to come and extract anything from my mind.'

'Haven't you read Orwell's *1984*?' Aparajitha asked Disha. 'About the police who are trained to extract information from the minds of people?'

'Didn't they ask you', Disha continued 'about your conversation that night?'

'No', said Aparajitha. 'But you have not spoken anything about that to them, have you?'

'They will find out when they scrutinise Niranjan's call list, the text messages he has sent you, his missed calls....They might question you again.'

'Um...let them ask', said Aparajitha.

'They might ask... why he was calling you at midnight ...'

'Oh, what's there in it? Can't he call me at midnight?' Aparajitha was defiant. 'I will tell them that we were having an affair.'

She tried to stop a passing autorikshaw. It didn't stop.

'You are hiding something.' Disha looked at her suspiciously. 'Actually, what did he discuss with you that night?'

'My darling sister-in-law, please stop', Aparajitha mocked her with folded hands. 'I just wriggled out from the questioning of that police officer. Now don't you start all over again.'

'All right, I won't ask anything', Disha's face shrank.

It was a night when moonlight filtered through the branches of the fragrant Champak tree. Both of them had been sitting under it. She sat leaning on the Champak tree and he sat opposite her. A flower fell on her head. She had picked it up and inhaled its heady scent. The moon hid behind the clouds. Crickets stopped their screeching orchestra.

'It's so late in the night!' she reminded him. 'Don't you have to leave early in the morning?'

'This night is not meant for sleeping', he said.

'But I am feeling sleepy', she complained.

'For my sake, just this one night', he pleaded.

'The melody of love you hummed has dissolved in the pure air of ...' she recited a line of poetry written by a well-known poet.

'Is that not the story of unrequited love?' he asked. 'Despite knowing about the heroine's deep love, the hero Divakaran abandons her to become a yogi? Even after his return, he is unable to recognise her love and give her back the love she has been longing for, for many long years.'

'Don't the yogi and the rebel follow the same path?' she asked, 'and the sting of neglected love… it's all the same.'

'What exactly do you mean?' he came close to her.

'Love humiliated!' She dropped the flower on the ground. 'Is that not what you are also doing now?'

'Did I humiliate your love?' he asked her.

'Um…' she said. 'Love nestled somewhere in the inner recesses of my mind… you were the one who stirred it up… unbeknown to me… and at the end, you….'

'Will I not come back?' He wrapped his hand around her shoulders. 'And then, together don't we have to journey to those far off places… through Cuba, Chile, Bolivia, Peru, to the heights of Machhu Pichhu?'

He held her tight.

Tumi Shundor she said in Bengali, 'You are so handsome.'

'Cling to my body like a magnet; hasten to my veins and to my words….'

His lips caressed her forehead and closed her eyes.

Nothing to Lose but Shackles

Pakkaran had reached the *Pattayam* house, jumping across a small canal. Somebody had told him that Prabhakaran had gone there for farm work. It was more than four days since he had seen him. The rumour was that he had also stopped working in the coir factory after Kaithara Pappy disappeared and had kept away from everyone. Anakhashayan also reported the same news. He had gone to Prabhakaran's house twice only to see the door locked. He had finished the roofing work of his house two weeks ago with coconut fronds woven into mats and there was an additional lean-to on the western side of the house which was a new extension. When Anakhashayan went inside the lean-to, he found a stump fixed to the floor, used for tying a cow. There were a few newly-planted flowering plants like jasmine of different varieties, marigold and other golden yellow flowers. By the side of the kitchen a few banana saplings were also seen. Comrade Karunakaran had reported to Anakhashayan that he had seen Prabhakaran coming from the nearby market holding a few household accessories like kitchen vessels, spoons, ladles, brooms, mats, and grocery.

'What happened to Prabhakaran?' Karunakaran quizzed him, 'why does he keep aloof from everybody after Kaithara Pappy went missing?'

'Oh, is that Pakkaran? How come you are here?' Pakkaran heard the sound from the top of a coconut tree. When he looked up, he found the toddy tapper Kochhappi descending from the tree.

'Oh, brother Kochhappi! When did you start tapping toddy?' Pakkaran asked.

Kochhappi was the youngest brother of Danavan, the toddy tapper of the village. When Danavan had become mentally disturbed, Kochhappi took over his work. Anakhashayan had told him that story. Both of them had been small kids. Danavan had absconded with his bride Thanka from a distant village and she was taken away forcibly by the landlord. As the landlord tried to molest Thanka, she bit him on his sensitive parts. As a punishment the angry landlord buried her neck deep in a pit on the ground. She was carrying a baby and could not withstand the torture. By the time Danavan came back, it was too late. From that moment he lost his mind. Anakhashayan was a witness to the incident along with Kochhu Kuttan Asaan.

Kochhappi came down with a pot full of toddy. Watching the toddy frothing in the pot, Pakkaran's mouth watered. Kochhappi knew that Pakkaran was yearning for the toddy. It was a common superstition that one should not allow a person to go without food after the person's mouth has watered at the sight of it. So, he decided to give Pakkaran a little toddy to satiate his yearnings. He also wanted to know something from Pakkaran. Kochhappi was clever enough to judge that this was the right opportunity.

'If you want to taste a bit of the freshly tapped toddy, you can have some', he told Pakkaran.

'But I don't see even a coconut shell to pour it into', said Pakkaran.

'You come along with me', Kochhappi invited Pakkaran. 'I am done with my work today. Both of us can go sit somewhere peacefully, drink a little and chat.'

Kochhappi started walking, his strong muscles moving in rhythm with his walk. Pakkaran was behind him.

'Okay, whom were you searching for here?' Kochhappi turned back and enquired.

'Oh, I came looking for our comrade Prabhakaran.' said Pakkaran. 'It has been more than three days since I saw him.'

'But what's the point in coming here to see him?'

'I was told that he came to this farm for work.'

'Oh, that was yesterday', Kochhappi reported. 'He came to my hut after his work and demanded a glass of toddy after paying one coin from his wages. I gave whatever stock I had and tried to give him back the change. But he refused to take it. Gulping the toddy in one swig, he walked off in a great hurry.'

'Has Comrade Prabhakaran taken to drinking?' Pakkaran was surprised. 'What happened to make him start drinking suddenly? He never used to drink before.'

'If you don't tell anyone, I will tell you something in strict confidence', said Kochhappi.

Pakkaran started walking abreast with Kochhappi.

'Are you aware that the Pulaya woman of Kaithara was abducted by the army?'

'Hm... I heard someone mentioning that', Pakkaran said.

'Was she not a firebrand?' Kochhappi continued, 'these two were a bit too close. People had started talking about them... that there was something fishy between the two.'

'Who told you all this gossip?' Pakkaran asked.

'Do you know when she was being dragged to the army vehicle, she was calling out his name, Prabhakaran Chetta, Prabhakaran Chetta...' Kochhappi put forth his proof of their relationship. Our neighbour Cheera Aunty, who pursued the vehicle screaming, heard her shouting.'

Pakkaran's pulse accelerated. Had Prabhakaran come to know about this? Is it because of this that he has gone berserk?

'Why are you quiet after hearing all this?' Kochhappi demanded. 'So, you also have heard about all that happened.'

Kochhappi opened the mud pot filled with toddy. Pointing to two shells of coconut, he asked Pakkaran to pick them up and wash them in the nearby pond. Pakkaran was hesitant, thinking that the pond water might be dirty if people had been using it for washing their bums after defecating.

'Oh, no... that pond is a new one. It was dug for the purpose of sun *pooja* just fifteen days ago.' Kochhappi clarified.

Pakkaran remembered. He had also attended the night pooja along with Anakhashayan to taste the sweet round rice cakes. All said and done, sweetmeats prepared as *prasad* for such night poojas were definitely more delicious than those they prepared for the routine temple pooja, he thought.

'Maybe it's like that because the moonlight is more beautiful than the sunlight, isn't it?' he asked Anakhashayan.

'No, sunlight is far more beautiful than the moonlight' Anakhashayan had objected.

Pakkaran brought both the coconut shells after washing them.

'Ok, now you pluck a peduncle from the coconut tree', Kochhappi told Pakkaran.

Pakkaran knew that it was meant for straining the freshly tapped toddy to remove the insects and beetles floating in it. Pakkaran drained the filtered toddy from the coconut shell into his throat greedily.

'This is the nature of our people', Kochhappi laughed. 'We don't mind drinking toddy that has been invaded by insects and flies, but if a fly floats in the drinking water, we will not touch it.'

Pakkaran extended the coconut shell to Kochhappi. While filling it again, Kochhappi asked him softly.

'Pakkaran, since long I have been thinking of asking you something.'

'What's it?' Pakkaran shifted his eyes from the toddy.

'Have you found anyone for Kochhu Paru?'

The coconut shell slipped from Pakkaran's hold.

Koman Kochhu Asaan had come to Kumaran Vaidyan's clinic early in the morning. The Vaidyan was busy stacking the wooden planks which served as the entrance door to the clinic when fixed adjacent to each other in the grooves. Asaan began helping him to arrange them in order.

'But why are you doing all this by yourself?' Asaan asked, lifting a plank with one hand. 'Who will take care of you if you happen to sprain your back? If the doctor himself falls ill, who will then treat him?'

'Vishuvappan was doing all these hard chores', the Vaidyan panted. 'To tell you the truth, I never knew this work was so hard. Only when we do the work, we realise how tough it is.'

'All labour is like that, my dear friend', said Asaan. 'Only when we try to do it by ourselves will we know the pain of it.

Turning the wheels in a coir factory is equally tedious. What about the labour in paddy fields and farm lands? Ultimately, the poor face untimely death on account of asthma and tuberculosis.'

'You are right Asaan.' The Vaidyan came to sit on his chair. 'Only now I realise that. The landlords and the rich happily lead a lazy life and enjoy themselves.'

'You have become a human being only now!' Asaan chided him.

'But, why are you here this early?' his friend enquired. 'Any health issues?'

'What sort of health issues can trouble me?' Asaan said confidently. 'I was busy working in my farm for two hours before walking all this distance to come here.' Asaan looked at the veins jutting out in his arms proudly.

'Were you not asking if I fall sick, who is there to take care of me?' the Vaidyan said. 'I at least have a wife to look after me. But, what about you? Whom do you have other than that young nephew?'

'Oh, are you asking me to marry… now in this old age…?' Asaan ran his eyes on his own body.

'I was not referring to you', the Vaidyan teased Asaan. 'I was talking about your nephew Sekharan.'

'But he is busy all the time with the party and the union office', Asaan complained. 'The other day, I tried to discuss this with him. But he does not listen to me. He left here for Alappuzha the day before yesterday. He has not returned yet. That is why I am here to spend some time chatting with you.'

'Oh, what's new in Alappuzha?'

'Comrade Pathrose has summoned a meeting there to discuss something serious. It was Comrade CK who asked Sekharan to accompany him. After all, like Pathrose, that guy also is a Stalin follower.'

'Who?'

'Our CK.'

'Oh, I thought Sekharan.' The Vaidyan got up from his wooden chair, came out and sat down on the easy chair kept in the verandah.

'Oh, he is also like that, at least no less than that. If the party decides something, he will unquestioningly follow it', said Asaan.

The healer opened a brass container, picked up two tender betel leaves and offered them to Asaan with slaked lime.

'No, thanks', Asaan declined, 'I seem to have ulcers in my mouth. This morning I chewed some green leaves of the jasmine plant.'

The Vaidyan made him open his mouth and extend his tongue. 'How is the bowel movement? There are white patches on the tongue. It could be a sign of arthritis. I will give you a herbal concoction when you leave.'

'Okay' Asaan replied. 'Did you see yesterday's *Kesari* newspaper?' he asked.

The Vaidyan pulled out a paper from the stack of newspapers arranged date-wise and read.

'It has been decided to conduct a countrywide strike at the Travancore Trade Union meeting from 22 October onwards. Like in the year 1938, this time also the strike will coincide with the grand birthday celebrations of the Royal King', the report said.

'Let's hope that at least this time, it will be conducted properly and seriously', said the Vaidyan after reading out from the paper.

'Oh, last time, it was because of a slip-up on the part of Comrade Sugathan', Asaan tried to explain. 'Finally, Comrade

AK Gopalan and P Krishna Pillai had no other choice but to support Comrade Sugathan in the interest of maintaining unity in the party.'

Asaan still remembered clearly P Krishna Pillai's dictation eight years ago, which he had written down in his neat hand writing, sitting in the house of author Keshavadev. Finally, Krishna Pillai and KV Pathrose had to painfully watch the failure of the strike. Kochhu Kunjan Asaan was sitting in the corner of the ground where they had conducted a meeting to discuss the strike.

Those days KV Pathrose was a worker in William Gudekar. Three of his younger brothers were employed in Darragh Smail. No one could beat Pathrose in spinning coir which was his skill. Comrade P Krishna Pillai had discovered him in a coir manufacturing factory. He had attended school till third standard. On account of poverty, he had to give up his studies and take up employment in the coir factory to take care of his family. P Krishna Pillai discovered the fire burning in him to fight against the injustice that ruled society. He found many others too; whose minds were ablaze. Those were the people who surged to the frontline of the trade union agitations in Alappuzha.

Study classes were conducted during the initial days by Comrade Krishna Pillai himself.

'How do the mill owner Gundert and the rich feudal lords amass so much wealth?' Comrade used to ask his students, with his eyes scanning over everyone and then answer himself. 'Comrades, that is done by accumulating the residual value of our hard work.'

They were hearing the terminology "residual value" for the first time.

Comrade would explain:

'The rich business owners export the mats and carpets woven by you to foreign countries by ship. Do you know how much they get as price for that? Five hundred or one thousand times the pittance of wages they pay you. But how were the mats and carpets made? What were the mats before you wove them?'

'Coir.'

'Even before that?'

'Coconut fibre.'

'And before that?'

'Outer husk of the coconut.'

'How did the coconut fibre originally grown on the top of the coconut trees become mats and carpets which fill the coffers of the rich businessmen?' A smile brightened his face. 'It's with your labour.' He paused and regarded everyone. 'So, who deserves its final value in terms of the price?'

'We!'

'But where does it go?'

'Into the pockets of the rich Mudalali, the capitalist.'

'Is that not rightfully ours? So, don't we have to fight and get it?'

'We should fight… fight and fight.'

'We are not claiming the entire value', continued Comrade. 'The fiber is from their farms. The coir factory belongs to them. The capital to run the factory also is theirs. All that we demand is the fair wages for our labour. Carl Marx defines that as the *residual value*.'

Major demands that Comrade Krishna Pillai raised in the labour strike were also the same. Fix minimum wages as Rs 30 per day. Sanction of maternity leave with wages for women workers. These were all unheard of in trade practices.

'But Comrade, during the period of delivery, women workers are not working', said Comrade Padmanabhan. 'In that case is it not injustice to ask wages for those days?'

'So, do you feel that the women workers should be starving during their delivery period?' Krishna Pillai asked, folding his mundu.

'Not exactly...', Comrade Padmanabhan scratched his head.

'Women are discharging a crucial function of nature by delivering children which is very important to sustain the human race.' Comrade explained. 'They need rest for at least three months. But now they are back to work by forty-one days. That's only because there is no other option for them to avoid starvation.'

Everyone clapped and accepted Comrade's arguments.

'In this struggle, the entire labour class should wake up like roaring lions, shaking their manes, and fight the capitalists and ruling classes and force them to bend their knees. Only through fighting for our rights can we snatch away the power we deserve.' Comrade Krishna Pillai became agitated.

'As the Russian rebels stated, all that we have to lose is the chains tied to our legs, but what we gain is a new world.'

'Coir factory workers, Union President PK Kunju and R Sugathan are in prison. Pathrose, you have to take care of things efficiently and effectively', he instructed.

Comrade Padmanabhan, retired from the army, was summoned to train five thousand red volunteers.

Comrade Pathrose had adopted the slogan, 'All that we have to lose is the chains tied to our legs, but what we gain is a new world'. The slogan echoed on the roads of various districts. All coir factories from Aroor to Vandanam struck work. Port workers also stopped work. Wheels of vehicles stopped turning. As the work was struck, movement of commodities also stopped.

Sir CP had decided to break the agitation. From the time the State Congress had called for agitation for 'responsible government', the country was flooded with goons known as the 'Five Rupee Police'. They took matters into their hands and attacked everyone. The jails were filled with agitators. There was no more space in the cells. CP found a way out of that crisis. The agitators were captured in groups, beaten down and dumped in faraway forests, a sort of putting them in exile.

The third day after the strike commenced, it was the birthday of the Royal Highness. Sir CP had then adopted a new strategy. He released all the leaders from the jails, as a gesture of goodwill on Maharaja's birthday. But CP kept in reserve bullets for the agitating workers.

A huge meeting of the agitating workers had been in progress on the seashore in Alappuzha. Comrade Krishna Pillai was addressing them. As he remembered the incident so many years ago, Asaan got goosebumps on his arms.

'What happened?' his friend asked, noticing it. 'Why are you getting goosebumps?'

'I remembered the day when the Alappuzha seashore turned into a red sea. Five thousand red volunteers trained in army discipline leading the procession. Behind them were women volunteers followed by ten thousand workers, holding red flags and standing in four lines. Roar of the human sea reverberating on the seashore…'

Comrade was standing on a platform made by joining four or five wooden benches placed closer to the sea and was addressing the rally facing them from the west. A few comrades stood on wooden tables in various places in the crowd and repeated the speech to make it easy for everyone to understand the gist of the speech.

The police force had waited for the labourers to return from the meeting, near the bridge by the side of the burial ground. The police attack came without any warning. Comrades who collapsed with fractured heads were dumped in the Commercial Canal.

Asaan could not return home that night. He slept on the verandah of the union office. Next day Comrade Krishna Pillai summoned an emergency meeting of the agitation committee which had around a hundred members. Only eleven members turned up. KV Pathrose, KK Variyar, CO Mathew, PA Solomon….

'What happened to the rest?' Comrade was disappointed.

'They may be scared of the police', said KK Variyar.

'By the time the gun fire was over the day before….' PA Solomon tried to explain reluctantly….

'That is CP's vicious trick', said Comrade. 'Release the leaders and shoot down the workers… tear down the worker's faith in the movement.'

'Even State Congress leaders are not returning to the strike venue. The dishonest rascals….' KV Pathrose was enraged. 'That Pattom and TM Varghese….'

'Everywhere they are organising welcome parties to receive those leaders released from jail. They are running around jubilantly, having forgotten everything', said Variyar.

'This is the treacherous nature of the national bourgeois. They are not trustworthy.' Comrade's face had become dark. 'That doesn't mean that the working class should retreat, accepting defeat. If this strike fails, the foundation of future struggles for our rights will become shaky. CP's next move will be to organise those renegades among us against strikes and defeat our struggle. We have to resist that. We have to start picketing from tomorrow. The first batch should consist of the members of the strike committee, including Keeran and Mathew. What do you say Keeran?'

KK Variyar had nodded his head in the affirmative.

'Who else is ready to join?' Comrade enquired.

'I am ready', PK Solomon raised his hands.

'I don't have to make a mention of my inclination, do I?' KV Pathrose raised his head from his seat.

Comrade made a long list of the members who were not present. 'Everyone should be informed today itself.' Comrade handed over the list to Comrade Pathrose.

'If Comrade had not taken that firm decision at that time', Asaan told the Vaidyan, 'they would have hammered the final nail on the coffin of the labour organisation. Sir CP would have demolished our movement forever.'

'Still, didn't the strike fail? Didn't Comrade Sugathan demolish it in total?' The Vaidyan reminded Asaan.

'Hm….' Asaan agreed.

Without the knowledge of the Agitation Committee, Comrade Sugathan had entered into an agreement with the mudalalis, the factory owners, and the strike call was withdrawn. All that the workers had got in 1938 was one anna, for one rupee. (16 annas made one rupee.)

Entire workers' community was opposed to the decision to withdraw the strike. Comrade along with AKG had called for an emergency meeting. Pathrose exploded and showered obscenities on Comrade Sugathan. Comrades were of the opinion that the agitation should continue. Comrade had listened patiently to everyone and spoke softly in compassion.

'It's true that Comrade Sugathan surrendered the movement, which we all had built up by spilling our blood and sweat for a pittance of one anna. But he is a senior leader. Under these circumstances, if we continue the agitation, our enemies will be the winners. There will be splits within us…'

It had taken a whole night for Comrade to explain and arrive at a consensus. As the day broke, the decision had been printed and sent over to all the wards.

'This time it won't be like that', said Asaan folding the paper. 'We will win our civil rights. Sir CP will have to step down. American Model will be flung into the Arabian Sea. You just wait and see.'

At night Mrinalda called.

'How far have you progressed with your writing?'

'Um… it is going on', Aparajitha said.

'Will it be over soon?'

'Can't say', she laughed. 'Aren't the characters emerging one by one from behind the screen of history?'

'Without your knowledge? Are they not coming from your mind?'

'Even I was under that impression. But experience shows otherwise', said Aparajitha. 'The characters are flowing down to my fingertips without my knowledge. They are the ones selecting the letters from the keyboard. They only are guiding the course of the story. I am just a toy in their hands.'

'But are they all not facts?' Mrinalda laughed. 'They will have many things to say, besides what is there in the official written history. Okay, have you named your novel?'

'No Mrinalda. I want you to think of a name.'

'Hm… is it not the story of that historic struggle?' Mrinalda enquired. 'What's the old name of the place?'

'Karappuram, meaning seashore.'

'Um…. Let me think about it.'

It reminded Aparajitha of one dusk in Dakshinapuri, in front of the Godavari Hostel, where they had a meeting sitting on a flat rock as usual. Mrinalda had arrived earlier and found a seat for himself. The discussion was on the thermal power plant in Koodankulam. Their friend Elengovan had just returned from his home town Thirunelveli after visiting Koodankulam. Elengovan had commenced his higher studies after his marriage. His pregnant wife Selvi was yearning for the famous milk sweet known as Agra ka Peda. He had gone home with a two-kg pack of the sweet to participate in their harvest festival Pongal.

The mobile rattled as Elengovan was firing away against the thermal plant. Mrinalda picked up the phone.

'Stop all the discussions', he looked very excited. 'Here's some happy news. Elengovan has got a daughter.'

Elengovan snatched the phone from Mrinalda.

'Don't we have to find a nice name for the baby?' Everyone together lifted up Elengovan. ' – a name in memory of this moment!'

'The name will be Kalindi', declared Mrinalda without having to think for a long time. 'We will call her Kalindi.'

Kalindi – the river that was poisoned by Kaliyan, a mythological negative character. Kalindi – who was restored to normalcy by Sree Krishna whose heart melted at the sight of the floating carcasses of cattle, who had drunk water from the river.

'I had called Disha...' Mrinalda woke her up from her reverie. 'She told me everything that happened there. I am making arrangements to make enquiries about him in Bastar. But how do you know that he has gone to Bastar?'

'Okay, then regarding what I called you for....' Mrinalda was slightly reluctant to continue. 'Well, let it wait. For the time being, you should stay with Disha.... In the present situation....'

'Mrinalda, why did you call me?' Aparajitha asked.

'You may have to come to Delhi.'

'Delhi? What for?' She was slightly puzzled.

'Oh, nothing. I will call later.' Wishing her goodnight, he rang off.

Invisible Wavelengths

Pakkaran wandered around searching for Anakhashayan. Finally, he came to know that he was attending study classes in the Chathanchira ward. The place was only two miles from the Ponnamveli Market where the army was camping. They could raid the place at any moment if they got scent of it. The class was conducted by a senior comrade in hiding who had come from the north. So, there were a few comrades kept on alert to protect him. They were questioning Pakkaran on the way. By then Comrade Karunakaran passed that way.

Around sixty comrades had assembled under the shade of the fully blossomed portia tree. There was a comrade wearing rosaries around his neck and dressed in a loose banian and mundu. His well-oiled hair was combed backward sleekly. His face was cleanly shaved. Pakkaran thought that he was in disguise. His mannerisms and body language didn't seem like those of a Christian. In the front row, Comrade Padmanabhan was sitting with his elbows resting on his knees. Next to him sat Comrade NP Thandar.

Pakkaran found a place in a corner.

'Comrades, so this is what I was trying to tell you.... We are being pushed into a big struggle by CP and these mudalalis and landlords. If CP is planning to confront the agitation of people with batons and guns, it is not going to work with the communist comrades. We will face the onslaught, standing together firmly, risking our lives. My dear comrades, the state of affairs is the same in Malabar too. What happened in Morazha?' Comrade looked around. 'Was it not because of the unbearable spiraling prices of essential commodities that our farming worker colleagues called for an agitation? The British collector banned all demonstrations, processions and public meetings. Farming workers' organisations, without paying any heed to the declaration, went ahead with the agitation. The government confronted the workers who were in a peaceful agitation with bullets. They shot two of our colleagues' dead, Comrades Abu and Chathu Kutty. In other locations too, there were similar confrontations with the police. One sub-inspector of police happened to die in one such incident. Police took into custody thirty-eight of our comrades for that offence and charged them with man slaughter; But what about the murder of two of our colleagues in Thalassery? It was not at all a matter of concern to them. That's how our lives are valued by them. The Special Court on investigation punished our comrades for a maximum of seven years' imprisonment. But the government went on appeal against that order in the Madras High Court and obtained an order from the British judges to hang KP Gopalan, unto death, and seven others including Comrade Vishnu Bharateeyan to be sent on lifetime imprisonment. People in Malabar were agitated at the order to the extent that Nehru and Gandhi had to intervene. At the end, on the twenty-eighth day, the Court had to revise its order, to quash the order to hang and reduce the punishment to lifetime rigorous imprisonment.'

Comrade picked up the water pot and emptied its contents into his throat, wiped his mouth, inhaled deeply and continued his class.

'Comrades, is this not the same bourgeois Court that hanged our comrades who lead the Kayyoor agitation? What was their fault? Wasn't it for resisting the police who barged into every house in the locality and assaulted everyone including the women? When a police constable got killed in the clash, they fabricated a man slaughter case and hanged our comrades Appu, Kunjambu Nair, Chirukandan and Abubacker. In spite of all adversities, what inspires us to get out into the streets holding red flags, braving the batons and guns of the police, thrusting our chest forward? It is only the intense desire to live like human beings; if at all we live, we should live like human beings. Rather than living as slaves, it's better for us to fight for our rights and die a hero's death. We will follow the path of the brave comrades who have marched before us and sacrificed their lives for freedom from exploitation.'

The audience sat frozen. The only sound that could be heard was the murmur of the wind caressing the leaves of the portia tree.

Suddenly there was a stir. Anakhashayan sprang up, throwing his fists to the sky. 'Long live the brave martyrs...Brave martyrs Zindabad Zindabad.'

'Don't repeat that anyone', Comrade Padmanabhan also scrambled to his feet. 'This is a study class. Remember, CIDs are sniffing around to catch the scent.'

'Senseless guy', Padmanabhan grimaced at Anakhashayan.

Anakhashayan shrank back. Pakkaran walked towards him.

'Come here', the man wearing the rosaries smiled at Anakhashayan. He went to him reluctantly. The man wrapped his arms around his shoulders. 'Bold guy! Have you heard of Comrade CP Krishnan Nair?' He asked the audience.

'He was active in the Kayyoor agitation. He was of the same age as you. Because of his tender age, the Court reduced his capital punishment to life.'

The man patted him on his shoulders and lifted his fists upward. Anakhashayan also did the same thing. His face, which was gloomy, brightened. Comrade Padmanabhan pretended to not see that.

'Come, we have to go somewhere.' Pakkaran got him outside the class.

'Where to?'

'To the house of that toddy tapper Kochhappi.'

'What for?'

'He asked me something yesterday.'

'Um...what's it?'

'Whether we have promised our Kochhu Paru to anyone?'

'What did you tell him?' Anakhashayan's face became pale. 'But isn't she too young for marriage?'

'Whether she is small or not, she is still a girl', Pakkaran said. 'They grow up very fast. Now itself she looks like a grown up girl.'

'Then what are you going to do about it?'

'Why don't we finalise it?' Pakkaran was thoughtful. 'Kochhappi will take care of her like gold. These days are not very good, especially after what happened to Kaithara Pappy. Drums are beating in my heart fiercely. I am happy that I had the presence of mind to leave her with my aunt, far away. Still, how long can she stay there? They are also poverty stricken.'

'So, you have already taken a decision?'

'That is why I want you also to accompany me.' Pakkaran took his hands. 'We will go there and finish that work.'

'I am not coming', Anakhashayan freed his hands. 'I have something else to attend to.' He walked away.

Pakkaran watched him walking away. Why did his face grow dark when he told him that? Pakkaran knew that the boy never liked Kochhappi. He was of the opinion that Kochhappi always minded only his own business and was very selfish. And that was true too. His only motto was to make some money in a short time. He never made himself available for any party activities and was very clever at slipping away. But he knew how to survive. That was the plus point in him as far as Pakkaran was concerned. Kochhu Paru will never be placed in a situation of starvation and deprivation.

Kochhappi's house was a little south of Pakkaran's village. Pakkaran walked briskly by the bund road bordering the canal, hedged by palmyra trees. This was the house from where Danavan was chased out by his father Kittanasan for the crime of abducting and cohabiting with a lower caste girl. Although Danavan was his son, he was not prepared to forgive him. Was that not the reason why when Kunjachhan Mudalali offered him a hut to live, he immediately fell for the trap? Otherwise, wouldn't his wife Kochhu Thanka have lived here quietly on the gruel given to her after everyone in the family had their food? Is that not the reason why all these undesirable events happened in the family? The villagers still accused Kittanasan for whatever happened to Kochhu Thanka. When he inherited some seventy cents of land from the ancestral property, he became arrogant. And didn't he suffer for his cruel deeds? Didn't he die heartbroken on the sixteenth day after Kochhu Thanka died? People also say that he was killed by the spirit of Kochhu Thanka, when he was coming from the house of Kaaliamma after a witchcraft ritual at midnight. That being the case, why did the spirit leave Kunjachhan Mudalali alone? Shouldn't he have been the first person the spirit fixed on?

Was not Kittanasan himself specialised in witchcraft? Was he not able to bring a roasted chicken alive and make it fly? How many evil spirits terrorising the villagers were brought under control by him? Clad in his red mundu, his forehead smeared with ashes collected from the cremation ground, matted hair forming a hallow around his face and holding his magic wand in his hands, was he himself not an awesome sight walking through the paddy fields majestically? When Pakkaran was a small kid, his grandmother used to threaten to call Kittanasan to hush him when he was throwing a tantrum.

That thought took him to the memories of his grandmother who was a very dynamic old woman who died at the age of 110 years. She used to hunt for small tortoises, knowing where they inhabited. On her way she would pluck medicinal herbs and come back home with big sized tortoises which would be cleaned and cooked for dinner to be eaten along with boiled tapioca. She would dry the herbs in hot sun and take them to the shop in the nearest market, which dealt with indigenous medicines.

Grandmother died of snake bite at the age of 110. While digging for tubers, she put her hands into the hole of a cobra which bit her fatally. When the family requested Kittanasan to conduct rituals to mitigate the evil effects of the unnatural death, he had refused to do so. Finally, they had to look for another wizard to do the needful.

Maybe, after the death of Kittanasan, his family has discontinued the outdated practice of untouchability, thought Pakkaran. Isn't that why Kochhappi came to him asking for Kochhu Paru?

Even otherwise, if upper caste Nairs and Namboodiris can have relationships with lower caste Theeyyas, what's wrong in Theeyyas getting into matrimony with girls from scheduled castes? Pakkaran tried to comfort himself. And Kochhappi was not a person who would jump into matters impulsively without discussing with his elder sister and her husband. So Pakkaran was sure that Kochhappi had thought about all the consequences. Lost in his reveries, Pakkaran didn't realise that he had reached the front yard of Kochhappi's house. Kochhappi was about to come out with his tools for toddy tapping.

A good omen thought Pakkaran.

'Oh, who is this? Pakkaran?' Kochhappi was pleasantly surprised. 'Come on in and take a seat', he invited Pakkaran inside. Pakkaran sat on the verandah.

'What would you prefer?' Kochhappi's elder sister asked from inside. 'Black coffee or tea?'

'If you can wait, you can have your lunch here', Kochhappi offered.

'Right now, I want nothing.' Pakkaran smiled at Kochhappi. 'We will have plenty of opportunities to eat and drink together.'

Kochhappi also smiled vaguely.

'Are you not getting ready to leave for work? I don't want to delay you.' Pakkaran was in a hurry to get to the matter. 'We have considered your proposal for Kochhu Paru and decided that since you have shown an interest in her, it would be better for us to accept the same.'

'In that case let's not delay anymore. We can fix a day in this month itself, Thulam. I will take the date from the astrologer today.'

'But Thulam is not an auspicious month.' Pakkaran was awestruck. 'Besides we need time to get the gold and other things ready.'

'You don't have to worry about all that.' Kochhappi surprised him again. 'All that will be taken care of by us.'

'That means....' Pakkaran was unable to continue.

'There is no time to waste thinking, Pakkaran', Kochhappi could not conceal his impatience. 'Isn't a big agitation being planned? God only knows who all are going to lose their lives. Are you also not a member of the Communist Party? Afterwards you will not get time for this kind of family matters. So, before that, now, when there is enough time, we should think about finalising such issues.'

'Look, Danavan is sneaking into the house, thinking that you have left already.' The elder sister spoke from behind the door. 'Please don't rake up anything with him. He may be hungry.'

Seeing Kochhappi, Danavan started sobbing miserably.

'Oh, please Kunjachhan Mudalali, don't harm me... don't harm my Thanka....'

Kochhappi waved his tapping knife and a scared Danavan scooted.

'This is the current state of affairs', Kochhappi complained. 'He was cured totally with our Vaidyan's treatment. Still, he goes berserk in my presence, thinking that I am the Mudalali who killed his wife. Otherwise, he is quite okay. Look at him, how neat he is, bathed and in a white mundu.'

'It's really sad.' Pakkaran became very unhappy at the fate of Danavan. 'Now what is the solution?'

'There is a way out', Kochhappi said. 'Vaidyan Kumaran told me.'

'Then do whatever the Vaidyan advises', said Pakkaran. 'You don't have to think twice.'

'Yes, so Kumaran Vaidyan said that he will be cured of his mental disorder if we get him married to a girl like Kochhu Thanka.'

A thunder cloud burst in Pakkaran's mind.

'Here's the black tea', jingle of bangles from inside.

Kochhappi got up and came back with two cups of black tea.

'It's sugared', Kochhappi said. 'I bought it at twice the price when I happened to be in the market in the city.'

'Then what about your proposal to marry Kochhu Paru?' Pakkaran enquired.

'Me! Marrying Kochhu Paru?' Kochhappi was stunned. 'When did I tell you that?'

Pakkaran came to his feet, leaving the tea cup on the floor.

'But what is the need for me to get married now?' Kochhappi continued. 'Once Danavan brother marries Kochhu Paru, won't she be here to take care of this household? And my sister doesn't stay here. My sister is in a hurry to go back to her marital home. How long can she hang around here?'

Kochhappi had a vulgar smile.

'Are you leaving without speaking your mind? Give another thought to this proposal. One third of this property belongs to Danavan brother.' He called out to Pakkaran from behind.

Unnikandan returned to the police station after his beat and parked his cycle, leaning against the wall. As he stepped inside the station, removing his cap and patting dry the sweat on his forehead, he saw four or five armed reserve policemen carrying in a young man of about twenty-five years. Unnikandan observed that the number of people in the lockup had gone up. Inspector Koshy had fulfilled the promise he had made to the DSP. As he lowered himself into his chair, he heard someone calling him.

'Sir….' A man in the lockup was standing close to the iron bars and looking at him pathetically.

'Yes, what is it?' Unnikandan twisted his moustache and barked.

'Sir, please save him', he pleaded. 'He is suffering from fits.'

'Whom are you talking about?'

'The one who the reserve Police have just carried in', said constable Nanappan. Nanappan was a fresh entry to the police force. Earlier he had been a postman. He knew everyone in the village.

'The poor man works as a beedi roller in the market', Nanappan told Unnikandan softly in his ears. 'He is somebody in the beedi workers union in Muhamma. The reserve police arrested him without any reason. Whole of last night, they were torturing him in the camp. They brought him to the lockup just now. He is suffering from fits. He is shivering all over. In spite of that, they have been beating him mercilessly.'

'You take back the word you said last. It is not meant for us the police', said Unnikandan. 'In our eyes all these are terrorists. Um… tell me the rest.'

'He cannot even move on account of his illness. Early morning, they dragged him out and plunged him in the canal.'

'Kind-hearted sir, please save the poor fellow from them', the man continued to plead from behind the bars of the lockup.

'Um….' Unnikandan got to his feet and placed his cap on the head. He stepped out, keeping his baton in the arm pit and looked into the darkness. The victim was being dragged to the canal which was used as a toilet area by the prisoners. Unnikandan caught up with them as they were about to fling him into the canal.

'Stop it!' he shouted. 'That fellow is totally sick.'

There was a scream from the banks of the canal. 'Please don't kill me.'

'You rascal, are you raising your hand towards the police?' someone howled.

Unnikandan saw them forcibly immersing his head in the dirty water.

'Gluk….gluk….' there was a sound of air escaping from him as he suffocated, forming bubbles on the water surface.

'Stop it', Unnikandan screamed loudly. All the four looked back stunned.

'Take him to the bank', he told them.

'Who are you to intervene?' they retorted. 'Do you know this bugger was raising his hands against us? He almost suffocated this Kuttikannan by strangling him.'

'So?' Unnikandan bawled. 'How can you be so inhuman? Get him out of the water.'

They dragged him out and pushed him. Unnikandan gave him a hand in support. 'Are you all human beings?' he stared at them.

'Please don't sermonise', the seniormost among the four sneered. 'We have seen what you people do inside the lockup.'

Unnikandan didn't reply. As he was crossing the road, the victim fainted. His mouth and nose frothed.

'Hurry up and take him to the hospital', ordered Unnikandan. The jail in-charge arranged a van and the reserve police themselves carried him to the vehicle.

Next day, in the afternoon, a bit of paper flew and fell in front of Unnikandan.

'Narayanan, son of Raman of Muhamma; twenty-four years, cause of death: aggravated fits.'

News reached her in the evening. The party had bailed out Dinar from the lockup.

The special investigation team confiscated Niranjan's bike. Dinar was taken to hospital immediately after his release. There was a blockage in his urinary tubes and the urine had to be taken out clinically.

When Disha entered her room to give the news, Aparajitha was talking on the phone.

'Ranbir', she drew a picture in the air to let Disha know.

'Ranbir', she spoke in Hindi, 'How many times I have told you, there is no place for such things in my mind. I have never felt that way about you....'

She kept one of the pins of the headphone in Disha's ear. Disha heard Ranbir's soft voice. 'Aparajitha, why are you running away from me? I know you have a soft corner for me....'

She looked at Disha helplessly. Inserting the other pin also in Disha's ear, she told her, 'I give up. Now can you explain to him?'

'Ranbir, I am Disha', she said into the phone 'Just leave her alone. There is nothing like you think. I know her.'

'Well, thanks for hearing from you. Bye', he kept the receiver down, at his end.

'Oh, what a relief!' Aparajitha sighed.

'He may call again', Disha said.

'No', her lashes were moist. 'He will never call.'

'Why are you looking so low?' Disha asked.

'Oh, it is nothing my dear.' Aparajitha dried her eyes.

Lotus in the Slush

Day was breaking gloriously, the rising sun painting the sky scarlet. Paddy fields slowly came out of their slumber with the sound of wheels drawing water. Before daybreak, the Pulaya youth, the untouchables started drawing water for irrigating the paddy fields.

Savaro Mappila was running towards the seashore through the narrow bund roads between the paddy fields, carrying the weight of a wooden ore and wooden containers. He had to go another four furlongs cutting across the paddy fields, canals and thickets to reach the shore where the people who owned the boats and fishing nets lived. If he reached late, others would hire the smaller boats and scoop up the entire day's catch required for the market, leaving him high and dry. With the descent of the army in the town, the fish market had moved closer to their camp. The entire lot of the big varieties of fish was taken away to the camp as soon the daily catch reached the market, leaving the locals to satisfy themselves with the smaller variety. But nowadays even that was not available to them because the camp demanded the small varieties too to make special dishes for nibbling at the time of their cocktail sessions in the evenings.

It looked like the army had no intention of moving out in the near future. As Mappila had returned from the market yesterday, he had seen a load of arms being unloaded near the camp from a lorry. 'God knows to take whose life….!' Mappila kept his hand on his head and looked at the skies.

Storks had lined up on the bunds, looking for small fish to prey on in the paddy fields. As they heard his footfalls they flew away.

'No need to fly away', Mappila assured the storks. 'I will not harm you. I am going to catch bigger fish than you can catch.'

As Mappila moved past, the storks returned and resumed their meal.

' Mappila, Whom are you abusing?' asked Kandan Pulayan standing atop the giant water wheel.

'Oh, these rowdy storks!' Mappila said, pulling his legs free from the slush.

'What did they do to earn that?' Kandan Pulayan asked kicking and turning the wheel.

'Not because they did anything', Mappila replied. 'Are they not sitting here blocking my way right from daybreak?'

Pulayan recognised the affection Mappila had for the storks. 'Why should they be scared of anybody, they are not like us; toiling from daybreak and always petrified about being spat upon and abused by the manager and the landlord.'

'Of course, what you said is true', Mappila turned back, looked at the Pulayan and admitted while heaving his load and moving forward in a hurry.

As Mappila walked past the paddy fields and moved through the pine thickets, he heard the howling of a fox. Near the thickets were the hutments of the Pulayas, who were still not up. His attention was drawn by the mayhem of a cluster of crows assembled on the banks of the canal. He saw something white lying on the ground. Someone drunk must have fallen there last night, he thought. It was very common in that locality. People used to drink and collapse on the ground. Mappila got close to the edge of the canal. The crows settled on the pine thickets. Two stray dogs were sniffing the body. Mappila chased them out. Putting his accessories down from his shoulders, he neared the body. He glanced at it and was stunned to see that it was a woman. Her nipples stood erect on large breasts which were swollen. Mappila looked around. There was no one nearby, other than Kandan Pulayan who was far away in the paddy fields.

Mappila stooped down and looked at the body once again but he was not able to figure out whether she was alive or not. With the face covered with hair turned to one side, the body was lying flat on the ground without a stitch on to cover her nudity. The hands were lying collapsed on both sides. Maybe the dogs have torn away the scanty clothes she had on. She looked around twenty, with a well-shaped body. Her mouth was open. She had thick lustrous hair and from the look of it, it appeared that she was from the Pulaya community. Both the legs were stretched into the flowing water in the canal. Her toes seemed to be on the verge of being eaten away by the fish and other water insects. She might have got caught in some grave situation. Or has she eaten some poison fruit to kill herself? But, in that case, why should she be lying here without any clothes around? No, definitely she would have been in some trouble.

Gods in heavens, he prayed looking at the sky. How come I am trapped in this situation early in the morning?

How can I leave her like this and walk off? If there is an investigation, they will immediately identify my foot prints. That's enough for further trouble. What am I to do? He felt miserable.

Maybe I should inform Kandan Pulayan. The moment one or two people come along, I can scoot with my baggage, he thought.

'Poo…hoy' he called out to Kandan Pulayan.

Hearing that, Kandan Pulayan responded 'Poo…hoy.'

The youth working in the paddy fields stopped pedaling and looked at the source of the sound. Mappila swirled his hands high and called again. Immediately Pulayan stopped his work and rushed to the spot along with a few others.

'God, is this not our Kaithara Pappy?' One among them started beating on his chest and wailing.

'Chathan, see whether she is dead or not?' said Kandan Pulayan.

'Oh here are two leeches stuck to her belly that have grown fat sucking her blood.'

Kandan turned her face straight and exclaimed. 'Oh, this is not Pappy.'

'Then who is it?' exclaimed the crowd.

'Isn't this Mara, Pappy's friend who was also abducted by the army?'

'Yes, definitely, she is Mara', another person confirmed.

'If the leeches have not left the body releasing their hold, it means that she is still alive.' Someone commented, holding his finger close to her nose.

'Look, she is breathing.'

Kandan Pulayan lighted a match stick and held it close to the leeches. Immediately they released their grip and fell down.

'Look at these insects', grunted Mappila. 'They have sucked away a whole lot of blood.' He ground them with his feet.

'Here, there are some more of them', said someone. Another one bent down and picked them up with a blade of casurina. 'Our Vaidyan was asking for two live leeches to suck out the clotted blood from the eyes of our Shanmugam who was tortured by the police.'

'Even in the midst of such a disaster, doc wants to make use of an opportunity.' Mappila was furious. 'Get out you guys.'

Kandan Pulayan scooped a handful of water from the canal and sprinkled it on her face. She grunted.

'See the wound under her nipples', another one pointed out 'somebody has bitten her there.'

'Other than those devils, who would have done that?' Kandan Pulayan said angrily. He lifted her up using his arms for support. 'We have to take her immediately to Vaidyan Maniyan. If there is even an iota of life left, he will revive her.'

Mappila covered her with a mundu and said, 'Okay, now you can take care of her.' Picking up his accessories, he started to walk off. 'I have to earn my day's food. It's time to bring in the fish.'

'How can you leave like this?' Kandan Pulayan objected. 'You summoned us, we who were busy doing our work rushed here and now you entrust us with this work and walk away?'

Kandan Pulayan and two others laid her in his fish basket.

Mappila didn't expect that. 'If you put her in that, she will stink of fish.'

'Fish stink is better than being left to die here', replied Kandan Pulayan.

'You don't have to carry her alone, two of us will support you', said Pulayan.

So Mappila positioned himself in the middle and the other two held the head and legs to carry her to the vaidyan's clinic.

Mappila bent down, realising that he had lost the day's earnings. He lifted the burden himself and said, 'I will carry her myself. Just make sure that her head does not get tilted this way or that way.'

The moment he felt the heavy weight on his shoulders, he was about to call out loudly, 'Fish… Fish, anyone wants to buy fish?' It was a habit, but he quickly swallowed his words before he said anything.

As the tripartite summit came to an end, the notification arrived from the Diwan's office, inviting everyone for a treat in the evening at the Bhakthi Vilasam Café.

'Is that a trap?' enquired Comrade Janardhanan Nair, as they withdrew themselves from the crowd and moved to the shade of a huge tree in the yard.

'What?' Comrade CK enquired without understanding what he meant.

'Invitation for coffee….'

'What's there in it?' Comrade Sreekandan Nair curled the tip of his moustache.

'There is a point in what Janardhanan Nair is saying', clarified TV. 'Isn't there an arrest warrant against him. By chance, if he happens to be spotted by the police….'

'No...No', Janardhanan Nair became alert.

TV said, 'CP is trying newer tricks. He has maneuvered the State Congress to his side. Now it is sure that they will not agitate against the American Model. So, they want to weaken the Communist Party by splitting the trade unions from the party. This conciliatory meeting itself is fraudulent.'

'I was equally surprised by CP's interest in the deferred wages as he explained the concept in the tripartite summit. The moment we were about to table the wage issue, he went on and on about the bonus for the workers, without allowing us much time to discuss our demands.'

'That's the reason why I keep on repeating... this is that Brahmin's crooked brain at work...', TV continued. 'Didn't you listen to what he said in conclusion; that the government will take a firm stand on the issue of workers, and the declaration of bonus is the precursor of that; a warning to the mudalalis that they should understand the stand of the government and to the workers that they should cooperate with the government.'

'Time for the treat', Sreekandan Nair said looking at the clock on the wall.

'Okay, then I will take leave of you.' Janardhanan Nair left the place.

At the beginning of the get-together, cigarettes appeared, followed by Sir CP. TV picked up a cigarette and lit it. The moment coffee was over; a uniformed daffedar (an attendant) with a red head dress approached TV and said, 'Diwanji is calling the two of you to his office'.

Sreekandan Nair was with TV. Sir CP was going through a file as both of them entered the room. He had removed his white head dress and placed it on a table nearby. Fragrance of cologne wafted through the room. On his table was a small portrait of Annie Besant. TV had heard of CP's connection with Annie Besant. Whenever the dynamic young man visited her, she used to treat him with a special cup of coffee made by her own hands. No one was allowed to touch that coffee. Some golden connection!

Along with Annie Besant, CP was the coordinator of the Home Rule Movement. From there he moved on to the cadre of a front-line Congress leader, working abreast Nehru.

'Welcome gentlemen. Have a seat.' CP waved his hands at the chairs kept in front of him.

As they sat, CP closed the file and looked into the eyes of the two of them. 'I hope you are happy about today's decision.' His severe eyes reflected a sneaking smile.

While arranging the white shawl wrapped around his neck on the white shirt, CP lifted his chin and asked again, 'What do you say?'

'We are absolutely happy', said TV.

'About the decision to give a bonus', Sreekandan Nair added.

'Of course, of course, I know that.' CP's lips held a smile.

'And tell me', CP sat back, leaning on the chair's back rest. 'Now, what is your attitude towards the government?'

'We will cooperate', said TV. 'We will cooperate with the government. Then only, we can confront the mudalalis and landlords, you see.'

'I know you are practical.' CP complimented them. 'And I expected that from you.'

His face brightened in the yellow light in the room.

'I want to tell you something very confidential.' CP started to say something with a foreword. TV and Sreekandan Nair waited to see the movement of his lips.

'I have reserved two seats for you in the Assembly, exclusively for you.' CP's words in English were soaked in honey. 'Don't you know, I am in the process of bringing out a new constitution for Independent Travancore?'

'Is it our old American Model?' TV asked with slight sarcasm.

A shadow fell over the smiling lips. The tip of the nose quivered slightly. Hiding that, CP pulled one end of his shawl to the front.

'What is your opinion about the provision for a permanent executive in the constitution?'

'We cannot agree with that', TV said bluntly.

'Nothing less than a complete responsible elected government ....'

'Oh', CP raised his voice. 'Are you supporting the anarchists in the Congress?'

'What do you mean by anarchism?' Sreekandan Nair was furious. 'We are ready for a debate on that.'

CP picked up the steel glass containing drinking water from the table and sipped some water and wiped his mouth.

TV gazed at the framed photo of the Maharaja fixed on the wall behind CP. The Maharaja seemed to be looking distantly somewhere else.

'Friends, please listen', CP spoke in his chaste and clear English. 'I would like to tell you something ... for your sake. This is a challenge to a legal government. I don't have anything personal in this. Whatever I am trying to do is in the interest of Travancore. Now itself, some people here are getting ready for agitations and unrest. That is not good. It is against the welfare of the land. Therefore, what I have to counsel you is that you should not associate with the political parties. By cooperating with us, you can gain much more than that. Politics will only damage you. It will damage Travancore….'

The moment TV heard this, he reacted; 'Forgive me Diwanji. That's the problem with your view point. The members of the working class also are the citizens of this land. Interests of the people include their interests too. That is politics. Not only here but anywhere in the world, separating working class from the people is not politics. For that reason, it is impossible for the working class to stay separated.'

Sir CP's face turned red. He lifted his head dress and fixing it on his head, he sat straight arrogantly.

'So, everything is well planned?' the tip of his nose quivered again. 'I must warn you that your stand is quite destructive.'

Comrade TV didn't respond.

'Are you aware that you are talking to the supreme commandant of both the forces?'

'I know', TV said fearlessly.

'You should remember that the eight thousand strong police and four thousand strong army of Travancore State are under my control', CP continued arrogantly. 'I am not only the Diwan now, but the highest Commandant of the defense forces.'

'That also is known.' TV concealed a ridiculing smile in the corner of his lips.

'Well, see you then.' CP opened the file that was kept aside.

Outside the door, Inspector General of Police Parthasarathy Aiyangar was waiting. A daffedar came in the office to inform CP.

As they climbed down the staircase, Sreekandan Nair said, 'Did you see the way he was trying to threaten us?'

'He understood that his threats will not work on us', said TV.

'If they make the Diwan the Supreme Commandant of the Defence, what is the job of the Maharaja?' Sreekandan Nair enquired.

'Isn't Maharaja the Colonel in Chief? His job is now restricted to receiving the ceremonial salute now and then. If there is any civil unrest in the land, the power to use the army to suppress it now rests on the Diwan', explained TV sarcastically

'We have to be alert', Sreekandan Nair cautioned. 'His priority areas for the launch of the attack will be Cherthala and Alappuzha.'

'Um....' TV said. 'We will see as and when it happens.'

It was almost dusk. Kandan Pulayan walked toward Maniyan Vaidyan's clinic by the bund road in the paddy fields. The moment the villagers came to know about Mara, they had only one question in their minds. What happened to Kaithara Pappy and Cheera grandmother's granddaughter who had also been abducted by the Army? They knew only one person could answer their questions; Mara, who was unconscious. The Vaidyan had assured them that Mara would wake up in twenty-four hours and he was always accurate in making such predictions.

As Pulayan turned to the narrow country road heading to the healer's house, three or four women came towards him, carrying bundles of braided palmyra fronds on their heads. As soon as they saw him, they bombarded him with questions.

'Is Mara able to talk?'

'Did she say anything about our Pappy?'

Kandan was irritated. 'Am I not going to the Vaidyan to find out all that? Before that, how am I to know anything?'

'No, we thought ….' The women left without completing the sentence.

As he was descending a small hillock on the way, another group of women who were engaged in de-husking the coconut shells accosted him. They were from his own community. He felt aggravated and grunted at them.

'Okay, all these days you were not concerned about Kaithara Pappy or what happened to her. Did you enquire whether she was dead or alive? Had one of you been abducted by the army like her, how would you have felt?'

'But what can we do about it?' The women complained.

'What you can do?' Kandan was enraged. 'Couldn't you women join together and go to the army camp in a procession holding flags in your hands, and demand to know what they did to Pappy and the other women? Would your bodies have melted down by doing so?'

The women looked at each other. They felt that there was a point in what he said.

'Um….' Kandan let out a long hum to let them know his displeasure and walked away.

•

There was a lotus pond where the hill ended in the property belonging to the feudal family 'Azhikkal'. Two years ago, when the landlord approached the Pulayas for their services at the harvest season, they had refused to comply. The enraged family decided not to cultivate paddy anymore and instead constructed a big pond in a two-acre land, to cultivate fish along with lotus flowers. Varieties of fish flooded the pond along with beautiful lotus blossoms. On alternate days, vendors came from Cochin town to pluck the flowers.

'Hello Kandan big brother, where are you going?' he heard a sound from the pond.

Kandan Pulayan turned to see who it was. It was Cherukka Pulayan who was trapping fish, using a cone-shaped trap made of reeds.

'Oh, I am going up to that Vaidyan's clinic', Kandan Pulayan said. In the middle of the pond where it was deep, there were a few lotus flowers blooming. His eyes widened, looking at them.

'Can you pluck two of them and give them to me?' He pleaded with Cherukka Pulayan. 'Mara is still unconscious. I want to give her the flowers when she opens her eyes.'

'Oh, I can't. The pond is dangerously deep.' Cherukka Pulayan pressed the trap in the muddy water.

'But what are you doing here?' Kandan questioned him. 'The Azhikkal family will cut you into pieces if you loot their fish. Don't complain later that I didn't warn you.'

'Big deal', Cherukka Pulayan muttered. 'If those soldiers can loot, why shouldn't we?'

'Soldiers?'

'So, are you not aware of anything?' Cherukka Pulayan asked. 'At the crack of dawn, the men camping in Ponnamveli will be here to catch all the fish. The Azhikkal family has leased out the entire pond to the army; there is not a single big variety of fish in the pond now.'

'What about the lotus flowers?'

'I don't know', Cherukka Pulayan shrugged.

Ever since the army had entered the area, the whole place has become crime-ridden, grimaced Kandan Pulayan. Nothing is spared, including the poultry, sheep or small kitchen gardens and banana farms maintained by ordinary small-time farmers who would have taken permission to cultivate the land by cajoling the landlords.

Kandan Pulayan passed the mud road and reached the Vaidyan's clinic. The Vaidyan was sitting in the verandah, with his legs extended, waiting for his attendants to apply oil and massage them.

Kandan Pulayan coughed softly to let the Vaidyan know of his arrival. The healer looked at him.

'She is still not fully conscious', said the Vaidyan. 'We are streaming ksheerabala (a herbal preparation made in milk) on her forehead.'

'I have something to ask her when she wakes up', Kandan submitted.

'But the army should give consent, you see?' the Vaidyan said, spitting into a brass spittoon. 'They came here in search of her.'

'But what business has the army got in this?' Kandan Pulayan was not clear.

'They claim that Mara escaped from their custody last night', he explained. 'They want to take her back when they come here tomorrow for fishing in the lotus pond. I told them that after she comes back to consciousness, we will think about it. Don't we have to ask her also?'

Kandan Pulayan knew that the Vaidyan was a sympathiser of the Communist Party and felt that he was right. He turned around and left the place.

It was Pothi Chothi, a woman from the Ezhava community, who saw it first in the lotus pond. In the centre of the pond, in the midst of the lotus buds, two frozen feet!

'Gods in heavens!' she screamed her guts out. 'My dear young woman, who planted such a thought in your mind?'

Locals, who were using the open space for ablutions, got up and craned their necks to see what was happening.

'Can anyone bear the pain of seeing that body lying face down like that?' she continued her laments.

'Is that Mara?'

'No, how can it be Mara? Is she not under treatment at the clinic?'

'Who else can it be?'

'Seeing the size of the body… isn't it Pappy?'

'My God….' The laments of the woman fell on the ears of the soldiers who were approaching the pond with their paraphernalia for fishing.

Indrani Sen is Still Singing

Comrade Prabhakaran saw Comrade Karunan, when he was standing in the tailoring shop in the Ponnamveli market. He tried to avoid Karunan by staying inside the shop. He had come to collect the two blouses he had given for stitching for Pappy. He had also purchased two colourful mundus for her, expecting her to step into his house any moment. He knew that if Karunan happened to see him with the packets, he would start questioning him in detail and then it would become the subject of gossip in the entire village.

'Tell those two boys that their shirts are ready', the tailor requested Prabhakaran as he stepped out of the shop. Prabhakaran knew that he was referring to Anakhashayan and Pakkaran. They had given the material for stitching long ago. They had wanted to wear the new shirts for Onam festival. Onam had come and gone, but the tailor had got time to stitch them only many weeks later.

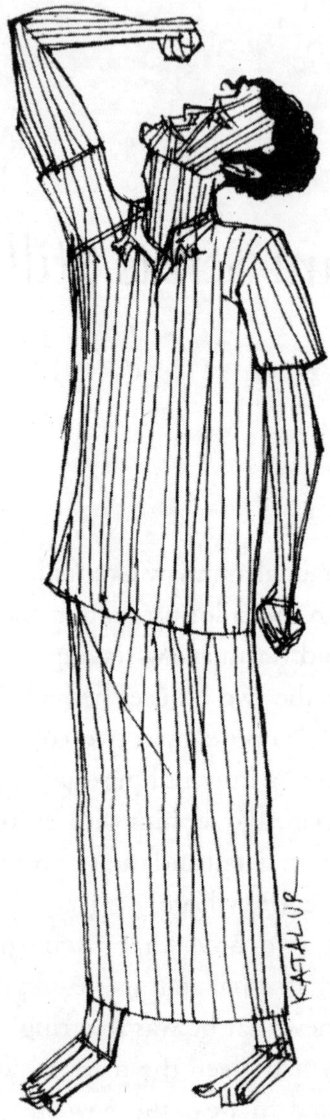
KATALUR

'Tell them, if they wear this, even the red flag will become humble', the tailor teased.

'Okay.' As Prabhakaran left the shop, he found himself face to face with Karunan.

'Where are you going in such a hurry, carrying this packet?' Karunan obstructed his path.

'Give me way Comrade; I have some important work to attend to.' Prabhakaran tried to avoid him.

'But I am also taking the same route as you.' Karunan walked abreast. 'I am going till that smithy.'

Both walked silently for a while. As the road forked, Karunan took the right. 'Whom are you trying to settle with, without talking or discussing with any of us', Karunan protested as he parted company; 'as if one of us offended you very badly!'

'You need to be frank about whatever you want to say and say it at the appropriate time; other than that…' Karunan spoke as if he was hinting at something.

'Um…go quickly… Mara has come back hoodwinking the army. But she is now unconscious and admitted to the clinic. Go and find out what happened.'

'Mara?' Prabhakaran looked rejuvenated. 'Did she speak about Pappy?'

'What's wrong with your head?' Karunan said with irritation. 'Didn't I say she is unconscious?'

Prabhakaran looked depressed again. Karunan looked at him pointedly and walked away. He knew that the whole village was gossiping about the affair between Pappy and Prabhakaran. They said he was going to marry her and take her to his house. And these days he was so gloomy and had distanced himself from everybody; especially after Pappy was abducted by the army. Karunan could see Prabhakaran sprinting towards the Vaidyan's clinic.

Prabhakaran wanted to ask Mara what happened to Pappy. Did she also hoodwink the army and escape? Is she hiding somewhere? Has anything bad happened to her? Wherever she is, I have to find her and get her back. Didn't grandmother Cheera say that at the time of abduction she had called out to none other than him for help?

Prabhakaran was confident that under normal circumstances Pappy was capable of handling anybody, but due to unforeseen circumstances if something bad did happen to her, how could she be blamed for it?

Never mind, he thought. The village abortionist Kochhu Kali can fix that without anybody's knowledge. Why should she bear the atrocities of some soldiers in her womb?

As he reached the lotus pond, drowned in unpleasant thoughts, he met Kandan Pulayan.

'Where are you going like a lighted firework?' Pulayan asked Prabhakaran. 'If you are going to find out Pappy's whereabouts from Mara, she has still not regained consciousness. You will have to wait patiently for the whole night.'

Prabhakaran was willing to lose his one night's sleep to find out about Pappy. In fact, he was willing to lose his whole lifetime waiting for Pappy. Pappy was his love, his treasure.

'Hello, see who has come?' The Vaidyan was in the process of bending and stretching his body after applying oil, as a part of his exercise. He was the kind of person who cared for his health.

'She has not mentioned anything about Pappy', the Vaidyan told Prabhakaran. 'But, how can she do that? She has still not regained her consciousness.'

'When will that happen?' Prabhakaran enquired.

'Can't say anything now.' The Vaidyan stretched himself, holding his hands up. Prabhakaran waited patiently.

'If at all she wakes up, it should happen within twenty-four hours', the healer continued. 'If not, things will be out of our control.'

'What happened to make her unconscious?' Prabhakaran enquired. 'Was she bitten by a viper?'

'Not one viper; several of them', the Vaidyan said softly. 'She was bleeding through the mouth incessantly. It stopped only now, after applying the herbal paste.'

'Is it because they stung her badly?'

'Yes... the devils had stung her... those vipers.'

Prabhakaran sat on the verandah without the strength to move.

'If this is Mara's condition', blood drained from his face, 'what will be the state of Pappy?'

In the night, when the healer came out to lock the gates, Prabhakaran was fast asleep on the verandah, keeping a packet under his head as a pillow.

Prabhakaran woke up at daybreak, hearing the screams of Pothi Chothi.

'Gods in Heavens... isn't this Pappy? Why did she kill herself by throwing herself into the pond?'

Prabhakaran sprinted towards the pond. Women stood in a circle screaming and beating on their chests.

Prabhakaran looked just once. Thick long curly hair spread in the midst of lotus blooms, feet above the water level.... Prabhakaran leaped into the pond, swam in the deathly cold water, scooped up her body on his shoulders and swam back. As he reached the bank, he fainted. The naked body was lying face down. Women continued to scream.

'Look there', Pothi Chothi pointed out. Pappy was holding a lotus with a long stem firmly in her right hand.

One of the men turned the body to see the face.

The Vaidyan came panting.

'Oh, she is not anywhere in the clinic', he said. 'I looked everywhere. Last night she regained consciousness. I told her to leave the place before the army came.'

Pothi Chothi looked at the face closely. 'Oh this is not Pappy; this is Mara of Mannanthara.'

Prabhakaran jumped up. The Vaidyan was dumbfounded.

'Last night, when she failed to revive, I made a concoction of buttermilk and gooseberry and streamed it on her forehead for two hours. Leaving my maidservant to take care of her, I went to have a nap for a few minutes. At midnight I heard a movement in the clinic. When I went in, Mara was up and sitting in a corner, leaning against the wall. The servant girl was fast asleep. As I entered the room she was petrified. I told her not to be afraid and that I was the Vaidyan. She asked me how she had reached the clinic. I told her that all those things could be discussed later, but for the time being, she had to take rest and escape early morning before the soldiers came looking for her. "You came here hoodwinking them, didn't you?" I asked her.'

'"Where can I escape from here?" she was desperate. She buried her face into her knees.'

'"Anywhere… see in that corner I have kept some broken rice gruel for you. I will give you medicine for one week. At daybreak, go somewhere where they cannot find you." I could hear her sobs as I came out of the clinic.'

The Vaidyan removed his shoulder wrap and covered her naked body.

'Gods... Mara of Mannanthara left us forever... she was a good girl...', the women beat on their chests and lamented. The soldiers who came with fishing tackles lingered on the way, reluctant to interfere.

Sekharan got off at a place called Kommadi, carrying a letter given by CK. After a long wait, he got a lift in a bullock cart carrying commodities to the market.

'Should I take the short cut or the narrow road?' Sekharan was not sure. Both the routes would take him to his destination. Some time ago, he had been there along with CK to meet Comrade Pathrose. At that time, they had gone by the narrow road and had returned by the shortcut as advised by Pathrose. Pathrose had said something in CK's ears. CK had not disclosed what he had said, to Sekharan. He too didn't ask CK. But he had heard that everywhere on the road, detectives were hanging around in disguise to check on the comings and goings of people to that place. Tucking the letter in his mundu at the waist, Sekharan took the short cut through the forest.

Big trees lined both sides of the narrow pathway. As he walked along, a man clad in nothing but a towel around his waist came forward, with a lighted beedi which was almost over, on his lips.

'I have never seen you around here', the man said, dropping the beedi on the ground and covering it with mud. 'Where are you from?'

'From a long distance', Sekharan said and continued to walk briskly.

Other than the chirping of birds, the place was absolutely silent.

It was close to the afternoon; yet darkness started filling the forest.

It was only after crossing the cashew forest and reaching in front of the 'Kaatungal House', that Sekharan could relax. A red-hooded woodpecker that had settled on a huge tree by the side of the paddy fields stared at him. Reaching the door, he knocked to let the inmates know of his presence, but there was no sound inside. He walked to the back of the house through rows of banana plants. A few hens were digging and kicking up the loose soil under the coconut tree. A mundu that had been drying on the clothes line had fallen on the ground. It may belong to the Comrade, Sekharan thought. He picked it up and folding it, he called out.

'Anyone around?' he looked in all the four directions.

'Who is that, my child?' a woman's voice was heard from inside.

'From Vayalar....' Sekharan waited.

Opening the door made of braided coconut fronds, an old woman peeped outside.

'Here', Sekharan handed her the folded Mundu. 'It was lying on the ground. The hens would have dirtied it.'

'Oh, he just left, saying that he is going to Kozhikode. God alone knows when he will be back.' Mother came out of the house. 'What's the matter my son?'

'I wanted to hand over this to him.' Sekharan pulled out the letter from his mundu. It was wet with his sweat and the writing on the envelope had got smudged.

'Will you drink something my son?' Mother asked. 'Shall I prepare some black tea for you?'

'No need Mother.' Sekharan turned and started walking.

'Oh, here comes Marian', said Mother. 'You can hand over that letter to him. He will pass it on.'

Marian jumped over the canal and rushed home. 'Old woman, I am famished; is there anything to eat?' He walked inside, without paying any attention to Sekharan.

Mother looked inside. 'If you are so hungry, you can eat coconut fodder kept for the cattle.'

Marian's anger and grief bubbled up. 'The coconut fodders! Don't make me say undesirable things. What did you do with that one measure of rice that was there in the house this morning?'

Mother stood in silence for a while and said. 'He went to Kozhikode after drinking the gruel made out of that rice.'

Marian cursed and flung the mud pot where the rice was stored into the courtyard. It broke into pieces and scattered everywhere. Mother stood helplessly. He leaped outside with a big knife.

Sekharan moved backward, petrified. Marian went to the southern yard.

'To tell the truth, even I ate only some coconut fodder this morning and drank water.' Mother looked at Marian. 'When he goes to Kozhikode for a good work for the country….'

'A very laudable matter', Marian said sarcastically. He uprooted a coconut plant from the ground.

'Are you mad?' Mother tried to stop him.

'Leave me alone', Marian hissed.

Marian cut down the coconut seed under the plant and ate the edible contents greedily. Mother's eyes became moist with tears. She looked at Sekharan. 'Okay my son, you may go now.'

Sekharan had heard about the uncontrollable hunger of the youngest brother of Comrade Pathrose. He was the youngest among the brothers. By the time he came back home after roaming around in the village, his elder brothers would have finished all the food that their mother cooked for the day. Then he would make a big racket in front of Mother, who herself would be starving.

Sekharan rummaged in his pocket. There was only half a chakram (a coin of minimum denomination which was prevalent in the Travancore kingdom). It was just enough for his expenses on the way back.

'Alright.' He walked towards the narrow road and turned back and looked at the thatched hut. It was time to renew the roofing made of braided coconut fronds.

Where does Comrade Pathrose have time to attend to all such domestic chores? thought Sekharan and started walking briskly. Sekharan tucked the letter again in the mundu.

CK had instructed him to reach Kommadi and hand over the letter to Comrade Pathrose before he left for Kozhikode. The decision to send him to Kozhikode was taken at the meeting of the Travancore Communist Party held in Alappuzha. The State Congress had not held their committee meeting on the twenty-fifth as decided earlier. Pattom did a somersault to please CP and devalued the decision of C Keshavan.

An emergency meeting was convened as demanded by Comrade Pathrose. 'Now there is no point in relying on the Congress', he observed.

The meeting was held in a closed room in strict confidence. Sekharan waited outside the room, waiting for CK to come out. Comrade TV came a little later along with Comrade Varghese. The moment PT Punnoose concluded the introductory part, Pathrose shot up.

'On one side, the government has let loose the police and army to demolish the party and trade unions. On the other side, the landlords have started evacuating the lands leased by small-time farmers and farm workers, using their goons. CP has already declared black regulations, denying common man all his necessities other than air and water.'

'The axe cutting down all the bare necessities of common people – was that not what C Keshavan said about the First Regulation?'

'If workers strike work, five years' rigorous imprisonment and a fine of Rs 1000; ban order on processions and demonstrations. No permission to conduct public meetings. The police can stop a drama or a music concert or a folk dance to entertain the public as they deem fit. The government can confiscate anybody's property; can put anyone in exile; monitor and control the press; in short CP has transformed Travancore into a prison complex. Is not the State Congress expected to fight against such black regulations? But what happens actually? They wait at Bhakthi Vilasam, where the administrative offices are housed, for negotiating a compromise; that too at a time when their Nehru's interim government has come into power. It is not possible for people like me to remain inactive in such a situation. It's time for an open confrontation.'

TV disagreed with that. 'On an impulse we can say such things.' He came to his feet and straightened the wrinkles on his jibbah. 'But without making appropriate arrangements, we should not jump into an open confrontation.'

Comrade Varghese also disagreed.

Comrade Pathrose bristled in anger.

'As TV says, if we keep observing the developments for a long time, we will have to search for the Communist Party in its burial place. Please don't drag the party and its leaders to such a disaster.'

'As we all know, when we stood under the banner of the Indian Communist Party, CP could not digest that. To cure his indigestion, we changed the name to Travancore Communist Party. But now, when CP has come to know that only the name has been changed and the principles remain the same, he wants to make the party non-existent. And the State Congress leaders like Pattom and TV Varghese are busy extending their support to him. Communist Party should not follow that practice. Let no one try to do that.'

'Comrade is misunderstanding...' TV tried to intervene. PT Punnoose was silent. Pathrose continued to spit fire.

'Let no one be under the impression that the State government is fighting for "responsible government". Also don't forget the fact that Pattom Thanu Pillai is the State Congress President. Pattom and CP, who were at loggerheads, are now hand-in-glove. This treachery was initiated in April last. After the cabinet mission, what did CP say at the press conference? "Pattom Thanu Pillai is a patriot of the highest order!" Who doesn't know about Pattom's meeting with CP in Delhi on his way back from Kashmir, after attending the conference of the Princely States? Can you forget his speech in the grand reception meeting given to Captain Lakshmi, the INA leader who visited Trivandrum after her release from jail, boosting CP by appreciating his policies? Didn't he say publicly that the American Model is worth experimenting with in Kerala? Was it not the same CP who banned collection of donations in

Travancore for defending the INA officers and soldiers, while this was being done all over India? Why did Pattom choose to forget all that conveniently?'

'Why should we make a mention of all that now?' TV objected. 'Later, didn't CP contribute rupees ten thousand to the INA Defense Fund?'

'That's known', Pathrose rubbed his calloused hands together. 'Was it not done when he went to attend the Chamber of Princes Meeting at Bombay? Was it not from there that he plotted with the Hyderabad Nizam and Bhopal Nawab for declaring Travancore as a Princely State? Is that not what we are fighting against? Travancore doesn't need a Diwan's rule in future. Travancore should become a part of the Union of India.'

As Pathrose sat down, CK stood up and said, 'I am also of the opinion that it's time for a confrontation. We cannot delay the public strike anymore.'

'It's true. It's time for confrontation.' The voices of KK Kunjan and Padmanabhan resonated in the hall.

'We will do one thing', Comrade Keeran, who had been silent all this time, made a suggestion. 'Shouldn't we discuss this with KC George who is in charge of the party? Isn't he in Kozhikode now, in Desabhimani newspaper? Don't we also have to discuss the issue with the leaders in Kozhikode? Will it not be appropriate to discuss this with EMS and AK Gopalan and arrive at a consensus?'

'Who will go?'

'Comrade Pathrose', called out the majority in a single voice.

Leaving the forest, Sekharan reached Kommadi junction and waited for the bus to Kozhikode.

That sight spread a red curtain before Aparajitha's eyes. The gulmohar tree on top of the Anakhan Hill had blossomed red, hiding the green leaves. Niranjan should have been with us, she thought wishfully. Disha also climbed the hill behind her. Kochhu Raghavan Sir and her childhood friends should also have been here, she thought. They were actually planning for such a reunion when Niranjan had gone missing.

The police raided the house again. That man, the Inspector, rummaged his room again, going through books and magazines neatly arranged in the almirah.... He had left by the afternoon train on that day. Till he had reached the Alwaye Bridge, his mobile had connection with the tower. From there on ... he could have flung the SIM card in the river or the call would have got rejected due to the wrong STD code.

'Camping in Bastar, Maoists are planning new strategies to reclaim the lost tribal lands. That should be the place where he is headed. He will call without fail.' He looked at Aparajitha. 'Haven't you heard of People's Liberation Army? Weapons for Maoists are reaching India through them... via Myanmar... through Kolkata... yes, we have to suspect a Kolkata connection here.' He smiled at her crudely. 'We may need one more sitting together.'

'Oh, sure', she was not at all worried.

Disha stopped under the tree which had spread a red canopy above her head. Aparajitha was searching for a song in her iPod.

She sat close to the tree. She could feel Niranjan's presence somewhere close by… his fragrance wafting through the air.

Kato bar bhebechinu, Apona bhulia,
Tomar Charane Deebo Hridaye Khulia

'Rabindra Sangeet…Tagore', said Aparajitha, 'rendered by Indrani Sen.'

'What's the meaning of those lines?'

'Many a times, I wanted to forget myself and wanted to surrender my heart at your feet.'

To reveal myself… were you aware of that?

A breeze went past the branches of the tree showering red flowers on them.

Disha's eyes became moist. Indrani kept singing… 'Apona bhulia….'

Intruders in Ippolith's Camp

Kochhu Kunjan Asaan became restless after hearing the news. It was Sekharan who told him. He had met Unnikandan last night on his way back home, who gave him a hint about the matter discreetly. Since he had heard that, there was a ball of fire in his stomach. Whole night he tossed and turned in his bed restlessly, waiting for daybreak. He wanted to reach Kumaran's house early in the morning before he started his routine work. What would happen in case he landed up there all alone? Sekharan had left home early in the morning itself and would return very late. Nowadays, it was so difficult to see him. CK always had him in tow. He wouldn't go anywhere without Sekharan.

As soon as it was the daybreak, Asaan finished his bath and put on his khadi jibbah, wrapped the malmal mundu around his midriff and picked up his long-handled umbrella as a caution against biting dogs. It was a long time since he had visited Kumaran's house which was three to four furlongs away.

Sir CP had taken his final decision. 'Burning down a house to get rid of a rat', was only an adage. But that was what CP had in his mind. He knew the communists were not rats but ferocious tigers and could not be eliminated so easily. That was the reason why he had declared the First Regulation. So that the police and army could do whatever they fancied. Since there was no war-time situation, Asaan strongly felt that there was an ulterior motive in CP's declaration of emergency.

In the month of September, about seventy thousand members of labour unions had struck work. That had enraged CP. Following that, communist leaders like R Sugathan, Punnoose, Shankaranarayanan Thampi and Bhaskaran were arrested. When the news of Punnoose's arrest came, thousands of workers went on a strike. He had heard from Sekharan that comrades Kakkachi and CK Velayudhan were also arrested.

Not only processions and demonstrations, even songs were banned. A song written by Comrade AK Das 'We don't want..., we don't want Diwan's Rule' was banned. The American Model was to be implemented on the Maharaja's birthday. The whole land was going berserk against the rule of the King and his Diwan. The government also took brutal steps to curb the unrest.

As Asaan passed the curve and reached the turning, he saw Vaidyan Kumaran coming.

Clad in a mundu, wearing a half shirt and with a smaller mundu on his shoulder, walking on a methiyadi (a footwear made of wood), the Vaidyan was on his way to his clinic.

'The creeper I was looking for...' Asaan started.

'...entwined the leg.' His friend completed the sentence. 'I was about to send for you, wishing for your company, to chat and while away some time', he added.

'You should be cautious', Asaan said.

The Vaidyan looked at him in panic.

'Things are not looking so good', said Asaan.

'Gods in Heavens!' the Vaidyan now looked petrified.

'It would be better if you don't open the clinic for a few days', continued Asaan. 'Your resignation from the Vigilance Committee has reached CP. Will he keep quiet when his loyalists change sides? If possible, move out from the locality for a few days.'

'Where to?'

'I have an ancestral house far away in the Koman island, unoccupied. I go there once in a while to clean up the place. Why not both of us go there? No one will know.'

Kumaran stood on the road closing his eyes for some time. He could see the cobra spreading its hood.

Unnikandan was parking his cycle against the wall after his routine night beat. He could hear Inspector Koshy and ASP Achyuthan talking in hushed tones. Unnikandan brought his ears close to the wall of the police station to overhear the conversation.

'The Communist Party has to be uprooted. That is the Diwan's order. They want to initiate action from the Ambalapuzha and Cherthala taluks. This was the decision taken at the confidential meeting held at Trivandrum...'

'Many bodies will fall...', ASP Achyuthan declared.

'If only the birthday of his royal highness gets over!' said Koshy. 'Till then....'

'By then we have to shake them badly... that is....'

'I got it... we have to smoke out all the bandicoots from their holes', said Koshy.

'Evacuate all the tenants from their huts'...said the ASP.

'Necessary orders for that have already been issued to the Federation of Landlords.'

'What about the Vaidyan's clinic?' Koshy asked.

'Didn't I tell you already?' replied the ASP. 'Diwanji is enraged. The clinic has to be closed and sealed down latest by tomorrow. No need for any soft treatment because he was a member of the vigilance committee.'

'The rumour is that he resigned from the Loyalist Group of Maharaja to join the Communist Party, according to a CID report. Though he is a landlord, he is still from the Chova community.' Inspector Koshy laughed. 'Birds of a feather flock together you see.'

'Um... wrong thoughts during adverse times', the ASP said.

Constable Unnikandan heard the screeching sound of chairs being dragged on the floor. He quickly moved towards the entrance and saluted the ASP who was stepping outside.

'Where were you?' Inspector Koshy regarded him sharply.

Unnikandan gave him a long salute.

'Um... go inside', Koshy joined the ASP in the jeep.

As he went inside, Unnikandan heard the squealing of a young boy. It was from the lockup. Unnikandan looked inside. Two of the reserve policemen were dragging someone from the lockup. There were some eight to ten new detainees in the cell. Outside, Appukuttan Nara Pillai, head constable from Alappuzha was standing with a nose-plier in his hand.

'All were captured from the Aroor Coir Factory Workers Union Office', reported constable Nanappan. The boy was banging his head against the bars of the lockup.

'What about that boy?' Unnikandan asked.

'He is the son of that moustached man', Nanappan pointed to the man who was being dragged out from the lockup. 'He was the one who tried to stab the ASP.'

Head Constable Pillai was getting ready to chew betel leaves with its accompaniments.

'Where is the nut-cutter? I had kept it somewhere here', he barked.

'Here it is', Nanappan produced the tool in a jiffy.

Policemen dumped the man in front of head constable Appukuttan Pillai.

'His punishment was ordered by ASP sir only.' Nanappan came near.

'What?'

'To pluck all the hair in his moustache and dab chili paste on the bruises... then stick paper pins on the toe nails ....'

The boy continued to scream his guts out, banging his head on the bars of the cell.

'Ayyo... please don't torture my father...he is a poor man....'

'Chhi... stop howling you rascal...' Nara Pillai threatened the boy, swirling the nut cutter. 'If you make any more sounds, we will cut off your penis, make it into pieces and feed the dogs.'

The boy was mortified. He ran to a corner of the lockup and hid his face.

'What is this, are you enjoying the fun?' Head Nara Pillai rolled his eyes and grunted at Unnikandan Pillai. 'Come and hold his head.'

The police in him woke up. Unnikandan shouted, 'stand quietly you Rascal.'

He got up and caught the man by his nape.

Benjamin, son of Nikolaou sat staring at the sea. An unexplained wave of misery crashed on the shores of his mind. After the police arrested Simon Asaan, he could hear only the sound of sea-gulls flapping their wings in his head continuously. After being the right hand of Simon Asaan all these days… on an impulse he got carried away by Mathayee. Benjamin's heart was throbbing with guilt. 'I shouldn't have betrayed Asaan… I shouldn't have resigned from the Fishermen's Union. Everything is over. Now what's the use of regretting it!'

Ben, Benjamin and Mathayee were the sons of three leading landlords of the seashore. They were the young ones who had stood by the communist leader Simon Asaan, disregarding the advice of their fathers, priests and leaders of the seashore. Mathayee was the son of State Congress leader Aplon Auraj, KS Ben, the son of Vaidyan Silva, and Benjamin, the son of Nicolas. The three of them had stuck to Simon Asaan at all times, like his shadow.

When he realised that the fishermen and workers working in the huge storages of the seashore were hesitant to join trade unions, Simon Asaan had a brainwave: to bring around the sons of the three rich men to the forefront of the party. Taking them as role models, a good number of young men from the seashore joined the trade union. They organised meetings on the seashore; stood along with Simon Asaan and addressed the gatherings. 'Fishermen comrades, stand united. All that we have to lose are the leg chains... but what we are going to gain ....'

Their fathers, families and the church reprimanded them, which they ignored.

Everything turned topsy-turvy from the time of the Alappuzha meeting of the State Congress held at the Punnapra market ground; a gathering of leaders who scrambled around. Pattom Thanu Pillai concluded his presidential speech with a question as to what was wrong in implementing CP's American Model in Travancore. Shankaranarayanan Thampi protested. That caused a furore among the party cadres. Pattom warned that the communists within the Congress Party who challenged him would be expelled and immediately there were catcalls and whistles from the audience.

Simon Asaan, Ben and others surged forward to the dais; people flung mud and stones on Pattom. Pattom closed the meeting and left the place abruptly. Congress Party was split into two; Socialists and Congress.

In the evening, the Union meeting held on the seashore ended up in dispute. Benjamin and Mathayee felt that the move to disrupt the State Congress meeting could not be appreciated. They alleged that Simon Asaan and his followers had conspired to disrupt the meeting. Mathayee felt intimidated, just like a female leopard that has just littered. He couldn't help it because the incident was like flinging mud on the face of his father Aplon Auraj, who was the Congress leader at the time and the State Congress leaders had come to his territory... Benjamin felt that there was a point in what Mathayee said; the heated argument ended in exchange of blows. Simon Asaan, Ben and his other followers stood together like a rock. Finally, Mathayee walked out. Benjamin also had to quit. Both were childhood friends. Both of them quit the trade union also together.

Now Benjamin felt that he should not have acted like that. He should have never quit the union; on the contrary, he should have stood by Asaan without deterring. Now the whole of the seashore community was paying for that. The police had already arrested Asaan, and Ben who had a vengeance towards the Arsakadavu Pollayil family, had taken his place and turned the Union to his side.

Sea breeze blew violently from the west. Seals came ashore, riding on huge waves. The sea turned tempestuous. Benjamin walked through the storage sheds built on the seashore.

It was during the last monsoon that Asaan was arrested by the police. For a long time, he had been under the surveillance of DSP Vaidyanathan Iyer who had fabricated a false case of violating the National Protection Rules against him.

This was done deliberately to trap Asaan. Mudalalis like Aplon Auraj, Anthappan Mudalali, Ippolith, leader of the Araya community, Chakrapani, Clarance Mudalali... controlled different sections of the seashore like Vattayaal, Vadakkal and Punnapra... the list was long. They were supported by the police in their atrocities.

It was only after the arrival of Simon Asaan on these shores that these atrocities against the fishing community workers were questioned and challenged. His presence assured the workers some kind of protection. In the absence of Asaan, once again, everything started turning topsy-turvy. The Punnapra seashore, which was peaceful till then, started smouldering with an imminent threat of a blazing blast.

It had all begun on Good Friday in April, when a few mudalalis caught hold of some fishermen, tied them to coconut trees and beat them black and blue for disobeying their order to take the boats to the sea for fishing. They started demonstrating their wrath on the workers, with one of the mudalalis whacking and hurling the body of his workman Srank Martin in the nearest forest for having joined the trade union.

A few days before that, when Vedappan Mudalali, Anthony Mudalali and Martin were passing through the Punnapra market fully intoxicated after a visit to the local toddy shop, they had chanced upon Kakkachi, a gutsy trade union leader, who was standing there with his mundu folded and sleeves rolled up. Kakkachi was the unchallenged leader of the union and so Martin unfolded his mundu and saluted him in respect. Vedappan Mudalali didn't take it very kindly.

'You useless scum, come here', He frowned at Martin. Martin disregarded his admonishments which enraged the mudalali. Emboldened by the liquor consumed, Martin started discussing union matters with Kakkachi very enthusiastically, till he pushed him away to go with the mudalalis.

Next day, women who were returning home from the market heard the sound of someone groaning and moaning in the thickets. Martin was lying there almost dead. His mudalali's goons had assaulted him, broken his spine and thrown him into the thickets. Martin, who was incapacitated thus, would never work on the boat again. Vedappan Mudalali fired him from his job.

Simon Asaan went to Vedappan Mudalali and questioned him about the assault on Martin. Both of them got into heated arguments.

'You senseless fellow who fights the church and clergy; I am going to teach you a lesson.' Mudalali challenged Asaan.

Asaan was unperturbed. Next day, he went to meet the mudalali again, along with Kakkachi alias Kakka Karunakaran. With Kakkachi entering the picture, the mudalali lost his nerves. Kakkachi stood there, six-feet tall in all his glory, thrusting his chest forward.

'What exactly is your demand?' mudalali asked in a subdued tone, 'You name it and it will be...'

'You assaulted Martin and fractured his spine', Kakkachi said. 'He cannot work anymore. So, you have to pay him his subsistence for the rest of his life; if you don't, you will get to know the consequences.' Kakkachi held up a fist. 'We came here to tell you that.'

Vedappan Mudalali nodded his head three times in agreement. That was the impact of Kakkachi who had beleaguered the army by demolishing the culverts and barricading roads by felling trees, in an earlier operation. In spite of two years' rigorous imprisonment, his might never faltered.

Asaan used to say that Kakkachi had double guts. In the jail, police had hit him on his chest with a stone. Each time they pounded him, he shouted more and more fiercely. 'Let imperialism be damned. Let Bharath Mata be glorified.'

Once, when the police were assaulting the leader-writer KP Keshavadev who had fallen on the ground, Kakkachi fell flat on him and received all the beatings nonchalantly. The policemen rained blows on Kakkachi's strong back which looked as though it was made of sturdy rose wood, till their hands got tired.

As he walked between the koodams (the storage sheds on the seashore) covering a long distance, Benjamin found a procession of seven or eight people carrying long ores on their shoulders, led by Kuttappan screaming obscenities at Pollayil Ippolith. Kuttappan called out the slogans and his followers repeated them. Kuttappan was an employee of Ippolith. He used to work in his boat but was a hard-core unionist. Ippolith owned the biggest boat in the three seashores. He was the second of the four sons of Pollayil Ambrose and was the reigning King of the Vettakkal seashore. With a sturdy body as if sculpted on hard rock, he walked, holding his head high to compensate for his short stature. Ippolith had a gang of goons comprising bold, dare-devil fishermen who were looking for work. No one in the vicinity would dare to challenge them either in the sea or on shore. Thus, Ippolith shone like an unchallenged monarch on the seashore. The rules and laws of justice to be followed on the seashore were defined and laid down by him and no one challenged them.

Kuttappan was a distant relative of Ippolith's wife Veronica's father Irani Moss. Benjamin knew that Ippolith owed money to Kuttappan in connection with the sale of prawns. Ippolith owed money to many like that. He would sell the prawns to the money lending traders of the seashore and sit on the money amassed in the trade without paying his suppliers. Kuttappan had approached Ippolith several times for the money and Ippolith asked for more and more time but never kept his promise. Kuttappan organised three or four other small-scale traders like him to whom Ippolith owed money and threatened him, pointing his fingers at him. In truth, because of Veronica's frequent nagging, Ippolith had been planning to give Kuttappan his money.

On the seashore, so far no one had dared to point fingers at Ippolith and talk. How did Kuttappan become so bold? Ippolith's hand itched to land a few blows on him but thinking of Veronica he restrained himself.

There is someone instigating Kuttappan, otherwise he wouldn't grow so impertinent, thought Benjamin. Now they were shouting all kinds of obscenities against Ippolith and going towards his house. Some disaster is impending. A storm is forming in the western sea. The sun hid behind dark clouds. Galloping breeze swirled coconut fronds in circles. Benjamin walked briskly behind them.

Disha and Aparajitha went to the library to see Dinar who had been bailed out from the police station. As soon as he saw them, he got up from the bench in the verandah on which he was lying flat and sat leaning against the wall. Disha sat opposite him and looked at him intently in total silence. Black finger prints on his cheeks were still visible and his eyes looked tired.

'I don't know what to say', Disha started talking. 'All this happened because of him.'

'No, no... what's his mistake?' Dinar stretched his legs. 'Whatever one is destined for... one has to go through.'

'Still how could he be so reckless?' Her eyes turned moist.

'Any idea where's he now?' he asked.

'They say he has gone to Bastar', Aparajitha said. 'But other than that....'

'Did they torture you a lot?' she laid her hand on his shoulders.

'Oh', a small smile flickered on Dinar's lips. 'After all, they are the police...till they get a lead....'

'What were they trying to find out?' Disha dried her eyes.

'Oh, my connections with Maoists.'

Disha wiped her tears.

'Dinar', she said bringing both her palms together in a gesture of pleading. 'Please, please don't curse him.'

'Come on, what's all this?' his eyes were also moist.

Leaving them, Aparajitha walked towards the almirahs where the books were kept. The books were all in disorder. Three or four racks were empty.

'Dinar', she called, 'where are the books which were here?' she pointed at the empty rack.

Dinar pointed his chin to a corner where a few books were lying scattered… with their red jackets.

'Pull out those labels', Dinar pointed to the labels. 'Marxism, Leninism, Maoism.'

'Why?'

'They made an issue of that', replied Dinar.

'But I don't want to do that with my hands.' Aparajitha was firm.

'You need a total body massage treatment', Disha came to her feet and looked at Dinar. 'Are you undergoing any ayurvedic treatment?'

'What for?' Dinar laughed away. 'Haven't they already given me a massage treatment? – The police….'

Three or four people reading newspapers in the library craned their necks to look at them.

As they walked out, Dinar called out to them.

'Comrade Vamadevan called. They have MR Nair's address.'

'MR Nair?' Disha looked confused.

'Dude, he is referring to that journalist who had written that Krishna Pillai had stayed hidden in your attic', Aparajitha reminded her.

'Is that so?' Disha was pleased.

'He is now living with his daughter in a flat in Idapalli.

Concert of the Crickets

Pakkaran spent the whole night tossing and turning on his mat as he could not sleep properly. He was disturbed by what Kuravan Damodaran had reported about Kochhu Paru, who was living with their aunt in a faraway village. Kochhu Paru was not at all happy with her stay and was desperate to come back here as she was not being treated properly by her aunt and her family. She had absolutely no freedom in that house. Her aunt had four children, three daughters and a son. Only the son, the youngest, was slightly warm towards her. Rest of them fought with her constantly. Her uncle was a very quiet person who left home at daybreak and went to the backwaters for scooping shells from the bottom of the waters and returned late in the evening. He never interfered in anything. Her aunt made all the decisions in the household. Though Kochhu Paru was her own brother's daughter, she was totally indifferent to her.

'You should immediately bring back Kochhu Paru, otherwise she may do something undesirable', Damodaran advised Pakkaran.

'But Damodaran…', Pakkaran said reluctantly. 'It is not so easy to bring her back abruptly like that.'

'Alright, I am leaving', said Damodaran, lifting his basket and placing it on his head. 'If she jumps into the backwaters or a pond… don't tell me later that I didn't warn you.' Damodaran started walking away briskly. Pakkaran ran after him.

'But did she say anything like that?'

'That's what I told you', Damodaran turned his head. 'She said she can't continue there because your aunt is very rude to her. She also said that you should go there tomorrow and bring her back.' Damodaran walked away swiftly, swirling his hands.

In spite of thinking for a long time, Pakkaran could not come up with a solution for the problem.

Just the day before, the goon Chandrappan had challenged him standing in front of the local toddy shop in the presence of the goonda, Kurukkal.

'Wherever you hide her, if I flag a woman for myself, I will definitely get her one day or the other', Chandrappan was completely drunk and was emboldened by the presence of his goon gang including Kurukkal.

'If Pattathil Chandrappan is a man, he will somehow taste the woman he desires', said Chandrappan as he came out from Achhamma's toddy shop.

Kurukkal added his own challenge. 'After all, she has to come back to this village one day.'

She was a fish he had trapped once, but she somehow slipped out. Chandrappan was frustrated because of that. Pakkaran did not want to get into an argument. He quietly avoided them.

At that time, the toddy tapper Kochhappi came out of the toddy shop, after making his regular supplies to Achhamma.

'If Chandrappan has decided to do something', Kochhappi warned him. 'He will do it. Did you decide anything about the proposal I put forward to you?'

'If you ask like this…' Pakkaran hesitated.

'After hearing about Kochhu Paru, my elder brother is very excited', Kochhappi said while counting the money the toddy shop keeper had given him. 'You consider it once again and give me a confirmation.'

While he firmly believed that Kochhu Paru should not be brought back to the village in the near future, Damodaran had given him a very disturbing report of her distress at the place where she was now. What should be done? If he brought her back from Koipuram, where would he keep her? Who could he discuss this with? These days Prabhakaran was going around as if he were in a trance. Anakhashayan also had not been very friendly since he had told him about Kochhappi's proposal. The only one left for support was Karambi Mamma.

At sunset, Pakkaran reached Karambi Mamma's hut. She was busy sharpening a sickle, rubbing it against a stone.

'Don't worry too much. You bring her here', she said when Pakkaran told her his woes. She moved forward and backward, sharpening the sickle. Pakkaran's attention was caught by her sagging breasts. After her mother's death, Kochhu Paru had grown up suckling on them.

'The time is not too good', said Pakkaran.

'So what? As long as there is a single breath of life within me, no one will be able to touch her.'

The sharpened blade of the sickle sparkled in the light of the tiny kerosene lantern.

There was a stir outside.

'Is there no one inside? Come out, you old Pulaya woman.'

Karambi Mamma covered her bare chest with a small cloth. 'You go and see who is outside', she told Pakkaran.

Pakkaran craned his head outside. In the dull light, he could see five or six people lingering in the yard.

'Who is that?' he asked.

'Come out', said the stoutest man in the group.

'What is the matter?' Pakkaran insisted.

'Before the crack of dawn, this hut should be vacated', they shouted. 'If you have any pots and pans to be taken out, do that right away.'

Pakkaran couldn't figure out who the people were.

'But you people don't belong to this place', Pakkaran challenged. 'Tell us who you are.'

'Phew, scoundrel, how dare you talk back to us?' the man growled. 'You better come out or…'

Karambi Mamma leaped outside with her sickle.

'Who the hell are you people to throw us out of our hut?' she said. 'We need to see who has come to evacuate us from our dwelling where our ancestors have been living for generations. All these farms and agricultural lands are the result of our hard work. And now you have come to evacuate us? Let me see how you do that.' She bristled with anger.

'You Pulaya woman', one goon rolled up his sleeves, 'don't give work to our hands.'

'By tomorrow at the crack of dawn, no one should be seen here.' The stout man threatened once again, 'I am giving all of you a final warning. There will be no more questions and answers.'

'Where can we all go?' Pakkaran came out. 'You tell us and then go.'

'Go and get lost anywhere', the man said. 'When we ask you to get out, just vanish. Otherwise…', he raised his hands at Pakkaran.

'Dare you touch him', Karambi Mamma leapt on him like a female tiger guarding her litter. 'If a pinch of dust falls on him…' she challenged.

'The old woman has gone nuts', the fat man raged and walked away.

They walked towards another area inhabited by seven or eight Pulaya families. Grandmother panted in suppressed fury. Pakkaran held her close and said, 'Don't worry grandmother. Tomorrow we will inform the union office and get a solution. Let the night be over.'

'But what right do they have to evict us?' Mamma continued to bristle with indignation.

'After all we are living on their land', Pakkaran said. 'That is why they are showing off their might.'

'Did your dead grandfather come and tell you that?' Grandmother bristled. 'This is the land allotted to us by the landlords during the days of our ancestors and we have been living here for generations. In those days, Thambrans measured and granted this parcel of their property for our usage without even our asking.'

'That's true', Grandpa Kelu, covering himself in an old blanket, came out and joined the conversation. 'Those days, when the Thambrans came and told us that this land is for our use, we were all so happy. We kept quiet when they came and measured the land and separated it for us as our tenements.'

Petrified men slowly started coming out one by one to join the conversation along with their women, who carried their babies on their hips. All their faces were shadowed by fear.

Pakkaran started walking fast. He wanted to meet Comrade Padmanabhan and brief him about the situation. It was very dark but since he knew the location of all the small roads and canals, he reached his destination quickly. But taking the effort to walk two or three hours jumping over seven or eight canals proved to be a waste since the Comrade had left for another village. He was told that Comrade would be late and would come back only by afternoon.

Pakkaran went back home but could not get a wink of sleep thinking of Kochhu Paru. What shall I do with her; should I bring her over here? he wondered.

By the time sleep slowly came to his eyes, he heard sounds of mayhem from the neighbourhood. Pakkaran leapt out of his mat and peeped through the holes in the braided coconut frond shutter of his hut. He saw a blazing fire through the gaps in the door. He knew that a hut was on fire. He ran out of his hut. People were running helter-skelter, holding lighted torches made of dry coconut fronds showering obscenities. Women and children screamed. Someone shouted in the crowd.

'Friends, they have cheated us. The goons and police are evicting our people from their huts in the scheduled caste settlements. Soon they will be here also.'

Kochhanian brother came running in panic and reported. 'They kicked and beat all of us. They are throwing out all our possessions.'

Pakkaran could hear the sound of pots and pans being hurled out. Police, with the peaked caps, ran everywhere, beating up men.

Sounds of men screaming, chorus of women and children wailing, 'All our possessions have gone…' could be heard everywhere.

Grandma Karambi leaped forward, swirling her sickle, 'They can enter my vicinity only over my dead body.'

A burning torch cavalry circled the huts in the settlement. Flames started blazing from the top of the hut in the center. Sea breeze blew from the western side, spreading the fire everywhere. The breeze blew in a fury, tossing up the flames and making them dance. Sound of dried bamboo pillars crackling in the fire could be heard. Sparks from the fire scattered everywhere,

'Before they reach here, try to remove all your possessions', Kochhanian brother alerted Pakkaran.

Pakkaran clasped his hands behind his head and stared at his neighbourhood, now under a blazing fire. His eyes bled. Devils of fire were fast approaching by the tank bund road.

Aparajitha was sitting in front of her laptop when Disha approached her with a book.

'How far have you gone?' Disha asked.

'Eviction', she took her fingers off the keyboard.

'Is this not Vyloppilly's collection of poems?' Aparajitha recited two lines.

Disha's fingers moved over her shoulders. Aparajitha looked at the book in front of her.

'This is the autobiography of Comrade Sreekandan Nair', said Disha.

'I read it', Aparajitha grimaced. 'Its horrible.'

Mother was at the door. She handed her a piece of paper and said, 'This has been sent by Comrade Vamadevan.'

Aparajitha looked at her. She looked as though she had been crying.

'What's that?' Disha looked into the paper. 'Oh, MR Nair's address.'

'Is there any phone number?' asked Aparajitha.

'No, only the address of the flat.'

'MR Nair should be a turning point', prophesied Aparajitha, 'My mind says so.'

'Is there any particular reason for your thoughts?' Disha enquired.

'Nothing like that', said Aparajitha. 'Still, I feel that he may know lots of stuff which would be of interest to us.'

Her mobile lying on the table began to ring. Disha lept and got it.

'Mrinalda', she spoke into the phone. 'Anything about Niranjan?'

'You tell him I am busy writing', Aparajitha said, burying her face in the laptop.

Disha walked out with the phone.

'As of date, we have no information from Bastar', he said. 'Village Sukma is in trouble. In Kasanpada village on the south of Bastar in the forest area, they shot fifteen men of the Border Security Force, keeping the villagers as human shields. This is a sort of getting-even in view of what happened about ten days ago at the same spot to the same number of Maoists. Surprisingly, the very next day, Chief Minister Raman Singh made a public statement that they will eradicate all Maoists from Chhattisgarh.'

'I read that in the paper', Disha said. 'Anything about him....?'

'He will come back', Mrinalda said, trying to comfort her. 'Okay, now I called....'

As soon as she had finished talking with Mrinalda, Disha came back into the room. Aparajitha was totally unaware of her entry. She was fully engrossed in the keyboard, writing....

Mrinalda had called to ask Aparajitha about her Delhi travel plans. He had visited her mother at the hospital. Her condition didn't seem so good. As soon as he sat by her side, taking both his palms together in her hands she had told him: 'There is only one wish left in my mind. I want to beg her forgiveness for having orphaned her.' Her eyes overflowed with tears. 'Once in life, at least once in life, will she not forgive me?'

'She will come', he had said, holding her hands together.

Disha walked into her room.

As she sat in front of the monitor idly, her eyelids grew heavy. A coal train moved behind the drooping eyes. Aparajitha was travelling in a third-class compartment, along with Pathrose, unaware of the destination. She was sitting opposite him, with her legs stretched on the wooden seat. His gaze was fixed on the passing scenery outside. Four or five north Indian Marwaris, their co-travellers, were engrossed in a card game. The coal train released streams of steady black smoke which entered the compartments through their windows, turning the faces of the traveller's black.

The rays of the sun slanting towards the west lengthened the shadows falling on the dried-up paddy fields. She also kept staring outside through the windows of the running train, like Pathrose. Pathrose had fixed his eyes beyond the paddy fields. She focused hers on the famished farmers whose legs dragged their energy-less bodies.

'What are you looking at unblinkingly like this?' she asked him.

Pathrose looked at her through his half-closed eyes.

'In Nalagonda and Telangana, the farmers are marching forward, capturing all the villages on the way. Can't you hear their triumphant songs?'

She couldn't hear anything. 'Um…hum', she replied in the negative.

'A stunned Nizam, his Razakar administration, the police and their goons are all standing still there. What you are hearing is the sound of the steady strides of our comrades. Listen to the slogans raised by the comrades throwing their fists up after touching their foreheads, "Let the revolution win… let feudalism be damned… let the Razakar rule collapse." The waves of October Revolution! Winds of change are blowing everywhere.'

She sharpened her ears to hear the sound. A red sky made his face luminous.

'My Travancore also will be released from the tentacles of feudalism. Days of the anarchist rule of the Diwan will soon be over. It will mark the end of the black days of the monarch's rule. Like in the streets in Moscow, like it is happening in Nalagonda and Telangana, my comrades in Travancore will also arm themselves for the release of my country… yes… It's time for an armed struggle.'

She was slipping back to sleep, resting her head on the wall of the train.

When Disha came into her room, Apu was in deep sleep, with her head resting on the keyboard. Outside in the darkness, crickets had started their concert.

Near the Palmyra Forest

'Silence becomes a crime at certain moments in history!' 'Silence can sometimes be a punishable offence. Presently Travancore is going through such a state.' Words of Comrade C Keshavan reverberated in the mind of Pathrose.

'If we assume silence without challenging the crooked Diwan's rule and feudal atrocities, history will never forgive us.' He remembered what Comrade BT Ranadive had advocated during a month-long military training programme conducted in Bombay in which he had participated.

'Only guns can confront guns. Words cannot. In the current situation in India, an armed struggle has become inevitable. Comrades, please get ready for that.'

It was Comrade Krishna Pillai who had selected the nine candidates for the training programme headed by Comrade Pathrose. From the Bombay Central Office of the party, they were taken to Pune by a military vehicle. During those days, when they were roaming on the steets of Pune in military uniform, armed with guns, their days began with transmissions from Moscow. As Ranadive repeatedly stressed on the inevitability of an armed struggle in India, Pathrose felt that it was not very far away. Excitement bubbled through their veins as they held their guns and went beyond the limitations of an unknown language. He didn't need the assistance of the translator, Shankar to understand the English-speaking European instructors. They regarded Pathrose very highly and their compliments prompted even senior Comrade Rajarajeswara Rao to hug him and say 'well done...well done....'

That's what he stressed upon during the discussions at Kozhikode between the senior leaders like Comrades Krishna Pillai, EMS, NC Sekharan and KC George.

'It is no more possible to remain silent like this; it's time for an armed struggle in Travancore.'

Comrade Krishna Pillai was also convinced of that. Earlier on, CK had spoken to him on the phone. The situation in Cherthala was becoming worse by the day. The police and the goons of the feudal lords had been extensively evacuating a large number of tenements. Hundreds of poverty-stricken families were roaming on the streets without food and change of clothes.

This was happening as a result of a cynical conspiracy by the police and the landlords; Sir CP's sly plan to displace communism by uprooting common man's solidarity.

Simultaneously, they were hunting leaders of the movement from the lower and upper cadres to arrest.

'Alappuzha also is chaotic', Pathrose said. 'As the President of the Travancore Communist Party, KC's presence is a must in Alappuzha from now onwards.'

Comrade Krishna Pillai listened patiently.

'In a stage like this, there is definitely a point in what Pathrose says', Comrade evaluated the situation. 'We have to become armed at least to protect ourselves. We don't believe in the philosophy of extending the other cheek for a slap if we are slapped on one. Our motto is an eye for an eye and a tooth for a tooth. Otherwise, not only our comrades but they will nail even our party on a cross. We should not let that situation occur by our silence.'

Comrade EMS stammered, wanting to say something. Comrade smoothly superseded him and said, 'Let George leave for Bombay immediately and brief our party general secretary PC Joshi about the situation and get the party's approval.'

Next day itself George left for Bombay. By the time he reached the party office he was given to understand that Joshi had left for Calcutta. Bengal was in deep trouble. Houses were being burnt down. Women were being molested. The State was in turmoil with the farmers clashing with the jotedars in the Tebhaga struggle.

The Tebhaga struggle had started in June 1946 in Malda. About fifty lakh farmers had joined the struggle from eleven districts demanding two-third of the agricultural yield. The farmers had been working in partnership with the landowners.

'The farmers work and produce in agricultural lands and the landowners enjoy the returns. These grains soaked in our blood should become food for our children. We will never compromise even at the cost of our lives.' Majumdar raised his voice in exhilaration. 'The landowners are asking, "Today you are demanding two-third of the produce; tomorrow if you ask for the entire quantity…?" We gave them a stern reply. "It will happen. Tomorrow this land also will belong to us; because the farmland belongs to farmers who work on it."'

'There also, the police and landlords put their heads together to suppress the struggle. In the end, the hands used only to hold yokes were forced to carry guns and turn them against their oppressors.' Everywhere women too came in the forefront to fight. They hugged paddy sacks while confronting the police and army.

'In truth we farmers were the owners of the farming lands earlier. About four generations ago, the land was forced out of our hands. It was Lord Cornwallis who, under the pretext of formulating a permanent legislation, had transferred the farming lands to the landlords. They held us as captives and exploited us as bonded labour. That will not be possible in future. We will win back our land even if it means risking our lives.'

Comrades George and Joshi spoke over phone from the party's central office. Comrade Joshi authorised Dr Gangadhar Adhikari to handle the situation. George knew Dr Adhikari very closely. Dr Adhikari was in-charge of the party's central committee office; the party's think tank. He had a PhD from Berlin University in Chemistry. From there, he had joined the German Communist Party. He was closely acquainted with Albert Einstein. He became a member of the Indian Communist Party soon after returning to India. He was arrested in the Meerut conspiracy case. Einstein wrote to Ramsay MacDonald, the British Prime Minister, urging that Dr Adhikari be released from custody. 'You have imprisoned a brilliant scientist'...is what he had written about Dr Adhikari.

Adhikari listened to KC George carefully and finally asked, 'We have to remember that we are planning to confront a powerful government. Will we be able to confront a powerful army?'

'We have no other alternative', George argued, 'even if it means sacrificing our lives'.

'The question is not whether an armed struggle is the need of the hour', Adhikari continued gloomily. 'The question is how far are we equipped.'

'That's the decision of the State party leadership', George said. 'That's the situation there.'

After thinking for a while, Adhikari nodded, 'If that is the situation in Travancore….'

Over telephone he gave instructions to various functionaries in Bombay and Madras to form supporting committees for the proposed armed agitation.

After the committee meeting in Bombay, Comrade George reached Madras accompanied by Comrade NK Krishnan. In Madras, Comrade Parameswaran organised a meeting of the party supporters.

'Don't we have to constitute a funding committee for the agitation?' Comrade Parameswaran asked.

'Of course', George responded.

'Shall we start from the arch enemy of Sir CP?'

'Who is that?' George and Krishnan chorused together.

'KC Mammen Mappillai', Comrade Parameswaran informed.

'But is he not the most prominent bourgeois from Kerala?' Comrade Krishnan expressed his doubt.

'Did I question that?' Parameswaran justified. 'Have you not heard of Chanakya's famous saying? Enemy of the enemy is a friend.'

George also felt that it was a truth. Two incidents that had happened at that time had driven Mammen Mappillai to CP's enemy camp. One, CP's action against the newspaper *Malayala Manorama* owned by Mappillai and second, liquidation of the National and Quilon Bank. The Diwan was enraged by *Manorama*'s articles supporting a responsible democratic government. The clash between the Diwan and the *Manorama* paper had started soon after the new prince, Chittira Thirunal had taken over the reign. Through his editorials, Mammen Mappillai had attacked the new Diwan's policies severely. The Diwan warned him several times, which was ignored by Mammen. Two news items that appeared at that time had enraged both the King and the Diwan equally. Firstly, on the undesired developments in the Sankumukham seashore and secondly the police shootout in Neyyattinkara.

'As we are convinced that the contents and title of your news items carried in your daily on Chingam 17 & 18th can trigger off people's wrath and disbelief in the government, orders are issued herewith to cancel *Manorama*'s license to continue the newspaper, and confiscate the press and machinery owned by the *Manorama*.'

It was a contingent consisting of the Kottayam District Magistrate, Superintendent of Police and a forty-strong police force who were detailed to serve CP's order on the *Manorama* and seal the press.

'I became an admirer of Mammen Mappillai for two reasons', said KC George. 'One, astounding even CP, he released his paper the next day from his Kunnankulam press, sitting in Madras; secondly, in spite of incurring a huge loss, he was not willing to compromise with CP, although the circumstances were in favour of that.'

'Wasn't he arrested and sent to jail on a false charge in that bank case?' Parameswaran said.

They had reached Mammen Mappillai's residence by afternoon.

'We condemn CP's action of sealing the press and stopping the paper as an attack on the freedom of press', said KC George.

'The King is aware of all the decisions made by Sir CP. He is just playing the fool, pretending ignorance', Mammen Mappillai said. 'I have a copy of the letter that CP wrote to the King even before sealing the press. After *Kaumudi* and *Samadarshi* closed down, there was no other paper to confront the government other than the *Manorama*. "If they also become troublesome, we will be taking action on them." That was the gist of CP's letter.'

'Sir CP has calculated all his moves well', said George. 'His hidden agenda is to turn the King into a puppet and bring Travancore under his feet.'

'This should be an agitation that should dig the grave of CP', said Mammen Mappillai. 'I will be with you in this endeavour.'

'If we live, we will live with dignity; otherwise we will die fighting for justice', said George. 'We have only these two options before us now.'

Mammen Mappillai went inside and came back with two hundred British rupees. He handed it over to George. 'Keep this with you for the time being. In case you need more in future, don't hesitate to ask me. I am with you.'

Thanking him, George and Krishnan got up.

'Everything should be done carefully', Mappillai reminded them as he bid them goodbye. 'Don't forget that your fight is against a State government. They will fight back with all their might.'

'We are aware', George said. 'This is a life and death struggle.'

'I pray that nothing untoward happens', Mappillai hugged George. 'And also, that I should meet you again.' George felt a shiver passing through him as he spoke those words.

'I will come back', George assured him, holding his hands tightly.

Mammen Mappillai stood there looking at him as if he didn't believe that. A shadow of sadness spread under his eyes. He kept waving his hands as if it was his last chance to bid George goodbye.

During his return journey to Calicut, the uncertainty in Mammen Mappillai's words kept haunting George. What guarantee is there that there will be a return journey? Who can predict who all are going to be the victims of Sir CP's guns? This is the Kurukshetra war for justice. Enemies are powerful personifications of injustice. They are stronger in terms of weaponry also. His mind kept on questioning whether he would be able to keep his word to Mappillai that he would return.

Pathrose sat in the party office waiting for his arrival. Sreekandan Nair and Janardhana Kurup were also present to discuss the general State-wide strike to be declared. Comrade EMS and Pathrose joined the discussions and came to a consensus. As the meeting ended, George suggested, 'Why don't we take a photo together?'

They lined up in front of '*Desabhimani*' and posed for the photo.

'George should return to Alappuzha today itself', said Comrade Pathrose. 'The mission in Kozhikode ends as of today. We will meet again. Lal Salam.'

Comrade Pathrose walked off, bidding goodbye to everybody.

Will they be able to see him again? There was no certainty. George bundled all the books he had collected during his wanderings and handed them over to NC Sekhar and gifted a good leather bag in his possession to EMS. All that he kept for himself was a set of clothes, a pen, a wristwatch and a small amount of money to meet his travel expenses. He started for Alappuzha by a night train.

Ippolith, son of Ambrose, mentally celebrated: 'Almighty God, what more blessings can you shower on me than this? Didn't the whole seashore witness the scene of the police handcuffing Kuttappan and his company for barging into Veronica's house and mouthing obscenities at her?'

'Benjamin, you are also a witness. When the police files a FIR, you better not falsify facts', he had told Benjamin.

Polycarp was worried. 'Benjamin is a senior trade union member. Don't forget that. If Simon Asaan is released from jail, he will change his stand. There is no point in saying that he is the son of Nicolas Mudalali.'

'But for that, shouldn't Simon be released from jail?' Ippolith tried to comfort himself.

'I do have ideas to combat the situation.' His crooked brain started working.

The police had reached Paravoor market by bus. There was no drivable road from Paravoor market. After getting off from the bus, one had to walk four to five kilometers by narrow village roads, by the side of Arsakadavu Thommankutty's house. Again, they had to take the same route back to Paravoor to take a bus.

'If the trade union people stop us what will happen?' The police group was apprehensive.

Ippolith told the police head, 'You give me a letter. I will get you a police vehicle.'

After taking the letter from the head, Ippolith handed it over to Benjamin. 'You take my younger brother Sebastian and go to Alappuzha police station. Come back here to Paravoor market with the vehicle.'

Benjamin left for Alappuzha along with Sebastian.

When Ippolith had visited the police station the previous evening with a pouch full of money, he had only one demand. Kuttappan and company should be hand-cuffed and paraded in front of the whole village while being taken to Paravoor market. Ippolith was bent on that. No one had challenged him so far in his glory. Kuttappan had made an attempt to do that. Kuttappan had the backing of the trade union. Polycarp had suggested that he could be easily eliminated by burying him in the depths of the sea overnight. That was Polycarp's expertise. He could eliminate a human with the same ease as pinching off the head of a prawn.

'We will do that later if required', said Ippolith. 'Now we will humiliate him in front of the locals by getting him hand-cuffed and dragged by the police.'

People crowded on both sides of the road to watch Koottungal Kuttappan, Chalithara Joseph, Palliparambil Ouseph and Moolankuzhi Joseph being herded away by the police. Scared of the police, no one uttered a word. A crowd of local people followed them. Ippolith and Polycarp reached Paravoor market through a short-cut and waited for them.

The police and the arrested men reached the market. Trade union workers stopped them on the way, asking the police the reason for the arrest. Both the groups got into heated arguments. The union workers started shouting slogans. The local people, who had not uttered a word till then, also joined them. Ippolith and Polycarp hid behind a petty shop. Suddenly a police vehicle roared and rolled into the market and halted in front of the native medicine shop. Along with the police, Benjamin also leaped out of the vehicle. As the police vehicle moved forward after picking up Kuttappan and company, the crowd circled Benjamin menacingly.

'Traitor, you are the one who brought the police, isn't it?' By the time Veera Pillai, the owner of the petty shop approached them, the crowd had trapped Benjamin.

'Hereafter, he will never be able to falsify his testimonials as a witness', Ippolith looked at Polycarp. 'How was my trick?'

'But where is our Sebastian?' Ippolith thought of Sebastian only when Polycarp reminded him. 'Is Sebastian also with Benjamin?'

By the time Ippolith and Polycarp reached the shore to organise a support group for them, around two hundred fishermen were moving in a procession shouting and abusing Ippolith, like a whirlwind raising tremors on the seashore. Ippolith hid away from their eyes.

'Sea breeze is moving in the opposite direction', Polycarp said to himself. 'The seashore is going to be set on fire.' He was getting signals of an imminent disaster.

Prabhakaran was running as if he had gone out of his mind.

'Kaithara Pappy has come….' Children were shouting and running in a frenzy. Prabhakaran also ran behind them. Others also joined the marathon from all directions.

'Where? Where is Pappy?' Prabhakaran asked anyone he came across.

'There, there she is', they continued to run.

'Did you see her?' Prabhakaran asked.

'Yes', they said 'Tailor Kochhanian Pillai saw her as he was going to the Ponnamveliyum market.'

'Then where did Pappy go?' Prabhakaran was growing feeble with anxiety.

'There are people who have seen her going towards her house.'

Prabhakaran sprinted through the mud roads, crushing the dry shells, through short-cuts running through the paddy fields. Before people crowded around, he thought, he should take Pappy away from there, to his place. He reached the front yard of Pappy's house, panting and sharpened his ears for the mooing of the cow and her song: 'Who plucked all the flowers in the tiny garden?'

He looked around in frenzy. He looked at the footprints visible on the sand. The second toe next to the big toe was longer than other toes. He recognised Pappy's footprints. Prabhakaran searched for her everywhere. As a tiny breeze swept the dried jasmine flowers from the base of the plant, he heard Pappy's song somewhere from behind the palmyra thickets.

Are you coming to pluck the flowers?
Are you coming early morning?

Isn't that Pappy's voice? Prabhakaran sharpened his ears. He bolted in the direction of the song, treading on the plants.

Whom do you need early morning?
We need our lover early morning.

Climbing down from the bus at Idapalli junction, Disha and Aparajitha crossed the road and started walking.

'We have to find the residence of MR Nair. This is going to be a turning point in my investigations.' She had a premonition. Aparajitha started getting a weird feeling as she took each step forward. 'What if he doesn't remember anything?'

Comrade Vamadevan had called again. MR Nair had just returned from the jaws of death. He had been living alone in a studio apartment in Mayoor Vihaar in Delhi, when he had suffered a stroke while he was in the bathroom. That was six or seven months ago. Fortunately, he had not bolted the door. Maybe he had been totally drunk and had forgotten. Anyway, that turned out to be a blessing. Somewhere in the passage between life and death, he was rushed to AIIMS where he had got good treatment. Now he was in Idapalli, in his daughter's house convalescing.

Why did MR Nair come back to life, leaving behind the narrow track to death? What made him forget to bolt the front door on the night he had the stroke and almost died, which made it possible for the rescue party to rush him to the hospital and save his life?

Aparajitha was lost in deep thoughts.

Disha waved at an autorikshaw.

The Script Changes

While the crowd approached Pappy's house by the bund road, Prabhakaran took a shortcut. As he got closer and closer to the house, Pappy's song reached his ears.

Little dragonfly, would you like to join me to pick the flowers?
Would you like to pick the flowers at the crack of dawn?

The familiar melody struck his ears like tiny arrows. But was there a discord in it now? What he had heard the last time before they were separated, was still lingering in his ears:

Thathayyam, thathyyam tharo,
Chimi Thathayyam, Thinthimi Tharo,
Thathinam Thinthayyi Tharo
Chimi Thathayyam, Thathayyam tharo…

The melody that had trapped his footfalls on the sand.... But why is there a discord in the melody now? He halted, panting on reaching the thickets. Why were his knees growing weak in front of Pappy? Pappy was singing and dancing in rhythm, standing in the midst of wild grass which had grown till the knees. Prabhakaran hid behind the clusters of leaves and looked at her.

Her hair parted into two sections, adorned by orange firecracker flowers streaming over her shoulders. With the mundu tied over her bosom with a knot, Pappy was singing loud enough to pierce a hole in the sky.

Whom do you need, ask as per your need, at the break of the day…

Pappi danced in rhythm.

My God what has happened to Pappy? She is dancing as if she is in a group, Prabhakaran was upset.

'Pappy', Prabhakaran called out to her, standing near the thickets. 'This is your Prabhakaran chettan.'

Pappy stopped her dance. The song also stopped. She stared at the thickets.

'Oh, Pappy has recognised her Prabhakaran chettan!' Prabhakaran came out of the thickets and walked towards her.

'Pappy, it is me.'

Pappy looked at Prabhakaran in stupor.

'Come on', Prabhakaran coaxed her, 'we will go to our house'.

Pappy stepped back with a jerk.

From nowhere a flock of jungle babblers flew into the thickets and chirped in chorus.

Prabhakaran tightened his mundu and folded it up.

'If you have any health problem, we shall go to the Vaidyan', Prabhakaran pleaded, walking towards Pappy…. Pappy, looking intimidated and frightened, retraced her steps and stood leaning against the portia tree, crossing her arms over her breasts. Her eyes spat fire at Prabhakaran as he tried to go near her.

'Don't get frightened. It is me. Your Prabhakaran Chettan', Prabhakaran tried to comfort her.

'Go away.' Pappy growled.

Prabhakaran trembled in trepidation. He could hear sounds of the approaching group of villagers, children and women shouting, 'Here's Pappy!'

The crowd stopped abruptly near the palmyra thickets. The jungle babblers flew back from the thickets and settled on the branches of the portia tree.

'Go away you harbingers of death.' Pappy snarled again.

'Look, Kaithara Pappy has gone mad', the crowd chorused. 'Kaithara Pappy has gone crazy....'

'Get lost you scoundrels', Prabhakaran waved his hands furiously. 'It's fun to watch when someone else's mother goes mad, isn't it?'

Pappy pulled out a branch of the portia tree and waved at them menacingly, 'Get lost.'

'Run, run for your life', the crowd retreated. Pappy came rushing with the branch.

Prabhakaran stood still, stunned to the core.

'This is not madness', someone commented from the crowd. 'This is possession. She has been possessed by the ghost of Mara.'

'What a senseless group of people!' Prabhakaran grit his teeth.

'See, didn't she detach that branch from the tree in one go? See the way she stares and the expression on her face? She looks as though she has not even seen us.'

'Prabhakaran, you better move out. This is not Pappy. This is the spirit of Mara.'

Pappy stormed close to Prabhakaran and asked.

'Did you kill, did you kill my Mara?'

Prabhakaran shook his head.

'Has my friend Mara left?'

'Our Mara drowned herself in the pond Pappy', Prabhakaran tried to explain.

'My Gods in Heavens!' Pappy cried out. The tree branch slipped out of her hold and she collapsed on the ground.

The coal train was speeding past spitting black smoke. As he was about to set on his journey, he took back one book from the bundle he had passed on to Sekhar. He needed something to read to pass the time during the journey. *History of the Communist Party of the Soviet Union* – the book was banned from circulation in Travancore as per the Sea Customs Act. Six or seven years ago, from somewhere, the book had reached Comrade Damodaran's hands. Damodaran had given it to George.

Once, he had seen Pathrose thumping through the book, a little disappointed. 'Why can't one of you who are educated, translate this into our language? Then comrades like me who are worthless, can go through it and learn how Stalin led an army against the ruling government.'

'Why not?' asked Damodaran. 'Can't Comrade George give it a try?'

'Let me see.'

On that day, he had taken it from Damodaran. A criminal negligence – what to do? How can one find time to make such attempts when life is so hectic? He thought.

The train reached Alwaye station very late. It had stopped almost everywhere for shunting. It had started very late too. He had to spend the whole night in Kozhikode station suffering mosquito bites. As he got out of the Alwaye station, a stranger approached him.

'I am here to take you to Vaikom', he said. 'I have brought a car.'

He greeted him and introduced himself. His name was Varghese. He was a practicing doctor running his own clinic and a party comrade too. Varghese informed him that they had arranged a boat to take him from Vaikom to Aryad. Comrade Thampi was waiting for him at Aryad at the pier from where he would take charge of him.

It was almost dark when the car reached the pier. As soon as the car pulled to the curb, the light of a glowing beedi came towards them.

'Do you have a beedi to lend?' the person asked. 'No. But we have matches.' George was slightly confused as he listened to the conversation.

'It's a code', explained Comrade Varghese.

'Is the boat ready?' Comrade Varghese asked the person.

'It will be here in a moment', he replied. 'Where is the comrade?'

'This is Comrade Thampi', Comrade Varghese whispered in his ears. 'My mission ends here. Thampi will take over from now. Lal Salam.'

'Lal Salam!' bidding goodbye to Varghese, he walked along with Thampi.

After assuming silence for a while, Comrade Thampi started talking. 'I couldn't do things the way I had planned. The boatman who had been arranged earlier didn't turn up. Patrol boats are scattered in the sea for surveillance. Nobody was willing to go to Alappuzha by boat for fear of them.'

'Now what shall we do in this pitch darkness?' George was scared.

'Comrade needn't worry', Thampi reassured him. 'We will find a way. After all, is this not the country of Comrade Krishna Pillai? You will have to stay here for a short while. Hide yourself from the eyes of the beat police. Don't allow them to catch you.'

George couldn't see his face clearly in the surrounding darkness. Thampi left him alone behind the petty shop attached to the pier.

After some time, he saw the round beam of a flashlight approaching the shop. What if it is the police? George moved to the other end of the shop. As it neared, the light turned red, with five fingers closing around the glass. Is that a signal?

'Do you have a beedi to lend?' That was the voice of Comrade Thampi.

'I have matches. Will that do?' George answered the question.

'It is enough.' The man who accompanied Thampi loosened his grip on the glass of the flashlight and flashed the light towards the ground. Light circled around his thin legs.

'Were there any police around?' Thampi asked.

'No', George replied.

'I had a tough time, getting a safe means of transport', he said. 'No one was willing to take the backwater route to Alappuzha. Finally found a cargo boat sailing from Kochi to Alappuzha.'

By the time he finished explaining, a boat came close to the pier.

'If the police patrolling in the backwaters ask you any question, tell them you are shifting tiles meant for Pooppalli village from Kochi to Alappuzha.' Thus giving his advice, the comrade turned back and walked away.

It was almost daybreak when he reached Aryad. Comrade Kochhu Narayanan was waiting for him by the backwaters.

'I am the liaison person for the Comrade', he said as he walked in front. Comrade Pathrose had arranged everything. Comrades from Alappuzha had briefed him about everything. Pathrose again proved to be a wonder.

Kochhu Ṇarayanan led him to a small house on the banks of the backwaters in the middle of a coconut farm.

'As long as you are here, no one will come to know about it. Neither deer nor monkeys stray around here', said Kochhu Narayanan. 'By night, Comrade Pathrose will reach here.'

'Pathrose?' George couldn't conceal his surprise.

'Um… Pathrose was also in the same train you travelled in. He got down at Kottayam. We got a message that the police had information that both of you are travelling together.' It might have been his idea to get down at Kottayam, a precautionary shift in plan to avoid anything untoward.

Pathrose came late in the night. He didn't say anything, nor did George ask him anything.

'Did you get bored sitting all alone?'

George closed the book he was reading in the light of a tiny kerosene lamp, *History of the Communist Party of the Soviet Union.*

'Have you started copying?' Pathrose was asking about the translation.

'Oh that's OK. We still have time.'

'Do we have time?' George asked doubtfully.

'Why this doubt? We will win this fight', Pathrose said confidently. Red light emitted by the tiny lantern scattered on his face

'Come, let's go somewhere.' Pathrose walked out. George didn't ask where, lest Pathrose got angry. He followed him. Kochhu Narayanan walked in front with a lantern which spread small circles of light in the darkness. They walked and reached the front yard of an isolated house. In the light of the lantern, Comrade CG's face became visible. The lantern hung on a roof panel, swinging gently in the night's breeze. Comrade Kunjan appeared in the verandah and behind him was Comrade PG Padmanabhan.

'Comrade CG Sadashivan has been living in hiding here for some time now', said Pathrose.

'Now Comrades PG and Kunjan will give him company. It is better to remain here for discussing future plans. No one will come to know of it.'

All of them sat in a circle under the cashew tree in the yard. Kochhu Narayanan moved to the kitchen to prepare black coffee.

'Hadn't we decided to strike work from the day after tomorrow?' Comrade Pathrose said, 'now TV is having second thoughts. He wants to discuss the issue once again at the party level.'

'Is it not second of the month *Thulam* today?' George asked. 'Wasn't that decision taken by the ATTUC? As the President of the joint trade union, shouldn't TV announce this?'

'All that is right', said Comrade PG, 'still, since Comrade KC has come to the scene, Comrade feels that it should be considered once again...'

Kochhu Narayan came out with glasses of hot steaming black coffee.

By midnight, Comrades TV Thomas and Vaidyan Varghese also came and joined the meeting.

'Pathrose has made all the arrangements in the style of the army', TV commented as soon as he arrived.

'In spite of the liaison person being with us all through the way, Pathrose's army stopped us and demanded the code', added Varghese amidst laughter.

Discussions became serious again. Only one issue was distracting TV.

'This is not an agitation that can be stopped by mutual consent. We will have to go ahead with the plans till we realise its political goals', said TV.

'That would be required', Pathrose said emphatically.

'If it becomes impossible…' TV looked at George.

'It will be possible', Pathrose barged in.

'We need to think once again', TV said. 'It is possible to do anything on an impulse….'

'What is there to ponder anymore? Has not the Central Committee given its approval for the move? As the Joint Union President, comrade has to give the final notification tomorrow', Pathrose gave an ultimatum.

'The steps we have put forward should now go only forward, whatever be the risk', George said firmly.

CG, PG and KK Kunjan agreed to that point.

'All of us, Kunjan, Pathrose and I will go in stealth. But Comrade's instruction is that no one among the top trade union leadership should go underground, including TV. They should firmly be in the agitation scene and undergo arrest boldly.'

TV didn't say anything for a while. Straightening the edge of his jibba he sat erect.

Oil in the lantern hanging from the roof panel dried up. The wicks burnt and slipped down. Circles of light shrank and disappeared.

Kuttappan's arrest triggered a tsunami of protest on the seashore. The police had handcuffed Kuttappan and his friends and taken them to jail, hung them upside down in the lockup, and thrashed them. When Comrade TV reached the seashore to make a truce between the fighting factions, the authorities promised that the fishermen would be released from jail the next day. But even after the lapse of four days, they were still in jail. Police raided the seashore again and picked up another eight men on a complaint lodged by Marian, an associate of Ippolith and Anthappan, at their instigation.

The seashore started smoldering. A crowd, carrying ores and machetes, marched to Anthappan's office. When Benjamin, who had been to the town for a hair-cut returned, the seashore was blazing. Anthappan's office had been gutted, all the storages were being engulfed by huge flames and Ippolith's house had been pulled down. Anthappan fled as soon as the assault commenced. Ippolith tried to resist and then fled and hid in Aplon Auraj's house. The crowd broke open the house and dragged him out. They assaulted him with ores and made sure that he was dead.

When Elisa, wife of his neighbour Ambrose, came to see what was happening, Ippolith was lying in a pool of blood. Elisa looked at him once again and felt that his lips that knew the taste and flavour of the seashore were trying to say something. She poured a few drops of water from a pot on to his lips. Suddenly his body came alive. Elisa lifted his head with both her hands and placed it on her lap. As she bent forward, her nipples pulsated. He opened his lips greedily. She poured some more water on to his lips. She was lost in memories. She covered his body with a few coconut fronds. She was scared his enemies would come back and see him alive.

The group who had moved southward were whacking Anthappan's father Paulongi. Elisa could hear his squeals. She could hear the screams of his wife, Isabelle also. They circled Dennis's house too. Elisa hid behind her door and listened. Ippolith's body was wriggling under the coconut fronds. On the western side, warehouses were blazing. Smoke coiled and rose up, shrouding the sky. Now they were attacking Ippolith's house. There was the sound of windows and doors being broken down. Flames went up from the kitchen. Elisa looked at Ippolith. The horned shark that terrorised the seashore was surrendering. She couldn't get over her mental agony at the thought of the strength of those arms of a man that crept inside her house in the darkness of the night when her husband Ambrose was away at sea.

Late in the night, sleepless Benjamin walked on the lonely seashore. Even the sea was silent. The stench of burnt fish waded through the breeze. The stench of ashes...the stench of burnt down huts.

Benjamin stopped walking when he heard the footfalls of someone running and fast approaching him. It was Yahiya.

'Things are going berserk, Benjamin', he panted. 'Three police trucks have come in. They are camping in Pollayil Mathayee's house. Mathayee has gone somewhere with his step-mother. No one knows the whereabouts of his father. Tomorrow they are going to bring in more police.'

Mathayee was the son of the State Congress leader Aplon Auraj by his first wife. Benjamin was wondering why Yahiya was talking in a roundabout way to get to the fact.

'Look at those storage sheds burning down. Nobody is there to extinguish the fire.' Yahiya went delirious. 'They set fire to Ippolith's kitchen also. This was done only to get even with the Pollekkar family.'

Who wants to get even? Benjamin gazed at the seashore engulfed in fire.

With both his legs drawn up, CK Kumara Panicker was reclining on his easy chair in the verandah of his family house

Kunthirisseri, with a growing sense of uneasiness. Not one or two, thousands of people have been thrown into the streets. The landlords and police have joined hands to evict them from their dwellings. The party had opened camps in four other localities apart from Vayalar. According to information obtained that evening, the number had exceeded two thousand in all the five camps. Arrangements were being made to provide food for all in the camps. But the question was, how long can one go on in this manner? Hundreds of famished people were coming into the camps every day. They have to be trained to use weapons at least for their own security. What was there for them to lose now, those who have lost everything?

VK Velayudhan and Sekharan came by the side entrance. They washed their feet and took their seats on the verandah.

'Have all the arrangements been made as discussed?' asked CK.

'Army trainer Kumaran will reach tomorrow morning', Sekharan said. 'You can discuss with him as to how the military training should be provided.'

'Don't we have other men also in the party who are retired from the army like that Soman Nair?' CK asked. 'We should include them also in the trainers' group.'

'All of them will reach here by tomorrow or the day after', said VK Velayudhan.

'Everything should be done in the army way.'

'Yes, yes.'

'Okay, did you know about the conspiracy in Ponnamveli?' Sekharan asked in hushed tones. 'We came to know of that when we were on our way.'

'Yes of course.'

He was referring to the secret decision taken by DSP Vaidyanathan Iyer in a meeting of landlords he had convened.

'Exterminate CK Kumara Panicker and CK Bhaskaran at the earliest.'

'You have to be careful', VK said. 'The decision is to do away with both of you some way or other.'

'We will wait and see', said Kumara Panicker.

'It was also decided that anyone who kills a communist leader will be employed in the police force or he will be given lifelong subsistence.'

'Oh, that's a good attempt', CK laughed. 'At least, like that a few in the country will escape from unemployment by getting opportunities in the police!'

'Okay, I heard something. I don't know whether it is true or not', VK ventured with a preamble. 'The joint trade union president is not in favour of this country-wide strike call.'

'Who, TV?'

'Um…Didn't Comrade KC get this approval from the Central Party Office by going to Bombay personally?'

'That's right', CK nodded.

He had heard of TV's last attempt to defer the general strike through Vaidyan Varghese.

He had also heard of a memorandum signed by the workers in Kollam sent by Sreekandan Nair through KCS Mani and Janardhanan Kurup to Pathrose in the secret camp. They had gone with a recommendation letter from Vaidyan Varghese.

'Go and tell that Sreekandan', Pathrose had torn the letter into pieces and trembled in anger. 'It's enough for the workers in Kollam to join the strike after one month. During that month, we will rule the area from Aroor to Kayamkulam single-handedly. After that, tell him to appropriate the portion of land south of Kayamkulam to himself.'

On hearing about the arrival of KC and Pathrose from Kozhikode, CK had visited them in their hideout. It was not very difficult to find out the hideout because CG Sadashivan had been camping there secretly for some time now.

'Are you ready?' Pathrose asked the moment he saw them. 'CK is the dictator* in Cherthala taluk.'

'We are ready.' CK said.

'It's difficult to predict what will happen.' Pathrose said. 'But we should be ready to face anything; inform all the comrades to be alert. All should be given good training.'

'We should be the soldiers of a war fighting only to win', his face was illuminated by a red glow.

'In Vayalar, we are ready to do anything', CK nodded.

'Lal Salam!' Pathrose threw up his right fist and said.

'Lal Salam!' CK also raised his hand.

It was while Aparajitha was taking a walk in the paddy fields after closing the laptop that Mrinalda's call came, breaking into the melodious Tagore lyrics rendered by Poulami Ganguly.

'It maybe to remind me about my Delhi travel', she thought. She didn't pick up the call deliberately.

Disha had disclosed the day before to her the reason why Mrinalda was insisting on her visit to Delhi. Why should Snehalatha Chatterjee, who had forgotten Sathyadas, remember her daughter now? Those were closed chapters of her life. Why should they be reread now? As she flew away, holding the hands of her lover on the wings of love, why hadn't she thought about

---

* This is the word the communists used for their area commanders in those days, according to some documents of those times.

this daughter who had spent her days with a tormented heart? Hadn't t she orphaned this daughter and walked off into a new life? Didn't she mar even the revolutionary dreams of Sathyadas? Finally, in the womb, in which she carried Sathyadas's daughter, she....

And now, lying helpless on the hospital bed, she seemed to want to apologise to her daughter with the lightness of editing and fine-tuning a half-written poem she had attempted to write in a trance! As if, trying to edit her own life in the light of her love for her daughter!

'No more Delhi', Aparajitha told herself – especially now, when her journey to look for the roots of Sathyadas had reached a turning point.

What would be the secret that MR Nair would disclose to her? Will he be able to pick up the threads of those memories, clearing up the cobwebs covering them?

Days Before the Revolt

Pappy was running vigorously on the bund road between the paddy fields holding a sickle in her hand. That was the scene Prabhakaran witnessed when he came back with Pakkaran. Shouting slogans and waving the sickle high, she was running on the road leading to Vaidyan Mani's house. A bunch of howling urchins followed her. The moment she turned back menacingly they retreated in fear.

Cutting across the areca nut farm of the Karthas, ascending the hill through the mini forest and then climbing down from the other side of the hill, she was nearing the lotus pond. Prabhakaran and Pakkaran followed her, keeping a safe distance.

'Thank God!' Prabhakaran thought. His plan was to bring Pappy somehow to the vaidyan and now, she herself was heading towards the clinic. The urchins came back intimidating her. Prabhakaran and Pakkaran chased them out.

KATALUR

'These rascals will make even a half-crazy person totally crazy', Pakkaran cursed the urchins.

'Who is half crazy?' Prabhakaran was infuriated.

'No…I was talking about Pappy…' Pakkaran said guiltily.

'There is nothing wrong with Pappy', Prabhakaran snapped at him. 'She has temporarily gone berserk after hearing about Mara's death. She can be brought back to her senses by treatment. Just wait and see', Prabhakaran resumed, walking swiftly.

'Oh, watch out…', Pakkaran alerted him.

'She is going towards the lotus pond. Is she going to drown herself like Mara?' Prabhakaran's heart skipped a beat.

'My God, she is getting into the water… holding that sickle.'

Pappy entered the water. Wading through the lotus plants, she was standing in waist deep water.

'My dear Mara, please tell me who killed you?' Pappy howled, her voice carrying to the depths of the pond. 'Whoever it is, I will cut him into pieces….'

'Pappy is thirsting for vengeance', thought Prabhakaran. 'She wants to take revenge not only on the army men but the whole world.'

'Pakkara, I will take care of her', Prabhakaran turned to Pakkaran, 'You go and inform the vaidyan. I will somehow get her to the clinic. She seems to have gone off her senses. The vaidyan will treat her.'

Prabhakaran slowly entered the water and quietly walked towards Pappy. His plan was to go under the water, pull her legs, topple her unexpectedly and snatch the sickle from her grip and fling it away into the deep waters of the pond. There is no other way we can get her to safety, he thought.

Pakkaran returned quickly and came closer to Prabhakaran, who was standing in the pond.

'The vaidyan is adamant that he won't take the responsibility of treating Pappy', Pakkaran panted. 'It seems the army registered a case against him for taking care of Mara, saying that he is responsible for her suicide.'

'Now what shall we do?' Prabhakaran sounded tired.

'Not to worry', Pakkaran said comfortingly. 'We have our Kumaran Vaidyan.'

'In that case, you hurry up and get Kumaran Vaidyan.'

He dived under the water.

Vaidyan Kumaran was getting ready to flee to Koman island. For the past three or four days, he had been living in hiding with Kochhu Kunjan Asaan. He knew that the police had gone to his house in search of him three or four times. They had spread word around the neighbourhood that he had gone to a relative's house in Thrippunithura. They were confident that Sir CP and the police would not enter the Kingdom of Cochin. Sekharan would gather information every day and report. It seemed, police constable Unnikandan had a soft corner for him. Kochhu Kunjan Asaan roamed around somewhere and came back home. He washed his legs and sat on the wooden bench on the verandah. The vaidyan was somewhere inside the room. He had been warned that he should never be visible outside till they reached Koman islet.

'Did you hear this?' Kochhu Kunjan Asaan opened the paper and read. 'The moment TV announced the general strike, Sir CP issued orders to ban the Communist Party and all trade unions.'

Asaan handed the newspapers to the physician who was still inside.

'Have they not banned about seventy trade unions!' he exclaimed. 'What are they up to?'

'He has taken a final decision', Asaan crossed his legs. 'All trade union offices have been locked and sealed. The police are taking away even the furniture.'

'Sir CP has issued an unusual notification', the vaidyan put on his spectacles and started reading. 'Communist activities have been on the increase in the country openly and covertly. Their violent activities in Cherthala and Punnapra Vayalar are the best examples. The workers instigated by the Communist Party are terrorising people in their localities and people who refuse to budge are being abducted, kept in illegal custody and harassed. We have been receiving reports to the effect that these Communist groups victimise those who report their atrocities to the authorities, by murdering them or gutting their huts. To spoil a harmonious relationship between the landlords and their workers, they have now called for a general strike....'

'My good Lord...what lies...' the vaidyan looked at Asaan.

'Read...go ahead read the rest...' Asaan prompted.

The vaidyan continued to read.

'It has been learnt from reliable sources that they are collecting lethal arms and weapons and threatening the peace-loving citizens and that to progress their terrorist activities, they are being supported from outside with a flow of money and weapons.'

'It's sad that Sir CP's press statement does not carry even an iota of truth and justice.' The vaidyan brought his hand to his chin.

'Is this not the person you people have been venerating all these days?' Asaan teased him.

The vaidyan assumed silence.

'Are you aware that another person has arrived to spy for CP?' Asaan asked.

'Who is that?'

'Our R Sankar, who else?'

'But Sankar is a person who has his own views', the vaidyan said as he looked at Asaan. 'Didn't he resign from the State Congress and take over as the General Secretary of the SNDP?*

They had heard that SNDP had decided in a meeting to depute R Sankar and four others to Cherthala to investigate the situation and report. He had PK Govindan, M Madhavan and Kumara Gopala Panicker to assist him in the investigation.

'All that is fine. But now he is a henchman of Sir CP. If there is a shootout or something, is it not our own people who are going to die? That's the forethought based on which, he has come over here. Yesterday evening, he visited Ponnamveli and Kalavankodu. There were three or four others also with him. Still, he didn't give even a cursory glance to the areas under eviction. He visited MK Krishnan in Vayalar, accepted their hospitality, and went back.'

'Oh, is not Krishnan now in SNDP? But we have to tell the truth. His wife Devaki is a sickle in true spirit. She will die for the party. How bold she is!'

'Oh, that reminds me', Asaan said, 'Day before yesterday, I went to meet Mother in the convent. They are planning to organise a rally of the comrades in the women's organisation, holding the sickle and the staff they use for de-husking the coconut shell, to express their protest against the Diwan's rule.'

---

* The Sri Narayana Dharma Paripalana (SNDP) movement was a movement for social uplift among the largest non-Brahmin caste group, the Ezhavas of Kerala, started in 1903. It was also known as SNDP Yogam, as it arose from a temple social reforms effort.

'Oh, that's not bad', the physician smiled slyly. 'That should be a scene to witness!'

Asaan looked angrily at him, to express his objection to what the physician had said.

Mother and the party had a long-time relationship. There was no comrade in the party who had not enjoyed her hospitality at the time of food scarcity. The women's organisation had its roots in that house. He recalled a day with her.

Mother was choreographing *Thiruvathira Kali,* a traditional dance form of Kerala, when Asaan had reached there on a blazing afternoon. A meeting of the women's organisation, presided by Devaki Krishnan, was in progress. Comrade CK Bhaskaran was also present at the meeting.

'Who is this? – Kochhu Kunjan Asaan? Come and take seat', Bhaskaran had invited him in. Asaan joined them.

Devaki stood up confidently and addressed the meeting.

'Gone are those days when we women remain subdued, suffering insults, humiliations and atrocities. From now on, we should not bear the atrocities and crimes of Sir CP's army, police and feudal landlords. It's time for us women also to carry weapons for self-defense. Our weapons will be sickles and the staff we use for de-husking the coconut shells.'

'On the seventh of Thulam month, a rally of our women comrades in the women's organisation has been scheduled', Bhaskaran whispered in his ears. 'About ten thousand women holding sickles will participate in the rally.'

Mother had come inside, carrying a pot full of butter milk.

'Oh, here's Kumara Panicker', she announced joyfully.

Kumara Panicker and VK Velayudhan came inside, fanning themselves with their shoulder mundus. 'Oh, how oppressively hot it still is', he said, trying to unbutton the top of his jibbah.

Panicker had looked at Devaki.

'On seventh, we the women's organisation, have decided to organise a rally', Devaki told him.

Mother poured the buttermilk into glasses.

Kumara Panicker had calculated.

'On fifth, the general strike; on seventh, the King's birthday; the same day a rally of one thousand volunteers from Olathala to Thuravoor. On the same day another rally of four hundred volunteers from Ponnamveli Army Camp to Menasseri. The sixth camp is there, at Menasseri.'

Sensing a movement at the fence, Asaan turned back. He was shocked to see Sekharan.

'This guy who normally leaves the house at the crack of dawn and comes back at midnight is here at this unusual time – how come?' Asaan asked.

'We need help from the vaidyan', Sekharan said as soon as he entered the house, 'and your support too', He turned to Asaan.

'What is the matter?' Asaan's brows knitted.

'It's regarding Kaithera Pappy who was abducted by the soldiers of the King's army.'

'Stop beating around the bush and come to the point', said Asaan.

'She seems to have lost her mind after being tortured by the men. We tried to take her to Maniyan Vaidyan. But he is not willing to treat her as he is scared of the army.'

'But, Kumaran Vaidyan is in hiding now', Asaan said. 'In addition to that, we are all set to leave for Koman islet late this evening.'

Sekharan stood gloomily. 'She is a spirited comrade. She was the one who conducted a rally of a handful of people and abused the police publicly.'

Asaan peeked inside at the vaidyan, wondering whether it was a health condition that could be treated through proper medication.

Kumaran Vaidyan said: 'When there is an imbalance between the three fluids in the body, *Vatha, Pitha* and *Kabha,* when the patient shows symptoms like thirst, excessive dislike for others, excessive temper and eccentricity, it can be concluded that he or she is suffering from a mental disorder. After applying medical procedures to bring out the excess kabha (phlegm) from the nose, and bringing out toxins in the body through vomiting and defecating, by administering medicines time to time and going through a strict diet regime, the ailment can be cured.'

'But now, at this time, that kind of a treatment may not be practical… we have to leave for Koman islet this evening', Asaan was uneasy.

'See whether it is possible to take her to Koman islet, without anyone knowing about it', suggested the Vaidyan.

'That's true', Asaan told Sekharan. 'After dark, we will start off. No one should come to know of it. People who accompany her also should be warned.'

'That I can manage', Sekharan assured.

Pakkaran was waiting outside the fence. 'What did the Vaidyan say?' he enquired.

'The Vaidyan has agreed. And remember, if this Vaidyan agrees, it will get done', said Sekharan. 'We will have to reach their place sometime after nightfall.'

From his house, Sekharan went directly to Kalavankodu. There was a small crowd assembled in front of a tiny prayer hall to the east of the temple. All the important party leaders were present.

'Where were you?' Comrade Velayudhan reprimanded him.

'I had to go somewhere on an urgent business', Sekharan replied. 'But what's the matter?'

'Ask there', KC pointed at CK.

All the comrades were standing around KC. CK Bhaskaran, PK Abdul Khader, CK Raman Kutty, PK Padmanabhan, NP Thandaar....

'By nightfall, we have to fell all the areca nut trees. Don't bother to ask or explain. We will need them. Whoever be the landlord, we will face him then and there.'

'From tomorrow we have to make arrangements to commence our work on shaping them into sharp spears in the camps', said CK Bhaskara Panicker.

'Splitting the trees, the pieces should be shaped into spears – the weapon of our soldiers – the sharp tips of which can pierce through an object like a pin', said CK.

'The length should be accurate', reminded Kumaran, the trainer who was a retired army person. 'At least eight feet! Then only it can be used against the army....'

'What can we do with the spears in front of the army's 303 rifles?' Chani Vakkachhan, another ex-military man countered. 'The guns are not filled with horse gram and salt, but with first class bullets.'

'No, the army will not shoot', fileman Keshavan said. 'Do you think our Maharaja will allow such a thing against us?'

'In case they shoot, they will shoot only below the knees', said Comrade Raman Kutty. 'Our Chithira Thirunal Maharaja is not all that heartless.'

'Initially, the army will shoot only in the air', said Kumaran. 'At that time, we have to lie face down on the ground. Holding the spears close to the heart, we have to start creeping forward. You should not raise your head high. You have to get close to them and pierce the spear into their stomachs.'

'We should have at least 600 spears ready by tomorrow', said CK looking at the comrades who had encircled him. 'We have to start training the first batch from tomorrow at the temple grounds.'

'To split the stem of the areca nut tree and make thin strips for the spears, we have to seek help of the trade union members of the coconut tree climbers.' Comrade Velayudhan looked at Sekharan. 'Today itself you should meet their leader Velu Mooppen.'

'OK.' Sekharan started to leave, with Pakkaran in tow.

He had heard that the spear was invented by Vadeparambil Narayanan, when unrest broke out in Alappuzha long ago. To punish a few men for molesting some Theeyya women, Narayanan organised an army of Theeyya men who carried spears with sharpened tips and attacked the opponents at night, piercing the weapons through their bodies. But actually, the spears had pierced through the innocent sleeping inside those huts.

'Have you heard of Sardar Bhagat Singh?' Sekharan asked Pakkaran. 'You may not have heard about him. He was hanged when you all were small children. He was hardly twenty four.'

'Who hanged him?'

'The English. Who else?'

'Oh, but what for?'

'They alleged that he hurled bombs at them. He was very bold, unlike our cool Gandhi.'

If one is a man, he should be like Bhagat Singh, thought Sekharan.

Sekharan visualised confronting the army with spears. Holding the spears close to the body, fighting comrades were creeping on the ground. As they got close to the army, like the roaring sea they sprang up shouting Inquilab, driving the spears into their throats.

'Don't we have to take Pappy to the healer?' Pakkaran was losing his patience. 'Comrade Prabhakaran would have lost his patience waiting for us.'

'Don't discuss this with anybody', Sekharan said. 'We are taking her to my uncle's house in Koman islet. The Vaidyan will come there.'

'What about comrade Prabhakaran?'

'He can leave her there and come back. The Vaidyan will take care of her.'

Pakkaran walked in long strides.

Thulam fifth.

The first siren of the morning went off in the coir factory at seven o'clock. Supervisor Kochhu Bhava Mooppan glanced at the road arrogantly. He was sure that at least some workers would come sneaking in, like it happened during the previous strike. Before the third siren at eight o'clock at least some twenty people....

The supervisor got busy getting ready the accessories for that day's production. The second and third sirens went off. The roads were still deserted. Not even a pedestrian was to be found on the road. The iron frames in the factory shed remained still. The wheels of the machines stopped spinning. The coir fiber arranged ready for spinning different products wove a web around him. 'It has been a long time since I have worked on those machines', he thought. He stomped on the iron frame left and right. He turned into a spider in the centre of the yarn, looking for a victim. Three or four police vehicles sped past on the mud road, kicking up a cloud of dust.

It was around ten in the morning when Benjamin was walking westward, dragging his legs in the sand, when he saw the parade of the armed reserve police on the Punnapra seashore.

DSP Vaidyanatha Iyer was in the forefront, with other high-ranking officers wearing cross belts across their chests. The parade was led by Velalyudhan Nadar from Parassala, well known for his big mustache. He was in-charge of the army camp recently started in the house of Aplon Auraj. Starting from the western side, marching through the fishermen's huts, the army was advancing like the roaring sea. Benjamin bolted by the side of the warehouses southward and reached the western side of the horse stable. Close to the church a group of people were sitting in a circle, a heated discussion was going on. It was the workers' camp which had started from the first of Thulam. He didn't want to be seen by them, lest they shower obscenities at him and manhandle him for being a traitor to the workers' cause.

The police were heading towards the church. Benjamin made some calculations in his mind. The moment the police close in on them, they will disperse and scoot. The police will chase them and whoever happens to be caught will be beaten up by the polilce. They deserve it for their arrogance. Didn't they, on that day, in the marketplace, without a trace of human compassion....

The police reached them but those who were sitting disregarded them without any fear.

'Move out from the way', the DSP barked at the workers.

'Not possible. You cannot go this way.' That sounded like the voice of the retired army man Devassy. Benjamin pricked up his ears. He had heard that he was currently training the volunteers in the workers' camps.

The police stood in attention as they could not proceed.

'Didn't you hear what Sir said? Move out from the way you scoundrels', Inspector Velayudhan Nadar roared. People rushed from the surroundings and crowded the place. Women and children created a human barricade on the road.

'Clear the route, immediately, it's my order', the DSP roared again.

'That's not possible you Vythi Pattar', Devassy stood like a rock. 'It's better for you to change your route.'

'What did you call Sir?' this time Velayudhan Nadar swung forward.

The DSP stopped him. 'I will shoot down each and every one of you.' He pulled out the hand-gun from his belt. 'Move out, you rascals.'

'Kill!' Devassy stood expanding his chest.

'Kill!' Comrade CK Bhaskaran barged forward thrusting out his chest.

The comrades jumped forward one by one and stood with their chests thrust forward and formed a human wall in a moment. Workers carrying long ores were encircling the police.

The DSP was reluctant. He put his gun back into the sheath, removed his hat and massaged his head. He changed his strategy.

'We didn't come here for a confrontation', he said in a diplomatic tone. Please move from the way a little. We will go.'

'Haven't we already told you that you cannot go this way', Devassy stood unshaken. 'If you want, proceed by the seashore.'

'OK.' The DSP grit his teeth and turned to his men. 'Left turn, quick march.'

The reserve police turned left, marched westward and turned north.

Comrade Bhaskaran threw up his fists, 'Inquilab Zindabad, Workers' unity Zindabad'.

People repeated the call. That became the roar of the ocean. The sea wind transmitted and carried it to Punnapra market, Paravoor, Kommadi, Muhamma and Vayalar. The western wind carried it to Kowdiyar and Bhakthi Vilasam. DSP Vaidyanathan had been forced to bend his knees in front of the fighting comrades.

Benjamin hid in the warehouse. 'God, even the DSP had to bend his knees in front of them, what is this going to trigger?!'

Saga of the Seashore

Firoza Begum was singing, *'Ashe Basanto Phoolbanye...'* (spring is coming in the forest of flowers ...)

Aparajitha woke up to the soothing melody from the ipod. Riding on the wings of music, she had reached the crowded streets of Calcutta. Rickshaws were racing; braving the rush on the road, she managed to get into one. Firoza Begum was still singing Nazrul's verses. Nobody could sing them better than her; Anjali Mukherjee, Subrata Sarkar, Susmita Goswami, Juthika Roy...no one.

The ten-year-old girl who came looking for Kazi Nazrul Islam; the one who carried Nazrul's verses to their zenith and showered them as a rain of ghazals...

'Apu, you should have descended to this earth a little earlier', her father had said, teasing her. 'You didn't have the fortune of seeing Nazrul!'

Father used to visit the lonely and bedridden Nazrul frequently with a tape recorder when he was in Calcutta; Nazrul, lying exhausted, propped up on the pillows; sharpening his ears for the death knell. When Firoza Begum's voice dissolved in his Alzheimer-affected brain cells in the form of his verses, his eyes would become moist. At that time Nazrul would be resurrected from the deep lagoons of fading memories.

When the great poet was laid to rest in Dacca,* Comrade Sathyadas was also one among his fans who had crowded at his funeral to pay their last respects. He had carried the memory of that last fistful of soil his hand had dropped on Nazrul's *kabar* (grave) till the end of his life. Maybe, that would have been the reason why one of his several journeys to Dacca was extended to the residence of Firoza Begum. Mother was with him also during this visit. It was a ride in a cycle-rickshaw by Father and Mother to the banks of the Buriganga river....When Mother and Father together hummed some of the Nazrul verses, Begum's eyes became moist. Finally, when they had visited Nazrul's tomb also, Father had hummed one of his verses.

'When I cease to exist, when I disappear in the web of lost memories...'

Her eyes were misty as she listened to that. In the nostalgia inspired by those memories, she travelled for a long time aimlessly. As she sat in front of the keyboard, she could see that little girl in white lingerie groping around, searching for the right path. Firoza Begum continued to sing, *Ami Jedin Roibo Na Go...* the music continued to play in Aparajitha's dream.

---

* Kazi Nzrul Islam died in 1976. Nazrul and his family moved to Dacca from Kolkata in 1972, following the liberation of Bangladesh.

Disha came running into the room panting…

Aparajitha woke up startled.

'He called.'

'When?'

'Last night… one of his friends… Dinar told me when I met him on the way.' She panted.

'Where is he?'

'He called somewhere from Chhattisgarh.'

'Couldn't you ask him for more details?'

'I asked. He evaded the questions, saying there was nothing more to say.'

'At least he called!' she sighed.

'Be careful', Disha reminded her, 'especially over the phone. You know those cannibals…' She walked towards the corridor.

'Um…' Aparajitha turned to her keyboard.

'Cannibals – what is the word in Malayalam…. Those who eat human flesh….'

Unnikandan had also heard of cannibals. Somewhere in the Andaman forests that kind of humans lived. They ate the raw flesh of other human beings. He had heard it from Kunjan Nair who had come back from the Andamans. He had gone there as a cook, to work in the Cellular Jail. The Tamils and those from Malabar who had been exiled by the British were kept under solitary confinement in the Cellular Jail, where they underwent horrendous torture. Kunjamu, a prisoner from Malabar, who had managed to escape the jail atrocities, had landed in the cannibals' hands. The Tamil soldiers who had gone in search of him had witnessed the scene, hiding behind the trees in the forest; Kunjamu being roasted alive on the fire, with his hands and legs tied apart on a bamboo split. His death screams as the cannibals approached greedily and ripped off his flesh, terrified even the trees in the forest. The Tamils had recounted the story after they came back to the jail and sat down for their dinner.

'A horrifying scene....' As they had told their story, a wild terror mirrored in their eyes.

Unnikandan had seen the same terror reflected in the eyes of Raman Nair also. When he looked at his own image on the faded mirror fixed on the station wall, he could see the same terror in his own eyes too. He felt he was just enacting the role of a policeman inside the khaki uniform as a matter of duty, as there was no other way to survive. If he had....

Sir CP's rule was devouring humans raw. Screams of the many Kunjamus hit his eardrums menacingly. Thirty to forty people were being brought to the station every day, poor guys. The Diwan's order was that all the jails and lockups in the land should be filled with communists.

That morning, advocate Kumaran, clad in his official robes, was brought to the jail in handcuffs. He had been made to walk some distance to the jail. Men from the reserve police force rolled up their sleeves to strike him as soon as he stepped into the station. Head Constable Narayana Pillai muttered something in their ears. They didn't beat him but pushed him into the cell, stripped off all his clothes and covered him with a single mundu. Their hands itched and they hit on the walls.

By afternoon he was taken to the court and brought back on a fourteen-day remand. The moment the lawyer kept his foot inside, Head Constable Narapillai signaled the policemen with his eyes; the policemen rubbed their palms together in glee.

That was when Unnikandan became aware of their plans. They had postponed the torture session for Kumaran Pillai to after his appearance in the court, lest there be tell-tale marks on his body which would be noticed by the court. 'How deviously cunning is this Narapillai', thought Unnikandan.

The policemen made the lawyer bend down by pulling his hair and started hitting him on his back. As his agonising squeals fell into his ears, Unnikandan left the station on his cycle for his routine patrol. By the time he came back in the evening, the station yard was flooded with placards which read:

'Put an end to the anarchy of the Diwan.'

'Dump the American Model in the Arabian sea.'

'We need responsible government.'

'End manhunt by the police.'

'Where are all these coming from?' Unnikandan enquired from the station security.

'They were picked from the union offices when the places were raided.' Around ten more people were stuffed in the lockup.

Head Narapillai was snoring away happily, with his legs stretched out on the table, his uniform unbuttoned and loosened. Flies swarmed around his mouth from where saliva treacled out.

Unnikandan turned his attention to the lockup. The lawyer was sitting in the corner, leaning his head against the wall.

'Have your porridge and then sleep.'

'How?' the lawyer looked at the bowl of wheat porridge kept by his side, which was covered with flies. 'Can't you see the worms floating in it?'

'And it stinks like shit.' Comrade Paraman kicked the bowl away.

'Is that true?' Unnikandan asked the constables. 'Are they being given worm-infested wheat gruel?'

'That's the order from the top', said PC Maniyan Pillai, 'that they should not be pampered. They have cut down their rations also; one measure of wheat to be shared between five. Make them starve and they will mellow… that's the idea. After all, isn't that the minimum punishment for revolting against our King?'

'Do you also need to add loose motions to all the torture they are undergoing?' Unnikandan was indignant.

SI Raman Kutty Nair came running from the next room. 'DSP sahib is arriving from Alappuzha.'

'Where? Where?' Head Narapillai bolted up from his seat, buttoned his shirt and tightened the belt. Placing his baton in the arm pit, he stood to attention.

'But where is this Inspector Sahib Koshy?' Raman Kutty Nair asked himself.

Unnikandan smiled to himself. Everyone knew about Inspector Koshy's tie-up with a Nair house in the locality. Raman Kutty Nair was perhaps unaware of what was going on in the village because he had come to the village only recently, after being discharged from the British army. 'Koshy Sahib will be in Ayyappancheri', said Narapillai sarcastically. 'Doesn't he have an account there?'

Soon, there was the sound of a jeep halting in the front yard; DYSP Usman leaped out of the vehicle.

'Has he come?' Narapillai ran towards the door.

There was the rigmarole of making routine courtesies to the higher officer. Koshy came in and sat on the Inspector's chair.

'Did you know?' he said, 'our Pattar (referring to DSP Vaidyanathan) went to Punnapra and was made to bend his knees in front of the fishermen. He wants all these communists to be pulled out and lined up. You know, the old adage goes, 'if one loses the fight outside in public, he will vent his fury on those inside the house!'

Raman Kutty Nair turned to the lockup: 'Get them all out of the lockup'

Unnikandan quickly opened the lockup.

'Come out and stand in one line', Narapillai yelled.

A dozen reserve policemen were also lined up by the side.

'What is this stench?' DYSP Usman closed his nose with a handkerchief.

'It is the smell of rotten, worm-infested wheat porridge', said Comrade Paraman. 'Sirs should come and try some.'

'No, it is not that sir', Narapillai bent down to the desk and said, 'It's from that pot ...the one kept in the corner...filled with the whole lot of what they have relieved.'

'Make them throw it away', the DYSP growled.

'Yes sir', Narapillai hastily moved towards the lawyer. 'Come.... Aren't you a great lawyer. You only should carry this.'

Unnikandan police ran and tried to stop Narapillai.

'Please don't do that. After all, isn't he a lawyer?'

'Get out of my way', Narapillai barked at Unnikandan and dragged the advocate to the lockup. 'Um...keep this on your head.'

Kumaran lawyer walked out of the lockup, carrying the urine pot on his head.

'Narapillai is trying to settle scores. He is carrying a grudge against the lawyer for cross-examining him in court.'

'God only knows when he is going to break that urine pot', PC Maniyan Pillai said. Before he finished his sentence, they heard the sound of the pot cracking.

'You son of a pig, will you intimidate the police in court again?' Narapillai roared.

Unnikandan rushed to the spot. The lawyer stood there, drenched in the stinking stale urine.

'Come on, get a few buckets of water and pour it over his head', Unnikandan told the police constables.

'Who are you? Are you his advocate?' Narapillai looked at him accusingly and went inside the station.

Three police vehicles rolled into the yard and DSP Vaidyanathan Iyer sprang out from one of them. Immediately, his attention was drawn to the posters.

'What is written on these posters?' He looked at advocate Kumaran. 'Read.'

'Will put an end to Diwan's rule, Dump American Model in Arabian sea', the lawyer read loudly. 'Put an end to the high-handed rule of Police, We don't need Diwan's Rule.'

'Who wrote this?' the DSP barked. 'Whoever has done this, he will be done away with. Idiots! Who is there? Come and flatten these guys.'

'Um…all of you…, break the backs of these scumbags…' Narapillai roared.

DYSP Usman stood to attention. Unnikandan rolled up his sleeves and looked around. Whom could he beat? All were familiar faces he saw every day.

'Come to TB', the DSP said, addressing DYSP Usman. Both of them stomped towards the vehicle.

'Rascals! All of you wait and see', he roared at the prisoners while getting into his vintage car. 'I will shoot you all down and gut your Moscow in two days.'

He was referring to Vayalar. Unnikandan looked at Kumaran lawyer.

'Boot them down and smash them all', Inspector Koshy howled.

'He has come wriggling out of Ayyappancheri', muttered Narapillai. Unnikandan frowned at the obscenity in what he said.

The agonising screams of the prisoners engulfed the prison. The King's Reserve Police were at work.

Comrade Pathrose folded his paper and sat looking into the backwaters. All over the country volcanoes were smoldering. No one could predict when they would explode.

Bengal was becoming a place of every-day strife on account of communal violence and the Tebhaga struggle. While Gandhiji held the view that women should be able to protect themselves, the women were forced to keep themselves submerged in water to protect their modesty. More than one-and-a-half lakh people were victims of crimes of varying degrees. About ten thousand families had fled to escape from atrocities, giving up their dwellings.

The communal conflict triggered in Noakhali spread disharmony in Shantipur. The crowd had thrown stones at Nehru who had visited the western border areas. Khan Abdul Ghaffar Khan had declared that the British were the hidden hand behind the attack on Nehru.

Intimidated by the surge of people's movements in Telangana, the ruling class let loose large-scale violence against hapless workers. A joint terrorising effort was staged by the

Nizam's administration, Qasim Rasvi's Razakar battalion and the police who were opposed to annexing Hyderabad to the Indian Union; there was widespread arson, looting and molesting of women in Telangana and Marathawada. The patriotic farmer comrades were forced to resort to guerilla warfare. Workers of textile and jute mills were getting ready to strike work.

And here, Sir CP was making all the moves to separate Travancore from the Indian Union under the American Model.

Thulam 7, the birthday of the ruling King.

Sir CP had moved all the pawns to get the American Model enforced by the King on that day. He wanted to rule Travancore as an unchallenged entity by turning the King into a puppet. He had already appropriated the support of all the Congress leaders, who were waiting at the doors of Bhakthi Vilasam for their share of power. The communists were the hurdle. They were concentrated in Ambalapuzha and Cherthala taluks – called communist territory, flanked by backwaters on the eastern and southern sides, Arabian ocean on the western side, and the Kingdom of Cochin on the northern side – that Sir CP wanted to eradicate. DSP Vaidyanathan Iyer was deputed to this area on that mission. All were waiting for Thulam 7.

Before that, the workers movement had to gain momentum. The concept of an armed struggle should gain currency failing which....

The workers evicted from their homes and workplaces were flowing into the party camps. The party had to open camps throughout the State.

Hearing a movement on the dry leaves, Pathrose turned back.

Comrade Kochhu Narayanan came up with a piece of paper in his hand. Without a word he handed over the paper to Pathrose, turned and walked away. It was sent by CG, a list of decisions taken by the Action Council.

The meeting was held in the front yard of Comrade Kumaran's house under the shade of a tree. It was preceded by a meeting of the trade union conveners in the morning. After lunch, fifty leaders sat in a circle and deliberated on the pros and cons of the decisions taken by the action committee. In his introduction Comrade CG, among other things, hinted that it had been decided to appoint Pathrose as the dictator in Alappuzha and CK Kumara Panicker in Cherthala. Future direction of the agitation would be in their hands. CK had not arrived. So Pathrose was made to take over.

Pathrose sprang up:

'Comrades, we are going to confront the torture experts of Sir CP. They will be armed with guns; not spears. We also need guns to confront them. The hands used to hold spears should hold guns.'

'Don't we need guns for that?' asked comrade Sreedharan.

'We will snatch the guns', Pathrose's voice echoed.

The wind blowing from the backwaters froze. Even a leaf didn't move. 'For that, we will attack their Punnapra camp tomorrow.'

'Tomorrow?' comrades looked at each other.

'Tomorrow, Thulam seventh, the day our food provider, the great King completes his thirty-fifth year', said Pathrose. 'Only those who have the guts need come. Who are all the fearless among us?'

'I am ready', Comrade Govindan stood up.

'We need only four gutsy comrades who can face a forty-strong police force', said Pathrose. We should be prepared for anything. If an army emerges from among us, I will be there to lead that force. Who all are with me?'

All the comrades stood up.

'Not four. Four thousand are ready', said comrade Chakrapani.

'All of you may please sit down', said Pathrose. 'Now, we have to think about our strategies. That task, we will entrust with our action council. Everything should be confidential. No one should come to know of our moves.'

The Conveners' meeting was dispersed. The action committee sat to discuss. Pathrose only presented the draft action plan to the action committee. Comrades armed with spears will move in a procession starting from the beach, covering areas southward to reach the police camp. Another group will head northward and a third group westward. The three groups were to encircle the camp from all sides.

'At the same time, we should deny access to any army battalions moving in from outside. We should be able to keep them away at least for four hours.'

'There is a way for that', said comrade PG Padmanabhan. 'We have to demolish the culverts in all the surrounding areas and build barricades on the road by felling trees; like what Kakkachi did some time ago.'

'That's not enough', Pathrose continued. 'We have to create confusion in the minds of Sir CP and his police chiefs. All will be busy making group presentations. They should be getting different kinds of reports from different places.'

'How is that done?'

'That's the agitation strategy.' Pathrose caressed his beard. 'From the beginning, they should get a feel that the labourers will demonstrate with their spears and disperse. Comrades from the southern areas should organise processions, assemble in the ground, register their protest and disperse. The police should get an impression that all they want to do is disobey the orders against mass gatherings.'

'In that case, let the processions from the northern sides assemble at the Bapu Vaidyar Junction and disperse', said MT Chandrasenan.

'That's a good idea', said Pathrose. 'Make sure that no army or police vehicles enter the area from Alappuzha town to Paravoor market.'

'There is a way for that too', said comrade Padmanabhan. 'We will make our ex-military comrades wear their uniforms and conduct a procession from the Paravoor market.'

'That's a good idea.' Comrade CG Sadashivan patted Padmanabhan's shoulders.

'Our target is the guns', said Pathrose. 'The whole lot of guns in the Punnapra police camp.'

Disha came to the room. 'Mrinalda has been calling you for quite some time. He is complaining that you are not picking up his calls.'

'I didn't know', Aparajitha picked up her phone, 'maybe, because it's on silent mode. He may want to remind me about my Delhi trip.'

'Any hints on Niranjan…' Disha hadn't even completed her question when the phone rang.

'Sorry Mrinalda…in the writing mood….'

'How far have you reached in your writing?' he asked.

'Isn't this history…it keeps slipping out of my grip.'

'I have hit upon the ideal name for your work', he said.

'Wow, tell me', she was excited.

'Is this not the story of a historical struggle; and of a place too?' He asked in Bengali. 'What is the name of that place? I forget.'

'*Karappuram…*Seashore.'

'Yes, yes. So "The Legend of the Shore", how is it?' he asked.

'Wow, The Legend of Karappuram', she repeated excitedly.

'*Karappuranthinte Ithihasam*', Disha translated that into Malayalam.

The First Spear

Srambikkal Karunakaran had started walking at the crack of dawn. Now it was noon. He needed to walk ten miles through several villages by roads and forests to go to Kalavancode to reach the camp where CK Kumara Panicker was.

Giving directions to reach the camp, Comrade Ayyappan had given him a letter to be delivered to Comrade Panicker.

'On your way, don't open your mouth to anyone who tries to make you do that. Don't tell anybody where you are going or why you are going. Whenever someone asks you, you should just say, "till there". If they still persist, just give them the name of a nearby village. Comrade will give you a letter in reply to this. Just take it and come back.'

Clad in a half-sleeved khadi jibba and folding up his mundu, Srambikkal Karunakaran had started walking. He used short-cuts through forests and villages to avoid the police patrolling everywhere. To be on the safer side, he kept the letter tucked into the fold of the mundu tied around his waist rather than in the shirt pocket.

By afternoon, he had reached the village where the camp was. But on reaching there, he learnt that Comrade was in another camp. He continued to walk on. After covering a short distance, he found someone waiting for him who also started walking along with him.

'Are you from Muhamma?' the man asked.

'Yes.'

'Who are you?'

'Techman.'*

'Whom do you want to meet?'

'Comrade Kumara Panicker.'

'Who sent you?'

'Comrade NK Ayyappan.'

'In that case come along with me.' The man walked ahead. 'Comrade is in a camp a little farther from here.'

Then there was no conversation. They walked by the mud roads running through coconut groves. Karunakaran continued to be restless till he met Comrade Panicker and handed over the letter. He knew the letter contained some very important information. After all, was not Panicker the appointed dictator of Cherthala taluk? He had seen the Comrade several times when he came to his village to visit Comrade Karunakara Panicker. That must have been the reason why Comrade Ayyappan had decided to send him to deliver the letter. He had gummed the letter closed, using his saliva. He could have opened the letter, read it and gummed it back. But he hadn't done that. After all, secrets

---

* In those days, messengers and informers were called 'Techman' by the party.

should remain secrets. If the matter could be disclosed to him, Comrade Ayyappan would have done that. But this was party matter. To him Comrade Ayyappan was the party itself. It was Comrade who gave him membership in the party. It was Comrade who made him the secretary of the union of beedi rollers.

As they walked ahead, passing thickets of portia, two people were waiting for them in two different places. The one who accompanied him whispered something in their ears.

'Where is he from?'

'Muhamma.'

'Okay', they said and gave way.

As he stepped into the compound of the camp, he could hear the sound of people marching.

'Left, right, left, right….'

Comrades were being given military training by ex-military Comrade Padmanabhan.

As he went ahead, he saw a large number of spears heaped into a small hill. Some twenty people were sharpening stems of areca nut trees to shape into spears.

'Oh, what is this for?' he enquired.

'These are the spears.' His guide explained.

'Look lad, we are going to demolish CP', Karunakaran turned around to see from where the sound came. It was CK Panicker with a white towel tied around his head, walking towards him.

Karunakaran released his folded mundu and let it flow to the ground as a mark of respect.

'Oh, are you going back?' asked the Comrade.

'Yes', pulling out the letter from his waist and handing it over, Karunakaran said, 'Comrade Ayyappan gave this to be given to you.'

'Don't keep standing after the long walk, take a seat', Comrade told Karunakaran. 'Give him whatever refreshments you have', he told his guide.

By the time Karunakaran had finished the porridge and side dishes served to him, Comrade had written his reply and had come back to him.

'Then don't hang around here', he said. 'Get going. Someone will come from here to show you the way.'

'But I know the way', Karunakaran said.

'No, don't take the route you came by. That may be dangerous', CK said. 'He will take you through a different route.'

A man from the camp accompanied him to show him the way out. Crossing backwaters in different places, when Karunakaran reached his own camp, Comrade Ayyappan was waiting for him. He handed over the letter to him. Comrade Ayyappan went through the letter and wrote another letter to be sent to the Gudekkar labour camp. As he reached Gudekkar camp, labourers were busy sharpening spears.

'From where you get so many areca trees?' Karunakaran asked in surprise.

'Oh, we gathered all the felled trees put up for sale near the backwaters and dismantled a new raft.'

'A new raft?'

'Yes, at night, as instructed by Comrade Ayyappan Panicker, a group went and dismantled a new raft tied to the pier near the backwaters', he said.

Next day, by afternoon it was given to understand that comrades TV and Varghese Vaidyan were visiting the camp. About 5,000 inmates of the labour camp, armed with spears and iron rods lined up to display the group power in front of the leaders –

Comrades CK Karunakara Panicker, Das, KG Chakrapani, C Madhavan, TK Narayanan, K Damodaran...

Comrade Ayyappan addressed them.

'Comrades, we are getting ready for an armed struggle to put an end to the monarchic rule and Diwan's atrocities. It may so happen that a few of us will have to give up our lives, but remember that it's being done in the interest of our country. Tomorrow's morning belongs to us. The morning of seventh of Thulam....'

Vaidyan Kumaran was enjoying a sightseeing trip conducted by Kochhu Kunjan Asaan on the Koman islet. The islet was fanned constantly by winds from eastern and western parts of the backwaters. Water chicks scattered and clucked without any fear. Seagulls basked in the sun on the banks blissfully. Two woodpeckers sneaked into the casurina thickets. Storks, kingfishers...different kinds of birds chirped in bliss.

'Sometime during our ancestor's time, this island was formed from the backwaters. It is actually below the sea level. One cannot predict when the sea will take over the island. That's the reason why nobody is willing to come and settle here', Asaan explained.

'But you should have told me about this place much earlier. A tidy small house...a few days' stay for a change....' Vaidyan Kumaran was very impressed with the place.

About ten acres of his land, Asaan explained, had been illegally appropriated by the feudal lord Kunjachhan. Asaan had barricaded the rest, planting a fence of casurina thickets on the boundaries. In the small canal flowing in the compound, varieties of fish glistened. Water snakes showed up their heads on the banks. Deadly venomous snakes like viper, cobra and other varieties ruled the casurina thickets. Once in a while, pythons would visit the island swimming across the backwaters; once Asaan had seen a water chick swallowed by one of them.

'Oh, this is not a bad place!' exclaimed Kumaran Vaidyan. Wherever one turns, herbal plants…all can be used for making valuable medicines for treatment of various ailments.

'If you know to fish, try to catch some fish', said Asaan. 'We will ask that girl to fry.'

He pulled out the fishing hook. 'When Sekharan comes, we will ask him to use the net and catch more fish.'

'It has been a long time', the Vaidyan took the hook. 'Still, I will make a try.'

Kochhu Kunjan Asaan looked inside the house through the open windows. Pappy was lying face down on the floor.

'She is blessed with perfect endowments.' Asaan looked at her narrow waistline, shapely rear and luxurious hair and thought of her everlasting spirit and confidence. She had had the guts to even confront the soldiers. That was the kind of woman she was. As Asaan turned after closing the window shutters, he came face-to-face with the Vaidyan.

'Will she come back to her senses?' he enquired.

'Definitely', the Vaidyan comforted him. 'I have applied a herbal paste on her forehead, that's the reason why she is sleeping like that. Let her sleep. Let her mind cool down a little. Okay, where is that herbal package I gave you to make the concoction?'

'That girl who came with Pappy has been busy in the kitchen since morning', Asaan replied looking into the kitchen. 'She was sent along with Pappy to keep her company. In a way, it is good she came. The taste of the red chilly chutney she made yesterday is still on the tip of my tongue.'

'Okay, but why is our Sekharan so concerned about Pappy?' the Vaidyan asked with a sly smile.

'Oh, there is nothing of that sort', Asaan denied emphatically.

'In that case, why can't you keep her?' he said deveining a betel leaf. 'She will be good company for you. After the army abducted her and spoiled her, it's not likely that anyone will marry her. If you consider it, you can give her a life. And in your old age too, you will have some company; somebody to wash your clothes and prepare food for you.'

Asaan looked at the closed window shutters and said, 'What are you talking about? Don't you have anything else to say?'

'Have I not been telling you all this time?' the Vaidyan didn't give up. 'You need someone to take care of you. Now think that God himself has brought someone to you.'

'Why don't you get lost?' Asaan walked out. 'I will just go around and see. God knows what this boy is up to. He left home yesterday in the middle of the night for Punnapra. The days are not so good. It is Thulam seventh tomorrow; things are going to happen tomorrow.'

Whenever he thought of Sekharan, his mind would be in turmoil. He was his only family on this earth. Asaan reached the main road after a brief boat journey. Then he hailed a bus to reach Kollam. When he reached the Ponnamveli market, a procession proving their loyalty to the King was moving, with Anakottil Kartha holding a garlanded photo of the King. A few people followed him holding flags made of cloth.

By afternoon, he had reached the Paravoor market. He walked southward after getting down from the bus. He was thirsty. He stopped in front of a petty shop and asked for a cold soda. The shop keeper picked up a bottle immersed in cold water and opened it with ease; soda foamed up with a sound.

'So, where are you from?' the shop keeper asked, trying to make small talk.

'From a little north.'

'Will anything happen today?', the shop keeper was anxious. 'I am asking because I am not able to understand what these people are up to.'

Kochhu Kunjan Asaan tilted the soda bottle towards his mouth and while looking up saw a poster of the King with paper garlands adorning it.

Beyond the road was a wasteland. On the roof tops of the houses beyond that, red flags flew high.

'All those houses belong to Theeyyas', the shop keeper said in a hushed tone. They are Communists.

'Oh', Kochhu Kunjan Asaan paid for a wrap of betel leaves and accompaniments.

'These fools are playing with our great monarch, Sir CP', said the shop keeper closing the money chest. 'I saw a procession of people carrying spears walking towards the Vadakkal seashore. A lot of them have assembled at the marketplace also.'

Asaan belched and brought up the soda. As he walked towards the market ground, he heard the thuds of marching feet. He hid behind a roadside tree. He was surprised to find a red flag flying at the head of the procession.

'How come the army is holding a red flag?' Asaan was bewildered. 'Oh, they don't have guns? They are all comrades in army uniform. The comrade who was walking in the forefront of the procession was holding the red flag. Two people were holding a sheet of cloth on which was written, 'If you beat us, we will beat you too'.

As the procession reached the flag post in front of the union office, the man in front held the flag horizontally and commanded.

'Parade, eyes left.'

The parade turned their face left and saluted the flag. Asaan felt goose pimples all over his body. They were all comrades who had retired from the military. They were marching in three files northward, filling the road. They might have been about two hundred strong. Slogans echoed in the premises.

'Dump the American Model in the Arabian sea', 'We will put an end to Diwan's Rule', 'We will have responsible government rule.'

The march proceeded. Kochhu Kunjan Asaan walked towards the Punnapra market grounds. Comrade KG Madhavan approached him, holding a sharpened spear.

'Did you see my nephew Sekharan anywhere?' Asaan asked him.

'He could be in that crowd.' Comrade Madhavan pointed out to a procession lead by Comrade PK Chandranandan. From the northern side a group, holding sharp spears with red flags fluttering on their tips, rushed past like a hurricane. Another group marched from Paravoor. A 3000-strong procession from Panakkal camp joined like rolling sea waves. All the processions merged together at the Punnapra grounds. Captains of the processions came forward. Asaan could recognise a few of them; PK Damodaran, TV Thankappan, Kunjalikkal Sukumaran, Manapprambil John….

A sea of humanity was closing in on the sea. Asaan knew Sekharan was somewhere in that sea.

Even if he happens to see him, Asaan was sure he had only one suggestion to give him.

Until not a single drop of blood or flesh remains, we have to fight against Sir CP's army. If anyone among us moves backwards, the other should smack his heel. Those monsters who molested our mothers and sisters should be killed. If we have to die, we will die with dignity.

'Lal Salam Comrades.'

'Move forward thrusting your chest out…Lal Salaam.'

Comrades ran westward. After crossing the canal, they turned north, heading to Aplon Auraj's house – the police camp. Asaan picked up a spear and joined the crowd.

Sub-Inspector Velayudhan Nadar was having his siesta in Anthappan's house. His police group was enjoying a game of cards. Suddenly they heard the sea roaring and closing in on them from three sides. The policemen peeped out to see the miracle.

A human sea carrying lethal weapons like spears, swords, batons and axes were closing in on the camp. Wearing his uniform, the SI came panting. The policemen lined up with their guns ready.

'Today is the birthday of our King', the SI shouted through the megaphone. 'All of you please disperse.'

'We didn't come for dispersing', Comrade PK Chandranandan shouted back. 'We request you to cast away your uniforms and join our fight.'

'Disperse decently', Nadar continued to shout, 'otherwise we will have to open fire'.

The comrades got closer and started throwing their spears forward as missiles. Nadar tossed his hat back as a sign to open fire. The police raised their guns and shot into the air three times. A warning bugle went off. The fourth time, as the guns were pointed at the comrades closing in, a whistle went off.

They fell on the ground flat and started crawling. As Nadar's fingers pressed on the trigger a spear split his throat.

'Fire', someone bellowed.

Mrinalda called again at night. Disha came with the phone.

'Are you going to sleep?' she enquired.

'I cannot sleep', said Aparajitha. 'I am busy writing.'

'You should be careful', Disha warned.

'All those concerns are only for those who have expectations in life', said Aparajitha.

'Let your book be finished', Mrinalda said into the phone. 'We have to translate it into Bengali.'

'Umm....'

'Your mother called', Mrinalda said hesitantly, 'just a while ago. She says she is willing to give up her relationship with the composer for your sake.'

'For my sake!' Aparajitha laughed, throwing her head back.

'What has happened has happened', said Mrinalda seriously. 'The mind has to forgive and forget.'

'What about that pregnancy?' she asked. 'The one he gifted her?'

Mrinalda kept silent for a while and asked impatiently. 'What shall I tell her?'

'Ask her, can she return Comrade Sathyadas, my father?'

'Don't talk rubbish', he disconnected the phone, feeling a sense of disquiet.

She heard the sound of approaching footfalls from behind. She turned back to see who it was. Mother stood behind, holding on to the back of the chair. Her fingers caressed her hair. Aparajitha lifted her face up. Mother looked into her eyes filled with tears.

'Mother, how come you have not slept yet?' She touched her fingers.

'I am not able to sleep my child. Whenever I think of him...' her voice broke.

'He will come', she said.

She held both Mother's hands together.

'A mother's mind...', Mother was struggling to say... 'the pain of the womb that gave birth...none of you will be able to...'

She lifted her face and looked at Apu. Tears were spilling over from those eyes. 'A birth meant only for shedding tears...' that was what Disha said about Mother. 'She has been crying her entire life.'

'Again, they came today to make enquiries', Mother said. 'Those police officials...maybe to dig up any news about him....'

'Mother, what did you tell them?'

'What do I have to tell them?'

Freeing her hands from Aparajitha, she quietly walked to the corridor.

'Will he be sleeping now?' Aparajitha pondered. 'Or roaming through the wilderness of Bastar, through the maze of shadows made by the moonlight?'

Che emerged once again from the wilderness of the Bolivian forests, with his rifle hanging on his shoulders and a book marked with the page marker in his backpack. He was getting closer to her, walking on the dry leaves. Then she recognised that it was him, Niranjan.

She turned to the keyboard. Fingers searched for words hiding in the gaps between the keys like tiny bugs.

First of the Martyrs

When Velikkakath Achuthanandan reached Panakkal camp in the afternoon, about 500 volunteers were getting ready to march, holding their spears. Captain Chakrapani, who was going to lead the march also had a spear in his hand with a red flag fixed to its tip. The sickle and hammer glittered in the afternoon sun. The red volunteers sang loudly in excitement.

> The tormentor, tormentor, listen to your death knell
> You are going to be buried in the holes you dug all over the
> universe
> You will be burnt down with the same weapon you use
> against us.

Comrade Achuthanandan came close to Comrade Chakrapani.

'Lal Salam Comrade, have you all come ready to die if necessary?'

'Yes, we are ready to die', The comrades shouted in chorus.

KATALUR

'Is there anyone here who is scared to die?' Achuthanandan addressed the group. 'If yes, he should quit and leave.'

'None of us came here to go back', they said. 'We are here to fight together against the oppressive rule of the Diwan; ready to meet both outcomes of the war.'

'Comrades', comrade continued to address them. 'Start fighting; be ready to die eventually. This struggle is for the good of our country. Lal Salam.'

Hundreds of red flags soared up to the sky. Tips of the spears were turned towards the sky. The procession marched forward.

Achuthanandan stood looking at the marching procession led by Chakrapani, lashing like the western wind from the sea. It was while he was hiding in Poonjar that the message from Pathrose came. 'Reach Punnapra immediately and take charge of the two camps in Punnapra and Kalarkode.'

The Kalarkode camp was in the house of Comrade Krishnan, and the other one in the house of Velikkakath.

He had gone underground after the Alissery public meeting. By the time he reached Punnapra after the meeting, somebody was waiting for him with a letter from Comrade Pathrose.

'There is an arrest warrant. Don't get caught. Along with the carrier of this letter proceed to Kottayam. Go and meet CS Gopala Pillai, the District General Secretary of the Party. Comrade will help you reach a place.' As soon as he reached Kottayam, Comrade Gopala Pillai had taken him to Poonjar.

The second son of Velikkakath Sankaran was also supposed to be a tailor like his elder brother Gangadharan. Gangadharan had bought him a sewing machine to start stitching. That was the time agitations were at their peak on the streets. Achuthanandan could not sit for a long time in front of the sewing machine. He became a worker in the Aspinwall Company at the age of seventeen. One day, Comrade came to the company to address the workers. He spoke looking into the eyes of the young men.

'To fight with the bourgeois powers, young comrades from our own midst should spring up, strong men with the smell of sweat, slush and coconut fiber.'

To confront the bourgeois, Comrade found young comrades from coir factories in Alappuzha. Spinner Pathrose, tailor PG Padmanabhan, MT Chandrasenan, weaver PK Chandrananda, CK Keshavan, CO Mathew, OJ Joseph, VL Thomas, tailor VS Achuthanandan....

When the last of the workers in the Panakkal camp left the gate, Achuthanandan's legs also craved to go along with them. He moved to the forefront of the march, holding a spear. But the warning from Pathrose kept him bound to his place, within the compound. 'On no grounds should you get caught. The arrest warrant is still in force. You should remember that.'

The red march roared towards the western horizon. Soon the horizon would turn crimson. He stood by the side of the tree spangled with red blossoms, his ears sharp for the war cry of changes.

Punnapra looked like it was celebrating a temple festival. The warring comrades left home as if they had taken their last meal. Their women had prepared a sumptuous meal for them with rice and fish curry. They also reached the market grounds along with the comrades, gazing steadfastly at them. Smaller processions merged with the crowd in the grounds. Ignoring the blazing afternoon sun, mothers waddled through the crowd with pots of drinking water. They filled mud cups with water and gave the comrades. They hugged them and kissed them on their foreheads. As the march moved forward, they waved at them with their eyes brimming. 'Fight and come back victorious my children.'

Processions coming from Vadakkal, Vandanam and Punnapra merged together and moved towards the south-eastern side of the huge palmyra tree which waved its thousand fronds and invited them, 'Lal Salam….'

Yahiya was running in panic towards the Vadakkal seashore as if carrying a brazier of fire on his head. He ran alongside the roaring sea. There was no sign of life on the seashore. Even the tiny crabs ran around in panic, searching for their holes to escape to safety.

He came face to face with police head constable Parameswaran Pillai who was twisting his moustache, when he reached behind Aplon Auraj's house.

'Come here rascal', the policeman caught him by his nape. Yahiya tried to struggle out of his grip.

'I am not taking you to harm you; I want to give you a job. By evening you can make some money for your refreshments', he said.

He took him inside Aplon Auraj's house. There were rifles kept in line, slanting against the wall.

'You have to wipe these rifles and clean them. Then fill them with bullets like this. Do you understand?'

The head constable showed him how to fill the bullets.

'Umm…you can start.' Pillai then emptied the liquor bottle kept in the corner of the room in a few huge swigs. He unbuttoned his shirt, pulled a wooden bench close to the window and rested his head on the windowsill. As his snoring merged with the sound of the aircraft zooming in from the south, Yahiya heard a roar from the eastern side. What Yahiya saw was a red sea roaring towards the camp. Thousands of spears with red flags flying from their tips, booming strands of slogans shouted by thousands of fighters, 'End the rule of the King', 'We don't need Diwan's rule', 'We want responsible government', the slogans went on and on.

A high-ranking police officer came to the verandah, tightening his cross belt. Twenty policemen lined up, taking aim with their rifles.

'We will have to shoot you if you don't disperse', the officer bawled.

'We didn't come to disperse. You better wind up this camp and leave', the mob replied.

At that moment, the officer removed his hat and flung it backward. That was a signal. The police fired shots at the sky.

'Don't lift your head. You will be shot.' A leader shouted from the front row. Comrade Kakkari Karunakaran raised his head slightly. Bullets swarmed around. There was a shout. The bullet hit Comrade Karunakaran right on the center of his forehead. Blood gushed out of the wound.

'You devil, you killed our comrade?' comrades screamed and crawled forward. One spear flew towards the throat of the head constable. As it struck his chest he howled, 'fire, fire….'

'Fill the gun and hand it over', Parameswaran Pillai shouted obscenities at Yahiya. As Yahiya extended the gun, Comrade Kunjunni leapt forward with his knife. The blades glistened in the sun and the SI Sahib fell down, wounded.

The agitators closed over the police camp and the police forces started dropping, many fatally wounded. Whosoever remained alive surged into the crowd with their rifles fixed with bayonets using which, they pierced to death seven or eight comrades. Blood pooled in the sand.

Comrades snatched the rifles from the men and Luis from the seashore smashed a policeman on the ground. He died instantly. Another policeman who tried to drive the bayonet into a comrade was caught and pinned to the coconut tree with the spear. Another spear sprang from somewhere and struck his throat. Comrades overran the camp like a firestorm.

'Load the rifles fast', head constable Parameswaran howled at Yahiya. Two policemen standing close to him were shooting continuously. Yahiya saw Comrade Puthan Parambil Damodaran crawling and approaching them from the west. Just when Yahiya thought that a bullet was going to hit him, Damodaran got up and drove the spear through the neck of the head constable. The head constable turned back to see who had stabbed him. Suddenly Damodaran sprang up and pierced another spear through his stomach.

'Kill him', shouted Parameswaran Pillai in his death pangs. The two policemen tried to aim at Damodaran, by which time two spears came and pierced them on their chests, killing them instantly.

'Confiscate the three guns', comrade Damodaran shouted. Comrade Krishnan Kunju snatched the guns from the dead policemen.

The comrades were snatching the guns from the police and killing them by piercing the bayonets into them. Yahiya looked through the slits in the window shutter. Five or six policemen charged into the hall and bolted the doors. Hiding behind the windows, they started shooting at the comrades left and right. A spear came in like a missile and struck the lower abdomen of one policeman so hard that the tip of the spear could be seen on the other side. Poor man, he died spitting blood.

Finally, when the ammunition was over, the gun shots stopped and the comrades carried away the bodies of their friends and relatives and left the place. The police opened the door slightly to take a look outside.

Yahiya jumped out. Everywhere, there were dead bodies. He saw Gregory bleeding and begging for water. Yahiya jumped over him and sprinted towards the sea. Even after diving into the sea and rolling over the waves, the brazier in his head continued to blaze. Finally, he came out of the sea and ran along the seashore. When he reached near blacksmith Krishnan's house, he saw two policemen followed by Krishnan, carrying two-three petromax lamps to the camp. It was so dark that they could not see anything. 'Where are you going?' Yahiya asked. Blacksmith Krishnan just stared, without giving an answer. Yahiya walked behind him. As they reached the camp, the blacksmith pumped the lamps up, lit them and hung them in different places. When Yahiya tried to walk in that light, he kept slipping on the blood and scattered brains. On looking closely, he found that it was Devassy and near him was Velayudhan Nadar.

That was when he witnessed that horrendous scene. The police were smashing the skulls of comrades, who were wounded but not dead, with the handles of their guns. They were being assisted by the local goon squads in the task. Yahiya looked around. There were about a hundred dead comrades. Around twenty policemen were also dead in the encounter along with them.

'Keep those bodies separately', a police inspector ordered, pointing at the dead policemen. 'Take the others to the big cremation ground; douse them in kerosene and burn them.'

Standing near the corpses of the policemen, he removed his cap and paid his respects.

Comrade Thankappan was trying to recollect from his fading memories, his role in the encounter. 'I was only twenty in those days. Comrade KS Ben came and told us, "We are going to attack the Punnapra police camp. You will have to cut across the canal with your spears and walk westward to reach the police camp." In those days, the canal was two times wider than this. Holding the spear in one hand we swam across the canal. We crawled on the ground towards the gun-bearing policemen. Bullets came from all directions and suddenly one hit me on the back. I became unconscious. Much later, when I regained consciousness, I was in the midst of corpses. Painfully, I crawled out and made it to my house through familiar routes. My family took me to a vaidyan who treated me, and I was underground for three years.'

'What else do you want to know?' he looked at Disha and Aparajitha.

'You said you attacked the police station to take away the weapons', Aparajitha asked. 'Then what did you do with the guns you had snatched from them?'

'The guns we had snatched were dumped in a well by comrade Gangadharan. But there were no bullets in them. All those efforts had been useless.'

'When he saw the rifles snatched from the police, it was said that Pathrose jumped up and down in excitement', Disha remembered having read it somewhere, as they left.

'The Spearman and Sacrificial Goat', Aparajitha said.

'They had arranged the six guns taken from the police camp in one line. Pathrose picked up one and took aim at the backwaters. By then Comrade Narayanan came and distracted him, handing over a letter.'

'Comrade George has sent a letter.'

Pathrose had opened the letter and read. 'Was not your question – what do we do with the guns taken away from the police? Under the present circumstances, all I can say is keep them safely and see that they don't fall into the enemy's hands again.'

Pathrose kept quiet for some time, staring at the letter.

'Didn't we grab those guns to shoot them back when they shoot us?' asked Comrade Kochhu Narayanan. 'But without bullets, how are we to shoot them back?'

Comrade Kunjan walked in. Seeing the guns, he said, 'It is rumoured that the police are looking for the guns. It is better to move them to a secure place.'

'Where?'

'There is a way to hide them.'

At midnight, a ferry boat leaped forward in the backwater. As it reached a turning, the boat stopped.

'Is this not the place where years ago, Chieftain Veluthambi Dalawa buried the white men?'

The other comrade looked around in the darkness. There were tiny circles of light visible at a distance in the backwater. 'I think the police and army are searching the backwaters.'

'They told us that they will be waiting for us at the point where the backwater and canal meet, isn't it?'

'True, but how will we reach there? If we go forward a little more, we will fall into the hands of the police. Then they will take care of us and the guns.'

'In that case shall we do something?' He uncovered the six guns kept under the tarpaulin. 'Shall we dump them here? When we need, we will retrieve them with the help of our comrades who are divers.'

'Was it for this that we sacrificed the lives of so many of our comrades and went through such a nightmare?' asked the other comrade.

The comrade assumed silence.

'How many would have died?'

'About a hundred?'

'That's what I was asking', he said, 'What did we gain by their deaths?

'All the decisions were taken by Comrade Pathrose.'

An aircraft flew above the backwaters. Twice it circled the area and went back. The buzzing sound of a wild bumble bee was heard at night. It was a bad omen, a forerunner of imminent disaster.

A man waited for a long time alone in a boat where the backwaters and the canal met, with a six feet long plywood box.

Instructions given to him were to receive six guns from two others who would come by a boat; pack them in the box, take it to the shore and bury it safely. Since no one came, although he waited the whole night, he rowed the boat till the curve. He found bubbles surfacing from the bottom of the backwater and presumed that it was a flotilla of sea turtles moving in large numbers under the water. Or could it be the spirits of the Englishmen who were buried by Veluthambi?

He decided to wait there for some more time for the boat to come.

'As the procession of the ex-militarymen reached near the big cremation ground, an army truck came from the northern side', Comrade Thankappan recalled.

'That truck must be going to the Punnapra camp', said Comrade Damodaran.* 'We should not allow them to reach the camp.'

The procession formed a barricade on the road not allowing the truck to proceed. The soldiers jumped out, pointing their guns at the procession menacingly.

'We will not allow the army to proceed. Go back', the procession shouted. 'It's better for you to disperse. We will shoot', said the soldiers.

'In that case, shoot.' Comrade Damodaran stood in front. Comrade Karunakaran joined him. The soldiers pulled the trigger. Both of them were shot and fell down. The procession circled the soldiers. They fought with whatever weapons were available to them. Sharp granite pieces flew like missiles. The army went back, without proceeding in the southern direction.

'The first of the heroic martyrs of the Punnapra-Vayalar uprising!' Aparajitha said.

'That was the time our comrades were encircling the Punnapra Police camp', said Disha. 'If the army truck had reached there by that time…'

---

* This Karunakaran and Damodaran were killed trying to prevent the army from reaching the police camp, where the other two comrades were killed.

'...hundreds of comrades would have been shot down', Aparajitha completed her sentence.

In Punnapra, Alappuzha and Vayalar, the police and the landlords' goondas had commenced their mopup two days before the King's birthday. They started hunting for the comrades, barged into their houses and molested their women. Their nails dug into the belly of young wives, teeth cut wounds on their nipples and children were held upside down to force mothers to come out with the whereabouts of their husbands. There were shootings in different locations, killing the bold comrades.

'At this rate, we will not be able to resist the King's forces for a long time', CG's throat cracked. 'Let us not create any more situations leading to the deaths of our comrades.' CG looked at Pathrose who was sitting with his head lowered, without uttering a word. 'So, it is better to wind up the camps', CG continued.

Pathrose did not respond. Comrade PT Chandrasenan agreed. 'It is not only that; where shall we hide so many comrades?' he asked.

'If we disperse the camps, it would be deemed as our failure and surrender', Pathrose roared. 'Why should the camps be dispersed? Not only that, what led to the formation of these camps? Has there been any improvement in the situation from what existed before?'

'To save our comrades from one more disaster and prevent loss of lives', CG said.

'But that's not the right solution. It will only destroy the confidence of our comrades. The government and people will consider it as our surrender', said KC George, agreeing with Pathrose.

Comrade Kochhu Narayanan came in like a spark to tinder. 'They have declared military rule in Cherthala and Alappuzha districts. The order is to catch Comrade Pathrose alive and drag him on the roads, tied to a police vehicle.'

'Whose order is it?'

'CP's order.'

The yellow Dakota cut across the sky.

The Suicide Squad

Yahiya was anxiously looking forward to daybreak. As soon the church bell chimed, he rushed to the church. The ringing of the ninth bell, the sacristan opening the door and Yahiya rushing inside the church, all these happened together. He knelt down in front of Saint Ouseph's glass case:

'My most revered Saint Ouseph, please keep my mind intact without causing any turbulence. It was only because the chief, Parameswaran, stared at me savagely and forced me to fill bullets in the gun that I did so. I am so unhappy that it was with those guns that those devil's messengers killed our people. Pathrose brother, who was not dead even after shooting, was beaten to death by the handle of the gun. I saw our Ouseph brother and Vareeth brother dead, lying flat on their back. In total they killed more than hundred of our people. Other than filling the bullets under duress and handing over the guns, I have not done anything wrong Father!'

'What is this, unlike your normal routine you are here even before daybreak? Father Ouseph wouldn't even have woken up.

Go and come at the time of the morning service...' Brother Kunjavara commented as he peeped into the church hall and left.

Sea waves rolled in his head...bullets whizzed in front of him...agonizing wails of people who were shot down echoed in his ears...policemen struck by spears screeching in pain... Kunjunnipparavan screaming murder....

'My Father, please erase all these unwanted thoughts from my head', Yahiya prayed, crawling on his knees. He went near the glass case and lit all the candles which were not lit and then began to pray.

'My Father, please protect me...'

In the light of the candles, the Saint's face brightened. It seems as if he understands everything, thought Yahiya.

Kunjavara Chettan came to the altar. 'What are you murmuring to Father?' he asked Yahiya. 'What happened to you today?'

Kunjavara Chettan lit the candles kept ready for the service and kept the wine and loaf at the altar.

'God knows how many will come today for the service', he murmured.... 'So many have perished.... All those who went around proclaiming there is no need for God and Church...now they will find their place in the "rogue's pit" for final resting.'

First bell for the service chimed. A few people came in alone or along with their families.

Without saying a word, Yahiya climbed down the church steps.

'But why are you leaving without saying anything?' Kunjavara Chettan asked from inside. 'At the time of service, pray to Saint Ouseph with your whole heart. This Saint is not like others. If he hears, he will act accordingly.'

Yahiya walked close to Ippolith's house. That was the only tiled house in the area and was behind the church. The burnt wooden roofing of the kitchen was still smoldering.

'But wasn't the fire extinguished long ago?' he thought. 'They may have not got extinguished inside yet.'

His mind was like that now. In spite of lying submerged in water, the smoke in his mind didn't settle.

He walked westward by the shoreline. There was not a single boat in the sea. Normally, there would have been at least thirty boats in the sea. There were no people on the seashore, except for the old men who dug small holes in the sand and excreted in it. All Ippolith's and Anthappan's warehouses had been reduced to ashes. Only a few of the warehouses in the southern side had not been gutted. They belonged to the Muslims who came to the seashore to buy prawns. When he walked close by, he heard a movement inside. Who could be inside at this time? As he looked through the braided door, someone who looked like Michael pounced on him with a sharpened knife.

'You son of a swine…, if you report me to the police, I will stab you and finish you off.'

Because there was no light around, he could not see the face properly. He felt it could be Michael because of his voice, which was like the growl of a buffalo being taken for slaughter.

'Don't let him escape', someone howled from inside. 'He was the one who was loading the guns for the police. Catch him.'

As he heard that Yahiya bolted.

The startled ducks dived into the sea. After running for some time, Yahiya saw Pathru dragging his swollen filarial legs behind him.

'You better not walk outside like this', Pathru steadied his legs. 'They are keeping an eye out for you.'

'The communist activists', Pathru stood, thrusting his chest out. 'Even the small kids on the seashore now know that you are the one who loaded the guns for the police.'

'But what did I do to get accused like that?' Yahiya was shaken.

'Go and tell that to the police', Pathru said and started walking. 'From Alappuzha scavengers have come to remove the dead bodies.'

Yahiya started walking eastward. He had barely moved a few steps when he saw a pack of stray dogs with big chunks of meat in their mouths, with blood dripping from them. Yahiya could not look at them more than once. 'But they are coming from the house of Auraj?' he wondered. The dogs had fought for the meat pieces.

When Yahiya entered the house, hundreds of crows were crowing and creating mayhem. Standing in the north verandah he looked at the west side. Scavengers were dragging away the corpses by their legs. The bodies were heaped up on coconut fronds spread on one side. Inside the rooms, corpses of policemen in khaki uniform were lying scattered. Head constable Pillachhan's belly was swollen and was about to burst.

The body of Laventhar, who had been shot on the chest, was being dragged in different directions by three or four dogs. Crows were pecking at the eyes of some comrades.

'Is this not Pathrose?' he thought.

'Gather them fast.' Yahiya stretched his neck to find out who was speaking. On the banks of the pond of the neighbouring house, under a huge tree, ASP Paul was sitting in style with one leg crossed over the other. The order was to gather the bodies of the activists and take them to the big cremation ground, douse them with petrol and burn them to ashes.

Marian and Peter were giving orders to the scavengers, standing along with the policemen. It was rumoured that Marian had gone to Alappuzha to inform the police about the attack on the police camp. Now they had become close aides of the police. Marian was holding the police baton in his hand. He was giving instructions to the scavengers, pointing with the baton.

Yahiya went near ASP Paul.

'Master', he called, scratching his head. The ASP turned his head away.

'This sir who is dead, had entrusted me with the task of handing the guns to the policemen', he pointed at the body of head constable Pillai. 'Now these communists are threatening to kill me. I want protection from you sir.'

The ASP looked at constable Sreedharan.

'Who is this fellow?'

Sreedharan looked at Yahiya and said, 'Oh, this guy, I was looking for you. Come here…' Sreedharan caught him by his nape. 'Yesterday, when you were asked to pass on the loaded gun, were you not fooling around, saying that there are no bullets?'

'Is this true?' the ASP rolled his eyes.

'Oh, no…master…' Yahiya was flabbergasted. 'The key of the trunk where the bullets were kept was in the pocket of the head constable. By the time I reached near him, Head Constable Pillai master was shot down.'

'When Head Constable Parameswaran Pillai asked, this guy didn't give him the loaded gun. That was the time those guys… I have a feeling that this fellow colluded with those guys….'

'Oh, no Master, it was not like that…' Yahiya was stunned at the allegation. 'I extended the gun but just at that moment, they hit Pillachhan.'

'Pillachhan?' Head Constable Sreedharan caught him by his nape. 'Who is your Pillachhan?'

'Take him away from here', ASP Paul growled.

'Come…' Head Constable Sreedharan dragged him through the scattered corpses.

Chakrapani also ran, along with the other comrades, immediately after the shootout. He didn't even stop to see who had died and who had survived from among those in the procession that had left from Panakkal camp.

Suppose someone asks, how did you allow them to be murdered? At least those who had been shot down, but were still alive, should have been brought to safety by carrying them on people's shoulders. He had seen five or six of them being carried and taken away. Even after reaching home, his mind was in turmoil.

'Were you not the one who made a sacrifice of our lives? And then you have come back to the comforts of your home.' The dead comrades blamed him, settling in his head. That was when he remembered about Thankachhan. He was with him, carrying the spear and calling him, 'Kochatta, Kochatta', (elder brother) frequently. Even the smell of the new red shirt he was wearing lingered around. What would have happened to him?'

When he couldn't sit any more, Chakrapani ran into the darkness. When he reached the ground there was total mayhem. He could smell blood, death and gun shots. Hundreds of comrades were lying dead. They were killing those who had survived by piercing bayonets through their bodies. He stood under the mango tree in the southern corner. Where is Thankachhan? In the light of the petromax, his eyes started searching the deathfield before him. There were corpses everywhere like a shoal of anchovy swept ashore. Was Thankachhan among them? Is he calling out 'Kochatta, Kochatta...?'

From the midst of the corpses, someone stood up.

'There, somebody is getting up and leaving.'

In the light of the petromax Chakrapani saw who it was – Kelan Velutha Kunju. He was a comrade from Panakkal camp who had come along with him.

Just when a policeman was about to stab him with the bayonet, the ASP stopped them.

'Don't kill him...we need him alive...to extract information.'

'Because the master says, I am not killing you now.' The policeman dragged him by his shoulders. 'Later, we will kill you painfully.'

Chakrapani recognised that policeman. He was the one who was standing by the side of SI Velayudhan Nadar, pointing the gun eager to shoot.

When Nadar said 'you have to disperse peacefully', Comrade Chandranandan had said, 'We will disperse, but before that you have to surrender laying down your weapons.'

At that moment Nadar had hurled his hat back and he was the one who had shouted 'Fire...'

He was the one who shot down Comrade Kakkiri Karunakaran.

'If only I could get one spear', Chakrapani thought frantically. 'Without any thought, I would have split the throat of that policeman.'

If only the police had left, he could have gone down and searched for Thankachhan.

It was morning. The scavengers came back. They were stacking the bodies and tying them with green coconut fronds.

Suppose Thankachhan is among them? Chakrapani felt a splitting pain in his throat. Sitting on the mango tree, he looked through the mango leaves.

Thulam Eighth.

It would have been around eight o'clock at night. In the fading memories of Comrade Karunakaran, those visions were surfacing from the haze and becoming clearer. He continued with his story: 'A comrade carrying a letter came running from the Aryad camp, which was four kilometers away from the Kannarkkad camp.'

'Comrade Pathrose sent this.'

Comrade opened the letter and read. 'From Thiruvananthapuram, four or five military vehicles are coming with an order to shoot in Vayalar tomorrow. Do the needful tonight itself. Don't waste time.'

'Demolish the Kannadi and Mararikulam bridges. Summon all the people from our camps. Send word to everyone to come over with all the necessary equipment to demolish the bridges. One set should demolish the Kannadi Junction bridge to the west of Muhamma Army camp. The other group should move towards Mararikulam. By the time the army comes, there should not be even a hair of the occupants left in the camps.'

From Kannarkkad the torch procession moved. Torches made of dried coconut fronds blazed in the darkness. Axes, hammers and other tools struck the pillars of the bridge. Both the bridges floated and drifted away in the canal. Early morning, the army vehicles stopped at the banks of the canals. The army which came for the shootout in Vayalar returned to Alappuzha.

Next day, two trucks full of army soldiers came to reinstall the bridges. They found that the new bridges were not strong enough. The army went back to Alappuzha to collect more accessories to strengthen the bridges. Meanwhile, the comrades went again and demolished the bridges and dumped them in the canal. Then the army didn't return. But by evening, however, news came that the army had come back again. Comrades met at the Kannarkkad camp.

'The bridge should not be rebuilt', said Comrade CK Madhavan. 'If the bridge is reinstalled, then the army will not leave a single comrade alive.'

'But only a few soldiers have come to construct the bridge.' Comrade Sadanandan stood up with his spear. 'Before more of them come, let us go and confront them.' All the young men joined him. All were youngsters of eighteen to twenty years with their blood boiling. Comrade Madhavan blew the whistle. The young men marched towards the bridge. A few army men were working on the bridge. There was an empty army vehicle parked nearby. The procession surged forward and reached the empty vehicle. Even after seeing around two hundred men with spears, the men working on the bridge were not perturbed. They continued to work.

'This is a trap, I said.'

'Hey, it's nothing',Thaithara Ramankutty surged forward.

'Suddenly we heard a gun shot. I tilted my head and watched; there were incessant gun shots. The soldiers were hiding somewhere. They surrounded us with guns. Comrade

Ramankutty's hand was wounded. With that hand, Comrade caught the gun held by a soldier. Carpenter Kumaran and Thoppil Kumaran barged into the midst of the soldiers with their spears. Comrades Bhanu, Sankaran Kutty, Raman Kutty and Padmanabhan fought with the army face-to-face.'

The army surrounded all the six of them and shot them to death. 'They threw the bits and pieces of their bodies in the flowing water under the bridge.'

Aparajitha and Disha had reached the Mararikulam Bridge, along with the old comrade. Holding the railing of the bridge with his shaking hands, Comrade stared at the water flowing under the bridge.

'Six of our comrades…in this flowing water…all the six of them dead ….' Comrade curled his fingers and shot up his fists skyward and shouted, 'Lal Salam. Comrades….' His eyes brimmed with tears.

'Three more of our comrades died in the shooting. I am not able to remember their names.'

'Those who wished no one should die in the shootout in Vayalar…gave up their own lives for that.'

Aparajitha bowed her head.

'Courageous martyrs.' Disha looked at the flowing water. 'How many of our courageous comrades have given lives to build up this movement!'

'What were you about to say?' asked Aparajitha.

'Oh, nothing, just remembered a few things Father told me.'

Anakhashayan finished his bath in the pond early in the morning and wore the new red shirt that the tailor Kochhanian Pillai had finally stitched for him. He applied oil and combed his hair, parting it in the center; applied powder on his face; he darkened his moustache with a burnt matchstick. In the mirror he found his image very impressive.

'It's a nice shirt', his mother Kalikutty Amma commented as she entered the room, after leaving the braided mat outside for drying. 'Remember that the money came from my tiny money reserve which was meant for buying a milligram of gold.'

'In that case, tell me how many milligrams of gold you need', Anakhashayan said dramatically. 'We will make goldsmith Gopalan make it for you.'

'Oh dear God, when is that going to happen!' Kalikutty said on her way inside.

'Then you wait and see', he told his mother. 'This year, by the time the flag is hoisted in the temple, you will have a five-stone stud in your ear.'

'My God…It's enough that you said this…. If only I could die now', saying that, Kalikutty went inside.

Raghavan came jumping across the narrow canal.

'Are you coming big brother?' asked Anakhashayan. 'I am going till the camp.' He picked up a basket hung on the wall.

Menasseri camp had been opened two days ago with four hundred volunteers.

'I will come. You go ahead. What is this?' he looked at the basket which Anakhashayan was carrying.

'I picked it up at the market junction; to fling at the army when they come', said the young fellow holding a sharp piece of granite. 'If one of these goes and hits their forehead…'

'Don't take them lightly', Raghavan warned. 'I have heard that three or four army vehicles have arrived. There will be a major shooting.'

'Let them come to shoot at us.' Anakhashayan started walking, balancing the basket on his head.

As he turned to the road leading to Menasseri, he saw Pattathil Kartha along with a few of his henchmen standing on the road.

'You low-caste young man, are you going to join the suicide army wearing red?' Pattathil Kartha caressed his beard and spat out a bit of chewed tobacco from his mouth, making a dirty sound. 'Your face looks as if your end is near.'

'Death has come near you, feudal lord', Anakhashayan retorted. 'The rumour is that women in your house have started using vessels in the house to urinate in the night.'

As he heard that, the feudal lord's dark face became darker. Rumour had it that the women in the feudal homes, scared of the comrades with spears, had stopped coming out of the house to answer nature's call at night.

'You....' The henchmen surged forward, making a fist of their hands, 'Remember who you are talking to....'

'Come along', Pattathil Kartha summoned his men, 'If we talk to such worthless guys, only our value will be lost.'

As Anakhashayan started walking forward balancing his basket, Kartha called out to him from behind, 'You.... You just count your days...your ego will be demolished in front of the army guns.'

When he reached Menasseri Camp, Comrade Prabhakaran was holding a class. Army had descended in all parts of Cherthala taluk. They had attacked all the camps on their way. Captain of one camp, Comrade Kochunarayan was shot dead there itself.

'With the impositionn of military rule, even if communists are shot dead at sight, nobody can question', said Comrade Prabhakaran. 'It is rumoured that CP has come down in army uniform to the Ponnamveli camp.'

'Not only Sir CP, let any mighty fellow come, we will confront', said all comrades together raising their spears.

As soon as he saw Anakhashayan, Pakkaran came out of the crowd.

'Oh, you are already wearing it?' Pakkaran asked, touching and feeling the red shirt Anakhashayan was wearing.

'Why didn't you wear?' he asked.

'Okay, I will wear it now. You also come.'

Leaving his basket under a coconut tree, Anakhashayan also walked along with Pakkaran.

Of the four red shirts which were stitched, one was given to Pakkaran, one to Comrade Prabhakaran and the last one to Raghavan.

'In Menasseri camp, if all the four of us wear red shirts and stand together, it will be a stunning sight', said Anakhashayan.

'Wearing the red shirt and holding the spear…it will be very nice to see', said Pakkaran. 'But they won't let you hold the spear.'

'Who said that?'

'Comrade Kaithavalappu Padmanabhan…' said Pakkaran, '…that you are a kid.'

'That fellow and I don't see eye to eye from the day we met.' Anakhashayan was angry. 'But he is not the one to decide. Isn't Prabhakaran, coming from Kalavankodu camp, responsible for our camp? Let him decide.'

'Even Comrade also said that', continued Pakkaran, 'only those who are above eighteen can hold the spear. That is the collective decision. In that case, they won't let me also carry the spear.'

'Whosoever may object, if the army comes to the Menasseri camp, I will hold a spear and stand in the front row.'

Anakhashayan tightened his mundu around his waist.

Four Red Warriors

Those days, when arguments were going on about the share of yield for tenants and workers of the Kundailatt Mallan family, the Mallans made it clear that no extra quantity of grain would be given to the workers other than what used to be given as per convention. Arguments reached the threshing floor too. Mallan's threshing floor was situated outside the household area to make sure that the lower caste Cheruman or Chovan would not pollute the family. The workers insisted that a decision should be arrived at before the threshing was over. Mallan was also stubborn. As the arguments reached a peak, five to six comrades barged into the threshing floor. A lean boy was the leader. He had folded his mundu above the thighs and asked, 'Has any decision been taken regarding the workers' share?'

'No', the workers chorused.

'In that case no worker is to leave the workplace without taking their share', said the lad. 'That's the decision of the union.'

'But for that, shouldn't the Kundailatt Mallan agree?'

'The masters need not give', the boy said, 'the workers will take. That's the right of the workers who worked and cultivated the crops. It is not a favour from the Kundailatt Mallan. Umm... each one of you come and pick up a bundle of stalks.'

The manager ran inside. The workers were leaving the shed carrying bundles of stalks to be threshed without any fear.

'Who is the one daring enough to enter my area and show his arrogance?' Mallan shouted at his manager.

'He is blind with arrogance', the manager said. '...A small kid...a student of Cherthala High school, Sadanandan. He belongs to the trade union.'

'I will fix his arrogance.' Mallan gritted his teeth.

Next day, in front of the Cherthala High School, a police jeep halted. They went directly to the headmaster's office.

'Umm..?' Headmaster Sivarama Panicker picked up his spittoon and spat into that.

The police saluted him.

'We came to take Sadanandan', said the police, 'he is the accused who looted bundles of paddy from Kundailatt Mallan's paddy fields'.

'Umm...take him right away', the Headmaster growled. 'From now on he won't step inside this school.'

Sadanandan, who was sitting on the half wall of the fifth form, heard the approaching boots of the police, jumped over the half wall and scooted. The police chased him. He knew that they would go looking for him in his house too. Then where could he go? How long could he stay hiding in the reed bushes?

So he ran to the party office. He stopped his studies. He became a communist.

'That was how SL Puram Sadanandan reached the Kannarkkad camp.' Comrade Karunakaran said as he walked down memory lane. 'Those days, Mararikulam Bridge was made of wood. Over the iron girders fixed on stone pillars, firm teakwood was fixed to form the bridge. Sadanandan was in the first batch which went to prevent the army from building the bridge. I was in the second batch of around 500 comrades from Karappuram and Puthannagady. Holding spears and burning torches, shouting slogans we ran towards the bridge. As we neared the bridge, we started hearing gun shots.'

'Isn't that the sound of gun shots?' We pricked up our ears, '...can hear the screams of our comrades too.'

'Run fast', I said, 'We will go fast and surround the army'.

We ran in the dark. As we reached the local library, comrades NK Ayyappan and CK Madhavan stopped us.

'No one should proceed', Comrade CK said, 'the army is hiding and shooting. We didn't expect that. Some of our comrades....'

'Are we not more than ten thousand strong...?' Comrades standing in the front row extended their spears together and started to forge ahead. 'We will go and get even with the army.'

'No!' ordered Comrade Ayyappan. He came forward and snatched two spears. 'Should we sacrifice precious lives knowingly? We are fighting for gains not for losses.'

'Go back', Comrade CK said.

We turned back and walked. We reached the Muhamma police station; an outpost.

'Doesn't that hitman Sathyanesan sit here?' Comrade Athikkadan Karunan asked. 'We have to finish him off today.'

'The hitman Nadar', said Comrade Keshavan. 'He is the one who hits our comrades without any mercy. Even when they are puking blood after being beaten brutally, he won't stop.'

'Comrade Kochhukrishnan was beaten to a pulp by him. At last unable to bear the torture our comrade spat on his face; for that...well, it is difficult to even explain how he tortured him.'

'If he gets comrades in custody, he first slaps them on the cheeks. They want to break the eardrum and stain their hands with the blood spurting out from the ears. Then, for the rest of their lives, the comrades will remain deaf.'

'Cruel man', the comrades got ready with their spears. 'He should be killed.'

'We will first throw stones and get him outside.' The stones hit the wooden walls and scattered.

'Stop, stop....' Comrade CK Karunakara Panicker came running. 'They are not here. They emptied the place the moment they heard that there was a shoot-out.'

The comrades were disappointed.

'Go.... Go.... All of you please disperse now', said Karunakara Panicker.

It was the old astrologer woman from Methara who came and informed Pakkaran at the Menasseri camp that Kochhu Paru had left her aunt's house in Koipuram, without telling anybody. Her aunt and daughters were making her life difficult there. 'It's our good luck that she didn't jump into the backwaters and kill herself. She came along with the lime vendor, Kuravan Damodaran. She has made it clear that even if her brother beats her to death, she won't go back to her aunt's house.'

'She came directly to my house when she reached Alunka. My daughter Kochhu Pennu is there for company. She is sitting in distress, saying that her brother won't come and pick her up. I told her that it's not like in olden days. Our huts and lands have been taken over by the Thambrans and we are all living in camps', said the woman to Pakkaran.

As Prabhakaran heard all this, he started walking along with Pakkaran to Alunka. On the way near a storehouse, an army truck came along kicking up dust.

'Hide… the moment they see red, they will shoot', said Prabhakaran.

Both of them hid behind a jack tree on the side of the mud road. A person jumped down through the front door of the military truck.

'There, he is the captain of the army. He is staying in the granary house', said Prabhakaran.

'For that matter, the news is that the people in Kattiyatt left the house for fear of the spearmen!'

'It was the talk of the village that Nalukettunkel Raman was killed and Kattiyadan fled to Thiruvananthapuram, fearing the comrades.'

'That's true', said Prabhakaran. 'Kattiyadan went to see Sir CP and never returned. From that time, their granary house is being guarded by the army. There are about thirty army men staying there. Let's not fall in their view. There is a shoot-at-sight order. See, there is no one seen on the road. All are sitting inside their houses out of fear.'

'In that case, how do we bring Kochhu Paru?' Pakkaran was worried.

'Oh, see who is coming.' Pakkaran looked where Prabhakaran was pointing.

Toddy tapper Kochhappi was coming out of the granary house with empty toddy pots after supplying toddy to the soldiers.

'Shh....' Prabhakaran called him, making a sound.

'Who? Pakkaran? What are you doing here?' Kochhappi asked. 'Oh, Prabhakaran brother also is here?'

'Came to pick up Kochhu Paru who has come to our astrologer grandmother Nanikutty's house', said Pakkaran. 'That's when the army descended.'

'Who, our Kochhu Paru?' Kochhappi salivated.

'Kochhappi, you go and bring her', said Pakkaran. 'We will wait here. The soldiers will not do anything to you....'

'You hold this pot', Kochhappi said, folding his mundu and tying it up. 'I will go there and bring her right now.'

Pakkaran envisioned Kochhappi and Kochhu Paru coming together. They would have been perfect for each other. If only Kochhappi had not mentioned Danavan....

As Kochhappi left, three to four soldiers came out of the camp and walked towards the truck parked on the road. Footfalls of heavy booted legs could be heard. The Captain came out of the verandah. He rested his right leg inside the truck and blew the whistle hanging from his shoulder. The soldiers came running.

'Quick...quick...' he ordered.

'Looks like, today there is going to be a shootout somewhere', said Prabhakaran.

'They can't do in Vayalar, what they did in Mararikulam and Punnapra', said Pakkaran. It is surrounded by backwaters on all the four sides. The moment their boats are seen from the land, our people will surround them. Not a single army man will go back alive. That is why, though they came in slyly last night, they could not come ashore.'

Prabhakaran had also heard that. 'Last night they came slyly at midnight by the backwaters. Thank God our comrades were standing on the shore, guarding. They had come to shoot down all the comrades who were in the camp.'

He remembered that the epics also mentioned that something like that had happened in ancient times. Slyly entering the enemy camp and severing the heads of several soldiers.

If the comrades had not chased them out with stones, by this morning thousands of dead bodies would have been strewn around here! God only knows whose brains are working behind all these treacherous activities!

Prabhakaran had decided to go to Koman islet early this morning to see Pappy. He was told that Pappy had started responding to Vaidyan Kumaran's medicines. The girl who was with her had told him that the previous day, she had come to her normal self as though she had woken up from a deep slumber. The girl had come from Koman islet to collect some medicines as instructed by Vaidyan Kumaran. Prabhakaran had told her that he would go along with her, when she went back to Koman islet. Only when he went to the pier did he come to know about the army showing up in the backwaters the previous night. Pappy's companion girl was nowhere to be found. So, Prabhakaran had returned to the camp. If Pappy becomes normal, he decided, the marriage should be conducted in Thulam this year itself. Panicker had promised that he would conduct the marriage at Kalangod temple. But it was already Thulam tenth. If the army nuisance got over, one could have breathed comfortably. He heard Panicker saying that the army would be chased out today. But how was that possible? Didn't comrade mention the previous night that the camps were going to be dispersed? Then everyone got angry with him. Comrade had said that because the army had shot dead more than a hundred comrades at Punnapra, not because he was scared. Many comrades were calling him Vayalar Stalin now. The trade union and party comrades were bound together in Vayalar only because of Comrade's strength. Otherwise the police, army and goons would have mauled them by now.

'Oh look there, Kochhappi is coming alone!' said Pakkaran.

Kochhappi, who had gone to get Kochhu Paru came alone.

'But where is Kochhu Paru?' asked Pakkaran anxiously.

'She has gone to take a bath', said Kochhappi. 'You do one thing. You get going. After she finishes her bath, I will bring her to you.'

Pakkaran looked at Prabhakaran.

'We are going to Menasseri camp', said Prabhakaran. 'You can bring Kochhu Paru to Menasseri camp.'

Pakkaran was not very comfortable about Kochhu Paru coming alone with Kochhappi. 'What will people think?' he thought.

'That's not right', said Pakkaran. 'Let her come after her bath. I will wait for her here.'

'In that case I am leaving', said Kochhappi. 'I didn't want you to stand here wearing this red shirt in the vicinity of the army. That's why I suggested. If it is not okay with you, I am leaving.' He got ready to leave, taking back his pot.

'What he said is true', Prabhakaran whispered in Pakkaran's ears. 'It's risky to stand here with the army around.'

'In that case…' Pakkaran said.

'In that case you may leave', Kochhappi said coming back. Under the jackfruit tree, Kochhappi waited for Kochhu Paru.

Kochhu Kunjan Asaan too didn't come back that night. The man who had left for Punnapra at seven in the morning saying, 'I will be back in a jiffy' had not returned yet. The Vaidyan waited for him till it got dark.

The girl who came as Pappy's companion poured kanji in the plate with a spatula made of the jackfruit tree leaf. Though extremely thin, she was very versatile and efficient. She prepared the kanji and chutney with grated coconut and red chilies, in no time. The moment the vaidyan had given her instructions on the preparation of the herbal medication, she had gone around the compound, collected all the herbs and prepared the concoction by morning. It was after administering that medicine that Pappy had regained her consciousness. He had seen Pappy in the evening, combing the girl's hair sitting on the front verandah. Clad in a mundu with square designs and a red blouse, Pappy looked stunning.

He had seen her walking by the banana farm to the pond. Her trim waist and abundant posterior were a sight to behold. After bath, he had seen her going to change her wet clothes. Her bosom rose up and down, chasing his sleep away.

He couldn't sleep even after midnight. He opened the textbook on *Ashtanga Hridayum* and went on reading in the light of an oil lamp. The book was written on palm leaves. It was about 300 years old and was crumbling to bits. He read through the entire night. It was almost daybreak when he finally fell asleep.

By afternoon, he sent off the girl to his village to pick up some medicines. Now in Koman islet there remained only two human beings – the vaidyan and Pappy. Pappy was sleeping in the room lying on a mat, turning to one side. Her dark hair curled around her face like earthworms.

He got worried about the medication he had given her in the afternoon. Though the medicine was meant for disorientation, if the herb was wrongly chosen, it could become toxic. Vaidyan Kumaran started getting worried looking at the way she was sleeping.

'Pappy, open your eyes', the Vaidyan called out to her, standing at the window.

She didn't move.

'Pappy, I am telling you…wake up and open your eyes…' the physician raised his voice. Still there was no movement.

He was worried. He ran inside the room. A small breeze from the lake entered the room, fanning her face. It caressed her hair. It moved down further to her lower parts, setting tiny hairs in that area erect.

'Pappy girl…get up', the vaidyan started shaking her.

Sitting on his knees, he raised her head and kept it on his lap. He remembered his good old younger days. How he used to swim across the backwaters and sneak into the hut of the blacksmith woman. Suddenly, the blacksmith woman came into the mind and called: 'Little master….'

He savoured that and suddenly the hooks of the blouse snapped, and her breasts sprang up.

'How many days have I been…' he started panting. His fingers ran through her hair, face, neck, and further down…a wild unbridled horse in the mind….

Pappy was still in deep slumber. Holding Prabhakaran's hands, she walked in a dream…by the bund roads between paddy fields…through paddy fields where purple kasithumba flowers bloomed….

She stirred a little. Her lips opened…inner eye opened to the sky. She held the wild horse tightly and whispered, 'Prabhakaran Chetta…'

Trees on the sides of the bund road swung in the breeze and bloomed….

When Kunjan Asaan came back to Koman islet it was getting dark. Water chicks raised a mayhem looking for a place to nestle. Water dogs that had come out to warm up in the sunlight dived into deep waters. A black rattle-snake slithering out of the aloe vera thickets hid under the stones in the water. Storks were busy cleaning their feathers with their beaks.

He had left on the seventh. It was three days since he had left. His dress was soiled. He had tried to wash it clean with the soap nut powder. Still, a sort of smell came out of the dress. He had started running from Punnapra. He hid in the attic of a house belonging to a comrade friend. There were three or four other comrades too. In the afternoon, he managed to get into a bullock cart filled with hill products. He came by a short cut. He wanted to have an oil massage and take bath as soon as he reached home. Getting out of the boat, Kunjan Asaan walked fast on his lean legs.

No one could be seen outside. There was no light inside. He climbed to the verandah and washed his legs. Where have all these people gone? From inside he could hear somebody's snoring. Opening the window shutters, he looked inside.

On the floor, on the mat, Kumaran was sleeping, tightly hugging Pappy.

'Kumara!' he roared. Kochhu Kunjan Asaan closed both the shutters of the window. 'Kumara, you scoundrel….'

A flock of birds nestled in the trees in Koman islet trembled at the sound.

Thulam Tenth.

•

When Anakhashayan reached the camp, comrade VK Thevan and his friends who had come from another camp were constructing a trench around the camp. It was meant for attacking the approaching army. They were to hide in the trench. When the army approached, the fighters were to spring on them and pierce them with the spears.

'We have to hurry up', said Comrade Prabhakaran. 'We have to finish before mid-noon. The army has reached Ponnamveli camp.'

Anakhashayan went near the Comrade.

'Oh, our messenger is here', Comrade held him by his shoulders with both his hands.

Anakhashayan felt so proud. It was the Comrade who had made him the informer of the camp. His job was to collect news from the surroundings and reach it to the camp.

'The army may surround the camp by afternoon', he said. 'I got the information from the Ponnamveli market.'

'Did you go to the market in this shirt?', Comrade Prabhakaran was shocked. 'If the army spots you, they will shoot.'

'Oh, no…' He replied, 'I removed and hid it. I went to the market without a shirt and got into the midst of the soldiers having their tea. That was when I heard them talking.'

'Oh, you are a smart guy.' Prabhakaran hugged him with affection.

'In that case, shall I take leave of you?' he asked, holding Comrade Prabhakaran's fingers.

'Where are you going?' Prabhakaran asked.

'To Ponnamveli', Anakhashayan said. 'I will find out from which direction the army is going to approach.'

Comrade Prabhakaran stood admiring the boy's sprit.

As Anakhashayan turned, the yellow Dakota aircraft came roaring. It flew over Vayalar once, dropping a bunch of pamphlets. One of the yellow papers dropped by the aircraft fell in front of Anakhashayan. He picked it up and brought it to Prabhakaran. Comrade grabbed it from him.

'Oh, this is the death knell from CP.' Prabhakaran read it loudly. 'It has been brought to our attention that in Cherthala and Ambalapuzha taluks, some individuals and organisations are trying to disrupt government activities and engaging in criminal activities. In view of that the government has declared military rule in these two taluks.' Prabhakaran looked at the comrades standing around him. Most of them had the yellow notice.

'The order is that all should disperse from the camps or else they will be shot down. Read further', said the Comrade.

Comrade Thevan continued to read.

'No one is permitted to convene meetings, deliver speeches or demonstrate, carry deadly weapons or explosives....'

'This is the forerunner of the army's forthcoming attack...' said Comrade Padmanabhan.

The aircraft flew in continuous circles. Anakhashayan didn't wait any more. He ran towards the Ponnamveliyum market. As he reached the Ponnamveliyum Bridge, he saw some twenty soldiers approaching. Hiding behind trees, he came back running. When he reached Parapalli bund, he looked back. The army was marching towards the Menasseri camp and nearing Parapalli bund.

Anakhashayan ran as if he had wings on his feet.

'The army is coming...there are about twenty of them. They have reached the Parapalli bund', he called out in a loud voice.

Menasseri camp lay south of the Parapalli bund.

Comrade Prabhakaran blew the whistle. Comrades came running.

Comrade Thevan and other comrades had finished digging the trench.

'Forty comrades armed with spears should go to Parapalli Bund. There you should hide behind the thickets', said Comrade Prabhakaran. 'Before the soldiers reach here, we have to attack them.'

'A few comrades armed with knives and machetes should hide in the nearby houses. The moment they enter, sever their heads then and there. The other comrades will hide with spears in the trench', said Prabhakaran.

Comrade Thevan and company rushed to the bund. Anakhashayan came carrying his basket with sharp granite chips.

'What is this for?'Comrade Prabhakaran looked at Anakhashayan.

'To fling at the army', he said as he emptied the stones into a thin bathing towel which hung on his shoulders like a shoulder bag.

'So, don't you need the spear?' asked a comrade.

'But I am not eighteen yet', he replied, looking at Comrade Padmanabhan.

'You have been eighteen for a long time now', said Comrade Prabhakaran. 'Are you not the strength of Menasseri camp, Comrade Anakhashayan?'

Comrade Prabhakaran gave him a sharpened spear with a red ribbon tied on it. Accepting it, Anakhashayan held it close to his heart and saluted comrade Prabhakaran.

'Lal Salam' Comrade Prabhakaran placed his hand on his head.

'It was not me. It was comrade Padmanabhan who kept this spear for you.'

'Is it?' Anakhashayan looked in astonishment.

Comrade Padmanabhan turned and walked away. 'Comrade!' Anakhashayan followed him.

Comrade Padmanabhan stopped, 'Hm...'

'Comrade…' he fumbled for words.

'Hmmm…. Be careful. Never be in a hurry. You are young. You have to take care of your family.' Comrade Padmanabhan said as he turned and walked away. Anakhashayan's friends, Raghavan, Pakkaran and Prabhakaran, came from somewhere in red shirts, holding their spears and stood around him. Four soldiers in red uniform!

The soldiers had reached the Parapalli bund. Spears flew towards them like missiles from the thickets.

'Fire!' the army roared. The first shot went to the sky.

In his daughter's flat in Idappalli, MR Nair sat in deep thought.

'We ran into each other after a long time during a train journey from Cochin to Delhi. We were in two different compartments. I was in second class AC. He was in second class sleeper. I saw him through the windows of my compartment, at a railway shop selling books and periodicals. Even in those days, there were one or two stray gray hairs in his beard.'

MR Nair's daughter Sumithra came with coffee. Aparajitha and Disha picked up the cups.

'Sir don't you take coffee?' asked Aparajitha.

MR Nair laughed, his lips twisting, 'I have been imprisoned by medicines, my child. I am on a diet…an extreme diet!'

'Oh, I forgot that.'

Aparajitha savoured her coffee.

He looked extremely tired. The stroke had paralysed his right side, leaving it totally motionless. A crooked smile spread through the corner of his lips.

'I might have used this organ of my body the most', he said, looking at his right fingers. 'Perhaps this is the punishment for having used them more than their capacity.'

'What I was telling is that …' MR Nair again went into a deep trance.

'Sathyadas was not his usual self. We had reached Nagpur where our train was held up for a long time. Some goods train had got derailed. The train was detained there for hours. It was oppressively hot outside my AC compartment. What would be the state of a second class non-AC compartment! I thought. I invited Sathyadas to my compartment. Oh, I didn't tell you, in Delhi, both of us had started our career together in *The Statesman.* Till then, I was in a news agency. Our office was in Connaught Place. The British corporate had transferred *The Statesman* newspaper to the Tatas. Pran Chopra was the first Indian editor. Have you not heard of him? Because he didn't go along with the Bengal interests of the management, he was sacked. That was the year Sathyadas joined the paper as an editorial trainee.'

In those days, I was the senior sub-editor. As soon as the training was over, Sathyadas was transferred to Calcutta; to the head office in Chauranghi Square. That was the turning point in Sathyadas's life.

Soon after that, I left *Statesman.* I heard that Sathyadas had moved to trade union activities. After that, we met for the first time during that train journey. He was very gloomy.

'What happened to you Sathya?' I asked him.

'This is my last journey from the land I was born in', he said.

'Were you not born in that land of the revolution?' I tried to recollect.

'Yes', he nodded.

'Then what happened?'

'My roots have been severed.' A shadow crossed his gloomy face. 'That land has become alien to me.' I saw his eyes moistening.

Death of a Comrade

Through the belching smoke of the Punnapra cremation ground, a flock of eagles flew away northward. Spreading their black blanket-like wings, they flew, looking for other scenes of death on earth. The red flags swaying in the breeze on the surface of the backwaters attracted them and they flew low, encircling the blood-dripping red flags and settled on the branches of the nearby trees.

In the big cremation ground, bodies were still ablaze. Stinging smell of burnt flesh and clotted blood wafted through the air. The stink of the cremation ground! Their eyes sharp, the eagles waited.

The army was about to reach the Parappalii bund. From Ponnamveli market, a flock of eagles flew above, circling its march to Menasseri.

Prabhakaran, Anakhashayan and Pakkaran, holding their hands together ran to the ridge around a coconut tree. Hiding behind the tree, the three peeped at the bund road.

'Comrade, Kochhu Paru has still not turned up.' Pakkaran said to Prabhakaran. 'Was she not supposed to reach the camp with Kochhappi?'

'What is this, at this time you are acting like an impatient bandicoot?' Prabhakaran was irritated.

'Kochhu Paru, till now…' Pakkaran's throat cracked.

'Don't think of that now and get worried', Prabhakaran tried to comfort him. 'Kochhappi has good presence of mind. Knowing about the approaching army, he would have taken her to a safer place instead of the camp.'

Pakkaran was somewhat consoled. He longed to see her. After all, she was his only sibling. How many days it had been since he had seen her? What if he never saw her again? He wished he could have seen her just once.

'About whom are you discussing?' asked Anakhashayan softly.

'Kochhu Paru', said Prabhakaran. 'She came back ending her stay in their aunt's place.'

'When?' Anakhashayan looked very disturbed.

'Oh, the army has arrived', Prabhakaran poised his spear. A gunshot from Pallichira was followed by the wail of a buffalo, as if it was being killed. Comrade looked at the scene, hiding behind the thickets. After the first shot at the sky, the bullet had hit the buffalo which was now wriggling under the coconut tree. After one last struggle for life, it died.

'There…' an army man jumped up. A three-and-a-half-feet-long spear was coming from the thickets.

'There, they are there', he said.

The soldiers surrounded the thicket.

'Fire' they screamed. The comrades lay down on the ground.

'Quickly jump into the water', ordered Comrade Thevan. 'In the water, the bullets won't hit us.'

Comrade Thevan dived into the water along with a few other comrades. The army circled the water. Comrades stayed under water, under the algae, keeping the tip of their noses above the waterline. Thevan could hear the death pangs of his comrades. He felt something on his right cheek. Blood and water gushed into his mouth. He had been hit by a bullet. When he surfaced to take a breath, another bullet struck him, this time on the left cheek. He wriggled and went deep under the water and stayed there holding on to a root. He lay there waiting for death.

The sounds of gun shots stopped. Three to four soldiers got into the water. They wanted to make sure that everyone was dead. Someone stirred under the water. Another gunshot. Making sure that everyone was dead, the men got out of the water. Gunshots from the land could be heard, followed by the screams of comrades. A tiny water snake came crawling through the water and licked the blood on his cheeks.

'Ptooey...' Comrade Thevan spat at it, using all his strength. Its tiny head was covered in blood. Schools of fish came to lick the bullet wounds and started biting away his flesh. He was not able to do anything.

'What can a deadbody do?' Comrade thought.

'Comrade Thevan is almost a deadbody now, with three fourths of his life gone. What can he do?'

'No, Comrade Thevan cannot die', someone said from the bottom of his heart. 'These hands have to hold the red flag for a long time to come. Comrade Thevan will resurrect. All those comrades who died will also resurrect. From every drop of blood, a thousand comrades will come up…' Comrade Thevan waited for the gunshots and screams to die down.

The army had gone haywire and the Comrades pounced on the soldiers with spears.

'Anakha!' Comrade Raghavan called out, 'Run and hide'.

'No…' Anakhashayan said, 'stay together and chase the army out'.

He was busy flinging the granite pieces, which hit the soldiers who were aiming at the comrades.

'Anakha, run, they will shoot you.' Comrade Raghavan called again.

'No big brother', Anakhashayan said, 'You may go and hide. Nothing will happen to me.' He ran in a different direction.

Raghavan turned back and looked. The comrades were writhing and dying. The army moved forward. More of them had reached the bund. The soldiers prodded the comrades who had been gunned down, with their bayonets. Comrade KK Prabhakaran and a few comrades were running northward, holding spears. Raghavan ran to them.

'Come, let's go and hide in the cellar', Comrade Prabhakaran ran to the nearby house and got into the cellar. Throwing away the spears, about sixteen of the comrades rushed inside. Because it was too dark, they felt they would not be recognised. Comrade Prabhakaran opened a small window in the corner and looked outside.

'Our comrades are being slaughtered by those monsters', said Comrade Prabhakaran fearfully.

Raghavan waded through the crowd and reached behind Comrade Prabhakaran and looked outside over his shoulders.

'Anakhashayan! The army may not harm him', thought Raghavan, 'after all, he is a small kid!'

Comrade Velayudhan rushed towards the soldiers poising his spear. He was a retired soldier himself. He struck down a soldier and then pierced him with the spear over and over again in a frenzy. The soldiers were approaching him fast with pointed guns; Comrades, poising their spears, also rushed to him.

'All of you needn't come. I will take care of them', Comrade Velayudhan shouted. A bullet hit him. He was further hit on the head by the handle of a gun. The Comrade started screeching. Raghavan closed his eyes.

Thirteen people inside a narrow cellar. They were all feeling suffocated. Raghavan tried to take a deep breath. How long could they remain here, in this cellar! Gunshots stopped outside.

'Oh, what a relief', said Comrade Gangadharan, keeping his hand on the chest. 'My baby is lying in the Vayalar camp, down with a fever. Don't know what happened. I was about to take him to Kunjan Vaidyan. Just then the army came. Comrade, if the army has left, may I get out?'

'Not now', Comrade Gopalan stopped him. 'The army will leave now. Wait till then.'

A bit of light crept into the cellar.

Now the faces of the comrades could be seen. Comrades NK Narayanan, Raman Kutty, Divakaran....

'Look', Comrade Prabhakaran said suddenly. 'The army is walking towards the cellar. No one should make any sound....Their guns are pointed to the cellar.' Soldiers surrounded the house. Sound of heavy boots came closer to the cellar.

'Is it here that they are hiding?'

'Don't watch and wait...fire...finish off everyone.'

Bullets came zooming inside. Ten men were shooting into the cellar at one time. Comrades shouted and screamed. The cellar was filled with gun smoke. Bullets hit the stomach of Gangadharan and brought his intestine out. He leaned on Prabhakaran's chest.

Smell of gun shots and hot blood.

Inside the cellar, corpses piled up. Wails and screams. Gunshots stopped for a while. There was no sound or movement.

Then suddenly, there was the sound of people running and reaching the cellar. They were comrades.

'Is there anybody alive inside?'

No one spoke. Comrades looked intently.

'Is that not Comrade Divakaran?'

'Comrade Divakaran was hit by a bullet', said Comrade Narayanan, 'but he is not dead'.

'Who else is there?' Comrade looked around again.

'The four of us...'

'...the rest nine ...?'

The cellar had become a burial pit... 'We came out of the cellar.'

Raghavan ran out. 'Did any one of you see our boy Anakhashayan?'

A comrade bleeding from his ears came running. He looked towards the courtyard of the Ayyangattu house. Raghavan looked there. Three comrades were lying hugging each other. Anakhashayan, Prabhakaran and Pakkaran wearing blood red shirts lay together even in death. There was a piece of granite in Anakhashayan's left hand and the other hand was resting on the bag made out of a bathing towel hanging from the shoulders.

'The army men surrounded him and shot him down', said the wounded comrade. 'The first bullet hit his stomach, next one on his chest and the third one on the left side of his neck.'

'He struck down the soldier who first shot him in one shot, with the stone', said the comrade. 'The stone hit him on the center of his forehead. At that time, another soldier shot him on his chest. As he fell down, he threw his fist up and shouted Inquilab…that's all…by then another bullet had hit him on the left of his neck and….' A drop of blood from the wounded comrade fell on the ground.

Raghavan sat on his knees and kept Anakhashayan's head on his lap. He didn't look like he was dead. With open eyes, he was staring at his brother's face.

'My dear baby', Raghavan wept aloud, 'Who did this to you?' Holding his brother's face smeared with blood and mud close to his face, Raghavan wailed uncontrollably.

The red flag fluttering in the breeze on the banks of the backwaters like a blazing fire in the hot sun suddenly became still.

Everywhere, there were corpses of comrades. Still their right hands were holding on to their spears. Warriors who were shot on the chest and forehead; they looked as if they were ready for another birth to fight again. They were bold warriors who had been alive and kicking till afternoon. No one fled. They fought with spears – face to face with Sir CP's army carrying automatic weapons. They, who fought for the good of the land they were born in, were lying dead on the sand unceremoniously.

What could be told to the people who were waiting for their return? Orphaned children, widowed wives, mothers who now had no one to protect and care for them. Raghavan scooped up a fistful of blood-soaked mud and brought it to his chest.

'Sir CP, you evil devil, you will have to account for all this, a time will come when the red flag will flutter on this soil....'

Raghavan lifted his fist up and shouted.

'Lal Salam, bold comrade...Lal Salam comrades....'

Hot tears poured out of his eyes. They dripped into the open eyes of his dead brother lying on his lap, staring at the sky.

In the front verandah of Chullickal House, Raghavan who was completing ninety years, was sitting holding on to the memories of Anakhashayan that had not yet faded.

'Anakhashayan's footprints must still be on that soil somewhere', thought Aparajitha.

'The scent of that burnt blood!' Raghavan said. 'As I drink my rice gruel, that scent still wafts through the air; the scent of that blood gushing from the wound on the chest of my Anakhashayan. Now also, when I fall asleep, he comes with that spear and tells me, "Brother Raghavan, it's time to wake up". When I open my eyes, he disappears. Seventy years have passed; he came on the tenth of last Thulam also. There was blood gushing down from the wounds on his chest and forehead. "Brother Raghavan, come out with the spear", he told me.'

'I spoke about Raghavettan's pension (pension paid to freedom fighters) to the Collector', said Aparajitha. 'There is no proof I believe!'

'Proof?' Disha wrinkled her face. 'Isn't he the only one alive among those who escaped from the massacre in the cellar?'

'Umm...' Aparajitha said in disappointment. 'That is also mentioned in the books written by the comrades who participated in the struggle. But that's not enough for the red tape, you see.'

'First Comrade PK Chandranandan, and later Comrade HK Chakrapani...both of them appealed for me', said Comrade Raghavan. 'Earlier I used to wish I could get it before my death, but...now...in this old age....'

Leaving Comrade Raghavan alone with his memories of Anakhashayan, Aparajitha and Disha left the Chullickal House.

Comrade CK Bhaskara Panicker came to Olathala camp in the evening with four or five comrades. Comrade CV Shanmugham bowed his head before the comrades who had been shot down.

'How many are there?' Comrade CK Bhaskaran asked, his voice breaking.

'Eight', Comrade Shanmugam stood looking at the soil soaked in blood.

The comrades came over to the dead bodies, lifted their fists up and paid their tributes to the martyrs.

'Where are the other comrades?'

'There....' Comrade pointed his finger to the shallow ridge around the coconut tree.

More than a hundred comrades came forward, holding spears in their hands.

Comrade Kumara Panicker sat on the floor supported by his elbows. He looked weak.

'In Vayalar, they killed around three hundred of our comrades...along with them the poor people who had come to the camp to drink some kanji.'

'In Menasseri also, they killed more than a hundred comrades', said Comrade Abdul Khader as he sat on the ground.

'How did so many of them escape without being shot?' Comrade Padmanabhan was astonished, looking at the comrades who stood holding their spears.

'We dug deep trenches around three sides of the camp. When the army came, all of us lay low in the trenches. When the bullets were over, the army got ready to go back. At that time, we sprang up and attacked them with our spears. They managed to kill ten of us but then had to flee for their lives.'

From the cowshed behind the camp, a few comrades came out carrying a bundle packed in banana leaves.

'Inside this is a small kid', Comrade Ramankutty looked up.

Comrades kept the bundle down; a ten-year-old kid. He had lost his memory. He was groaning and wailing. He had been shot on his knees.

'His kneecap has been smashed into pieces', said Comrade Shanmugam.

'He was standing by my side. Seeing the army approaching from far, he picked up some granite stones and kept them near me, asking me to strike the army with that. "You run away", I told him. "They will shoot you down." But he didn't care. "Let them shoot me comrade", he said unperturbed. "The other day, didn't they shoot down my father?"

'There was no time to ask him who his father was and his whereabouts. I made him stay behind a coconut palm. I don't know when he was shot. Seeing him bleeding, I managed to move him to the cowshed and cover him with a plantain leaf. The soldiers might have thought that he was dead and left him alone.'

'Let's not delay', said Kumara Panicker. 'Take him to the vaidyan.'

Comrades lifted him up.

For sometime, no one spoke.

After sometime, Kumara Panicker told himself, the camps should have been dispersed long ago. But now, what's the point in talking about it?

'Tomorrow, everyone should go into hiding', said Comrade Bhaskaran. 'They must leave in groups of two or three.'

'The camps should be dissolved by tomorrow', said Kumara Panicker.

'That may not be possible.' Comrades who stood around came forward. Comrades who were standing at a distance also roared and came near. 'We have to get even with the army', they said angrily.

Kumara Panicker sprang up. 'Are you not fed up comrades? I said this the day before itself, when I came to the three camps and instructed you to disperse. No one agreed. See, what has happened now? So many people have died. Do you want to continue to sacrifice your comrades? If you say yes, we will do so.'

Comrades calmed down. They put down their spears.

Darkness spread. There were no lights in the houses nearby. From the heaps of corpses, Comrade Veliyil Kumaran crawled out. In the darkness somebody came near and struck a matchstick.

'Who is this? Comrade Kumaran? Oh, blood is gushing out of the bullet wounds.'

He helped him up. He was taken to the house of Kaayipalli Narayanan. At night, vaidyan Parappalii Kochhuvava Asaan came. He sharpened a knife and heated it up till it was glowing red in the fire. Two people held Comrade Kumaran firmly. Kochhuvava Asaan slit the thigh and removed the bullet. As they bandaged the wound, someone knocked on the door.

'Who is it?' Narayanan picked up a machete.

'Courier from Karuvaayi camp. There is a letter to be delivered to Panicker.'

Narayanan opened the door, holding the machete behind him.

'I am coming from South Karbala junction', he said trembling in fear. 'My name is Kothattu Viswan. I am coming as per the instructions of Comrade TG Sivaraman.'

He extended a letter.

'Who sent this?'

'It was sent from Alappuzha to be passed on to Comrade Panicker yesterday itself. Because of police and army all along the way, it reached here just today. I started off immediately.'

Narayanan opened the letter and read: 'Camps should be dispersed immediately. Please do not postpone; do it today itself.'

Narayana looked at Kochhuvava Asaan. 'We should have got this letter yesterday itself. Now, what is the use?'

Kaayipalli Narayanan, along with Kothattu Viswan, started off to Kunthisseri in the darkness of the night.

'Didn't Comrade KC George say that the action council had not decided to disperse the camps?' Aparajitha asked expressing her doubts.

'If that letter had reached there on time…' Disha said.

'Haven't yous read the *Kerala Kaumudi* daily brought by Dinar; which carried the interview with MT Chandrasenan?'

Disha tried to recollect the interview. 'If that letter had reached there… because of the police force and the army, that letter couldn't reach Cherthala.' When he had said this, tears had rolled out of MT Chandrasenan's eyes. He had sat leaning on the chair, unable to talk for some time. Then he had got up, washed his face and come and sat down before them once again. He had said, 'The camps from Alappuzha to Vandanam were dispersed by me. If it had been done in Vayalar… this type of a massacre could have been avoided.'

'Then why is KC George denying that?' Aparajitha continued to wonder.

Dusk.

Disha had a bath and then came to sit before her computer. In the Inbox there was a mail from Mrinalda which was unusual. She opened it:

> Disha, Sathyadas did not die of natural causes. He was murdered. Chemical investigation reports have been released. The reports mention a fatal toxin called Polonium 210. It might have been injected through the IV fluid.
>
> Comrade Sathyadas was involved in an uncompromising fight against mafias and corporates. Comrade was a thorn in their sides. He was a communist who never bent his knees in front of threats or bribes. So many people came to visit him in the hospital. Was one among them the messenger of death? He could have injected the toxin into the IV. Or they could have hired someone from the hospital to do that.
>
> Polonium 210: You might have heard of that. It is fatal. Do you remember Palestine Liberation Organization leader Yasser Arafat's death? Arafat died in a military hospital in Paris following a brain hemorrhage. Later, when a doubt was raised about his death, the

body was exhumed and reexamined? They found traces of polonium in the brush used by Arafat and the scarf he used on his head. The American spy network also used Polonium 210 for executing communist leaders.

Haven't you heard of the Curie couple; the Nobel laureates Mary Curie and Pierre Curie? Both of them together discovered this chemical – a lethal poison containing radioactive elements. If polonium gets into the human body above a specific quantity, death is certain. The patient will experience a splitting headache, followed by uncontrollable vomiting and dysentery; finally all the hair on the head will start falling.

Comrade Sathyadas's case sheet was examined by the Sub Divisional Magistrate. Sathyadas also had gone through all these symptoms. When the body was taken out, it was noticed that all his hair had fallen. Somebody has murdered Comrade Sathyadas.

We have to find out who is behind all this.

It's not easy to take further steps without Aparajitha's presence here. Don't we have to find out the murderers of Comrade Sathyadas? Who can trust the Delhi Police? – Even if they see the murder in front of their eyes....

'Let the CBI take up the investigation. The party is thinking in that direction. For that, Aparajitha has to stand along with us. Its better she doesn't know all this till she reaches here. When you are alone call me. I have certain things to discuss with you.'

Disha dialed the number. As soon as he picked up, he enquired.

'Is she around?'

'No'

'She has to reach here immediately', he insisted.

'How? What shall I tell her?'

'You have to find a way out', he said. 'Next Monday, Parliament session is commencing. The party and citizen groups together are initiating a demonstration programme to demand a CBI enquiry into this. She must be with us.'

Disha stood doubtfully.

The Head with a Price

The bullet embedded in the chest was pulsating inside, trying to force itself out. While writhing in pain, lying on the rough floor of the Cherthala Tourist Bungalow, Sekhran's eyes searched for his uncle. He knew his uncle would surely come, after gathering information from here and there.

His chest was on fire. He gritted his teeth. Pressing his ankles on the floor and thrusting his chest forward, he tried to bend like a bow to expel the bullet. But the bullet continued to pulsate, making him very uncomfortable.

'You monsters...kill me...kill me once and for all...' he screamed. 'I am not able to bear this pain.'

Captain Prasad came inside and growled at him, 'you rascal, shut your stinking mouth'. He hit him with the rifle butt.

'You devil's servant... kill me!' Sekharan screamed.

'Phew...you rascal... stop your death screams.' Prasad kicked him with his booted legs.

Ptooey.... Sekharan spat out the blood filling up in his mouth. 'Kill me....' Blood splattered the captain's trousers.

'You dirty bastard.' The Captain raised the butt of the rifle, 'You people are not to be killed in one shot....'

Screaming his guts out, Sekharan's body bent like a bow. Sounds of bones cracking inside were heard. His mouth frothed and saliva dripped on the floor.

That scream echoed in the ears of Kochhu Kunjan Asaan.

'What has happened to my boy?' Asaan got up in shock. It was almost daybreak. He opened the shutters of the window and looked at dawn breaking on the surface of the backwaters. Last evening, he had heard at the Junction that the army had attacked and massacred more than ten thousand comrades and camp inmates in three locations. His heart had started pounding in fear.

'What would have happened to Sekharan?'

It had been three or four days since he had seen him. He had heard that he was with Comrade Panicker. He had also heard that Panicker was unhurt and was in one of the camps. Then Sekharan also should be with him. Still, from that time, a fire had burned in his heart. He had planned to leave immediately. Then he remembered there was no ferry boat to reach Vayalar after dark. Then, what about the two girls inside? How could he leave them alone at night?

He had never thought that Kumaran would betray him in this way. He had got into a verbal fight with him. It was as if he had entrusted a lamb to a wolf to safeguard. Kumaran had picked up his trunk and left the place then and there.

Let him go, Asaan thought. He should have slapped him, the man had no character.

The day before yesterday, when he was coming from Punnapra he had heard on the ferry boat that Pappy and Prabhakaran had a soft corner for each other and that their marriage was to take place in Thulam month itself at a temple. Otherwise, Asaan had plans to make Sekharan agree to marry her. Though of a scheduled caste, she was very efficient and had impeccable character. The physician had given her some herbs to disorient her and put her to sleep. Then the wretched man, making sure that there was no one around by sending her companion somewhere ....

Someone knocked on the door.

'Who is it?' Asaan called out.

'Coffee'....it was Pappy's companion girl.

'Come inside girl.' Asaan got up.

She came inside and kept the coffee cup near him.

'Pappy chechi was asking whether she can go now that her ailment has been cured.' She stood in the corner of the room with respect.

'Where can she go? And who told her that the ailment has been cured?' Asaan asked.

'Yesterday Prabhakaran chettan told me that he would be coming today to discuss with you about taking her with him. He didn't come yesterday. In case he comes today, she is thinking of leaving with him.'

'What is their relationship, for her to leave with him?' Asaan asked as if he didn't know anything.

'Ah...', the girl she drew a picture with her toes on the floor. 'What shall I tell chechi?'

'Let him ask me. Then I will tell him.' Asaan said.

The girl left the room. Will Prabhakaran come to fetch Pappy? Even if he comes, will he be able to safeguard her?

Who knows who died in the shootout and who are still alive!

The backwaters still remained in slumber. From the western side, a boat was approaching – maybe a fisherman. The Kaithapuzha backwaters had ten to twelve varieties of fish.

Asaan walked towards the bathing ghat with his tooth powder and towel.

Must leave for Vayalar in the morning itself, he thought. Have to find out the present situation.

Finishing his bath, as he was hanging his wet clothes on the clothesline, when he heard a discussion in hushed tone from the western side of the house. It was between Pappy and the girl. He sharpened his ears. Were they discussing what happened yesterday? Was Pappy aware of anything?

'What is this you are saying chechi, is it true?'

'It is true', Pappy's voice answered, 'Yesterday Prabhakaran chettan came to see me. Clinging on to me, he slept with me. After taking that medicine, I was in a daze and not in my proper senses. By the time I woke up, he was gone.'

'Then what about Prabhakaran Chettan telling me yesterday morning that he was coming here today?'

'Ah....' Pappy didn't know what to say.

'Maybe true; that could be the reason why he didn't come in the evening yesterday. There was a big fight yesterday at the Kadakkara Church junction. Prabhakaran chettan went to hit that crooked-toothed Vasu for saying that the soldiers spoiled you.'

'I told whoever came to ask me: If they have done that, how come she is getting her monthly periods? Wouldn't she have got pregnant?'

'Spoiling me? Anyone who comes to spoil me will be cut into pieces with my sickle.' Pappy's voice rose.

'She is still in the fantasy world of her disease. In a way it is good. At least she will not know about Kumaran's treachery. She doesn't even have a doubt that it was him. She thinks it was Prabhakaran who was with her.'

'Thank God!' Asaan was relieved. At least no one knows.

Asaan changed his clothes. 'I should reach Vayalar at the earliest. Sekharan should be brought back immediately. What would have happened to him?' In his ears, Sekharan's voice echoed…'Uncle…Uncle…'

At night when Asaan came back after roaming, Pappy was waiting for him at the front verandah. As soon as she saw him, she went inside and got a vessel full of water to wash his legs. The lighted brass lamp kept at the front door spread light in the verandah.

'Where is that girl?' Asaan washed his legs and got inside the house.

'She is sleeping', Pappy said handing over a bath towel to him.

Asaan walked to the southern verandah and reclined on the easy chair. As soon as the day breaks tomorrow, I must leave for Alappuzha, he thought. Sekharan might be taken to the hospital on the seashore to extract the two bullets. Then he will be presented in the Alappuzha court. If the court remands, he will be put in jail.

He had met Unnikandan on the way, who had given him this information.

In a way it was good that he was hit by the bullets. Otherwise they would have tortured him in the cell; not that he had escaped even now.

'Still, some relief', said Unnikandan. 'I am fed up with this job, Asaan. I cannot live on this blood money any more…the next ten generations of my family will suffer because of my deeds.'

Unnikandan had removed his cap and dabbed his sweat. 'There is discontentment among the army too. A group of them have turned against CP. There was a writing on the wall saying "Killer CP, go back". Who other than the soldiers could have done that inside the army camp? They are keeping mum out of fear. How can they put up with such things? After all, they are also human beings with a conscience. Have they not shot down more than six hundred humans? What will they do to atone for all these sins? All these things are being done just to cling on to power.'

Asaan came to know from Unnikandan that Vaidyan Kumaran had again joined the loyalist group of the King. From Koman islet, he had gone directly to Kartha. He had confessed all his lapses and opened his medical shop and clinic in the afternoon itself. The glass cobra spread his hood again.

Hearing footfalls, Asaan turned around. Kaithara Pappy was standing behind the door. She had something to say.

'Come, come here.' Asaan called out to her. She stood half hidden behind the door. She had tied her mundu up to cover her bosom.

'What is the matter?' Asaan put his feet down. 'Tell me without any hesitation.'

'She went to sleep after making rice gruel', said Pappy. 'Shall I bring it here?'

Only then did Asaan think of food. He had forgotten about hunger and thirst.

'No, I will come there', Asaan went inside.

She gave him a wooden plank for sitting. As he raised the ladle made out of the jackfruit tree leaf, filled with kanji to his mouth, suddenly she asked, 'Is he alive or dead?'

The ladle fell back to the plate. 'What did you ask?'

'The old woman who came to cut the grass said…' she kept her head lowered, 'in the Vayalar area, everyone has been slaughtered by the army.'

'Who are you asking about?'

'Prabhakaran Chettan', she looked at him with worry in her eyes.

'Its true', he said, 'more than six hundred people died. But we don't know who all died or who are alive. Those who survived ran away when the shooting got over.'

'He promised to come and fetch me', her voice cracked, 'but he has not come till now. If he is alive anywhere on this earth, I am sure he will come.'

'He will come.' Asaan got up without being able to take his kanji. 'Where will he go without coming here?'

'It would have been enough to know whether he is alive or not.' She sat in a corner of the room with her head lowered.

Asaan went close to her. 'Don't you have all of us? You don't have to go anywhere. You can stay here. I had only him as my son and daughter, my Sekharan. I don't know when he is going to come back after his jail sentence.' Asaan caressed her hair. 'You are like my daughter. From now on you can stay here with me, like my daughter.'

Pappy lifted up her face. Her eyes brimmed with tears. She leaned on to his arms.

SI Ponnayya Nadar was not leaving anyone alone. The Diwan had fixed a price for the head of Pathrose. An order has been issued to catch him alive and present him to the authorities. The police were scrupulously searching for him in all the houses in different localities. Police had received a secret intelligence report that Pathrose had been camping somewhere in the vicinity.

Pathrose was living in hiding in the same locality. The police had alerted everybody to keep an eye on those who were suffering from corn on their legs. As a matter of fact, corns had started troubling him very badly. An old pair of footwear he used also had worn out. His only intention now was to escape somehow from the police barricade. Pathrose looked around. He found a group of lower caste men and women wearing thick red bath towels, carrying bundles of dried fronds on their heads walking on the road. Old people were wearing footwear made of dried bark of palmyra and dragging their feet along, because of the weight of the load on their head. Pathrose removed the mundu he was wearing, rolled it and placed it on his head. He wrapped a small bath towel around. He kept a bundle of fronds on his head. The group passed the bridge and one among them walked in a different direction to safety, hoodwinking the police.

'It is dangerous to live here now', said comrade Kunjan who was waiting for him, 'You will have to shift somewhere else'.

'Where should I go?' Pathrose asked.

'If you don't leave, both of us will go mad.'

'Why do you say that?' Pathrose looked at him offended.

'Aren't you the leader of the party? Don't you see what is happening around you? Our comrades are standing in front of the factory gate, confessing their faults and getting back to work.'

'Why are they doing that?' asked Pathrose. 'Has the trade union withdrawn the strike?'

'That's not the issue. Sir CP and the bourgeois are turning our comrades into slaves.' Comrade Kunjan hit his forehead with his palms. 'Should we stay here watching all this?'

Comrade Kunjan had seen the pathetic begging for work when he was passing by the Aspinwall Company in disguise.

The supervisors were making the surrendered comrades sing *Vancheesa Mangalam* as repentance for having been involved in activities against the royal King. The supervisors sang and the former comrades repeated the song in the loudest possible voices.

'Long Live Sir CP Iyer', the supervisor shouted raising his fist to the sky, 'We want Diwan's rule. We want CP's Rule.'

The comrades repeated the slogans after them.

'They are uttering these slogans with the same tongue that used to call out inquilaab…' Pathrose bristled with indignation. 'Shameless. Can't they go and hang themselves?'

'There is no point in blaming them', said Comrade Kunjan. 'What can they do if they lose the very ground they stand on? I am sure, if there is a spark of fire deep inside, one day or the other it will be rekindled…the last conquest will be ours. This failure is not at all a failure.'

'What failure? Who failed?' Pathrose didn't like that statement. 'I have not failed at all.'

Comrade KK Kunjan didn't respond to that.

By then Comrade Divakaran came running, 'Do you know? Police have arrested Comrade TV and Comrade Padmanabhan. Both of them have been taken to Civil Jail.'

TV had taken the entire responsibility of the Punnapra-Vayalar struggle on his shoulders.

Pathrose looked at KK Kunjan with a sort of discomfort writ large on his face.

When they reached the library *Swadeshabhimani*, it was Dinar who said, 'The old leaders who led the struggle are meeting at the Vayalar hills this evening.'

'Oh, we didn't know!' Aparajitha said looking into her mobile. 'How can we reach there? At what time is it?'

'We will find a way', Dinar comforted her. 'Shall I arrange a two-wheeler?'

The Vayalar hills of massacre. Aparajitha pulled her vehicle to the curb. Under the *Elanji* tree, comrades Karunakaran, Vasu, Gangadharan, and seven or eight other comrades were gathered by the statue of the solider holding a spear. Aparajitha sat near its feet, leaning against the small platform.

'There were about a thousand people in the Vayalar camp', said Karunakaran as those days came alive in front of his eyes. 'Most of them were farm workers, coir workers and other petty workers.... To tell the truth, the camps had not been started for the purpose of attacking the army. When the police and landlords made it difficult for them to survive...' Comrade got lost in thought.

Comrade Gangadharan was the informant of one of the camps. His job was to carry secret messages to the camp. The comrade remembered. 'At different points, our people stood guard to prevent any police, goons or secret agents from entering the camps. There were code words to recognise the comrades who came from outside. If they came with a handkerchief tied on to their right hand, then one could conclude that he was a friend.

During the night, they had to keep their flashlight downward. Then there were questions and answers in code words. Not even a fly could enter the camps without following all these formalities.'

'We didn't foresee that the army would come with automatic guns.' Comrade Karunakaran returned to his memories. 'As the comrades in two camps including Punnapra and Kattoor were shot down, it became evident that the army would barge into other camps too with guns and death was imminent.'

We told each other, 'We will die but with our death, the Diwan's rule also will come to an end.'

A breeze from the backwaters came up and shook the elanji tree which swayed from top to bottom, trying to peer into the violent memories of one morning.

'On those days also, this tree was there', Comrade said looking at the leaves swaying in the breeze.

'Looks like it also has something to say', Aparajitha said laughing.

Through the whispers of the leaves, the tree was trying to say something.

'Come on tell us something', Aparajitha pleaded with the tree silently. 'Don't you also have many things to say?' She sat for a moment closing her eyes.

'A day the dark rain clouds trapped the afternoon sun! The small girl holding a plate with broken edges walking in unsteady steps... Where did she fall down and lie wriggling when the red hibiscus flower on her chest scattered?'

She came home after wandering around, very late in the evening.

'Where were you roaming around, all alone?' Disha pulled a long face.

Swadeshabhimani, said Aparajitha 'In between, I also went to see Vasudevan Master.'

She sat on the half-wall.

'Couldn't you have called me?' asked Disha.

'You were sleeping like a buffalo', said Aparajitha. 'Anyway, Vasudevan Master enquired after you.'

'Can you take a printout of whatever you have written so far?' Disha asked. 'We could read it together.'

'Oh, I thought so too', said Aparajitha 'Do you have a spare pen drive?'

'Oh... have you not copied it yet?' Disha asked. 'I have been telling you to do that since so many days.'

'It's on the desktop... the short cut...' she said.

'Other than that...isn't there a risk?'

'What risk?'

'No, in case....' Disha started to say something.

'No, don't say anything with your black tongue.'

She looked around and said cautiously, 'then, there is something very confidential.... Both of us have to go to Anakhan hill tomorrow evening.'

'Dinar said', she said softly, 'a few of his friends will come there tomorrow. He will call them on their phone.'

'Really?' Disha's face brightened.

'Umm...' said Aparajitha, 'don't tell anyone on the phone... even when Mrinalda calls...and Dinar specifically said, not to tell Amma also for the time being.'

'Oh, Mrinalda called', Disha said as she remembered his call. 'Did he call you?'

'No.'

'There is some good news.... The occasion calls for a treat... you have got a baby brother...but your mother's condition....'

Disha noticed the change of expression on her face. 'Mrinalda called to ask you to go there…'

'A new heir for the womb that gave birth to me', her face paled,.'an encroacher!'

'I am in two minds about your weird philosophy', Disha wrinkled her nose. 'If I were in your place…in this short life, Sarangi, should you be so stubborn?'

Aparajitha walked out without any reply.

Branches of the Big Tree

Che came galloping on a brown horse and halted near her. He whispered in her ears.

'When it comes to freedom struggles, there are no boundaries till death. We cannot be indifferent to such struggles, be it happening anywhere in the world because any conquest made over the imperialist fascist forces will be our conquest; similarly any defeat suffered anywhere will be our defeat too.'

The brown horse galloped away, leaving the echo of its hooves. After running a long distance on the tracks of time it came back; in the place of Che, now it was Niranjan.

In her ears, in Che's intense tone he said, 'Either in death or victory, we have to keep a constant eye on our adversary. It's not enough to have a desire to fight and win, but we have to be conscientious in these fights. These fights are not games played in the arena, to be watched and enjoyed by an audience….'

The horse carrying him galloped away through the narrow wild tracks.

The phone stirred in the jacket's pocket. It was Disha.

'Are you not coming?' she asked.

'I have just reached the town', said Aparajitha. 'I don't know in which godown that courier fellow has settled.'

Disha disconnected the phone immediately.

Dinar had specifically said that these people were coming from different places. They would have to leave for some other place by the night train… 'there should not be even a trace of suspicion.'

'Who are they so scared of?' Disha asked, '…these friends of Niranjan?'

'They are not scared of anyone', said Dinar. 'We are the ones who should be scared. Haven't we had a bad experience recently?'

Disha was waiting to reach Anakhan Hills. That afternoon, the courier service had called to inform her about the arrival of the package from MR Nair. Since they did not deliver to remote areas, the package had to be collected from their office.

As Aparajitha got out of the courier office, after taking the delivery of her package, her mobile started ringing. Was it Disha again? She looked at the phone…no … It was Mrinalda.

'Hi Mrinalda…'

'Namoshkar' he said in Bengali. 'So, when are you going to be in Delhi…you have no other option but to be in Delhi… heard that your viva date has been fixed.'

'I didn't know', she said. 'What about Disha?'

'Not yet', he said. 'But her faculty is different.'

He switched over to her writing. 'The history of the Shore', '...is that not what's holding you there?' he said. 'You may please complete that fast. There are many things to be attended to after you reach Delhi. Disha may have told you...'

He seemed to be in a hurry to finish the discussion.

'Mrinalda, have you been to the hospital?'

He didn't speak for a moment.

'Is it you who is asking this?' he broke the silence. 'I can't believe it.'

'Disha said...her condition...'

'Whose', he raised his voice, 'your mother's? Ask: how is my Mother's condition? I want to hear that from your mouth.'

'Umm...how is she?'

'Can't say better; she is fine. Yesterday also, she was asking when you will come...', the voice broke. The phone was disconnected. When she dialed again, he was out of range.

She was waiting for the vehicle on the roadside. Disha's phone was switched off. Aparajitha could not wait, she began what MR Nair had written on the road itself:

> Meeting with the daughter of Sathyadas was the most unexpected development: a mission life had left for me for my last days. I never expected that. Life opens such boxes of small wonders and strange events off and on. This unexpected meeting also was something like that. Sathyadas's daughter coming to know about me and visiting me to dig into those memories archived in me, some missions in life left for me to complete before this journey comes to an end. Life itself will set the stage for that. Sumithra might have taken a lot of trouble to retrieve those small notes I had jotted down about Sathyadas; it would have never seen light if his daughter had not come looking for that. Has death given me a reprieve only to hand them over to you? If it was not so, I would have left this earth long ago. Had I not completed all

my missions? Even my right hand reminds me that there is nothing left for me to do!

The notes I have attached to this note were written for a leading weekly in Malayalam…sorry I am not able to recollect its name. How long it has been since I have read or written Malayalam! The weekly's editor Viswanathan was part of our Delhi gang of olden days, along with me and Sathyadas. He was more than a journalist. He was a typical professional manager; a management loyalist.

'Ramunni, why can't you write about our Sathyadas?' he asked me once. I tried to evade the matter smartly because I had lost touch with Malayalam. He started calling me everyday.

'Ramunni, have you started writing? Language need not be a problem. You write in whatever language you like. Or write in English. I have smart trainee boys around. I will make them translate it.'

I felt that memories of Sathyadas should have the fragrance of Malayalam. So, for many days, sitting on the wings of two pegs, I put together whatever he told me during that last train journey…. Whatever he said when he opened his heart to me. Those are the only things I knew about him. In the meanwhile, they threw Viswam out of his office, and before long Sathyadas also left this earth forever. Consequently, I too gave up my plans to write about him.

MR Nair's letter was coming to an end.

Aparajitha felt like calling Sumithra to thank her. The phone was answered by an unfamiliar voice.

'I am Sumithra's husband Chandramohan', he sounded tired. 'Father is in ICU…a little critical.'

'Sorry' her lips trembled.

'Is there anything you want to tell Sumithra?'

'Nothing special, just that I got the package she sent by the courier service.'

'That package' his throat cracked. 'When I went out to send that parcel, I got Sumithra's call. Till then he was very active.'

'How is he now?' she asked.

'He is on the ventilator', he said. 'In this situation, doctors say, there is no scope for a surgical intervention. Let's see.'

'My prayers', she put the phone back into her handbag. The bus came and she got in.

A bunch of papers turning yellow ripped off from a diary; tiny handwritten notes. She turned the pages. MR Nair's face came up on the pages:

> I met Sathyadas on one of my return journeys to Delhi. His ever cheerful face was gloomy.
>
> 'Sathya, what happened to you?' I asked.
>
> 'Ramunni, this is my last return journey from my land of birth.'
>
> The whole day we talked about that.
>
> 'Ramunni, what would you do if you get to know that the person you were told is your father, is not actually your father?'
>
> 'Sathya what are you saying?' I took his hands into my hands.
>
> 'Yes, Ramunni', he cried uncontrollably. 'The person who I had called Father all my life, is not my father. That big man...he happens to be nobody to me.'
>
> 'Don't cry like a child', I patted his shoulders.
>
> 'I am not able to bear this', he sobbed. 'I don't want anything. I don't want even a grain of sand. All that I want is my Father...the person who I called father all these years...'
>
> He leaned on to my shoulders.
>
> 'Do you know, I have never known what a mother's love is? The moment she delivered me, my mother.... I lived under his shadow.

The one who brought me up …the one who helped me reach this status in life… finally when I got the call letter from *The Statesman*, the one who with a broken heart sent me off to Delhi…. He said, "your life is not meant to be wasted away in this islet…. Go, go and see the world outside."'

'Before leaving, he took me to a place where purple kasithumba flowers danced in the wind… a deserted plot of land where wildflowers bloomed.

"This was where your mother lived. Later, the landlord took away the land forcibly. It was from here that the army abducted your mother…. Had she been alive, as per the Land Reformation Rules, she also would have gotten ten cents of land. But she didn't wait for that. She never came back here. She was with me for less than a year. Entrusting you into these old hands…." Father's eyes looked tired when he said that.'

'Ramunni, he was the only link that connected me to this world. My father! That link also has been severed. My father never believed in after-death rituals. Still, I performed the rituals for him. Is that not the done thing in the village? But no crows came to peck on the ritual rice I kept for him, in spite of calling them repeatedly by clapping my hands. Uncle Sekharan, who passed by, commented in the presence of everyone:

"Isn't it a known fact that only when children of same blood offer the ritual rice, the crows will come to eat? How can one blame my uncle, for having adopted a child born of an illicit pregnancy? One should consider it a great deed that he brought up the baby safely." A secret that I never knew till that day! I was left alone near the ritual rice, which was not acceptable even to the crows.'

'I understood the meaning of what uncle Sekharan told me in my ears, when I was getting ready to light his pyre.'

"You can light the pyre and all... but don't come here claiming a share of his property etc. Uncle owned half of the property in that island. But what's the point in talking about all that? Has not the entire property gone under the water now?"

'When the Koman island submerged under the water, Father had moved in with uncle Sekharan. In fact, all the small islands had gone under the water. Father's letters to me when I was in Delhi, expressed his hope that one day the backwater would give back the land it had claimed. That never happened.'

'Finally Father wrote, "You know the space where our house stood? All the surrounding areas have gone under the water. We can't say when our house also will be submerged. Therefore, I made arrangements to dispose off our property to trader Chandi who bought it for the price of timber. I have deposited that money in your name in our cooperative bank."'

The next time when he went to his hometown for his annual holidays, Sathya had gone to Sekharan uncle's house where his Father was living. Uncle had been in prison for a long time for participating in the Vayalar struggle. It was only after the Communist Party came into power that he and many others were released from prison. After coming from jail, uncle got engaged in farming activities and withdrew totally from the party. Father was still active in the party. In those days, once he left the house from Koman island early in the morning, he would return only late at night. Even when he was laid on his pyre his whole length stretched out, covered by the red flag on which the sickle and hammer were embroidered, embers still glowed in his sunken eyes. Every cell in his body was that of a communist leader till death hunted him down.'

She stood there looking at those papers. A song from the marotti treetop breezed into her ears.

Parrot damsel, why have you come,
Do you have something to tell me?
Thatthinam thanthayee tharo,
Thatthinam thanthayee tharo.

She got out of the bus at the junction and got into an auto. The driver asked 'Where to?'

She told him the route.

The auto stopped with a splutter in front of Disha's house. There was no one in the portico. She ran inside the house.

'Disha' she called out.

She heard a movement in the kitchen. It was Mother.

'She left long ago', Mother said. 'She waited for you for a long time!'

Aparajitha turned back and ran. The autorickshaw started and sped past, kicking up dust. She called out from behind. But it went fast and disappeared.

As she was walking towards Anakhan Hill, she saw the purple kasithumba flowers blooming everywhere on the way on the bund roads between the paddy fields. She looked at them in surprise. Where is that paddy field hedged by the purple kasithumba flowers? Where is the Koman island submerged in water?

She started walking past the village roads where wild plants grew dense through which Disha had guided her once.

'The Saga of the Seashore' is coming to an end. She was engrossed in the thought of how to end the book. The previous evening, she had sat with Vasudevan Master, thinking about it along with him. Master hummed from the famous

Malayalam lyrics 'Vayalar Roars' written by popular poet P Bhaskaran:

> 'Vayalar is not just a village now,
> It is a poem of immeasurable value.
> A poem scribbled by the harassed
> With their life blood
> On the bosom of Malayalam.
> Dear Historian of the land
> Please stir with your pen,
> Those smoldering ashes....'

'Okay, let me ask you a question', Vasudevan Master had flung a question at her. 'Who was the actual villain in this story?'

'Was it the Diwan or the King', she pondered, 'or both of them?'

'Sir CP cannot deny his role in this bloodshed but neither can the Royal King shed his responsibility', said Aparajitha.

'Definitely not.' Vasudevan Master nodded. 'Telegram messages which had gone from Sir CP to the King himself are the proof that the King was aware of everything.... Deploying the army, massacring his own citizens with automatic guns...but....'

She looked at him.

'The real villains were neither of them', continued Vasudevan Master.

'Then?' she stared at him.

'IG Parthasarathy, DSP Vaidyanatha Iyer and four or five of his associates – landlords of Cherthala were behind that massacre.'

'But without shifting the blame on anybody, Sir CP took full responsibility. After the Vayalar shoot out, Sir CP wrote to his son Pattabhiram, living in Madras: 'In a way it was good that the Communist riot took place at this moment. Had I been in Delhi for attending the Constituent Assembly, wouldn't the King have been put in a difficult spot? So, I took over the responsibility myself and issued a statement; because I don't want to say that I have no responsibility in the action of the army. After all, the King had given me that position equivalent to the Army General on my own explicit request. The shootout would have never happened without my orders. In the name of this massacre, if the people of Thiruvithamkoor want to blame anyone, let it be me.'

'Are you glorifying Sir CP?' asked Aparajitha.

'No, no, no', Master said. 'In truth, initially Sir CP was trying to avoid bloodshed. He told leaders like Pattom Thanu Pillai and R Shankar to intervene in the matter. He had sent a peace mission under the leadership of R Shankar. But the police and landlords wanted to uproot the Communist movement; and covertly that was what the State Congress and some of its leaders also wanted. They cleverly made their moves to make it possible. They heartlessly threw out the tenants and workers from their settlements, subjected them to starvation and forced them to move into the camps. Then they instigated the Diwan to send the army to the camps with automatic guns for a massacre. This is the fascist strategy of the hunter, trapping the prey and killing it.'

'Was not Sir CP's agenda also to destroy the Communist Party – the Communists Party which had critiqued the American Model severely and thoroughly? Were they not bragging that the Communist Party would not raise its head for the next twenty-five years in Travancore?' asked Aparajitha.

'There was a person who had advised the Diwan and the King that emptying automatic guns into unarmed people is barbaric', said Vasudevan Master. 'The head of the Army, VVN Parameswaran Pillai, who was the Commanding Officer, had told Sir CP on his face that Vayalar should not be made into another Jallianwala Bagh.'

'That's true', said Aparajitha. 'He came to know of Sir CP's hidden agenda much later. Actually, he had advised Sir CP that by just seeing the army flagmarching, the people would be hesitant to get into violent activities. But the Diwan didn't heed his advice. Instead, he gave powers to DIG Parthasarathy Ayyangar to supersede the General Officer Commanding (GOC). Didn't the hurt GOC submit his resignation to the King?'

'Sir CP's lone agenda was to eradicate the Communist Party', Vasudevan Master nodded, 'like the all-time agenda of fascism all over the world'.

The uprising did not come to an end with the shootout on Thulam tenth.

Ambalapuzha and Cherthala taluks came under army rule.

A total of sixty organisations were banned. Many leaders were arrested, but the uprising had still not come to an end. It was continuing inside and outside the jails.

In the hideout, Comrade KC George was waiting for someone anxiously. Towards midnight, someone knocked on the door. KC George opened the shutters of the window and looked outside. It was Comrade KV Pathrose.

'Oh, haven't you still gone into hiding?' asked KC George opening the door.

'First, it is your turn', said Pathrose. 'All of us are going in different directions. A boat is waiting for us at the jetty.'

Wearing a dirty mundu and vest and a head band made of a white cotton bath towel, George came out and started walking.

'Don't I look like a tapioca trader?' he asked.

'All you lack is a rosary around your neck', Pathrose commented, standing on his toes. Corns on his feet were troubling him a lot and he had to drag himself forward.

'The boatman has not been told where to go', said Pathrose, 'that can be decided by you.'

Keeping a pair of braided coconut fronds on the wooden bars inside the boat, George sat on it.

Pathrose waved him off, standing on the banks.

'Everywhere the police are keeping a watch on us. It is like jumping from the hot pan into the fire.' Comrade Kunjan had alerted everyone. 'It won't take much time for them to get a scent of our shelters.'

What next? Pathrose tried to reflect. The messenger who had gone to meet the Comrade, had not come back.

Police were searching for Pathrose everywhere. It was necessary to smuggle him beyond the state boundaries. The comrade who had gone, promising to send him a boat, also had not arrived yet. Comrades CG Sadashivan and PG Padmanabhan were ready to move on to the next shelter.

'Where are you going', Comrade Kunjan asked CG.

'Kannarkkad', he said.

'Before the crack of dawn tomorrow, everyone should have reached one shelter or the other', said Pathrose. 'Our fight against the monarchy and American Model is not over yet. It will continue visibly as well as in hiding. Now onwards, we will have to strengthen our movement secretly. Drawing energy from the people, our movement has to grow stronger.'

CG and PG Padmanabhan bid goodbye and started their journey.

There was no sign of the ferry boat although they waited for the whole day. After being convinced that it was not going to turn up, both of them started walking through the narrow lanes of a small town. Pathrose struggled to walk with the corns on his feet.

'How far do we have to walk?' Pathrose started growing impatient due to the pain.

'Till the border', said Comrade Kunjan. 'From there we will go to Kozhikode via the neighbouring State.'

Pathrose sat down and looked at his corn-infected leg.

'Dragging this leg?' he looked at Kunjan. 'I get a stabbing pain even when I just lay my foot on the ground.'

Kunjan lifted the Comrade on his shoulders. 'We will find a place to halt for the night. Tomorrow we will find a way.'

'I have hopes for tomorrow', Pathrose's eyes glowed. 'The time is not very far away when we are going to witness the red flag flying high in front of the High Court.'

Sitting under the blooming Gulmohur tree on the Anakhan hilltop, Asuthosh Yadav, a frail young man continued his discussion.

'Yes, our strategy is to sabotage the bourgeois governments, by lying low and hidden. Since the enemy is too strong, only through this strategy can we strengthen our movement to resist their power and exploitation. Comrades, we have to draw the energy required for this from people. Their aspirations to get freedom from exploitation should give energy to our movement and it has to be their struggle for freedom from their own sufferings.'

She was sitting on the red carpet of flowers, in the midst of strangers who had come from unknown parts of the country. Except Dinar's, there was not a single familiar face.

'Comrade is a Kanpur IIT product. He became like this after getting caught in a police action. During a third-degree torture, they broke two of his ribs. He was detained in the jail for two years.' A woman comrade, Paushi hailing from Palakkad, explained to her, when he paused for breath.

'Niranjan has still not called!' Disha said in dismay. 'I can't wait for long. Mother is alone at home.'

'He will call as soon as he gets back to the camp', said Paushi.

'Camp?' Disha was perplexed.

'Yes, he is in action', she said, 'a routine surge. He will call as soon as he gets back to the camp.'

'In action?' Disha asked. 'Where is he?'

'There, comrade…' Paushi diverted her attention to Asuthosh who had become cheerful and ready to address them once again:

> 'Comrades, our goal is not to create martyrs. At least a few of you might have read about the strategies Che had put forth. Why we opt for flash attacks is only because we are less in number. We don't have the arms or number to put up a direct fight with the powerful enemy. Cause severe loss to the enemy, at the same time reduce loss of our people; that's our strategy When there are 1000 people on the enemy's side, we have only some twenty people to resist them. So, avoid loss of lives. One guerilla fighter from our side is equivalent to one hundred men from the enemy's side. So, they are very valuable to us.'

'Comrades, a revolution has to come up from an exploited group of people. So, our next stage is to organise those people who want to free themselves from exploitation, especially from the economic exploitation of the corporates and open a powerful warfront. Che's intention also was to build up a force like that. Che's announcement to the mineworkers is relevant here. "There is no point in standing in front of the guns baring your chest, colleagues", he said. Even building up a powerful defensive force, on the face of automatic guns, will not help us in any way. In a country like India where we have expansive agricultural lands and a strong rural foundation, we have to progress revolution through the villagers. Keeping the villagers as a front, the frontline fighters and guerilla fighters have to fight jointly. They have to forcibly capture their highly-sophisticated weapons and grow powerful at the enemy's expense. Even if it takes time, situations have to be created which would antagonise the people against the bourgeois. We have to kindle the fire of rebellion in their minds. It is foolishness to divert them to struggles which are not assured of victory. Any struggle without knowing the power of the enemy is inviting wasteful self-martyrdom. The real concept behind the rebellion is not sacrificing one's own life in front of the enemy. On the contrary, it is to make people the weaponry and dissolve the bourgeois in the torrent of changes.'

'That was the basic strategy of Mao's guerilla struggle in China. The revolution that gained strength in North China was brutally suppressed. Establishing in the villages and strategising surges, holding the hands of the farming population was the methodology that succeeded there. Weren't the farming workers, the populace who were subjected to the power and suppression of the French colonial rule the strength of Ho Chi Minh, and in Cuba did we not fight the brutal rule of Spain, allying with the farmers there? It is the same strategy, the Communist Party of India (Maoist) is also following. Victory is like a night train running late. But, however late it runs, it is bound to reach the station at least later in the afternoon. In our great surge forward, we will have along with us a massive population. The revolution is on new routes of blazing ember. Yet, I have no doubt that the days when the red flag flutters on the Red Fort are not far away.'

In the peak of excitement Asuthosh started panting.

'Dinar', Disha prodded, 'Niranjan…?'

'He will call.' Dinar tried to comfort her.

'It's getting late Dinar', she became uncomfortable. 'Aparajitha also has not yet come….'

Paushi got up and came near Disha. Wrapping her hands around Disha's shoulders, she walked her to another corner.

'Niranjan wants to communicate a very important matter to both of you. He wants you to become a part of our movement. New wings of the organisation are under formation, centered around the old battlements. Both of you should participate in that. We have to travel together a long of distance for the final destination of our national freedom.'

'National freedom', Disha looked at her sarcastically, 'through becoming a colony of China?'

'Disha, what do you mean?' Paushi looked into Disha's eyes.

'To keep India from being a threat to China in the world market, where China is now growing very strong; to convert India into a market for China and to keep her under control…. With that purpose they are giving you money and weapons…. But comparing this with Che's guerilla encounters in Cuba and Bolivia….'

'You are thoroughly mistaken', Paushi's face turned red. 'The India you are talking about is under whose feet? A collaboration of imperialist bourgeois, corporates and dishonest and highly corrupt political crooks? Is it not their collective trading taking place here? Are they not the ones making India a trading commodity?'

'I am not ready for an argument', Disha walked away, 'but my direction is different'.

'I am in a hurry to leave', Disha said. 'If Niranjan calls, tell him I am not with him on this.'

She started walking fast, down the hill through the cashew thickets.

Along with the sun's rays that were slanting towards the west, Aparajitha started climbing the hill swiftly.

Niranjan's friends, she thought, would they have arrived? Would he have called? Would his fragrance be lingering in the reed thickets?

Hearing the roar of vehicles, she turned back with a start. Three or four police vehicles halted on the road where the paddy fields ended. Policemen armed with guns leapt out of them and ran towards the Anakhan Hill, cutting across the paddy fields.

Prisoner of Dreams

'The social norms are turning points in the path of change.' Aparajitha tried to recollect the words of Vasudevan Master while giving shape to her thoughts, sitting in front of the keyboard:

> 'In the process of liberating the human race, there was a lot of change between the Marxian concepts and Lenin's point of view. The basis of Communism followed all over the world was the Bolshevik point of view conceptualised by Lenin. Finally, history proved their inadequacy through what happened in Soviet Russia. The Bolshevik party failed in maintaining democratic norms among the disillusioned members who were denied their rights within the tight framework of Party rules. They disregarded the great word that Marx glorified in his discourse, "The Man". The Maoists are opening a new path of norms, a democratic path leading to a more liberal society. "What is needed is not to define the universe but to change" – this Marxian thought still holds good in the present context. A rebel's responsibility is to

rewrite the course of history. Only Marxian concepts can transform the world.'

'Sir, are you a Maoist?' Aparajitha asked.

'Me?' His smile spread through the grey beard and moustache. 'Am I not a poor soul dreaming of the welfare of the human race all over the world; A prisoner of dreams?'

Disha sat on the bed propped on the pillow. Her heart was still pounding. The way she had sprinted down the Anakhan Hill as the police surrounded the hill was still haunting her. At night, party Comrades had called and informed her that Dinar had been arrested. All others had escaped. Asuthosh Yadav, Paushi, they had the agility to escape the enemies. That was the first rule of guerilla warfare. The enemy can surround you at any time; be alert.

Asuthosh had started with an alert. People were posted around to alert in case the enemy turned up. He had also detailed the ways to escape the enemy.

'Life of every member is valuable for us. Try never to fall into the hands of the enemy. In case any one of you gets caught, use one bullet on him. It is better to die at the hands of a Comrade rather than being tortured at the hands of the enemy. If one among us gets killed in an encounter with the enemy, make sure that his weapon is retrieved. It is valuable for us. Discard the body at the disposal of the enemy. Let them feast over it. The martyrs are immortal. They will continue to live in the spirits of the living members like Che continuing to live in our psyche immortally.'

'Yes, the important point in our context is about escaping from the hands of the enemy. We are not interested in fighting wars with the enemy. We are on a democratic war path. In a semi-feudal country like India, it is desirable to tread on a democratic war path. On the face of people's will power, any strong enemy will bend his knees. That's what history is teaching us.'

Asuthosh Yadav transferred his energy to the minds of his followers.

The Gulmohur tree spread a red carpet under her. Shedding its leaves, its empty branches staring at the sky, she felt the tree was singing a song.

I will soar up to the sky
I will spread all over the country
Reviving her with a new life
To rise above the skies.

She sat on the thick jutting roots of the tree, leaning against the rough surface of its trunk looking upward. Shedding the leaves and flowers, the tree was standing tall, exposing its branches to the sky where white clouds drifted. Here and there a red hue spread in circles, forming a beautiful design. She was wearing a yellow chudidar with red polka dots. Her red duppatta fluttered in the breeze. If only Van Gogh was around with his palette and brush; she tried to visualise that painting.

'Why are you not saying anything?' asked Aparajitha.

'I was thinking how lucky it was that you didn't turn up there!' Disha said as if in a nightmare. 'If you were also there, both of us would have hung around together and the police would have arrested us also, along with Dinar. I came down only because you didn't turn up.'

'History is repeating itself, isn't it?' Apu lowered her head to the keyboard.

'Umm…' said Disha.

'Revolution in its new path', said Aparajitha, 'the police in the old costumes of hunters.'

'No movement can sustain without finding a place in the hearts of people', Disha started saying.

Before she completed, Aparajitha interrupted, 'It's time for a democratic socialist revolution in the country. Shoot the corrupt politicians and the bureaucrats. They are the people who are destroying this country.'

'Annihilation? Destruction of class enemies? – that was an idea this country gave up long ago', Disha said.

'That was not the right direction. We have more class cheaters around us than class enemies. We will change the word annihilation and give a new name; an anti-virus operation to eliminate those viruses who are not allowing the system to work.'

'It's not likely to happen', said Disha.

'But we have to make it happen.' Aparajitha bristled. 'Then only will this country change. One of these days, there is going to be a democratic movement organised by the people to make it happen.'

'We have to be careful. Since Dinar has been caught by the police, there are chances they may come again to conduct a search. Poor fellow, this time there will be no one to bail him out.'

'No chance…. Dinar will not let us down.' Aparajitha ran her fingers through the keyboard.

'Cannot be sure of that; especially in the face of police torture; their third-degree tactics; for the time being it will be wiser to move out of this place.'

'Where shall we go? Where shall we leave Mother?' Aparajitha asked.

'Delhi', said Disha. 'We will be in Delhi till the viva is over.'

'Mother here, all alone?' asked Aparajitha.

'We have to find a place for her.'

'Where?'

'We will meet Vasudevan Master', said Disha. 'He will find a way.'

Aparajitha's fingers drew a portrait of Sathyadas on the monitor.

Asaan walked briskly; stretching his thin legs and holding on to his shrunken fingers, the ten-year-old Sathyadas tried to keep pace with him. There was a red flag in his left hand. They walked past cashew thickets, areca farms and narrow bridges made of split palm tree stems. They had to reach the bus stop well on time to catch the bus to Punnapra to be present at the historic moment; the moment when the aspirations of twenty-five years came to fruition; moments written with the life blood of thousands of martyrs. If at that moment, they were not able to scream Inquilab Zindabad in a full throated voice, along with everyone, there was no point in continuing with their lives anymore, thought Asaan.

'My son, walk a little faster', Asaan tried to hasten Sathya. The boy pulled up his shorts which were slipping down.

'Your mother should have been here now.' Asaan wiped a drop of tear from his eyes. 'She would have carried you on her two wings to Punnapra.'

'Oh, Mother should not have died, isn't it Father', little Sathya said wishfully.

'Umm…you are right. She shouldn't have died.' Asaan dried his eyes with his shoulder mundu. 'But we cannot fight our destiny.'

Everywhere on the sides of the road bright red flags fluttered. Asaan's mind went back ten years to the day India got independence and the Tricolor flag fluttered on the Red Fort.

The village midwife had come rushing and handed over a white bundle into his hands and said: 'It's a boy but he has been born at an inauspicious time ready to eat away his mother. Please try to get a vaidyan immediately. I tried my level best but have not been able to stop the bleeding.'

Asaan went to Vaidyan Kumaran's house reluctantly and pleaded with him to save Pappy. Kumaran showed his true colours, saying, 'I cannot attend to a woman who has delivered an illegitimate baby. Is it not you who wants her to live? I know what's in your mind. Go and find out some other vaidyan to attend to her.'

Without getting any medical attention, Pappy had closed her eyes forever, leaving the new born in the hands of Asaan. From that day, Asaan became his mother and father.

'Why is my Father so sad?' The ten-year-old enquired.

'Oh, nothing my son… I thought of the olden days.' Asaan dried his eyes and thought, how fast Sathya has grown up. On the fifteenth of August, this year he is completing his tenth year.

VS Achuthanandan was arrested and brought to the lockup. A thin man in the cell approached him.

'Oh, you're a comrade, isn't it?' he asked.

'Umm…'

'I heard police saying that your profession is making spears.'

Achuthanandan looked at him and asked. 'What's your profession?'

'Oh, I am a petty thief', he said. 'Then I do certain small and essential services for the police masters. People call me thief Kolappan.'

The Head Constable came near the lockup and asked. 'Are you the Achuthanandan from Alappuzha?'

CID Vasu looked into the cell fiercely.

'Yes master.' It was Kolappan who answered the question.

'So you should know', the Head Constable said, 'where is your leader Pathrose hiding?'

'I don't know', said Achuthanandan.

'Oh, you don't know? I will make you talk like a parrot.'

'You drag his feet and put them outside the bars', he told Kolappan.

Kolappan complied. He asked a police constable to place a baton in between his legs and tie it to the bars so that his feet were exposed; then they started beating Achuthanandan on his feet. Blood splashed on to Kolappan's face. The legs became swollen. Achuthanandan screamed off his guts, wriggled once and fainted.

'Looks like he is dead', said the constable.

'Is that so? Then drag him to a vehicle, drive him down to that forest, dig a hole and bury him.'

The vehicle waded through the darkness. Kolappan sat near the dead body, with a pickaxe and shovel. As the vehicle took a curve there was a movement behind Kolappan.

He turned back and told the driver, 'Looks like he has come back to life'.

Kumara Panicker shaved his head bald, slipped a rosary around his neck, hoodwinked the police and left his house. After one week, unable to find him, the police and army came to his house and ransacked it. They looted all the possessions inside the house, demolished the house and staked all the wooden panels used for the house. They then filled the basement of the house with water and made a pond where the house once stood.

Night.

Asaan had missed the last ferry boat to Koman islet. He walked around the backwaters a long distance and reached his house and collapsed in fatigue. He was woken up by barking dogs. When he looked out through the shutters, he saw the police. There was no way to escape. The moment he opened the door, DYSP Achyuthan barged into the house and squeezed his neck.

'Where have you hidden that scoundrel Kumara Panicker?'

When he said he didn't know his whereabouts, he was slapped several times.

'Dump this rascal in the vehicle', he ordered.

Asaan was arrested and taken to the police station. They searched the house and attic but didn't find anyone. CID Sanku Pillai had tipped them that Kumara Panicker was hiding in Sekharan's house. They whacked him in the lockup and stuffed him in the overcrowded jail, along with other prominent leaders. At midnight they were taken to the jail superintendent OM Khaddar, a giant of a man, who was sitting in the southern yard of the police station under a yellow light. The police dumped them at his feet one by one.

'Where is the Vayalar lion hiding?' He placed one leg on the back of his prey and kicked the face with the other one. Blood splashed everywhere.

'Bring the next one', he growled.

Next day, Comrade Padmanabhan was crushed by the booted legs mercilessly. They wanted to find out where Pathrose was hiding.

They beat Comrade Thommachan and fractured seven of his ribs. Next day, at midnight Khaddar and a few policemen came to the lockup. They dragged Nicolov through the cell bars, tied his legs and beat him with batons. They wanted to know where the stolen rifles from Punnapra police camp were hidden. Finally, they pierced a bayonet through his thigh. He writhed in pain and his screams woke up the leaders in the next cell. MN shouted at the police loudly.

Next day, early morning they dragged Thandar to the southern yard for torture. That was the time prisoners were sent out to attend to their morning chores. As they heard Thandar's screams, MN tied his towel around his head and rushed to the place.

'Stop it', he shouted in a full-throated voice. 'Stop beating my comrades….'

'If we beat?' asked the police superintendent.

'I will go on a hunger strike unto death', said MN.

The superintendent looked around. The comrades had formed a barricade around MN. He dropped his cigarette, stomped on it and walked away.

After two days the warden came with two barbers. The prisoners were to be taken to the magistrate's court. Before that, the jail authorities wanted to make them presentable by shaving off their lice-infested stinking hair. The barbers sharpened their knives and started their work. On the wounds on their heads, they dabbed thick turmeric paste.

After one month they were bailed out.

He reached Koman islet by night. Pappy didn't come to the front verandah. Instead, her companion girl came and said, 'Pappy sister is not keeping well. The village midwife says she might be three months pregnant.'

Asaan walked inside. Pappy stood up with her head lowered. He caressed her hair and said, 'At least, this way, we can see a pair of tiny legs trotting in this courtyard! My daughter, you don't worry, you can stay here for the rest of your life as my daughter.' She leaned her head on his chest and sobbed, heartbroken.

Both of them were still walking briskly. Another scene flashed in Asaan's mind. Fourteenth of August 1947. At midnight, two colleagues went to the Union office and hoisted two flags. One Tricolor and the other one Red, with a sickle and hammer embroidered in the middle. His fingers automatically touched his forehead in a salute. My country has been liberated from foreign rule. A song breezed in:

Saare Jahanse Acha, Hindustan hamara

(Of all the places in the world, my Hindusthan is the best.)

'It's too late', Disha got up and walked into her room, 'try to get some sleep.'

'I have not finished writing Dashu...' she said, raising her hands backward and yawning. 'There is an important work pending.'

'What's that?'

She showed her a pen drive. 'I bought this when I went to town today. Let not what was uttered by your black tongue come true.'

'Are you planning to copy the entire thing now in the middle of the night? Are you crazy?' Disha was shocked.

'Umm...sometimes I too feel so', she yawned and closed the laptop. 'May be, I will do it tomorrow. I am feeling too sleepy.'

Vasudevan Master sat on his easy chair with his feet pulled up. Nearby on the half-wall, Disha and Aparajitha sat leaning against the wooden pillars facing each other. Fragrance of elanji flowers wafted through the verandah along with the mesmerising musical notes of santoor played by Pundit Shivakumar Sharma.

Vasudevan Master picked up a sheaf of papers from the top of a stool kept nearby and placed it on Aparajitha's lap. They were foolscap papers in which Master had written in ink.

'This reminds me of what Arthur Schopenhauer said, "If I maintain my silence about my secret, it is my prisoner.... If I let it slip from my tongue, I am its prisoner. My secret and I have decided to jump the prison together."'

Disha looked at the papers on Aparajitha's lap.

> 'My Holy State Congress, you have been cheated. Your pet sons, Raghavan, George, Kochhu Pillai and Kochhu Krishnan who threw open their chest in front of the bullets have been hanged to death. Sivaraja Pandyan of Tamilnadu, who wanted to uphold your prestige, breathed his last on the cold prison floors. Thousands of comrades fell dead in the war fields fighting for you and became martyrs. Comrade KK Kunju Pillai died of tuberculosis. Comrade Janardhanan died alone in Calcutta without his family around. Your ethical energy and sense of justice drawn from all these sacrifices are now being

commoditised by those nefarious forces for money. My Dear Venaad, your life blood is being sucked away by these power mongers.'

'These lines....' Disha tried to recollect.

'Yes' said the Master 'from *The Cheated Venaad* written by Comrade Sreekandan Nair'.

'Oh, isn't this a novel?' Aparajitha looked at him in surprise.

'You can define it that way also', Master said. 'That is the foreword. I borrowed it from Sreekandan Nair. A novel based on Punnapra-Vayalar, which I had started writing a long time ago.'

'Is this the secret of jumping the jail?' Aparajitha turned the pages marred by a lot of corrections and deletions.

'It was written on ruled notebook sheets, listening to the sound of the nib moving on the paper. I have not tamed the keys of the keyboard the way you have done you see....'

'How long did it take?' Disha asked.

'Years together. I had deliberately left it incomplete. I didn't want it to turn up as a historic novel.'

'Then what happened at the end?' Aparajitha turned over to the last pages.

'It's not finished,' said Master. 'I will complete within the next two days. The characters have to finish playing their roles you see...'

'The characters...?' Disha and Aparajitha looked at him curiously.

'The two of you', he said looking at both of them. 'You are the two leading my novel. Not over... Niranjan, Dinar, Mrinalda...' Master burst out laughing. My theme is about the new generation turning back and taking a look at that historical event. When I narrate the story through your eyes, it becomes a contemporary novel.'

'Like characters searching for the writer, is it not?' Disha smiled at Aparajitha.

'Hats off', Aparajitha folded her hands to the Master. 'You really surprised me.'

'Then what about the climax of the story?' Disha asked.

'That can wait', Master said. 'Why don't you hurry up with your preparations to take your flight to Delhi tomorrow? Your flight is at 1.30 in the afternoon.'

'It would be wise for both of you to take off to Delhi before the police comes searching', said Master. 'The police can arrive at any time. Don't fall into their hands. These are the days when the 'burden of proof' backfires on the victim. It becomes the burden of the prey to prove his innocence. I have already made arrangements for your stay in Delhi with Mrinalda. It is better not to stay in the campus too. Mother can stay here with me. I am short of a sibling. She will be the light of this house.'

'I hope you are aware that protecting those who have committed a crime is also a crime', Disha reminded him.

'I am not protecting criminals. I am protecting the innocents', Master defended himself. 'I can argue that out in any court.'

'Will it not be smarter to leave this evening itself?' Master asked. Suddenly Disha's mobile rang.

'From home', she said.

'When?' she spoke into the phone.

'When?' her face became pale.

'What happened?' Aparajitha got panicky.

'Police raided our house again', Disha said. 'Your laptop….'

'My laptop…?' Aparajitha sprang up, 'My writing…my *Saga of the Seashore*'.

'They seized it and took it along with them.'

'My damned black tongue', Disha cursed.

To Death's Pyer

Night.

Mallikarjun's soul-touching music along with the fragrance of medlar flowers wafted through the room.

Aparajitha had not slept. In the round yellow light of the hurricane lamp, she drifted into the concluding parts of Vasudevan Master's novel. That was the time when Travancore was going through turmoil, facing monstrous treatment at the hands of a tyrannical government with the barbaric rule of Sir CP reaching new heights. From the day he laid his foot on the soil of Travancore as an adviser to Maharaja till 25 May 1947… seventeen years of scorching heat. He had no hesitation in dumping even his close allies like Mannathu Padmanabhan, if they happened to incur his displeasure.

After the massacre in Punnapra and Vayalar…

The socialist leaders who escaped arrest had met in Alappuzha.

'Has it not been decided that Travancore should stand apart without joining Indian Union?' Sreekandan Nair raised his voice. 'This is an act of sedition.'

'Is it not declared in Diwan's statement that when India gets her freedom, Travancore also will become independent?'

'Who doesn't know that behind the "Independent Travancore" proposal is the Diwan's vested interest to keep Travancore always under his feet?'

'If someone could do away with that Ramaswamy Iyer, it would be a blessing for Travancore.' Comrade KR Gopala Kurup made a wish in distress.

'Who will be ready to do that?' Mathai Manjuran enquired.

'I am ready', KCS Mani came forward.

Sreekandan Nair looked at him sternly. Mani was his neighbour.

Who will answer for the recklessness of youth? No one, he answered himself.

'Is there not a proverb about using a thorn to dig out a thorn stuck to the foot?' asked Mani. 'He is an Iyer. I am also an Iyer.'

'If you want you can go ahead', warned Comrade KS Joseph. 'But don't ever think that you will remain alive thereafter.'

'Remember that if you are caught you will be sent to the gallows', added Comrade G Janardhana Kurup.

'I am not scared even a little bit of death', declared Mani. 'The country is not going to gain anything by my being alive. On the contrary, if I could do this, that will be a great service to my country.'

'My cooperation will be there in any movement against CP', said Gopala Kurup. 'To demolish the statue of CP in front of the "CP Inn" in Trivandrum, Comrade Sanku Pillai also will join hands with us.'

It was Comrade Sanku Pillai's cherished desire to demolish the statue. He had made an attempt to do that with the help of his friend Comrade Narayana Pillai, which however, had not worked out at that time.

'First we will destroy the statue', said Gopala Kurup. 'Then we will think about finishing off the man.'

Gopala Kurup paid ten rupees to Mani for his travel expenses. KCS Mani boarded a bus to Trivandrum and reached there in the middle of the night, around 1.30 am. There was a slight drizzle. He entered the compound of the inn by jumping over the southern wall.

Next day the newspaper *Yuva Keralam* (Kerala's Youth) carried the following news:

'Sir CP's statue has been demolished.'

Next day the *Yuva Keralam* press was shut down forcibly.

'Only Mani can kill Sir CP', declared Gopala Kurup as he learnt about the fate of the statue.

The Rebel Committee met. 'When is the assassination going to take place?'

'It's not like cutting off the nose of the statue', said Janardhana Kurup. 'How do we get him in our hands?'

'We will get him', said Mani confidently. 'On 25 July. It is the day of the centenary celebrations of His Highness, the composer Maharaja Swathi Thirunal. On that day, Sir CP will escort the present King to the music concert in the Music Academy…on his way to the kingdom of death.'

'Come back victorious.' Gopala Kurup blessed him and embraced him.

He was paid Rs 65 towards his expenses.

25 July.

At the Thycaud venue where the concert was to be conducted, Mani sat in the front row on the left side, waiting for his prey. The weapon he was to use was hanging from his waistline under his mundu. By 5.30 in the evening, the Diwan came to the hall with his escorts. He stood at the entrance, waiting for the King.

'This is the right opportunity', Mani's hand reached for his weapon. Suddenly, the Diwan turned back instinctively and looked at the front row of chairs.

Has death a smell too? Mani wondered. Well, this is not the time.

The King arrived.

'The King will leave soon. The concert will begin. That will be the time.' Mani waited patiently.

On the dais were the King and the Diwan.

Mani looked at the watch of his neighbour. Suddenly it turned back and stopped at Thulam tenth. The army stamping on the shot down bodies of comrades, hundreds of comrades, wails of widows and orphaned children….

The Diwan got up from his seat and moved toward the exit. Mani moved out of the hall and waited in the shadows outside. Mani tightened his grip on his weapon, a machette. War cries echoed in his ears… war horses galloped… Mani leapt forward, lowering his mundu to pull out the machette from its sheeth. Suddenly, the lights went off. There was darkness everywhere. The machette went up and down several times.

IG Parthasarathy Iyer, who was exchanging pleasantries with dignitaries, growled in the darkness: 'catch him'.

Early next morning, the King's government released a press note:

> Yesterday, around 7.30 in the evening, there was an attempt on the life of Diwan Sir CP Ramaswamy Iyer who was walking towards his car from the venue of the concert. A stranger with a knife sprang on him and stabbed thrice on his neck, wounding his cheeks and neck. As he raised his hands to block the attack, his fingers were also wounded. There are totally seven wounds. And three of the nerves near the left ear have been slashed, causing severe bleeding. The assassin fled and escaped.

On the fourth day after India got her independence, Ramaswamy Iyer relinquished his powerful position, lowered his hood of arrogance and left Travancore forever.

Vasudevan Master came inside. 'You have still not slept?'

'I was reading', Aparajitha got up. '...things I still have to write about...Sir CP's flight... Calcutta Thesis, Comrade's death...'

Vasudevan Master sat on a chair. Aparajitha also sat down.

'Was not the idea of independent Travancore raised by Sir CP after Punnapra-Vayalar? An argument raised by right-wing leaders!' said Aparajitha.

'A Travancore that stood separate from the Union of India; that was always the dream of Sir CP. What else is the American Model – other than a conspiracy to take over the power, keeping the King as a dummy; like the American President – an autonomous ruler not accountable to the legislature or judiciary of India.'

'The bullets that pierced through the chests of Punnapra-Vayalar comrades demolished the very foundation of the Diwan's rule.'

'What about the British rule that lasted for two centuries in India? Do you think they were forced to leave India by her non-violence movement? The right-wing historians have recorded it like that, knowing that it is not true. But in truth, was not the communist movement the real reason for that?'

Vasudevan Master turned out to be an impassionate historian.

Days prior to her independence, most of the struggle India had witnessed was organised by the Communist Party. The Navy revolt in Bombay, Tebhaga revolt in Bengal, Revolt of those wrongfully detained, the Railway workers' agitation in the Goldenrock workshop in Tiruchirapalli, the farmer's agitation in Worli, Textile workers agitation and strike in Coimbatore, Kanpur, Bombay and Calcutta, the tribal farm workers' agitation in Bihar, Telangana agitation, the Punnapra-Vayalar uprising....

When the Indian navy workers tore off the Union Jack and hoisted the flags of the Congress and Muslim League in Mumbai, the Congress and League parties condemned their action. It was only the Communist Party who hailed and justified their action.

When they knew that the naval workers revolt would spread among army men too, the white army got into the streets of

Bombay in protected vehicles. Courageous patriots were shot down and their hot blood pooled in the streets of Bombay.

What about Travancore? While some power-hungry Congress leaders had secret understandings with Sir CP in closed rooms, the Communists were arguing for an armed confrontation against monarchy, the Diwan's rule and the American Model. Just like the Bolsheviks declared war against the Czar from St Petersburg, by shooting at the winter palace, Comrade Krishna Pillai had lead all those movements remaining invisible in the party office in Kozhikode.

14 August 1947. The Tricolor flew jubilantly on the Red Fort. As they returned after hoisting the national flag in front of a party office in Kerala, there was an untold sadness in the minds of the Communist leaders.... An incomplete armed struggle... what a lot of hardships they had to go through for that...how many courageous leaders had given up their lives for that...all over Kerala....

After independence, the bourgeois government took over at New Delhi under the leadership of Jawaharlal Nehru.

Comrade did not participate in the Second Congress of the Communist Party held in Calcutta where the armed struggle strategy was tabled by BT Ranadive. Following the Calcutta Thesis, Nehru declared the Communist Party as illegal in India. Comrade went underground in Chouvara near Aluva.

Pattom Thanu Pillai took over as the Chief Minister of Kerala. The fire started by the Calcutta Thesis spread all over the country. Many leaders were imprisoned. CK Kumara Panicker and Varghese Vaidyar were caught in a lodge in Kochi. The police started their manhunt throughout the State. Secret police arrived at the scene to trap underground comrades. Most of the leaders had gone underground

On 10 August, at night nine o'clock, near Mararikulam Bridge, Comrades Vasu and Sadanandan were waiting as per the instructions they had got from the secret wing of the party.

'Comrade Raman is arriving. He should be protected like the apple of the eye.'

'Who is this Comrade Raman?' asked Sadanandan.

'I don't know', Vasu replied. 'Even if I know, I wouldn't say, that's the kind of instruction from the party office.'

At 9.30 pm a car came and halted near the bridge. Sadanandan flashed the torch in his hand thrice.

One old man and three women emerged from the car. From their midst a thin dark person with a narrow mustache and closely-cropped hair, holding a bag, walked forward. It was difficult to figure out who he was, still seeing the glow in his eyes Vasu asked, 'Comrade Raman?'

Instead of replying to the question, he asked a counter question.

'Has Comrade Menon arrived?'

'He reached last night itself.'

'What about others?'

'They will be here by tomorrow or the day after.'

'What about the arrangements for the Committee meeting?' the question sounded as if he knew everything.

'Everything has been done.' It was again Vasu who answered.

'Where is my shelter?' Comrade Raman held his head high and walked.

'Kannarkkad.'

'Deshabhimani library….?'

'Closer to that', Vasu said.

'The house Comrade CG and Comrade Kumara Panicker had occupied till yesterday.'

'Then where did they go?'

'To a place closer to that', he said.

'Comrade give me that bag. I will hold it.' Sadanandan tried to take the bag from the Comrade.

Comrade tilted his head and looked at Sadanandan.

'Comrade, are you making me a capitalist lord?' He smiled. 'Is this not the requirement of those capitalist bourgeoisie – servants to hold his luggage, spittoons and other accessories? Are we all not comrades?'

Comrade Sadanandan retreated.

Comrade Raman doesn't seem to be an ordinary person, he thought. From the moment he got down from the car, he had been attracted to him as if drawn by a magnet. There was an unusual commanding power in those eyes.

'A high-powered leader who had access to information on the entire secret moves of the party; he has come down from somewhere in the north. But he seems to be quite familiar with this locality. Anyway, let him be anyone. After all, hasn't he been entrusted to us by the party for safe keeping?'

The car left. Vasu, Sadanandan and Comrade Raman started walking to the shelter in Kannarkadu. Vasu walked in front as a guide, followed by Comrade Raman and Sadanandan behind him. They had gone to the house of Comrade Nanappan. At night, another comrade came, one Menon. Both of them were closeted in a room for a long time in discussion. During the following days comrades Gopalan, Ananthan, Ravi and John joined them. Sadanandan recognised three of them at first glance itself – CG Sadasivan, Kumara Panicker and PG Padmanabhan. All were waiting for the young man Hari who was underground.

'How can we convene the meeting without Hari?' Comrade Raman enquired repeatedly.

'We need six or seven young comrades to provide security for the meeting', Comrade CK Madhavan came and said.

'Where?'

'Around our Desabhimani library, our Committee is meeting there. The security should be tight.'

By eight o'clock that night, comrades who were staying hidden in different houses, assembled there for the meeting. Deliberations and discussions continued till two in the morning. Thereafter, all of them went back to their respective shelters.

It became a practice to hold meetings every night. Comrade Raman spent his day-time reading and writing without getting into a conversation with anybody.

'Comrade Hari is coming to meet Comrade Raman', Vasu came and warned everyone. 'Don't allow anyone inside till they finish their discussions.'

Comrade Hari came. Sadanandan recognised him immediately. It was Comrade KC George.

Comrade Sadanandan stood guard till their discussions were over. When he went inside to serve them tender coconut water, the discussions were still on. They were discussing the Calcutta Thesis. Armed struggle all over India ... the new line of thought pursued by the party propagated by BT Ranadive, verbal attacks on the new democratic union government as the government of peace-makers at the new party congress at Calcutta, 'the basic motto of the labour class and party will be to fight the bourgeois government incessantly, which has been cited in italics in the Calcutta Thesis. Our goal will be to install a government of the working class, farming communities and other sidelined masses in place of the bourgeois government; a government with a leftist outlook.'

After the Calcutta congress, Nehru started hunting the Communist Party leaders all over India. Party offices were sealed.

'Comrade, there is something wrong with our party policies', said Comrade Raman. 'No new memberships; whoever are members are not willing to actively involve in our action programmes.'

'Even the new government of Pattom Thanu Pillai is pursuing Sir CP's aggressive policies in Kerala. To topple us, that Nehru is encouraging the same policy all over India.'

'The party should give more importance to those young members who have genuine party spirit. Everyone should consider party above their personal priorities. People may come and go but the party should remain forever.'

'Okay…but why is Comrade discussing all this now?'

'My mind has been asking me to discuss all these issues from the past few days', Comrade Raman said. 'In tomorrow's Travancore Party Committee, you have to discuss all this discreetly. Comrade CG and Kumaran have met all the members alone and in groups. Nobody is willing to get involved actively. It has become so difficult to get even the shelters.'

'The reason could be that their self-confidence has eroded', said Comrade Hari. 'Is not every day spent in torture, court cases and allied problems?'

'There will be a change', said Comrade Raman optimistically. 'The wind will start blowing in the opposite direction. Comrade, the day when the workers' party will form a democratic government and take over the power is not far away', Comrade prophesied.

'Are you not changing the shelter?' Comrade Hari asked. 'I am moving into another one.'

'Thought I will do that tomorrow', Comrade replied. 'I am waiting for that messenger. I sent a note to Kumaran, asking for a few of Stalin's books and ten rupees. He is not back yet.'

'I am taking leave of you now', Hari bid goodbye. 'We will meet again after the Central Committee meeting.'

As he looked back Comrade was still standing there looking at him. He waved his hand. Comrade lifted his strong fists skyward.

Next morning, Comrade Kochhukuttan came looking for Comrade Sadanandan, panting. Veins on his face stood tight.

'Comrade, please come fast.'

'What happened comrade?' Sadanandan leaped out.

'Our Comrade Raman has been bitten by a snake... a deadly poisonous one.'

'Then how is he now?'

'I don't know all that. Please come fast.'

He dragged Comrade Sadanandan to Nanappan's house. As they got close to the shelter, they could hear a chorus of wailing.

Che's Mirror Image

Vasu reached Nanappan's house running and panting. The two-roomed thatched house was surrounded by unkempt ponds and thickets. The snake seemed to have sneaked in from the casurina thickets into the hut through the gaps between the braids of coconut fronds which formed the walls.

Comrade Raman was lying on a mat on the floor with his head resting on Comrade Madhavan's lap. The vaidyan for snake bite treatment was dabbing a green herbal paste on the wound.

Comrade Narayanan was standing a little apart. He called Vasu and asked, 'Do you know who is lying there?'

'I recognised him at first sight when he got down from the car. But I didn't want to ask you because it was a party secret.'

'But did you figure out who he is?' Narayanan asked and said softly, 'He is our Comrade Krishna Pillai. Don't tell anybody.'

Vasu was stunned. Not any ordinary comrade – the most honorable comrade of the party in the whole country.

Not an ordinary man, it is a great tree that has been uprooted, Vasu thought.

'Speed of a cavalry horse, courage of a soldier, alertness of a rebel and a patriot's pride in his country – that is Comrade Krishna Pillai', Comrade Narayanan recalled what someone had said, describing the Comrade.

'When did it bite?' Vasu asked.

'May be around nine o'clock in the morning, it was Nanappan's mother who found out first.' But she was lying unconscious in one corner of the hut. Nanappan's father, his brothers and he had gone for work in William Gudekkar factory.

'Comrade was writing some report.' Nanappan's mother had seen him lying down on that bench when she went out to clean fish. Suddenly she heard a call from the hut. 'Family members, please come fast with a knife.' When she went inside, he was standing there holding tightly below his elbow. 'I think I have been bitten by a snake, please make a slit with that knife under the bite and tie a thread tightly above the bite'. Nanappan's mother screamed loudly and gathered people from the neighbourhood. She dabbed thick lime over the wound. Someone rushed to call the vaidyan.

After some time, Comrade bent down and picked up the report he was writing. He wrote, 'I am blacking out. My body is growing weak. I know what is going to happen. Comrades, move forward. Lal Salam.' The pen slipped from his hand.

Comrade collapsed on the floor.

'I don't think I can manage this', the vaidyan said. 'I have done whatever I can. It's not working. The snake is highly venomous. It is better to take him to a hospital.'

By that time Nanappan and his brothers and father had come from the factory. They lifted him on to the cot. In that blazing hot sun the Comrade's sparkling eyes were focused on the sky. Suddenly his face lit up and a flash of light went up to the sky.

As the mourning procession of the comrades moved towards the big cremation ground, Comrade's voice whispered in their ears, 'Comrades, move forward.'

Vasudevan Master came into the room. 'Have you finished reading?'

'We finished the last page of what you have written; till the death of Comrade.'

'The rest has to be written in two days, by today and tomorrow.'

'Then why can't you finish it before we leave', Disha asked. 'We could have read it before we left.'

'But the future course of the story is not in the hands of the writer, isn't it?' A smile lit up his face.

'Okay, what happened to the 'Saga of the Seashore?' Disha asked. 'Will we get back her laptop?'

'I don't see any possibility', said the Master. 'It is in the custody of the special investigation team.'

'But what is there in it for them to dig it so much?' Disha was enraged.

'Definitely there is', Vasudevan Master said. 'Everything about the Maoist movement in India till now.'

'But all that was downloaded from the net.' Aparajitha was agitated.

'Is this going to be a trap, Sarangi?' Disha said fearfully.

'Looks like it's going to be, for the time being', Master smiled.

'Let's see.' Aparajitha regained her confidence.

'Yes, we will see', said the Master.

'Has Mother slept?' Master asked.

'No. She is always praying; maybe for him. I have never seen her eyes dry.'

'Even if he comes back, he should be careful about a few days and not fall under police scrutiny', said the Master. 'I heard that Dinar has been remanded for two weeks.'

'It would be better if he doesn't come back', Disha said. 'We suffered so much because of him.'

'Niranjan, where are you?' Aparajitha called out to him. 'Don't we have to go on a long journey; to Santa Clara in Cuba? Didn't you say that that's where the memorial is where Che's mortal remains are kept?'

From Cuba to Bolivia to Peru to the heights of Machu Pichhu.
From Air to air like an empty net,
Cling to my body like a magnet
Hasten to my veins and my mouth
Speak through my words and my blood.

Like Neruda you and me, through the nervous system of the earth.

She was trying to recollect the slice of light shining in his eyes. Where is he?

The picture that she had sketched of him in her mind flashed clearly on her mind's monitor.

His horse was galloping down the mountain peaks. A breeze coming from the Auro River caressed him. Beninjo and Pachho had gone searching for water a long time ago. The team members were craving for a drop of water. The white horse he discarded, collapsed and died on the spot. His group got busy eating its flesh raw. He was roaming through the wild palm trees. She ran behind him with a leather bag filled with water. She called him from behind 'Ernesto….' He didn't hear her. Three or four fighter aircrafts circled the forest. She tried to hide behind the palm trees. She saw him also trying to hide. She called him loudly 'Ernesto….'

On their ride to Nedumbasseri Airport, Disha asked Aparajitha.

'How would you have ended the 'Saga of the Seashore?'

'Can't say', she said, 'when the writer is guided by what is written.'

'That's right.' Master agreed. 'The writer should be guided by what he has written.'

Sitting on the back seat, mother was engrossed in her prayers.

'Little Sathya's long walk clinging to Asaan's fingers', Disha said. 'That's where you had stopped.'

'Yes, they were going to the big cremation ground. That was the day the first elected Communist Party came into power after the formation of Kerala State.'

5 April 1957.

That was the day the government functionaries were going to take their oath after the formation of the communist government. It was fixed at 10.30 am at Trivandrum. Before leaving for Trivandrum, they had come to the big cremation ground in Punnapra for paying homage to the martyrs of the uprising.

Sathyadas walked briskly with his father. A group of about fifty women joined them, wearing checked mundu and red blouses and holding their lunch carriers.

'They all are our comrades working in Darragh Smail', Asaan told Sathya.

'Lal Salam', Sathya greeted them. They smiled at him.

From the south a group of comrades came shouting slogans and holding red flags.

'Is it time for the comrades to come?' Asaan asked them.

'Of course, it is time', said one among them.

'Father and son have been walking for quite sometime now.' One among them recognised Asaan.

'Okay, do you know this person who is with me?' the man asked and made the introduced. 'This is Gallows Damodaran.'

Asaan greeted him.

'Don't you know me?' the man asked. 'I am Kakkariyil Phalgunan. I was in jail for a long time.' He turned to Gallows Damodaran, 'He had stood by my side with his spear when we were attacking the Punnapra police camp'. He turned to Asaan, 'But I don't know your name'.

'My name is Kochhu Kunjan Asaan but people call me Asaan.'

'Okay, I am in a hurry and have to get going', said Gallows Damodaran and walked ahead.

Phalgunan slowed down to keep pace with Sathya and Asaan.

'He was condemned to the gallows in the Inspector Velayudhan Nadar murder case along with two other comrades.' He told Asaan. 'As they were being taken to the Central jail, leaders MN and TV were waiting at the entrance.'

'Go with confidence', they had told him. 'We are going to the higher court to appeal to reduce the intensity of the punishment.'

The leaders kept their words. The Higher Court reduced the punishment to lifetime.

Still, when friends visited him at the jail he complained, 'It would have been better to be hanged, than this. At least my sufferings would have come to an end in a moment.'

Leaders consoled him. 'Don't worry, we will find a way out.'

That was the time the ruling party, lead by Pattom lost its majority. He got into a discussion with the Communist Party for support. In the discussions, the Party put down their conditions.

'We will give support, but all the Punnapra-Vayalar prisoners should be released unconditionally.'

'Punnapra-Vayalar prisoners?' Pattom frowned, 'but don't you know their charge is sedition? How can we release them just like that?'

'How can you say sedition? What is their fault? They all are patriots who shed their blood for the freedom of Travancore. It was their lives which were sacrificed in this struggle that lead to a democratically-elected government in this land', MN broke down emotionally. 'There should be a decision by tomorrow and they should be released immediately.'

Pattom thought for a while, got up and shook hands with MN and said, 'Done...done...'

'Have you come across Comrade Pathrose recently?' Phalgunan asked Asaan. 'It's said that he is going around on a cycle selling coir mats. How very unfortunate! He should have been a Minister by now.'

'He was demoted to the local party cell from the position of party secretary for his wrong decisions and for leading the party in the wrong direction', Asaan thought. Even after losing his position he used to visit the party office, sit on a bench looking far away in total silence. After a while such visits also stopped.

'Once upon a time, was he not the uncrowned King of the party?' Phalgunan turned into a philosopher. 'Then he was reduced to being called spear-legged Pathrose. Life is life. In a jiffy everything changes.'

'After Comrade left the world, there was nothing left', Asaan said. 'I am referring to Comrade Krishna Pillai. Had he been there, he would have protected Comrade Pathrose somehow.'

'That's true', Phalgunan agreed.

Four or five Ambassador cars sped past, heading to the big cremation ground.

'Comrades have arrived', Phalgunan bolted.

Ocean of humanity roared. The cremation ground turned crimson with thousands of red flags fluttering.

Asaan lifted Sathya to his shoulders. 'Look my son.... That is EMS, next to him is Comrade TV, then Comrade Achyutha Menon...Comrade KR Gowri....'

The leaders were paying homage to the martyrs with flowers. After that they went to the memorial of Comrade Krishna Pillai and raised their fists skyward 'Lal Salam...comrade Lal Salam. Inquilab Zindabad....'

At the entrance to the airport, Aparajitha stopped and turned back to address Master.

'Shall I tell you a name for your book?'

Master looked at her inquisitively.

'Scorched Earth.'

As he was exiting the airport, he saw a crowd in front of the TV in the foyer. Master craned his neck.

'Clash between Maoists and Border Security Force in Chhattisgarh. Ten Maoists killed in the encounter.'

A clip of the shotdown Maoists. One among them resembled Che.

Master turned back.

Mother was sitting on the back seat of the car, lost in her prayers.

Glossary

AIIMS—All-India Institute of Medical Sciences

Chakara—a peculiar marine phenomenon in which a large number of fish and prawns throng together during a particular season as a part of mud bank formations, on Kerala coasts seen from April to after the rains.

CIDs—police detectives

Goons--goondas

Inquilab Zindabaad—Long Live Revolution

Jalebi—an Indian sweet

Jibba—an Indian-style shirt

Kalari—martial art

Kanji—rice gruel

Lal Salam—Red Salute

Mundu—wraparound

Pattar—a Tamil Brahmin from Malabar coast

Pooja—worship

Prasada—god's gift, special food offered to dieties

Ramacham—The Vettivar long grass, also called Khas

Tambaran—Master, Lord, Landlord in Tamil and Malayalam

Thortumundu—a towel

TTUC—Travancore Trade Union Congress

Bibliography

History of Punnapra-Vayalar Revolt: A Brief Narrative by PK Chandranandan.

Memories of Revolution by Puthupally Raghavan.

Punnapra Vayalar: Blazing Chapters by MT Chandrasenan.

Communist Movement in Kerala: Through Initial Days by NE Balaram.

Communist Movement in Kerala: Origin and Development by EMS Namboodiripad.

History of Travancore Revolt for Independence by C Narayana Pillai.

Portrait of the Bygone Era by A Sreekandan Nair.

Punnapra-Vayalar and the History of Kerala by A Sreedhara Menon.

Punnapra Struggle: Story Behind History and History in the Story written by AM Josy.

Arsakadavu, Punnapra-Vayalar Struggle: Through Experience edited by Father Aloscious D Fernandez.

The Eighth Ring: An Autobiography by KM Mathew.

https://www.epw.in/journal/1977/53/uncategorised/punnapra-vayalar-rewriting-history.html

https://www.insightsonindia.com/2016/10/28/2-discuss-objectives-significance-punnapra-vayalar-revolt-1946/

Translator Manjula Cherkil is a Research Associate for the Five College Women's Studies Research Center (FCWSRC), Mount Holyoke College, South Hadley US. She has translated KV Mohankumar's award-winning Malayalam novel, *Pranayathinde Moonnamkannu* (The Third Eye of Love) into English and *Ushnaraashi.*

KV Mohankumar is a distinguished novelist and short story writer. A member of the Indian Administrative Service, hc has written fifteen books and is the author of best-selling novels in Malayalam like *Ushnaraashi* (Manhunt: The Seashore Saga of the Punnapra-Vayalar Uprising), *Sradhasesham* (Beyond Salvation), *Jaaranum Poochayum* (Paramour and the Cat) and *Ezhamindrium* (The Seventh Sense). *Pranayathinde Moonnamkannu* (The Third Eye of Love), a fictionalised philosophical quest based on Tantric Buddhism bagged several literary awards in Malayalam. **Manhunt** is a translation of *Ushnaraashi - Karappurathinte Ithihasam* which received the 2018 Vayalar Ramavarma Literary Prize.

The first Communist ministry in Kerala, 1957 to 1959.

Memorials to the Punnapra-Vayalar Uprising

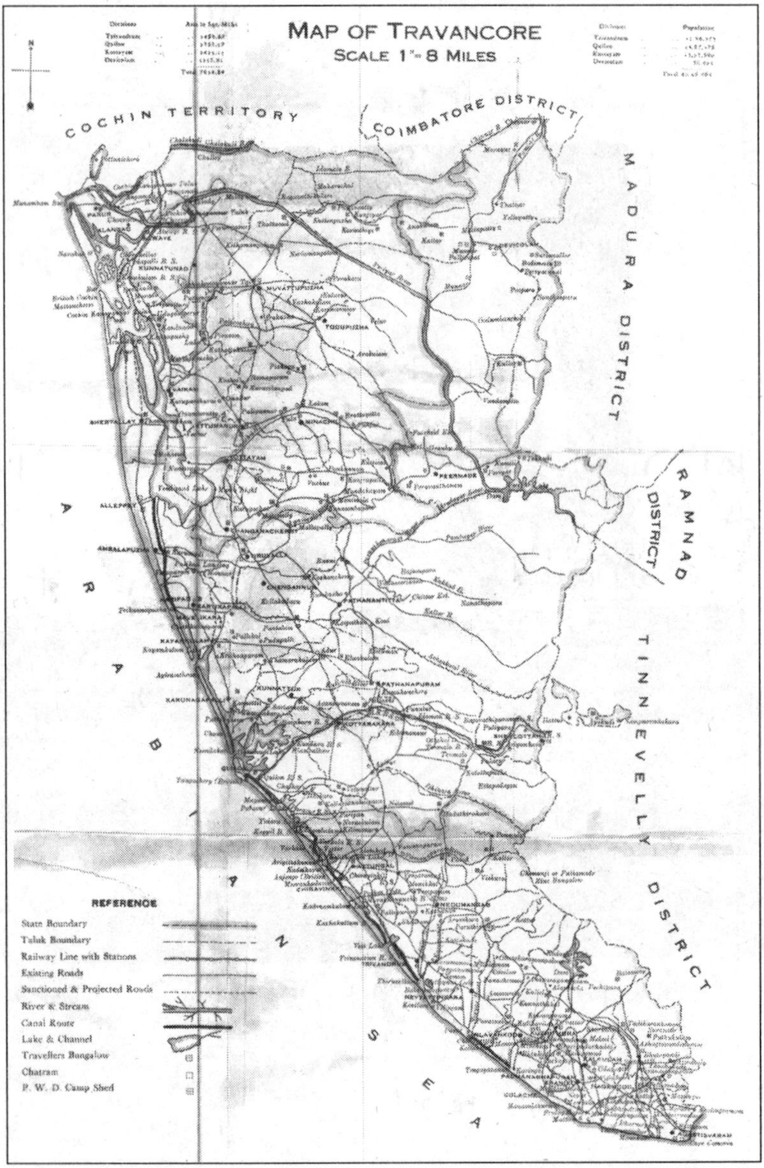
MAP OF TRAVANCORE
SCALE 1"= 8 MILES
COCHIN TERRITORY
COIMBATORE DISTRICT
MADURA DISTRICT
RAMNAD DISTRICT
TINNEVELLY DISTRICT
ARABIAN SEA
REFERENCE
State Boundary
Taluk Boundary
Railway Line with Stations
Existing Roads
Sanctioned & Projected Roads
River & Stream
Canal Route
Lake & Channel
Travellers Bungalow
Chatram
P. W. D. Camp Shed

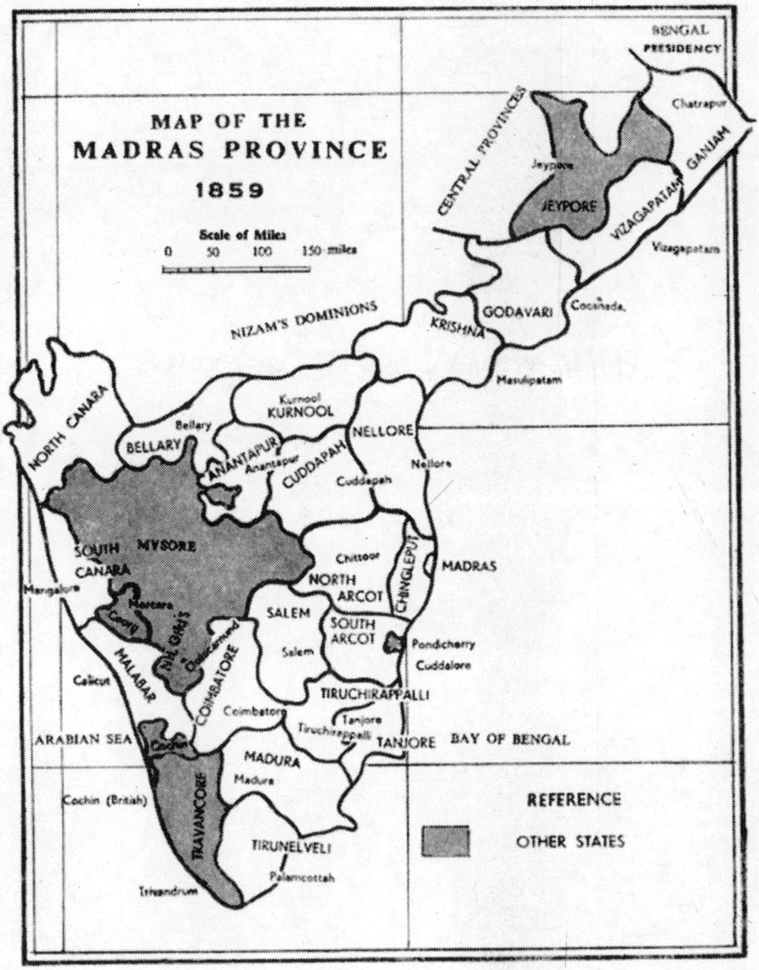

MAP OF THE
MADRAS PROVINCE
1859
Scale of Miles
0 50 100 150 miles
BENGAL
PRESIDENCY
Chatrapur
GANJAM
CENTRAL PROVINCES
Jeypore
JEYPORE
VIZAGAPATAM
Vizagapatam
GODAVARI
Cocanada
KRISHNA
Masulipatam
NIZAM'S DOMINIONS
NORTH CANARA
Bellary
BELLARY
Kurnool
KURNOOL
NELLORE
ANANTAPUR
Anantapur
CUDDAPAH
Cuddapah
Nellore
SOUTH
CANARA
MYSORE
Chittoor
NORTH
ARCOT
CHINGLEPUT
MADRAS
Mangalore
Mercara
Coorg
NILGIRIS
Ootacamund
SALEM
SOUTH
ARCOT
Pondicherry
Cuddalore
Salem
MALABAR
COIMBATORE
Calicut
TIRUCHIRAPPALLI
Coimbatore
Tanjore
Tiruchirappalli
TANJORE
ARABIAN SEA
Cochin
BAY OF BENGAL
MADURA
Madura
Cochin (British)
TRAVANCORE
REFERENCE
OTHER STATES
TIRUNELVELI
Palamcottah
Trivandrum